Hmg B

D1744231

This collection of original essays by leading western and Russian specialists gives an overview of key issues in Russian women's writing and of important representations of women by men, between 1600 and the present. This volume contributes to the contemporary feminist project of rediscovering many hitherto unjustly neglected Russian women writers and sheds further light on the literary construction of women's identity by Russian men. It combines a study of the history and biography of women writers with close readings of literary texts, and explores certain controversial issues in Russian women's literary studies, such as whether there is a separate women's literary tradition in Russia, whether the treatment of the woman question by Russian male writers reflected women's interests and experience, and whether a feminist reinterpretation of Russian women's literature is possible or even desirable.

CAMBRIDGE STUDIES IN RUSSIAN LITERATURE

GENDER AND RUSSIAN LITERATURE

For a complete list of books in the series, see the end of this volume

GENDER AND RUSSIAN LITERATURE

LITERATURE

New perspectives

TRANSLATED AND EDITED BY

ROSALIND MARSH

*Professor of Russian Studies and Director of
the Centre of Women's Studies,
University of Bath*

CAMBRIDGE UNIVERSITY PRESS
Cambridge, New York, Melbourne, Madrid, Cape Town,
Singapore, São Paulo, Delhi, Tokyo, Mexico City

Cambridge University Press
The Edinburgh Building, Cambridge CB2 8RU, UK

Published in the United States of America by Cambridge University Press, New York

www.cambridge.org
Information on this title: www.cambridge.org/9780521174947

First published 1996
First paperback edition 2011

A catalogue record for this publication is available from the British Library

Library of Congress cataloguing in publication data

Gender and Russian literature: new perspectives/translated
and edited by Rosalind Marsh.
p.   cm. - (Cambridge Studies in Russian Literature)
Includes index.
ISBN 0 521 55258 3 (hc)
1. Russian literature - Women authors - History and criticism.
2. Women in literature.
1. Marsh, RosaiindJ.11. Series.
PG2997.R86 1996
891.709/9298 - dC20   95-30646   CIP

ISBN 978-0-521-55258-5 Hardback
ISBN 978-0-521-17494-7 Paperback

Contents

Notes on contributors

Eva Buchwald studied at the School of Slavonic and East European Studies of the University of London, where she obtained a doctorate in 1990 for her dissertation entitled 'Ideals of Womanhood in the Prose and Drama of Finland and Russia, 1894–1914'. Since then she has lived in Finland, where she teaches courses on Finnish and Russian literature at the University of Helsinki. She is also currently employed as a literary manager by the National Theatre of Finland.

Pamela Davidson is a Lecturer in Russian at the School of Slavonic and East European Studies of the University of London. After taking her first degree at the University of Cambridge and doing postgraduate research at St Antony's College, Oxford, she held a Junior Research Fellowship at The Queen's College, Oxford, and lectureships at the Universities of Birmingham and Surrey. She is the author of *The Poetic Imagination of Viacheslav Ivanov* (Cambridge: Cambridge University Press, 1989) and *Viacheslav Ivanov: a Reference Guide to Literature* (New York: G. K. Hall Reference, 1996), and the editor of an anthology of poems dedicated to Anna Akhmatova, *Posviashchaetsia Akhmatovoi* (Tenafly, NJ: Hermitage Publishers, 1991). She has published articles on a number of twentieth-century Russian authors, including Ivanov, Akhmatova, Gumilev and Bulgakov, and has also written on Russian food and translated nineteenth-century opera libretti and modern poetry.

Ol'ga Demidova is a Reader (Dotsent) of Herzen University in St Petersburg. She graduated from an institute of foreign languages in 1977, specializing in English and German, and in 1986–9 was a postgraduate student in the Department of Foreign Literatures at Herzen State Pedagogical Institute. In 1990 she obtained a Candidate's degree (PhD) for her thesis on 'Charlotte Brontë, Elizabeth Gaskell and George Eliot in Russia (from the 1850s to the 1870s)'. Her major publications include twenty-six articles in Marina Ledkovsky, Charlotte Rosenthal and Mary Zirin, eds., *Dictionary of Russian Women Writers* (Westport, CT: Greenwood Press, 1994); 'George Eliot in Russian translation', *Russkaia literatura*, 2 (1992); 'The reception of Charlotte Brontë's work in nineteenth-century Russia', *Modern Language Review*, 89, 3 (July 1994), 689–96. She is currently working on a book on Russian women writers of the 'first-wave' emigration based on the material gathered in American archives while on an IREX grant in 1993–4.

Helena Goscilo, currently the Chairwoman of the Slavic Department at the University of Pittsburgh, specializes in Romanticism, contemporary Russian literature and culture, and Slavic women's writing. Her numerous publications include articles on Pushkin, Lermontov, Tolstoi, Bulgakov and Tolstaia. She is the editor of *Russian and Polish Women's Fiction* (University of Tennessee Press, 1985); *Balancing Acts: Contemporary Stories by Russian Women* (Bloomington and Indianapolis, IN: Indiana University Press, 1989); co-editor (with Byron Lindsey) of *Glasnost: an Anthology of Literature* (Ann Arbor, MI: Ardis, 1990) and *The Wild Beach and Other Stories* (Ann Arbor, MI: Ardis, 1992); editor of *Skirted Issues: the Discreteness and Indiscretions of Russian Women's Prose* (*Russian Studies in Literature*, Spring 1992); *Lives in Transit* (Ann Arbor, MI: Ardis, 1993); and *Fruits of Her Plume: Essays on Contemporary Russian Women's Culture* (Armonk, NY and London: M. E. Sharpe, 1993). She is currently working on a book on recent women's fiction for Michigan University Press.

Jane Gary Harris is Professor of Russian Literature at the University of Pittsburgh. She is the editor and co-translator of *Osip Mandel'stam: The Critical Prose and Letters* (Ann Arbor, MI: Ardis, 1979; 2nd edition, 1991; British edition, Collins and

Harvill, 1991); the author of *Osip Mandel'shtam* (Boston, MA: G. K. Hall, 1988); editor of *Autobiographical Statements: Essays on the Autobiographical Mode in Twentieth-Century Russian Literature* (Princeton, NJ: Princeton University Press, 1990); *American Contributions to the Xth International Congress of Slavists* (Columbus, OH: Slavica, 1988) and of *Lidia Ginzburg: In Memoriam, Essays*, special edition of *Canadian-American Slavic Studies*, 28, 2–3 (Summer–Fall, 1994). She has published articles on Petr Bitsilli, G. R. Derzhavin, Lidiia Ginzburg, Osip Mandel'shtam, Aleksandr Solzhenitsyn and problems of autobiography and fiction; her translations include works of Ginzburg, Mandel'shtam, Boris Pasternak and Iurii Tynianov. She also wrote Lidiia Ginzburg's obituary for the *Slavic Review* (Winter, 1990). She is currently writing a critical literary biography of Lidiia Ginzburg, working on a translation of *The Literary Hero*, and preparing a volume of Ginzburg's *Selected Writings*.

Rosalind Marsh is Professor of Russian Studies and Director of the Centre of Women's Studies at the University of Bath. She was awarded an MA at Cambridge and a D.Phil. at Oxford. She taught at The Queen's University of Belfast from 1977 to 1987, and at the University of Exeter from 1987 to 1991, where she was Director of the Centre for Russian, Soviet and East European Studies from 1989 to 1991. She is the author of *Soviet Fiction since Stalin: Science, Politics and Literature* (London and Sydney: Croom Helm, 1986), *Images of Dictatorship: Stalin in Literature* (London and New York: Routledge, 1989) and *History and Literature in Contemporary Russia* (Basingstoke: Macmillan, 1995), and the editor of *Women in Russia and Ukraine* (Cambridge: Cambridge University Press, 1996). Her articles on women's issues and women's literature in Russia include 'The birth, death and rebirth of feminist writing in Russia', in Helena Forsås-Scott, ed., *Textual Liberation: European Feminist Writing in the Twentieth Century* (London: Routledge, 1991), pp.130–63.

Rosalind McKenzie is engaged in doctoral research into the secularization and modernization of hagiographical traditions in medieval Russia at the School of Slavonic and East European Studies of the University of London.

Mariia Mikhailova is a lecturer in the Department of Twentieth-century Russian Literature at Moscow State University. She graduated from the Philological Faculty of Moscow State University in 1969 and obtained her Candidate's degree in 1974. She has written more than a hundred scholarly works on the 'Silver Age' of Russian literature, especially on the life and work of women writers, the contribution of 'minor' writers such as G. Chulkov and N. Nikandrov, and the development of literary criticism. She is co-author (with A. G. Sokolov) of the reader *Russkaia literaturnaia kritika kontsa XIX–nachala XX veka* (Moscow, 1982) and author of *Istoriia russkoi literaturnoi kritiki kontsa XIX–nachala XX veka* (Moscow, 1985). She has contributed to Ledkovsky, Rosenthal and Zirin, *Dictionary of Russian Women Writers*, and has published extensively in Poland, in such journals as *Przeglad Humanistyczny* and *Slawia Orientalis*; her most recent publication in the collection *Studia Litteraria Polono-Slavica* (Warsaw, 1993) was devoted to the life and work of Lidiia Zinov'eva-Annibal. She has contributed a postscript, 'O schastlivoi zhenshchine', to a new edition of a famous novel of the Silver Age, Evdokiia Nagrodskaia's *Gnev Dionisa* (Progress-Liter, 1994), and is currently working on editions of Lidiia Zinov'eva-Annibal's *Tritsat' tri uroda, ili Golova Meduzy* (Moscow: Moskovskii rabochii, forthcoming) and Georgii Chulkov's *Valtasarovo tsarstvo* (Moscow: Respublika, forthcoming).

Graham Roberts is Lecturer in Russian Studies at the University of Strathclyde. A graduate of Manchester University, where he obtained a degree in French and Russian, he was awarded a D.Phil. from Oxford University in 1992 for a study of the self-conscious fiction of three members of the 'Oberiu' group, namely Daniil Kharms, Aleksandr Vvedenskii and Konstantin Vaginov. His major research interests are Russian and Soviet literature, Soviet cinema, twentieth-century Russian drama, and literary theory, and he has published articles on Vvedenskii and Kharms. He is currently completing a book on 'Oberiu' and the Leningrad literary avant-garde.

Arja Rosenholm is Academic Assistant in Slavonic Languages at the University of Tampere in Finland. She obtained a Master's degree in Russian and German literature from the Freie Universität Berlin, and the postgraduate degree Fil.Lis. in Russian literature from the University of Jyväskylä in Finland. Her licentiate thesis focused on the Russian writer Nadezhda Khvoshchinskaia. She is one of the editors of *Gender Restructuring in Russian Studies. Conference Papers – Helsinki, August 1992*, Slavica Tamperensia, II (Tampere: University of Tampere, 1993), and editor of two anthologies of Russian women writers in Finnish translation. She has published articles on Russian women writers, on film and gender, and is currently working on a monograph on Russian women writers and the 'woman question' of the 1860s.

Charlotte Rosenthal is Associate Professor of Russian at the University of Southern Maine. Her area of specialization is the 'Silver Age' in Russia. She has published articles on Remizov and Sologub, and on women writers of the period, including 'Achievement and Obscurity: Women's Prose in the Silver Age', in Toby W. Clyman and Diana Greene, eds., *Women Writers in Russian Literature* (Westport, CT and London: Greenwood Press, 1994). She is co-editor (with Marina Ledkovsky and Mary Zirin) of the *Dictionary of Russian Women Writers*, which won the 1994 Heldt Prize for the 'Best Book in Slavic Women's Studies' from the American Association of Women in Slavic Studies.

Wendy Rosslyn is Reader in Russian Literature at the University of Nottingham. She has written numerous articles on Russian poetry, and is the author of *The Prince, the Fool and the Nunnery: the Religious Theme in the Early Poetry of Anna Akhmatova* (Amersham: Avebury, 1984), editor of *The Speech of Unknown Eyes: Akhmatova's Readers on her Poetry* (Nottingham: Astra Press, 1990) and translator of Anatoly Nayman, *Remembering Anna Akhmatova* (London: Peter Halban Publishers, 1991). She is now completing a biography of the poet Anna Bunina.

Stephanie Sandler is Associate Professor of Russian and Women's and Gender Studies at Amherst College, Massachusetts. She has published numerous articles on Russian poetry and gender, and is the author of *Distant Pleasures: Alexander Pushkin and the Writing of Exile* (Stanford, CA: Stanford University Press, 1989), and a co-editor of *Sexuality and the Body in Russian Culture* (Stanford, CA: Stanford University Press, 1993). She is currently completing a book entitled *When We Look at Pushkin: Russia's Myth of a National Poet*.

Gerald S. Smith is Professor of Russian at the University of Oxford and Fellow of New College, Oxford. He taught previously at the universities of Nottingham, Birmingham, Liverpool, Indiana and California (Berkeley). He has written numerous articles on Russian eighteenth-century literature and twentieth-century poetry, and is author of *Songs to Seven Strings: Russian Guitar Poetry and Soviet 'Mass Song'* (Bloomington and Indianapolis, IN: Indiana University Press, 1984); editor of *Contemporary Russian Poetry: A Bilingual Anthology* (Bloomington and Indianapolis, 1993); co-editor (with A. G. Cross) of *Eighteenth-century Russian Literature, Culture and Thought: a Bibliography of English-language Scholarship and Translations* (Newtonville: Oriental Research Partners, 1984) and *Literature, Lives and Legality in Catherine's Russia* (Cotgrave: Astra Press, 1994); translator of Alexander Galich, *Songs and Poems* (Ann Arbor, MI: Ardis, 1983); and co-editor (with Archie Brown and Michael Kaser) of *The Cambridge Encyclopedia of Russia and the Former Soviet Union* (Cambridge: Cambridge University Press, 1994).

Elena Trofimova is a literary critic, deputy editor of the literary and scholarly women's journal *Preobrazhenie*, and the author of a numerous publications on contemporary women's literature and the poetry of the Russian underground. She has contributed fifteen articles to Ledkovsky, Rosenthal and Zirin, *Dictionary of Russian Women Writers*; an introductory article to the collection of women's stories, *Chego khochet zhenshchina?* (Moscow: Amrita, 1993); and articles on the poetry clubs of the 1980s for *Oktiabr'*, 12 (1991) and *Istoriia russkoi literatury*, 2 vols. (Rome, 1994). Journals to which she has contributed since 1991 include *Russkaia rech'*, *Novoe literaturnoe obozrenie*, *Slovesnik*, *Voprosy literatury* and *Druzhba narodov*.

Faith Wigzell is Senior Lecturer in Russian Language and Literature at the School of Slavonic and East European Studies, University of London. She is the author of a monograph on the writer Epifanii Premudryi and of numerous articles on Russian literature and folklore; the co-editor (with Jane Grayson) of *Nikolay Gogol: Text and Context* (Basingstoke: Macmillan, 1989), and editor of *Russian Writers on Russian Writers* (Oxford: Berg, 1994). She is currently completing a book, *Reading the Signs: Fortune-telling and Fortune-telling Books in Russia.*

Acknowledgements

I gratefully acknowledge the financial support offered by the British Academy, the Ford Foundation, the ESRC, the British Council in Russia and Ukraine, South West Arts, and the Council for Co-operation in Russian and Soviet Education to enable the conference on 'Women in Russia and the Former USSR' to be held at the University of Bath in March–April 1993, at which earlier versions of many of the chapters in this volume were presented. Special thanks are due to Celia Dyer for ensuring the efficient organization of the conference.

I should also like to thank the British Council for enabling me to do research in St Petersburg; the Kennan Institute for Advanced Russian Studies, Washington, DC, for awarding me a research fellowship; St Antony's College, Oxford, for making me a Senior Research Associate; and the University of Bath for awarding me the study leave essential to complete this book.

I am especially grateful to all the contributors to this volume for the prompt delivery of their manuscripts, and their courteous responses to my queries. The comments of Barbara Heldt, Catriona Kelly and a number of anonymous readers for Cambridge University Press have been of particular value in preparing this volume. I am also grateful for the insights of my colleagues in the feminist literature study group of Bath University, and for the technical assistance of James Davenport and Christopher Williams. Finally, I should to thank all the participants in the 'Women in Russia' conference, who helped to make the occasion so successful and to stimulate debate and further reflection on many issues discussed below.

CHAPTER I

Introduction: new perspectives on women and gender in Russian literature

Rosalind Marsh

This selection of essays provides an overview of key issues in Russian women's writing and of important representations of women by men, between 1600 and the present. The book has two main aims. Firstly, it hopes to make a contribution to the contemporary feminist project of rediscovering the 'lost continent of the female tradition'[1] of Russian literature, which forms part of the wider interdisciplinary initiative by social historians, political scientists, psychologists, art and film historians to reconstruct the political, social and cultural experience of Russian women as a whole. Secondly, it incorporates some new thinking on gender issues in the works of Russian male writers, in order to shed further light on the patriarchal Russian literary tradition. Unlike most previous feminist studies of Russian literature, which, to borrow Elaine Showalter's terms, have tended to concentrate on either 'the feminist critique' ('revisionary readings' of masculine texts and criticism)[2] or 'gynocritics' (the rediscovery and analysis of literature by Russian women),[3] it is hoped that this comparative study will facilitate an exploration of the historical and cultural context of women's writing, and the differences, if any, between the writing of women and men in Russia, which no book focusing entirely on women's writing can achieve.[4]

Many of the essays presented below are revised versions of papers first presented at a conference on 'Women and the Former USSR', held in the University of Bath in March–April 1993, but others have been offered specially for inclusion in this book. There is no unanimity of viewpoint in the collection, although all the western contributors are influenced by the theory and practice of feminist criticism. Many of the essays have a strong theoretical basis and make use of much secondary material; while others, such as Elena Trofimova's, rely on close readings of texts for which few secondary sources are available. Both methods are valuable, and reveal different aspects of women's creativity and the position of women in Russian society.

PREVIOUS RESEARCH INTO WOMEN AND GENDER IN RUSSIAN LITERATURE

Until the 1990s, feminist criticism of Russian literature had lagged some way behind the recuperation and reinterpretation of writing by American and European women, initiated in the late 1960s under the influence of the second wave of the feminist movement in the USA and western Europe. Feminist criticism of Russian literature had also failed to keep pace with research into the history and contemporary situation of Russian women by historians, sociologists and economists, which began in the mid-1970s.[5]

Until very recently, most histories of Russian literature paid scant attention to women writers, as the majority of critics who established the Russian literary canon, masculine and feminine, in both Russia and the West, were conditioned by the patriarchal Russian cultural tradition.[6] The irredeemably patriarchal nature of Russian and Soviet society, in which power has always been in the hands of men, has been amply documented by historians and political scientists,[7] and, to a lesser extent, by literary scholars, although there is as yet no systematic history of Russian misogyny or of the suppression and distortion of women's writing in Russia.[8] Russian male writers and critics have frequently been unduly harsh and dismissive in their judgements of women writers, probably because they have felt threatened by them or have had little interest in the themes they have chosen to treat. Moreover, journals, publishing houses and literary criticism in Russia have always been dominated by men, although some women critics in the nineteenth century, the Silver Age and the 1920s, such as 'Evgeniia Tur', Elena Koltonovskaia and Aleksandra Kollontai, have managed to express views which differed from those of their male contemporaries. Yet, as Barbara Heldt has shown, 'women's writing in Russia has proved especially vulnerable' to male-dominated literary criticism, creating on the part of women writers 'a peculiar awareness of their otherness'.[9] Such criticism has sometimes undermined the confidence of Russian women writers, leading them to conformity, silence, or even suicide.[10]

The fundamental assumptions of patriarchal ideology – the perception of woman as object, 'immanence', 'nature', passivity or death, as opposed to man as subject, 'transcendence', 'culture', activity and life,[11] have dominated all aspects of Russian social, political and cultural life. Many Russian women writers and critics too – along with western critics of Russian literature – have internalized this objectified vision.[12]

In recent years, under the pressure of western feminist criticism, some male critics in the West have been persuaded to include sections on women writers in general studies of Russian literature, although in a book published as recently as 1989, dealing with a period which had witnessed a great resurgence of women's writing, N. N. Shneidman claimed that: 'The number of Soviet women writing today is indeed small. The index of any history of Soviet literature does not list many female authors who merit attention'.[13] The masculinist version of the Russian literary canon has also been accepted by some women critics, such as Xenia Gasiorowska, who argues that: 'Women writers, though widely read in Russia, contributed but little to the greatness of Russian literature, which has no George Sand, Jane Austen or George Eliot'.[14] Until very recently, the study of Russian women's literature has also suffered, with some honourable exceptions,[15] from what John Gross calls 'residual Great Traditionalism':[16] a tendency to reduce and condense the range and diversity of Russian women writers to a small band of 'the great', which has usually meant Karolina Pavlova in the nineteenth century, and Anna Akhmatova and Marina Tsvetaeva in the twentieth century.

It was not until the late 1980s that pioneering feminist research on Russian literature by western scholars eventually

got under way.[17] One advantage of the relatively belated
rediscovery of much literature by Russian women is that
Slavists have been able to learn from an impressive body of
feminist scholarship and theory amassed by scholars working in
other disciplines, fruitfully adapting their insights to the
Russian context.[18] Yet, even in the 1990s, it is still fair to say
that the 'feminist critique' of masculine texts and criticism has
only just begun in relation to Russian literature. 'Gynocritics'
was in an even more embryonic state until 1992–4, when a
number of important new works of bibliography and criticism
were published almost simultaneously, adding tremendously to
our knowledge of Russian women's literature and necessitating
a radical reinterpretation of Russian culture as a whole.[19]
These introductory works, however, have still left ample scope
for further research.

MAIN THEMES OF THIS BOOK

Whereas most previous feminist critiques of the image of
women in Russian literature have focused on a reinterpretation
of nineteenth-century Russian literature, or on socialist
realism,[20] the critics represented in this volume who engage in
a feminist re-evaluation of twentieth-century texts by Russian
male writers suggest that stereotyped images of woman also
abound in 'alternative' literature written outside the confines of
the socialist realist tradition. Eva Buchwald and Graham
Roberts analyse the stereotypes of feminine passivity, silence,
confinement and hysteria portrayed in the modernist works of
Leonid Andreev and Daniil Kharms, demonstrating that avant-
garde literature in Russia can be as misogynistic, if not more so,
than realist fiction. Gerald S. Smith's study of Aleksandr
Velichanskii, a poet of the glasnost era whose work is almost
entirely concerned with the portrayal of women, sheds more
light on the contemporary literary construction of women's
identity by Russian men. Smith's analysis, along with female
images in the works of such contemporary male prose writers as
Anatolii Kurchatkin and Eduard Limonov, suggests that
glasnost and the sexual revolution in Russia have intensified the

innate male chauvinism and voyeuristic tendencies of many Russian writers, who have simply shifted their focus from woman as mother or symbol of virtue to a more explicit portrayal of woman as sexual object, even as victim of rape.

In its study of Russian women writers, this book seeks to complement and build upon the valuable new works of bibliography and criticism which have appeared in the 1990s. While the *Dictionary of Russian Women Writers* (1994) has accomplished the basic task of identifying forgotten women writers and reclaiming their work from oblivion, encyclopaedia entries are no substitute for a more extended discussion of the lives and works of individual women writers. This collection is a response to the continuing need to establish a more accurate and systematic history for Russian women writers, to facilitate the rediscovery of the many minor women writers who were the links in the chain that bound one generation to the next, and to provide full and close readings of certain Russian women writers whose work remains insufficiently studied, or who have been partially misrepresented by other critics. Extensive footnotes are needed in many of the articles, because the study of Russian women writers is still such a new field that very few assumptions can be made about it, and much fresh information must be included as an essential aid to future researchers.

Some contributors, such as Demidova, Rosenthal and Goscilo, provide general surveys of women writers in the nineteenth century, the Silver Age and contemporary Russia; while others, such as Rosslyn, Marsh, Gary Harris and Sandler, analyse individual women writers hitherto little known in the West. Such an exploration of Russian women's writing in a historical context may well help to corroborate the view that some western feminists have expressed since the late 1960s, that 'a special female self-awareness emerges through literature in every period'.[21]

This collection combines a study of the history and biography of women writers with close readings of literary texts. These themes are predominantly treated in Parts One and Two of the book respectively, although the present thematic grouping is imperfect and indicates only bias. Whereas Catriona Kelly, in her monumental *History of Russian Women's Writing, 1820–1992* (1994) largely eschews biography in order to concentrate on textual analysis,[22] many contributors to the first part of this volume acknowledge that it is important not only to unearth and reinterpret 'lost' works by women writers, but also to document their lives and careers, which have exerted a significant influence on their fiction. As Virginia Woolf argued in her 1929 essay 'Women and Fiction': 'In dealing with women as writers, as much elasticity as possible is desirable; it is necessary to leave oneself room to deal with other things besides their work, so much has that work been influenced by conditions that have nothing to do with art'.[23]

Our study makes it clear that many women writers in Russia, as in other cultures, have been disadvantaged, harassed and marginalized, and that their unjustly neglected works contain much of interest both for literary historians and contemporary women readers.[24] To the objection that male authors too have been subject to considerable persecution from censorship and political tyranny in Russia and the USSR,[25] it can be argued that, while this is undeniably true, some women writers have been unfortunate enough to suffer twice over, from both political and patriarchal persecution (to name only a few, the lives of Karolina Pavlova, Anastasiia Verbitskaia, Anna Akhmatova, Marina Tsvetaeva, Ol'ga Berggol'ts and Iuliia Voznesenskaia are cases in point).

As Toby Clyman and Diana Greene have noted, the former obscurity of women writers in Russian culture can be attributed to three main factors: the bias of Russian critics;[26] the impact of adverse social conditions;[27] and the creation of literary theories by later critics who retroactively eliminated them.[28] One such theory was the conception of 'committed literature' and 'the new woman' which prevailed in the 1860s, excluding the works of many women writers before that date; another was socialist realism, developed in 1934, which imposed a monolithic, male-dominated ideology on male and female writers alike.

Most feminist historical research into Russian history and culture has hitherto concentrated on the modern period since 1800,[29] but the essays by Rosalind McKenzie and Faith Wigzell help to bridge this gap, contributing to the rediscovery of the significant place which women and 'women's literature' occupied in Russian culture long before the 'woman question' was put on the political agenda of the nineteenth-century Russian radical movement. Whereas much previous research has focused on the history of gender inequality, female oppression and male dominance in Russian and Soviet culture, McKenzie suggests that in some seventeenth-century texts women began to be portrayed with greater realism and psychological motivation than we have hitherto been led to believe. While adding to the documentation of women's marginalization and subordination in Russian society, Wigzell's essay exploring the roles of women as readers of fortune-telling books and as amateur and professional practitioners of magic in the eighteenth and early nineteenth centuries also helps to establish a specific urban market of Russian women readers from the 1790s, and to recover the private sphere of women's experience, yielding insights into the role of sexual difference in Russian society, and of patterns of female ritual and sociability.

Many contributors to Part One, such as Marsh, Rosenthal and Mikhailova, seek to investigate the relations between literature by women, women writers' lives and the changing status of women in Russian society. This results in a historical, political, sociological and economic analysis which is rather different from Kelly's modernist aim of identifying 'texts which ... execute the task of representing female creativity', laying an 'emphasis on the text as representation of varying forms of literary identity, of a fictional self'.[30]

However, some contributors, especially in Part Two, also share Kelly's interest in the nature of female identity and creativity, and provide new interpretations of texts by Russian women. With the exception of Stephanie Sandler's new study of Ol'ga Sedakova, a major contemporary poet about whom little has hitherto appeared in English, the writers chosen for detailed treatment here – Anna Bunina, Nadezhda Khvoshchinskaia, Lidiia Zinov'eva-Annibal, Anastasiia Verbitskaia and Lidiia Ginzburg – are different from those selected for close reading in Kelly's *History*, and have hitherto received little

critical attention in English. Anna Bunina is of particular
interest, because she is a rare example of a Russian noble-
woman who, early in the nineteenth century, managed to
achieve an independent life, educate herself and gain a considerable poetic reputation. Lidiia Zinov'eva-Annibal and Anastasiia Verbitskaia represent two different strands of women's
literature of the Silver Age: Symbolism and feminist realism.
Mariia Mikhailova reinterprets Zinov'eva-Annibal's *Tridtsat' tri
uroda* (*Thirty-three Abominations*, 1907), previously known as one of
the first Russian works openly to treat lesbian themes in
literature,[31] in the light of the author's strange and tragic
biography; while Pamela Davidson reinterprets Zinov'eva-
Annibal's little known verse play *Pevuchii osel* (*The Singing Ass*,
1907) as a satire on the views of her husband Viacheslav Ivanov,
and on Russian Symbolism in general. My essay on Anastasiia
Verbitskaia, who is generally disparaged as a writer of sensational blockbusters, argues that Verbitskaia deserves reassessment for her realistic treatment of women's issues and her
feminist publishing activities. Jane Gary Harris's study of the
early journal of the prominent literary scholar Lidiia Ginzburg
represents the first analysis of the feminist and lesbian elements
in her writing, which have formerly been taboo in Russian
discussions of her work. Ginzburg's previously unpublished
writings afford a striking illustration of one of the most
pervasive themes in lesbian criticism, that 'woman-identified
writers, silenced by a homophobic and misogynistic society,
have been forced to adopt coded and obscure language and
internal censorship'.[32]
   Feminist research on Russian literature is still, unfortunately,
being pursued more vigorously by foreign critics than by
Russian women themselves. Nevertheless, since the inception of
glasnost a number of texts by Russian women of the past and
present have been published in Russia, although these have
rarely been presented from a feminist point of view.[33] Although
a few articles on the history of women's literature by Russian
female scholars have now reached an international audience,[34]
and 'women's courses' and seminars are conducted at two
Moscow universities,[35] there is as yet no institutional backing

for such isolated endeavours comparable with the Centre for Gender Studies in Moscow which promotes the feminist analysis of contemporary Russian society, and access to feminist critical sources is still quite limited.[36] One aim of this book is to encourage the development of feminist literary criticism within Russia by including three articles by Russian critics which reflect the advances which are now being made in the understanding of the history of Russian women's writing by Russian women themselves. The juxtaposition of essays by Russian and western scholars frequently serves to highlight interesting similarities and differences in their approach to Russian women's literature.

In rediscovering their own feminine literary tradition, contemporary Russian women critics sometimes accept assumptions widely established in Russian literary criticism which have now been challenged by western feminist critics. Whereas Ol'ga Demidova, for example, accepts the usual Russian view that male critics welcomed women's literature in the 1820s, western scholars, including Wendy Rosslyn, have argued that the tendency to idealize the female sex and to attribute moral superiority to it could be interpreted as an example of Russian male critics' patronizing attitude to women writers.[37] As Linda Edmondson has pointed out, such views of women's moral superiority are close to the anti-feminist argument that women are obliged to be better than men in order to deserve equal status, and that women must remain on their moral pedestal if they are to retain the respect of men.[38] Demidova also claims that Romanticism had a wholly positive influence on the development of women's literature in the nineteenth century, whereas Catriona Kelly contends that Romanticism's impact on women writers was ambiguous, to say the least, since it emphasized the masculine nature of inspiration and the role of the male genius.[39] In her study of women writers of the Silver Age, Mariia Mikhailova has to a certain extent internalized the essentialist notions of men and women prevalent at that time, in the works of Otto Weininger and Elena Koltonovskaia,[40] notably the view that women are more inclined to all-embracing passionate love than men, and that creativity in women may be a substitute for an unsatisfactory love life. Sometimes Russian critics do not comment on the feminist implications of texts by Russian women: for example, Elena Trofimova, in her analysis of the contemporary poet Nina Iskrenko, does not refer to her playful deconstruction of gender stereotypes, which has been emphasized in western criticism.[41]

KEY ISSUES IN THE STUDY OF WOMEN AND GENDER IN RUSSIAN LITERATURE

It will be useful here to explore certain general questions which have been raised by previous feminist criticism of Russian literature, with the aim of stimulating further debate without in any way pre-empting the views expressed by other contributors to this volume. One particularly controversial issue is whether there is a separate women's literary tradition in Russia – a claim which cannot be conclusively proved or disproved. On the one hand, literary influence is always difficult to establish in any culture, and there is no doubt that many Russian women writers were also deeply influenced both by individual male writers and by the masculine culture of their time. Many nineteenth-century women writers did not know each other,[42] and their domestic isolation made it difficult for them to form any kind of 'movement' until the early twentieth century. Moreover, the severe criticism, distortion and neglect to which Russian women writers have been subjected has meant that every successive generation 'has found itself, in a sense, without a history, forced to rediscover the past again, forging again and again the consciousness of their sex'.[43] The greatest historical discontinuity has been caused by the Bolshevik Revolution and Stalinism: only since the advent of glasnost have some women critics and writers begun to rediscover their own literary tradition as a whole, not to mention their feminine literary subculture.[44]

Notwithstanding all these obstacles, a certain tradition in Russian women's poetry and autobiographical writing has been tentatively postulated by other feminist critics.[45] In the twentieth century, particularly in contemporary Russia, women poets often refer to prominent women in history and myth-ology,[46] or acknowledge their debt to Pavlova, Akhmatova, Tsvetaeva and other prominent women poets.[47] Although most previous critics would not go as far as to hazard the existence of a separate tradition of Russian women's prose,[48] some essays in this volume, such as Ol'ga Demidova's and my own, suggest that, perhaps more than has generally been realized, women writers in pre-revolutionary Russia were influenced both by each other, and by foreign women writers, particularly George Sand and Charlotte Brontë. Some feminist writers at the turn of the century, notably Anastasiia Verbitskaia, were particularly influenced by foreign models, to some extent corroborating Ellen Moers's view that women's writing was an international movement 'apart from, but hardly subordinate to the main-stream: an undercurrent, rapid and powerful. This "move-ment" began in the late eighteenth century, was multinational, and produced some of the greatest literary works of two centuries, as well as most of the lucrative pot-boilers'.[49] It could be argued that, in Russian culture, as in other countries, some women writers at least 'studied with a special closeness the works written by their own sex'.[50] In any case, even if precise influences cannot always be proved, a women's tradition does emerge in Russian literature, in prose writing as well as poetry, if 'tradition' is interpreted to mean a commonality of themes, patterns, problems and images which persist from generation to generation.

The whole question of Russian women's prose merits further attention, since, apart from the growing interest in contem-porary women prose writers,[51] most critics have hitherto focused on poetry and autobiographical writings by Russian women, as there has been general agreement that there have been no outstanding Russian women novelists.[52] This book, while offering valuable new studies of women's poetry and memoirs by Sandler, Trofimova, and Gary Harris, also re-considers many previously forgotten Russian women novelists, who, although not major talents like Jane Austen and George Eliot, nevertheless deserve attention, since they were at least as well known as most of the male writers of their day. Rosenholm shows that in the 1860s women writers such as Nadezhda Khvoshchinskaia treated the 'woman question' primarily in prose fiction, not in essays, which were the predominant discourse of male advocates of sexual equality, perhaps because they did not wish to be dictated to by men, or could not imagine simplistic utopian solutions to intractable human problems.[53] Mikhailova, Marsh and Rosenthal suggest that by the end of the nineteenth century and the beginning of the twentieth century a flourishing prose tradition by Russian women – or rather, two traditions, one realist and one anti-realist – had evolved.[54]

It is somewhat curious that there is no great tradition of women novelists in Russia, as there is in England and America, especially in view of the frequently voiced argument that women's talents are best suited to novel writing. But as Barbara Heldt has argued, Russian women writers in the nineteenth century, and to a lesser extent in the twentieth century, have tended to favour genres other than the novel, which has remained a largely masculine medium shaping the mainstream literary canon. There are a number of possible explanations for this, including the lack of time at women's disposal for large-scale prose fiction, and Russian women writers' attempts to avoid criticism by concentrating on 'minor' genres rather than male-dominated 'major' ones;[55] but another significant reason is undoubtedly the fact that Russian women writers are heirs to a problematic prose tradition.[56] In classical Russian literature women have generally been presented through male eyes, in terms of the age-old opposition of Madonna and Whore, or, in the more complex perceptions of feminist critics, as Russian versions of Coventry Patmore's stereotypical 'Angel in the House'[57] and the 'Madwoman in the Attic'[58] portrayed in nineteenth-century English literature. Prominent examples of Russian 'Angels in the House' are such domestic paragons as Fenechka in Turgenev's *Fathers and Sons*, Dolly and Kitty in Tolstoi's *Anna Karenina*, Natasha Rostova in the Epilogue to *War and Peace*, and the saintly prostitute Sonia in Dostoevskii's *Crime and Punishment*. The Russian equivalent of the hysterical 'Mad-woman in the Attic'[59] is often known as the 'demonic woman', whose many incarnations include the eponymous heroine of Turgenev's *Asia*, Zinaida in Turgenev's *First Love*, Nastas'ia Filippovna in Dostoevskii's *The Idiot* and numerous other Dostoevskian heroines. Other male writers chose to portray a more specifically Russian character, the 'strong woman' who acts as mentor or muse to the weak 'superfluous man': for example Tat'iana in Pushkin's *Evgenii Onegin*, Natal'ia in Turgenev's *Rudin*; and Elena in *On the Eve*. Because of the prevalence of the 'strong-woman motif in Russian literature',[60] many Russian critics insist that the Russian novelistic tradition by no means denigrates women, but, on the contrary, places them on a pedestal. However, as mentioned above, idealization can be interpreted as simply another form of sexism, since literary heroines are expected to conform to what Barbara Heldt has called 'terrible perfection'. These paradigmatic images of women as angels or monsters have deeply influenced Russian women writers,[61] although some, such as Elena Gan, Karolina Pavlova and Nadezhda Khvoshchinskaia, while feeling an 'anxiety of authorship' in the face of the masculine cultural tradition, have been able simultaneously to conform to and subvert these images.[62]

Recent works by feminist historians and critics have emphasized that even writers conventionally considered to be sympathetic to women's problems in nineteenth-century Russia, such as Ivan Turgenev or Russian radicals of the 1860s concerned with the 'woman question', have sometimes adapted women's writing to their own purposes,[63] or abrogated to themselves the natural right to speak in the name of women, mapping out paths to their liberation which may not always have suited women themselves.[64]

Another reason why prose fiction is problematic for Russian women is that 'women's prose' *(zhenskaia proza)*, and *a fortiori*, 'women's literature' as a whole *(zhenskaia literatura)* are terms coined by male critics which sound pejorative in Russian, suggesting a literature devoted exclusively to love and trivial themes, and a preference for a simplistic, over-emotional, even hysterical style (the Russian equivalent of Mills and Boon romances). However, as Nancy Miller has noted, the term 'women's literature' is generally 'applied to such fiction by those who do not read it'.[65] As Mariia Mikhailova and I demonstrate below, such popular 'middle-brow fiction' could be valuable to Russian women writers as a form of self-expression, and to Russian women readers for the sexual, moral and social issues it raised.

Perhaps the most significant obstacle to a feminist reinterpretation of Russian literature is the persistent lack of interest in women's literature as a distinctive genre within Russia itself. Russian women writers and critics frequently deny that there is such a thing as 'women's literature'; or, if they do acknowledge its existence, they denigrate it in terms similar to those used by male critics.[66] The highest praise that can be accorded to a Russian woman writer is that she is a 'poet' rather than a 'poetess', a 'writer' rather than a 'woman writer', and that she writes with 'a masculine hand' or 'a masculine pen'. Brought up in this tradition, and eager to be accepted into the cultural mainstream in a society which has disadvantaged, marginalized and excluded them,[67] many Russian women writers have adopted a view similar to that of Marina Tsvetaeva: 'In art, there is no woman question. There are only women's responses to the human question.'[68] Such a view is implicitly accepted by many contemporary women writers, who prefer to regard themselves as individuals rather than as women, and take pride in their choice of humanistic themes transcending the allegedly narrow range of those considered typical of 'women's literature'.

Such ideas can be irritating to western feminist critics, who espouse the view that gender, along with other factors, such as age, nationality, religion, ethnicity, education and experience, cannot fail to exert some influence, if only subconsciously, on a writer's work.[69] As Virginia Woolf maintained, 'A woman's writing is always feminine; it cannot help being feminine; at its best it is most feminine; the only difference lies in defining what we mean by feminine'.[70] It is somewhat curious that the essentialist notions of gender propagated in the USSR and contemporary Russia have always maintained that women are influenced by their sex in every other activity they undertake, while implying that this influence miraculously disappears as soon as they take up the pen.

It is, however, necessary to remember that Russian women writers' denigration of 'women's literature' is a natural product of their own repressive, patriarchal culture. The fact that such terms as 'women's literature' and *'poetessa'* have a pejorative ring in Russia means that this may simply be a quarrel about semantics, rather than substance: Russian women writers correctly perceive that such labels denote inferiority in their culture. If in Russian 'women's literature' is nothing but a synonym for 'bad' or 'trivial literature', it is not surprising that good women writers do not wish to be part of it.

Moreover, lack of sympathy for the concept of 'women's literature' on the part of prominent Russian women writers has sometimes also sprung directly from their need to defend their work, sometimes even their lives, against hostile attacks by male critics. Tsvetaeva's view, for example, was a forceful response to a highly patriarchal, politically charged society in which a prominent member of the Soviet government, Lev Trotskii, had denigrated the 'very small ... lyric range of Akhmatova, Tsvetaeva, Radlova and other real and near-poetesses'.[71] Similarly, when considering the provocative remark attributed to Lidiia Chukovskaia: 'What does "women's literature" mean? You can have a women's sauna, but literature?',[72] we need to bear in mind that Chukovskaia, for all her individuality, was nevertheless a product of Stalinist society, where patriarchal values were all-pervasive.[73] She was, moreover, deeply influenced by her father, the prominent literary critic Kornei Chukovskii, who brought her up to conform to male standards,[74] and had a well-developed sense of art as service to a cause (in her case, bearing witness to Stalinist injustice) which she perceived as wider than mere 'women's issues'. Given her attitude, it is somewhat ironic that Chukovskaia, along with Akhmatova, who hated to be regarded as a 'poetess', and was denigrated by Stalin's spokesman Andrei Zhdanov in offensive misogynistic terms as 'part-nun, part-harlot', did more than any other writer to bear witness to the real situation of Soviet women in the 1930s.[75]

Even the greatest Russian women writers appear to accept the patriarchal view that to be seen to treat 'women's themes' somehow diminishes their work, narrowing their purview to a mere half of the human race. Russian writers and critics seem impervious to the argument that the depiction of female characters and the discussion of issues of concern to women in such works as Akhmatova's *Requiem*, Chukovskaia's *Sof'ia Petrovna* and the memoirs of Evgeniia Ginzburg are not necessarily incompatible with the exploration of such traditionally 'masculine' themes as the plight of the Soviet intelligentsia or the destiny of Russia. If Turgenev, Tolstoi and Dostoevskii can use female characters as a vehicle for the expression of general truths about the human condition, what, apart from the strictures of unsympathetic male critics, prevents Russian women writers from doing the same? The denigration of 'women's literature' by many Russian women writers suggests that they have internalized the patriarchal values of their culture, and, in the words of Simone de Beauvoir, 'still dream through the dreams of men'.[76] But, as Toril Moi points out, 'the fact that women often enact the roles patriarchy has prescribed for them does not mean that the patriarchal analysis is right'.[77]

The prevalence of such anti-feminist views in Russia nevertheless suggests that it is important for western critics to take account of the real historical and political circumstances in which Russian women have written, and still write today; and not to seek to impose arbitrary western feminist models on the very different experience of Russian women.[78] That is not, however, to say that feminist criticism cannot add considerably to our understanding of texts by Russian women, even those usually considered typical products of socialist realism, such as the works of Galina Nikolaeva and Vera Panova, or little different from the 'masculine literature' of the post-Stalin era, for example the stories of I. Grekova. Writers are not always the best judges of their own work; texts by Russian women writers who do not consider themselves to be 'feminists', such as Baranskaia, Petrushevskaia, and even the vociferously anti-feminist Tolstaia,[79] frequently afford penetrating insights into women's alienation in Russian society or deconstruct conventional gender stereotypes, and can thus legitimately be interpreted in a feminist manner.[80] At all events, the post-modernist theory of the 'free play of the signifier',[81] which encourages readers to discover a multitude of possible meanings in a text, legitimizes such interpretations (as well as their opposite).

AN OVERVIEW OF RUSSIAN WOMEN'S WRITING

Western feminists have frequently pointed out that the commonly accepted periodization of literary history is not appropriate to women's writing in Western Europe and the USA.[82] Similarly, this volume suggests that a considerable divergence also existed between significant periods of masculine and feminine writing in Russia.[83] There was no 'Golden Age' of Russian women's writing in the 1830s and 1840s; but the 'Silver Age' of men's writing from the 1890s to the Revolution did prove to be an important period for women's culture too, since it witnessed the emergence of a varied group of talented, *avant-garde* women writers and actors, who criticized outdated notions about men and women and the nature of their roles.[84] Perhaps a more satisfactory general periodization of Russian women's fiction might to some extent follow Elaine Showalter's[85] classification of English women's fiction into the 'Feminine', 'Feminist' and 'Female' stages.[86]

In modern Russia the 'Feminine' phase of women's writing, defined by Showalter as a period in which 'women wrote in an effort to equal the intellectual achievements of the male culture, and internalized its assumptions about female nature',[87] began in the eighteenth century, in the reign of Catherine the Great, herself a writer and a promoter of secondary education for women. In pre-revolutionary Russia, however, women generally found it difficult to penetrate into the mainstream of Russian culture, not only because control over most forms of artistic expression was in the hands of men, but also because of their lack of formal education, low social status and the many preconceived notions which prevailed about 'feminine' psychology and experience. Nevertheless, exceptional women in

Russia did manage to make some contribution to their country's culture in the late eighteenth and early nineteenth centuries, even if their success was often dependent on obtaining
the support of influential men – either by finding a patron, like
Anna Bunina, or by establishing a salon, as in the case of
Evdokiia Rostopchina and Karolina Pavlova. Another, exceptional method of entering the world of men was adopted by
Nadezhda Durova, who assumed the dress of a hussar and
fought in the campaign against Napoleon. Other women
writers, who were not of noble birth and lacked influential
connections, such as Elizaveta Kul'man and Nadezhda
Teplova, did not always survive male indifference or persecution, and are only now being discovered by feminist critics.[88]
Recent research, including the essays of Rosslyn, Demidova
and Rosenholm presented below, has made it clear that the
nineteenth century did not merely witness a disparate succession of unconnected women writers, as had previously been
thought, but that these women shared many common themes
and experiences, notably their sense of alienation and marginalization in Russian society and culture.

Although as early as the 1840s and 1850s feminist ideas
current in Europe took root very quickly in the economically
backward society of Russia, the 'woman question' was, as
Rosenholm suggests, rapidly appropriated by radical male
writers and critics, who established their own agenda which did
not always correspond to that of Russian women,[89] concentrating on political demands for equal rights with men,[90] and
establishing a close link between the personal liberation of
women and the liberation of society as a whole.

Showalter's characterization of the second period of
women's writing in Britain and the USA as the 'Feminist' stage
is equally true of Russia.[91] Just as the first wave of the Russian
feminist movement remained largely unknown in Russia until
pioneering studies by western scholars brought it to the attention of Russian feminists,[92] it is also not generally known, and
less in Russia than in the West, that Russia possessed a
flourishing tradition of feminist writings which appeared from
the 1880s to the Revolution and beyond, into the 1920s. The

major difference between feminist writings before the Revolution and after, and between feminist writings in Soviet Russia and elsewhere, was that, since legislation promoting women's equality was introduced much earlier in Russia than in many other countries, feminist writings of the 1920s, such as the essays and novels of Aleksandra Kollontai, were concerned not with the struggle for emancipation, but with the problems attendant on it. This feminist phase of women's writing, embodying ideas far ahead of their time, deserves to be better known: most modern Russian women do not even know of its existence, since it has been perhaps more successfully buried by patriarchy and politics than that of any other country.[93] Russian women are unaware that long ago such writers as Anastasiia Krandievskaia, Tat'iana Shchepkina-Kupernik, Anastasiia Verbitskaia, Ol'ga Shapir and Aleksandra Kollontai addressed themes which are still of concern to women of their own and other cultures in the late twentieth century, depicting the complexities of the modern woman torn between a desire for independence and such 'atavistic' female emotions as the need for love and security.[94] The neglect to which this literary tradition has been subjected in Russia has little to do with its intrinsic merits or demerits; it springs from the general hostility to feminism embedded in the patriarchal culture of Russia and the USSR, and particularly from the view which held sway for much of the Soviet period, that the 'woman question' had already been solved.

It is in the late 1920s that analogies with western Europe and the USA begin to break down. The third period of 'Female' writing defined by Showalter as 'a phase of *self-discovery*, a turning inward freed from some of the dependency of opposition, a search for identity', which in Britain began with the writings of Virginia Woolf in the 1920s and has continued to the present day,[95] was not accompanied by a similar development in Russia, where women writers were doubly shackled by Stalin's anti-feminist revolution and the harsh political controls imposed on all Soviet writers. In the Stalin era a new concept of Soviet womanhood emerged, which all writers and artists were expected to promote: a glorification of maternal and wifely

values, coupled with demands that women should be economically productive. As women's liberation had allegedly been
achieved in the USSR, the history of women's writing in
metropolitan Russia since the 1920s represented a retreat,
rather than an advance, from the point of view of the airing of
women's issues, until the accession of Gorbachev in 1985.
Women writers in emigration were also subject to certain
intellectual constraints, such as essentialist notions of gender
inherited from the Silver Age, although these were less severe
than those affecting Soviet women writers.[96]

   Although the publication of Natal'ia Baranskaia's novella
Nedelia kak nedelia (*A Week like Any Other*, 1969)[97] led to a certain
revival of interest in women's issues in literature and the press
in the late 1960s and 1970s, Russian literature has not yet
progressed through a new, genuinely feminist period, as occurred in the West in the 1960s and 1970s. In Russia patriarchal
attitudes have persisted unabated until the present day: even
after the inception of glasnost, little interest was evinced by
major literary journals in publishing the work of Aleksandra
Kollontai and other prominent first-wave feminists, and,
whereas most other *samizdat* and *tamizdat* works had appeared
earlier, in the late 1980s, Iuliia Voznesenskaia's *Zhenskii dekameron* (*The Women's Decameron*, 1986) along with other controversial *émigré* publications, had to wait until 1992 before at long last
achieving publication in Russia. Such classic feminist works as
Simone de Beauvoir's *The Second Sex* and other key feminist texts
are only now appearing in Russia in the post-communist
period.

   In the perestroika and post-perestroika eras, Russian
women's fiction has to some extent bypassed the second wave of
feminism and progressed directly to the third, autonomous
'Female' phase of women's writing. As Sandler, Trofimova and
Goscilo demonstrate, the 1980s and 1990s have witnessed a
great flowering of women's poetry and prose, which now
represents some of the most interesting literature being written
in Russia today. Glasnost has brought to the fore some
examples of independent female creativity and intimations of a
feminist point of view. Although contemporary Russian women

writers do not call themselves 'feminists', many present believable women in recognizable settings, not the positive or negative stereotypes which still proliferate in masculine literature. Women of all ages, social backgrounds, occupations and characters are represented in women's fiction, counteracting the masculine tendency to concentrate on the sexy young woman or the wise old woman. It is difficult to generalize about recent writings by Russian women, but women's prose and drama in the 1970s and 1980s have tended, not surprisingly, to be written from a feminine point of view and to provide a realistic picture of women's everyday lives, focusing on the problems of combining work and domestic duties, and on relationships with men, children and family members. Women's prose provides a detailed, often bleak picture of Russian society, exposes the disintegration of morality and family relationships, and the daily indignities with which Russian women have to contend.

Since late 1987, glasnost and post-modernist concepts of literature have enabled Russian women poets and prose writers to speak in a plurality of voices, to employ predominantly masculine genres, such as the philosophical lyric,[98] and to break out of the Romantic paradigms of woman as moral being (the 'Turgenevan maiden'), as Virgin Mary or Mother Russia. As Helena Goscilo has shown, contemporary writers such as Makarova, Vaneeva and Petrushevskaia have begun to 'write the body', often featuring horrific or masochistic aspects of female physical being, to reject gender stereotypes, and elevate their own conceptions of female space.[99] Post-modernism has proved liberating for Russian women writers, since it has enabled them (at least in their texts)[100] to break free from the essentialist notions of man and woman which are so deeply embedded in their culture. In the words of Julia Kristeva, 'What can "identity", even "sexual identity", mean in a new theoretical and scientific space where the very notion of identity is challenged?'[101]

Critics have, however, pointed out that post-modernism is not necessarily compatible with feminism,[102] and this is certainly true of contemporary Russia. Discussions of women's creativity at the Second Independent Women's Forum at

Dubna in November 1992 and the Bath conference in 1993 suggested that many Russian women writers do not know what 'feminism' is, although some seemed unwittingly to be groping towards a consciousness similar to that expressed in much western literature and literary criticism since the late 1960s. Many have a feeling of alienation, of being 'the other' in a world not made for them; they feel uncomfortable with the patriarchal family, the male-dominated political system and the current exhortations to Russian women to return to traditional values of home and family, even though they do not call their ideas 'feminist'. In much contemporary women's writing in Russia, as in western women's literature, there is an indefinable sense of emptiness, of loss, or of an absence of stable identity, and a desire to escape.[103] There is also a significant confusion about gender: Helena Goscilo shows that contemporary women writers often choose to set their fiction in confined spaces such as hospitals or prisons, but these could be interpreted not so much as autonomous feminine settings, but rather as patriarchal images of constraint and passivity.[104]

Although there has been a great upsurge of women's writing in contemporary Russia, women writers have sometimes found it difficult to achieve publication, as editors, who are still predominantly male, sometimes criticize them in the same way that they have done since the late eighteenth century: for a concentration on the 'personal life' and the treatment of allegedly trivial themes.[105] For a female observer, it is difficult to understand why such 'eternal' themes as birth, love, family life, human relationships, suffering and death, should be considered more trivial than conventionally 'masculine' themes such as politics and history, which, in the Russian context at least, have proved to be far more mutable and ephemeral.

Some advances have been made in post-communist Russia: there are now some women editors, such as Natal'ia Perova, the editor of the English-language journal *Glas*; and some contemporary women's writing has received international recognition, in that three works by women writers have been nominated for the Russian Booker Prize in 1992 and 1993,[106] but no woman has yet won the prize, even though some critics considered

Petrushevskaia's *Vremia noch'* (*Night Time*)[107] the most interesting novel of 1992.

CONCLUSION

While emphasizing the profound misogyny of Russian and Soviet culture, this book also explores the various ways in which Russian women writers have adapted to, or attempted to resist, the patriarchal society and culture of their country, both in their texts and in their lives. Although much research still remains to be done into the image of women in Russian literature and the works of Russian women writers, amply justifying the separate presentation of essays on these subjects, it is to be hoped that an understanding of gender difference and the lives and work of Russian women writers will ultimately be integrated more closely into 'mainstream' studies of Russian literature, thereby redefining the literary canon and presenting a more balanced view of Russian culture as a whole.[108]

NOTES

1   Elaine Showalter, *A Literature of Their Own: From Charlotte Brontë to Doris Lessing*, revised edn (London: Virago, 1992), p. 10. Except in direct quotations, I adopt the established usage in feminist criticism whereby the word 'female' is used to mean women's biological sex, whereas 'feminine' is used to refer to social and cultural constructs of womanhood.

2   Elaine Showalter, 'Towards a feminist poetics', in Mary Jacobus, ed., *Women Writing and Writing about Women* (London: Croom Helm, 1979), p. 25. On the image of women in Russian literature, see Barbara Heldt, *Terrible Perfection: Women and Russian Literature* (Bloomington, IN: Indiana University Press, 1987); Joe Andrew, *Women in Russian Literature, 1780–1863* (Basingstoke: Macmillan, 1988); Sigrid McLaughlin, *The Image of Women in Contemporary Soviet Fiction* (Basingstoke: Macmillan, 1989); Xenia Gasiorowska, *Women in Soviet Literature, 1917–1964* (Madison, WI: Wisconsin University Press, 1968).

3   For the rediscovery of texts by Russian women, see Frank Göpfert, *Dichterinnen und Schriftsellerinnen in Russland von der Mitte des 18. bis zum Beginn des 20. Jahrhunderts: eine Problemskizze*

(Munich: Otto Sagner, 1992); Uta Grabmüller and Monika Katz, *Zwischen Anpassung und Widerspruch* (Berlin: Osteuropa-Institut, Free University of Berlin, 1993); Marina Ledkovsky, Charlotte Rosenthal and Mary Zirin, eds., *A Dictionary of Russian Women Writers* (Westport, CT: Greenwood Press, 1994); Catriona Kelly, *A History of Russian Women's Writing, 1820–1992* (Oxford: Clarendon Press, 1994); Toby W. Clyman and Diana Greene, eds., *Women Writers in Russian Literature* (Westport, CT: Praeger, 1994). Barbara Heldt's *Terrible Perfection* ventures into both fields, although it is primarily concerned with the feminist critique of nineteenth-century Russian literature; and Joe Andrew's *Narrative and Desire in Russian Literature, 1822–1849: the Feminine and the Masculine* (London: St Martin's Press, 1993) discusses both male and female writers in the nineteenth century. Previous interdisciplinary studies combining essays on history, politics and culture include Linda Edmondson, ed., *Women and Society in Russia and the Soviet Union* (Cambridge: Cambridge University Press, 1992); Marianne Liljeström, Eila Mäntysaari and Arja Rosenholm, eds., *Gender Restructuring in Russian Studies*, Slavica Tamperensia, II (Tampere: University of Tampere, 1993); Jane T. Costlow, Stephanie Sandler and Judith Vowles, eds., *Sexuality and the Body in Russian Culture* (Stanford, CA: Stanford University Press, 1993). I am greatly indebted to all these works. For excellent and informative general introductions to women's literature in Russia, see Marina Ledkovsky, Charlotte Rosenthal and Mary Zirin, 'Introduction', in Ledkovsky, Rosenthal and Zirin, *Dictionary of Russian Women Writers*, pp.xxvii–xli; Toby W. Clyman and Diana Greene, 'Introduction', in Greene and Clyman, *Women Writers in Russian Literature*, pp.xi–xvii; Susan Hardy Aiken and Adele Barker, 'Afterword: Histories and Fictions', in Susan Hardy Aiken, Adele Marie Barker, Maya Koreneva and Ekaterina Stetsenko, *Dialogues/ Dialogi: Literary and Cultural Exchanges between (ex)Soviet and American Women* (Durham and London: Duke University Press, 1994) pp. 357–92; on post-Stalin fiction, see Helena Goscilo, 'Introduction', in Helena Goscilo, ed., *Balancing Acts: Contemporary Stories by Russian Women* (Bloomington and Indianapolis, IN: Indiana University Press, 1989), pp.xiii–xxvii.

4 On the value of such a comparative approach, see Annette Kolodny, 'Some notes on defining a "feminist literary criticism"', *Critical Inquiry*, 2, 1 (1975), p. 78; Myra Jehlen, 'Archimedes and the paradox of feminist criticism', *Signs*, 6, 4 (1981), p. 584. The contemporary trend in feminist literary criticism is to

focus on gender – cultural constructions of masculinity and femininity – rather than specifically on women writers.

5 See, for example, William M. Mandel, *Soviet Women* (Garden City, NY: Anchor Books, 1975); Richard Stites, *The Women's Liberation Movement in Russia: Feminism, Nihilism and Bolshevism, 1860–1930* (Princeton, NJ: Princeton University Press, 1978); Gail Warshofsky Lapidus, *Women in Soviet Society* (Berkeley, CA: University of California Press, 1978).

6 Very few women writers are mentioned, for example, in D. S. Mirsky, *A History of Russian Literature* (London: Routledge, 1949); Mark Slonim, *The Epic of Russian Literature* (New York: Oxford University Press, 1964); Charles Moser, ed., *The Cambridge History of Russian Literature* (Cambridge: Cambridge University Press, 1992). On the way in which literary canons have excluded women, see Tillie Olsen, *Silences* (London: Virago, 1980); Dale Spender, *Women of Ideas and What Men Have Done to Them* (London: Routledge, 1982).

7 On autocratic pre-revolutionary Russia, see Barbara Evans Clements, Barbara Alpern Engel and Christine D. Worobec, eds., *Russia's Women: Accommodation, Resistance, Transformation* (Berkeley and Oxford: University of California Press, 1991); on the Soviet period, see Mary Buckley, *Women and Ideology in the Soviet Union* (New York and London: Harvester Wheatsheaf, 1989); on the construction of gender in the USSR, see Lynne Attwood, *The New Soviet Man and Woman: Sex-Role Socialisation in the USSR* (Basingstoke: Macmillan, 1990); on the development of a new kind of patriarchal system in post-communist Russia, see Rosalind Marsh, ed., *Women in Russia and Ukraine* (Cambridge: Cambridge University Press, 1996).

8 Tat'iana Mamonova's *Russian Women's Studies: Essays on Sexism in Soviet Culture* (New York: Pergamon, 1989) is rather slight and disappointing. However, many examples of misogynistic Russian thought emerge from the books mentioned in notes 2 and 3; and from this volume. See, in particular, the references below to *Domostroi*; the patronizing attitudes of men to women writers in the early nineteenth century; Belinskii's influential attack on women writers; Shelgunov's complaint of 1870 that women were not taking part in the discussion of the 'woman question'; the widespread acceptance of the essentialist views of Weininger in the Silver Age and beyond; criticisms of Verbitskaia and the suppression of her work; the views of political figures such as Trotskii and Zhdanov.

9 Heldt, *Terrible Perfection*, p. 3.

10 See Rosenthal, and Marsh below, pp. 136–7 and 191.

11 Analyses of these issues are too numerous to mention, but the specific references are taken from Simone de Beauvoir, *The Second Sex*, trans. and ed. H. M. Parshley (Harmondsworth: Penguin, 1988); Sherry Ortner, 'Is Female to Male as Nature is to Culture?', in Michelle Rosaldo and Louise Lamphere, eds., *Woman, Culture and Society* (Stanford, CA: Stanford University Press, 1974), pp. 67–87; Hélène Cixous (with Catherine Clément), *La Jeune Neé* (Paris: Union géneral d'éditions, 1975), p. 115.

12 On women's unconscious internalization of sexist attitudes and desires, see Toril Moi, *Sexual/Textual Politics: Feminist Literary Theory* (London and New York: Routledge, 1985), p. 92; Cora Kaplan, 'Radical feminism and literature: rethinking Millett's *Sexual Politics*', *Red Letters*, 9, p. 10.

13 N. N. Shneidman, *Soviet Literature in the 1980s: Decade of Transition* (Toronto: University of Toronto Press, 1989), p. 169.

14 X[enia] G[asiorowska], 'Women and Russian literature', in Victor Terras, ed., *Handbook of Russian Literature* (New Haven and London: Yale University Press 1985), p. 520.

15 Exceptions include Temira Pachmuss, trans. and ed., *Women Writers in Russian Modernism* (Urbana, IL: University of Illinois Press, 1978); Charlotte Rosenthal, 'The Silver Age: highpoint for women?'; Marina Ledkovsky (Astman), 'Russian women writers: an overview. Post-revolutionary dispersion and adjustment', in Edmondson, ed., *Women and society in Russia and the Soviet Union*, pp. 32–47, 145–59. This comment is not meant to disparage the many illuminating studies of Akhmatova and Tsvetaeva.

16 John Gross, *The Rise and Fall of the Man of Letters: English Literature since 1991* (Chicago: I. R. Dee, 1991), p. 304. The weakness of an approach which moves from 'Great Woman' to 'Great Woman' and derives all theories from only four or five writers is highlighted in Showalter, *A Literature of their Own*, pp. 6–7. Although the appearance of the *Dictionary of Russian Women Writers* and Kelly's *History of Russian Women's Writing* have begun to set this to rights, there are still few book-length studies of Russian women writers other than Akhmatova and Tsvetaeva. Recent exceptions are Beth Holmgren, *Women's Works in Stalin's Time: On Lidiia Chukovskaia and Nadezhda Mandelstam* (Bloomington: Indiana University Press, 1993); Sonia I. Ketchian, *The Poetic Craft of Bella Akhmadulina* (University Park, PA: Pennsylvania State University Press, 1993) and Diana Burgin, *Sophia Parnok: The Life and Work of Russia's Sappho* (New York: New York University Press, 1994).

Books on Anna Bunina and women writers of the 1860s are in preparation by contributors to this volume.

17 Heldt, *Terrible Perfection*; Andrew, *Women and Russian Literature*.

18 On the benefits of being 'late to the feast', see Helena Goscilo, 'Introduction', in Helena Goscilo, ed., *Fruits of her Plume: Essays on Contemporary Russian Women's Culture* (Armonk, New York and London: M. E. Sharpe, 1993), pp. xvii–xviii.

19 See note 3 above. The *Dictionary of Russian Women Writers* contains infomation on 448 Russian women writers and activists. For an excellent survey of recent feminist research into Russian literature and history, see Barbara Heldt, 'Feminism and the Slavic field', *The Harriman Review*, 7, 10–12 (November 1994), pp. 11–18.

20 Exceptions include the critique of Pasternak's *Doctor Zhivago* in Heldt, *Terrible Perfection*, pp. 146–9; on the stereotyped images of women in Solzhenitsyn's *V kruge pervom*, see Rosalind Wells, 'The definitive Solzhenitsyn?', *Irish Slavonic Studies*, 1 (1980), p. 118.

21 Patricia Meyer Spacks, *The Female Imagination. A Literary and Psychological Investigation of Women's Writing* (London: Allen and Unwin, 1976), p. 3.

22 For her justification of this approach, see Kelly, *A History of Russian Women's Writing*, pp. 4–5.

23 Woolf, *Collected Essays*, 2 (London, 1967), p. 141.

24 Showalter, *A Literature of Their Own*; Sandra M. Gilbert and Susan Gubar, *The Madwoman in the Attic: the Woman Writer and the Nineteenth-Century Literary Imagination* (New Haven and London: Yale University Press, 1979), pp. 3–92; Dale Spender, *Women of Ideas and What Men have Done to Them* (London: Routledge, 1982); Joanna Russ, *How to Suppress Women's Writing* (London: The Women's Press, 1984).

25 See, for example, Osip Mandel'shtam's famous statement that 'Poetry is respected only in this country – people are killed for it. There's no place where more people are killed for it': Nadezhda Mandelstam, *Hope against Hope*, trans. Max Hayward (Harmondsworth: Penguin, 1975), p. 190.

26 See note 8 above. As in other countries, women writers prominent in the realist, Symbolist and Decadent movements of the immediate pre-revolutionary period, while sometimes enjoying the support of husbands and patrons, were largely neglected, misinterpreted or condemned by male critics of their day for their feminism or alleged immorality – as they have been in Russia to some degree ever since. For male critics' hostility to English 'decadent' women writers, see Elaine Showalter, 'Introduction', in Elaine Showalter, ed., *Daughters of Decadence: Women*

Writers of the Fin de Siècle (London: Virago, 1993), pp. ix–x. On
male critics' ploy of attributing immorality to women writers, see
Joanna Russ, *How to Suppress Women's Writing*, pp. 25–30.

27 This is evident from many writers' biographies in Ledkovsky,
Rosenthal and Zirin, *Dictionary of Russian Women Writers*.

28 Toby W. Clyman and Diana Greene, 'Introduction', in Clyman
and Greene, *Women Writers in Russian Literature*, p. xi; their analysis
is based on the discussion of American women writers in Nina
Baym, 'Melodramas of beset manhood: how theories of American
fiction exclude women authors', *American Quarterly*, 33 (1981),
123–39.

29 Exceptions include Clements, Engel and Worobec, *Russia's
Women*; N. L. Pushkareva, *Zhenshchiny drevnei Rusi* (Moscow: Mysl',
1989); Joanna Hubbs, *Mother Russia: the Feminine Myth in Russian
Culture* (Bloomington: Indiana University Press, 1988); Eve Levin,
Sex and Society in the World of the Orthodox Slavs, 900–1700 (Ithaca,
NY: Cornell University Press, 1989); Margaret Ziolkovski,
'Women in Old Russian literature', in Clyman and Greene,
Women Writers in Russian Literature, pp. 1–15.

30 Kelly, *A History of Russian Women's Writing*, p. 9.

31 For a lesbian critic's attack on Zinov'eva-Annibal's decadent
treatment of lesbianism, and her 'misogynistic and anti-Lesbian
moral', see Diana Lewis Burgin, 'Laid out in lavender: perceptions of lesbian love in Russian literature and criticism of the
Silver Age, 1893–1917', in Costlow, Sandler and Vowles, *Sexuality
and the Body in Russian Culture*, pp. 182–4.

32 See Bonnie Zimmerman, 'What has hever been. An overview of
lesbian feminist literary criticism', in Elaine Showalter, ed., *The
New Feminist Criticism: Essays on Women, Literature and Theory*
(London: Virago, 1986), p. 207. For further discussion of the
relationship between lesbian criticism and feminist criticism, see
Adrienne Rich, 'Compulsory heterosexuality and lesbian existence', *Signs*, 5, 4 (Summer 1980), 631–60. As yet there are few
studies of lesbian themes in Russian literature, apart from
Burgin, 'Laid out in lavender'; and studies on the lesbian poet
Sof'ia Parnok, such as Diana Lewis Burgin, 'Sof'ia Parnok and
the writing of a lesbian poet's life', *Slavic Review*, 51, 2 (1992), 214–
31; Sof'ia V. Poliakova, *Nezakatnye ony dni: Tsvetaeva i Parnok* (Ann
Arbor, MI: Ardis, 1983). See also Simon Karlinsky, 'Russia's gay
literature and history (11th–20th Centuries)', *Gay Sunshine* (San
Francisco), 29–30 (1976), 1–7.

33 See, in particular, M. Sh. Fainshtein, *Pisateli pushkinskoi pory*
(Leningrad: Nauka, 1989); criticized by Diana Greene,

'Nineteenth-century women poets: critical reception vs. self-definition', in Clyman and Greene, *Women Writers in Russian Literature*, p. 107, n. 3 for 'referring to Kul′man, Teplova, Rostopchina and Pavlova by their first names and devoting a great deal of space to their physical appearances and relations with men'. On women's fiction of the nineteenth and early twentieth century, see the three volumes edited by V. Uchenova, *Dacha na Petergofskoi doroge: Proza russkikh pisatel′nits pervoi poloviny XIX veka* (Moscow: Sovremennik, 1986); *Svidanie: Proza russkikh pisatel′nits 60–80-kh godov XIX veka* (Moscow: Sovremennik, 1987); *Tol′ko chas: Proza russikh pisatel′nits kontsa XIX – nachala XX veka* (Moscow: Sovremennik, 1988). These selections may have been influenced by Russian critics' predilection for 'committed literature'. Among several collections of women's fiction published in Russia in the 1990s, perhaps partly in response to interest from western feminists, some, have, unfortunately, been given titles suggestive of Russian women's 'terrible perfection': see, for example, A. V. Shavkut, ed., *Chisten′kaia zhizn′* (*A Very Pure Life*, Moscow: Molodaia gvardiia, 1990); and Larisa Vaneeva, ed., *Ne pomniashchaia zla* (*A Woman without Malice*, Moscow: Moskovskii rabochii, 1990). In the post-communist period another collection has appeared, Elena Trofimova, ed., *Chego khochet zhenshchina* ... (Moscow: Amrita, 1993), whose title is a response to Freud's famous question 'What do women want?'.

34 See, for example, Alla Gracheva, 'Russkoe nitssheanstvo i zhenskii roman nachala XX veka' and Viktoriia Uchenova, 'Formirovanie zhenskogo nonkonformizma v Rossii i ego otrazhenie v tvorchestve pisatel′nits XIX veka', in Liljeström, Mäntysaari and Rosenholm, *Gender Restructuring in Russian Studies*, pp. 87–98, 229–42; Alla Gracheva, 'Estetika russkogo moderna: zhenskaia proza nachala XX veka (A. A. Verbitskaia)', in Frank Göpfert, ed., *Russland aus der Feder seiner Frauen. Zum femininen Diskurs in der russischen Literatur. Materialen des vom 21/22 Mai 1992 im Fachbereich Slavistik der Universität Potsdam durchgeführten Kolloquiums* (Munich: Otto Sagner, 1993); Ol′ga Demidova, 'The reception of Charlotte Brontë's work in nineteenth-century Russia', *Modern Language Review*, 89, 3 (July 1994), pp. 689–96. See also the collection of contemporary Russian critics on women's writing, Helena Goscilo, ed., 'Skirted issues: the discreteness and indiscretions of Russian women's prose', *Russian Studies in Literature*, 28, 2 (Spring 1992), special issue. Collections of conference papers on women's culture by Russian scholars have begun to appear: see *Rossiiskie zhenshchiny i evropeiskaia kul′tura* (St Petersburg, 1993) and

30   ROSALIND MARSH

Zhenshchina i svoboda (Moscow: Nauka, 1994), but few of these are presented from a femininist point of view.

35 Moscow State University (MGU) and Russian State Humanitarian University (RGGU).

36 For a collection of feminist writings on contemporary society by members of the Moscow Gender Centre, see Anastasia Posadskaya, ed., *Women in Russia: a New Era in Russian Feminism* (London: Verso, 1994). The Gender Centre possesses a good library which has been largely stocked by foreign well-wishers.

37 Cf. Demidova, and Rosslyn below, pp. 93–5 and 55–9.

38 Linda Edmondson, 'Women's emancipation and theories of sexual difference in Russia, 1850–1917', in Liljeström, Mäntysaari and Rosenholm, eds., *Gender Restructuring in Russian Studies*, p. 51.

39 Kelly, *A History of Russian Women's Writing*, pp. 36–43.

40 Otto Weininger, *Geschlecht und Charakter* (Vienna, 1903); E. Koltonovskaia, *Zhenskie siluety* (St Petersburg, 1912).

41 Carol Ueland, 'Women's poetry in the Soviet Union', in Clyman and Greene, *Women Writers in Russian Literature*, p. 244, singles out Iskrenko's poem 'Chelovek – ona ne ptitsa' ('A person – she is not a bird'), which parodies the misogynistic proverb 'A chicken is not a bird, a woman is not a person' and other traditional assumptions about gender: see Nina Iskrenko, *Ili* (Moscow, 1991), p. 31.

42 For the lack of contact between the three prominent women members of the 'Society of Lovers of the Russian Word', see Rosslyn below, p. 73, n. 51.

43 Showalter, *A Literature of Their Own*, pp. 11–12. For this reason, Showalter calls British women's writing a 'subculture', not a 'movement'.

44 Ellen Moers, *Literary Women* (London: W. H. Allen, 1977), p. 63. On the rediscovery of previously suppressed Russian culture under glasnost, see Julian Graffy, 'The literary press', in Julian Graffy and Geoffrey Hosking, eds., *Literature and the Media in the USSR Today* (Basingstoke: Macmillan, 1989), pp. 107–58; Rosalind Marsh, *History and Literature in Contemporary Russia* (Basingstoke: Macmillan, 1995).

45 On the women's poetic tradition, see Charlotte Rosenthal, 'Achievement and obscurity: women's prose in the Silver Age', in Clyman and Greene, *Women Writers in Russian Literature*, pp. 164–5; for a subtle exploration of how Ol'ga Sedakova fits into the tradition of philosophical poetry in Russia, see Sandler, below, pp. 317–19. For the direct influence of Karolina Pavlova on Anna Prismanova, see Kelly, *A History of Russian Women's Writing*,

pp. 277–8. On the tradition of women's autobiographical writing in Russia, see Heldt, *Terrible Perfection*, pp. 64–102.

46 See, for example, the Petersburg poet Elena Chizhova's poem 'Kassandra', translated in Catriona Kelly, ed., *An Anthology of Russian Women's Writing, 1777–1992* (Oxford: Oxford University Press, 1994), p. 334, and her verse play *Tragediia Marii Stiuart, korolevy Shotlandii* (Petersburg, 1992); an extract is translated in Rosalind Marsh, 'New developments in Russian poetry: Elena Chizhova', *Essays in Poetics*, 18, 2 (1993), 88–110.

47 The debt of contemporary women poets to Akhmatova's *Poema bez geroia* has frequently been acknowledged: see, in particular, Inna Lisnianskaia, *Muzyka 'Poemy bez geroia' Anny Akhmatovoi* (Moscow: Khudozhestvennaia literatura, 1991), which also suggests that Marina Tsvetaeva is a crucial, hidden addressee in Akhmatova's poem. See also Stephanie Sandler's study of women poets' treatment of the image of Lot's wife, 'The canon and the backward glance. Akhmatova, Lisnianskaia, Petrovykh, Nikolaeva', in Goscilo, *Fruits of Her Plume*, pp. 113–33.

48 Rosenthal, 'Achievement and obscurity: women's prose in the Silver Age', pp. 151, 164–5 denies the existence of a prose tradition, of a conscious continuity between women writers.

49 Ellen Moers, 'Women's lit.: profession and tradition', *Columbia Forum*, 1 (Fall 1972), p. 27.

50 *Ibid.*, p. 28.

51 For collections of contemporary women's prose fiction, see Goscilo, ed., *Balancing Acts*; Helena Goscilo, ed., *Lives in Transit: Recent Russian Women's Writing* (Ann Arbor, MI: Ardis, 1993); *Soviet Women Writing*, ed. Jacqueline Decter (New York: Abbeville Press, 1990); *Women's View, Glas: New Russian Writing*, 3 (1992). Valuable essays on contemporary women writers are Helena Goscilo, 'Introduction', in Goscilo, *Balancing Acts*, pp.xiii–xxvii; Barbara Heldt, 'Gynoglasnost: writing the feminine', in Mary Buckley, ed., *Perestroika and Soviet Women* (Cambridge: Cambridge University Press, 1992), pp. 160–75; Goscilo, *Fruits of Her Plume*.

52 Heldt, *Terrible Perfection*, p. 7.

53 The latter reason is suggested in Jane T. Costlow, 'Love, work and the woman question in mid nineteenth-century women's writing', in Clyman and Greene, *Women Writers in Russian Literature*, p. 63.

54 For fuller discussion, see Catriona Kelly, 'Configurations of authority: feminism, modernism and mass culture, 1881–1917', Chapter 5 of her *A History of Russian Women's Writing*, pp. 121–80.

55 Joanna Russ, *How to Suppress Women's Writing*, p. 100 suggests that

many women writers have followed the injunction to 'get out of the "major" genres and into the "minor" ones. Stay on the periphery of culture'.

56 This is the main theme of Barbara Heldt's pioneering feminist work *Terrible Perfection*.

57 Discussed in Virginia Woolf, 'Professions for Women', in *The Death of the Moth and Other Essays* (New York: Harcourt Brace Jovanovich, 1942), pp. 236–8; Alexander Welsh, *The City of Dickens* (Oxford: Clarendon Press, 1971), pp. 164-95.

58 This phrase refers to the first Mrs Rochester in Charlotte Brontë's *Jane Eyre*, who has been interpreted by feminist critics as a symbol of the darker side of the Victorian woman's nature, particularly her repressed passion and sexuality: see Gilbert and Gubar, *The Madwoman in the Attic*.

59 Slavists have sometimes playfully adapted these terms to a Russian context: see Joe Andrew's reference to the 'Madwoman in the Garden' in Gan's *A Futile Gift* (see below, note 62); and Helena Goscilo's allusion to the 'Floosie in the Field' below, p. 328.

60 Vera Sandomirsky Dunham, 'The strong-woman motif', in Cyril E. Black, ed., *The Transformation of Russian Society* (Cambridge, MA, 1960), pp. 459–83.

61 There is a difference of opinion between Barbara Heldt, who believes that such images have always inhibited Russian women writers, and Catriona Kelly, *A History of Russian Women's Writing*, p. 13, who believes that they only became constraining on women writers in the era of 'committed literature' from the 1840s onwards.

62 Gilbert and Gubar, *The Madwoman in the Attic*, p. 59. Analyses of the simultaneously conformist and subversive nature of Russian women's texts include Joe Andrew, 'A futile gift: Elena Andreevna Gan and writing', in Liljeström, Mäntysaari and Rosenholm, *Gender Restructuring in Russian Studies*, pp. 1–14; Rosenholm below, pp. 117–28; Karolina Pavlova, *A Double Life*, trans. and ed. Barbara Heldt (Oakland, CA: Barbary Coast, 1987). Following the analysis of Mary Jacobus, 'The Difference of View', in Catherine Belsey and Jane Moore, eds., *The Feminist Reader. Essays in Gender and the Politics of Literary Criticism*, pp. 49–62, a close study of Russian women's writing enables us to establish the 'awkward breaks' in the text when the author's real feelings, often of despair or anger, break through.

63 Jane Costlow, 'Speaking the sorrow of women: Turgenev's "Neschastnaia" and Evgeniia Tur's "Antonina"', *Slavic Review*, 50, 2 (1991), 328–5 suggests that Turgenev borrowed, but radically

transformed, the heroine of Tur's *Antonina*. It could also be argued that the heroines of George Sand, who sees economic independence as crucial for women, may have exerted more influence on Russian women writers such as Nadezhda Khvoshchinskaia than Turgenev's 'new women'.

64 See Rosenholm below, pp. 112–25; Edmondson, 'Women's emancipation and theories of sexual difference in Russia, 1850–1917', pp. 39–51.

65 Nancy K. Miller, 'Emphasis added: plots and plausibilities in women's fiction', in Showalter, *The New Feminist Criticism*, p. 348.

66 Heated debates on this subject between Russian writers and western feminist critics took place in the 'Glasnost in Two Cultures' conference at New York University, 1991, and at the 'Women in Russia' conference at Bath, 1993.

67 On this problem in western culture, see Sandra M. Gilbert, 'What do feminist critics want? A postcard from the volcano', in Showalter, *The New Feminist Criticism*, pp. 29–45.

68 Cited in Simon Karlinsky, *Marina Tsvetaeva: the Woman, her World and her Poetry* (Cambridge: Cambridge University Press, 1986), pp. 96–7.

69 As Helena Goscilo argues, 'Paradigm Lost? Contemporary women's fiction', in Clyman and Greene, *Women Writers in Russian Literature*, p. 205, feminist critics in the West are discussing *how* gender affects writing, whereas in Russia they are still arguing over *whether* it does. For a similar view, see Aiken and Barker, 'Afterword', p. 383, n.2.

70 Virginia Woolf, *The Times Literary Supplement*, 17 October 1918.

71 Leon Trotsky, *Literature and Revolution*, trans. Rose Strunsky (Ann Arbor, MI: Ardis, 1968), p. 41.

72 Cited by Helena Goscilo, 'Introduction', in *Balancing Acts*, p.xiii.

73 Buckley, *Women and Ideology in the Soviet Union*, pp. 108–38.

74 See Beth Holmgren's entry on Chukovskaia in Ledkovsky, Rosenthal and Zirin, *Dictionary of Russian Women Writers*, pp. 133–4.

75 See Lidiia Chukovskaia, *Sof'ia Petrovna*, written in 1939–40, first published in Russia in *Neva*, 2 (1988); Anna Akhmatova, *Requiem*, written in 1935–40, first published in Russia in *Oktiabr'*, 3 (1987); *Neva*, 6 (1987).

76 Beauvoir, *The Second Sex*, p. 132.

77 Moi, *Sexual/Textual Politics*, p. 92.

78 For a recent expression of this viewpoint, see Larissa Lissyutkina, 'Soviet women at the crossroads of perestroika', in Nanette Funk and Magda Mueller, *Gender, Politics and Post-Communism: Reflections*

from Eastern Europe and the Former Soviet Union (New York and London: Routledge, 1993), pp. 274–86.

79 On Baranskaia, see McLaughlin, *The Image of Women in Soviet Fiction*, pp. 10, 112; on Petrushevskaia, see *ibid.*, 98–9; for a particularly virulent anti-feminist statement, see Tat'iana Tolstaia, 'Notes from underground', review of Francine du Plessix Gray, *Soviet Women: Walking the Tightrope, New York Review of Books*, 31 May 1990, pp. 3–7.

80 See Helena Goscilo, 'Monsters monomaniacal, marital and medical: Tat'iana Tolstaia's regenerative use of gender stereotypes', in Costlow, Sandler and Vowles, *Sexuality and the Body in Russian Culture*, pp. 204–22. Goscilo notes, however, that it is important to acknowledge the difference between women writers' texts and their public personae.

81 Jacques Derrida, *L'Ecriture et la Différance* (Paris: Seuil, 1967), adapted by Toril Moi to mean complete flexibility in thinking about gender, in *Sexual/Textual Politics*, pp. 172–3.

82 Elaine Showalter, 'Feminist criticism in the wilderness', in Showalter, *The New Feminist Criticism*, pp. 243–70.

83 For a discussion of why the periods of Sentimentalism, Romanticism and Realism commonly applied to masculine culture do not fit Russian women's writing, see Kelly, *A History of Russian Women Writers*, p. 23. The periods of women's writing she distinguishes are 1820–80, 1881–1917, 1917–53 and 1953–92.

84 See Pachmuss, *Women Writers in Russian Modernism*. Rosenthal, 'The Silver Age: highpoint for women?', p. 32 argues that the 'Silver Age', generally used to refer to the achievement of Russian male poets, 'was more of a Golden Age for women writers, particularly for female lyric poets'.

85 Elaine Showalter's work is considered suspect in some circles, but her historical approach to women's writing in *A Literature of their Own* is more appropriate to the historical overview of Russian women's writing attempted here than the ahistorical, psychoanalytical insights of French feminism, which are unable to study the historically changing impact of patriarchal discourse on women. See the critique of Luce Irigaray by Moi, *Sexual/Textual Politics*, pp. 147–8; Kelly, *A History of Russian Women's Writing*, p. 12. French feminist theory has, however, proved valuable to some contributors to this book in their analysis of specific texts, particularly modernist ones, and in deconstructing male writers' attempts to suppress women's voices (see Goscilo, Roberts below, pp. 326–7 and 249–50). Although Catriona Kelly, *A History of Russian Women's Writing*, pp. 6–7, correctly points out that 'The

facile equation between writing and experience which one finds in some Anglo-American feminist criticism has been very adequately critiqued by Toril Moi', Moi is nevertheless very complimentary about Showalter's *A Literature of their Own*, praising her emphasis on 'the rediscovery of forgotten or neglected women writers', her 'wide-ranging scholarship' and 'admirable enthusiasm and respect for its subject'. Moi regards Showalter's main shortcomings as unstated theoretical assumptions about the relationship between literature and reality, and between feminist poetics and literary evaluation. She is accused of a tendency to establish a separate canon of women's writing rather than the desire to abolish all canons, and is perceived as more successful in analysing realistic fiction, particularly that written between 1750 and 1930, than modernist texts by women writers: Moi, *Sexual/Textual Politics*, pp. 56, 75–80.

86 This is, of course, a very broad-brush approach to the subject, and should be refined by the more detailed categories suggested by Catriona Kelly (see note 88). For a subtle redefinition of Showalter's categories (and hence a possibly implied criticism of Showalter's approach), see Toril Moi, 'Feminist, female, feminine', in Belsey and Moore, *The Feminist Reader*, pp. 117–32. Showalter's categories cannot be directly translated into Russian, as *zhenskii* means both 'female' and 'feminine' in the senses Showalter means; *feministskii* has a pejorative tinge; and *zhenstvennyi* means 'feminine' or 'womanly' in a conventional sense which cannot easily be applied to literature.

87 Elaine Showalter, 'Towards a feminist poetics', in Mary Jacobus, ed., *Women Writing and Writing about Women* (London, 1979), p. 35.

88 Diana Greene, 'Nineteenth-century women poets: critical reception vs. self-definition', in Clyman and Greene, *Women Writers in Russian Literature*, pp. 97–9, 101–3.

89 For further discussion, see Edmondson, 'Women's emancipation', pp. 39–52.

90 J. Kristeva, 'Women's Time', in Toril Moi, ed., *The Kristeva Reader* (Oxford: Blackwell, 1986), pp. 193–4 regards such egalitarian demands as typical of those of the first generation of feminists in Western Europe; but in Russia feminist concerns have hardly progressed beyond this first stage: see Rosalind Marsh, 'The birth, death and rebirth of feminist writing in Russia', in Helena Forsås-Scott, ed., *Textual Liberation: European Feminist Writing in the Twentieth Century* (London and New York: Routledge, 1991), pp. 130–63.

91 Of course, the Silver Age also featured an anti-realist women's

tradition, in prose as well as poetry, notably the writings of Zinaida Gippius, Lidiia Zinov'eva-Annibal and Anastasiia Mirovich (see Davidson below, and Kelly, pp. 152–80). Symbolist writers, although generally not interested in the feminist movement, were also concerned with themes which today would be interpreted as feminist, such as woman's right to happiness through sexual and artistic fulfilment.

92 In a personal interview of 1991 the Petersburg feminist Ol'ga Lipovskaia admitted that she found out about the first-wave feminist movement in her own country through the works of western historians, such as Stites, *The Women's Liberation Movement in Russia*; Linda Edmondson, *Feminism in Russia, 1900–1917* (Stanford, CA: Stanford University Press, 1984).

93 Sandra M. Gilbert, 'What do feminist critics want?', in Showalter, *The New Feminist Criticism*, p. 43 argues that in other countries too the first-wave feminist movement as a whole has been 'massively and I think deliberately forgotten until recently ... because it is central to most aspects of all our lives – central, crucial and volcanically influential'; see also Theodore Roszak, 'The hard and the soft: the force of feminism in modern times', in Betty Roszak and Theodore Roszak, eds., *Masculine/Feminine: Readings in Sexual Mythology and the Liberation of Women* (New York: Harper and Row, 1969), pp. 87–104.

94 See the two works by Aleksandra Kollontai translated by Cathy Porter, *A Great Love* (London: Virago, 1981); *Love of Worker Bees* (London: Virago, 1988).

95 Showalter, *A Literature of their Own*, p. 13.

96 See Kelly, *A History of Russian Women's Writing*, pp. 255–60.

97 N. Baranskaia, *Nedelia kak nedelia, Novyi mir*, 11 (1969); English translation Natalya Baranskaya, *A Week like Any Other: A Novella and Short Stories*, trans. P. Monks (London, 1989).

98 See Sandler on Sedakova below, p. 318. This is also true of Elena Shvarts, *Trudy i dni Lavinii, monakhini iz ordena Obrezaniia serdtsa (ot Rozhdestva do Paskhi)* (Ann Arbor, MI: Ardis, 1987).

99 See Goscilo below, pp. 326–43; Goscilo, 'Paradigm Lost?'; and Helena Goscilo, 'Inscribing the female body in women's fiction: cross-gendered passion à la Holbein', in Liljeström, Mäntysaari and Rosenholm, *Gender Restructuring in Russian Studies*, pp. 73–86.

100 Catriona Kelly, *A History of Russian Women's Writing*, p. 8 points to the paradox that for Russian women, writing has sometimes been a substitute for political power.

101 Julia Kristeva, 'Women's time', in Belsey and Moore, *The Feminist Reader*, pp. 214–15.

102 See the volume of essays on this topic, Linda J. Nicholson, ed., *Feminism/Postmodernism* (London and New York: Routledge, 1990).
103 This is true, for example, of the stories of Galina Skvortsova, who was present at the 'Women and Creativity' session at the 1992 Dubna Forum.
104 Mary Ellman, *Thinking about Women* (New York: Harcourt, 1968). For other examples of such confusion, see Aiken and Barker, 'Afterword', pp. 381–3.
105 Discussions among women writers at the 1992 Dubna Forum. The Moscow poet Larisa Miller complained to me in 1991 that she could not get her work published because she did not treat 'sensational' themes, although this problem has now been partially rectified. Many women writers, even if they achieve publication, do not get adequately reviewed, and sink without trace.
106 Liudmila Petrushevskaia's *Vremia noch'* was nominated in 1992; Liudmila Ulitskaia's *Sonechka* and Valeriia Narbikova's *Okolo ekolo* were nominated in 1993, although Narbikova's work was later withdrawn, because it had been published in 1991.
107 L. Petrushevskaia, 'Vremia noch'', *Novyi mir*, 2 (1992), 65–110.
108 This is one of the avowed aims of Catriona Kelly and David Shepherd, eds., *Russian Cultural Studies: an Introduction* (in preparation for Oxford University Press).

PART I

Historical and biographical perspectives

CHAPTER 2

Women in seventeenth-century Russian literature

Rosalind McKenzie

The seventeenth century is generally accepted as a period of major transition in the history of Russia: the 'Time of Troubles' (1598–1613) eventually gave way to the dynastic continuity of the Romanovs; invasion and civil war were ended when Muscovy gathered up the reins of political centralization and power, becoming at last the undisputed capital of all Russia; and the Orthodox Church suffered many decades of heretical dissent from splintering factions before the great Schism of the second half of the century left it scarred forever. In cultural fields it was a time of transference of ecclesiastical pre-eminence to secular, and the transition from medieval to modern began in earnest.[1] This was a period of much uncertainty and introspection, yet also of great literary innovation and creativity,[2] and specifically, a period when the image of woman in literature underwent radical transformations which not only significantly advanced her own status, but also produced pioneering literary works, challenging accepted generic and ideological conventions.

The parameters of this essay have necessarily been limited, as space, unfortunately, does not permit detailed analysis of all areas and aspects of literature. Therefore the main focus will be upon native Russian works, wholly independent of or minimally influenced by the translated literature from Poland, Czecho-slovakia and France which was beginning to appear in Russia, especially in the second half of the century.[3] The female role in folk and oral traditions is far too extensive to approach here, but will be referred to when required.[4] Finally, although no works of civil or canon law will be examined, as the treatment of woman in this area is of more socio-historical interest than literary, it is crucial to remember that the depiction of the female image is intrinsically bound up with her social and legal status.[5]

The Orthodox Church was the vehicle that brought the learned men from Byzantium to Rus' where monasteries remained the almost exclusive seat of all literary activity until the middle of the sixteenth century. The written word was, in the medieval mind, uniquely God's word and even blind copying, let alone composition, of manuscripts a sacred task. No reliable evidence exists of literacy in convents,[6] and, although some written records do indicate a possible presence of literacy among aristocratic females,[7] such documentation is arguably tendentious and must be approached with more caution than credence. It is highly improbable that any more than a totally insignificant minority of women were literate prior to the seventeenth century. The subsequent absence of a female authorial perspective produced the tendency for woman to be portrayed in a dangerously imbalanced, often misogynistic, manner: for example, in *Molenie Daniila Zatochnika* (*Supplication of Daniil the Exile*), the author considers that suffering a fever is better than suffering a bad wife, for one may recover from the former while the latter haunts one to the grave;[8] and the *Slovo o zhenakh o dobrykh i o zlykh* (*Discourse on Women, both Good and Evil*) has little better to say about women: «Жена почитающая своего мужа, всем мудрой кажется, а злая жена — это храм дьявола, жилище сатаны! Бесстыдное животное, неукротимая ехидна — злая жена.»[9] ('A wife who honours her husband is considered wise by everyone, but an evil wife is the devil's temple, Satan's abode! A shameless beast, untameable and venomous – that is, an evil woman.') It is also worth noting that, of all the grammatical structures which were to become stylistic clichés in ecclesiastical composition, none are feminine; this serves only to reinforce the commanding stance of the ever-present male author.

One reason behind such consistent imbalance in female literary depiction is that from the tenth to the sixteenth centuries in Russia, woman suffered from the traditional,

dualistic ecclesiastical concept of the female image – the pit or
pedestal formula: either woman walks in the footsteps of her
ideal image (Mary, Mother of God in the case of the Orthodox
Church), or else she wallows in the pit of whoredom and pagan
witchery.[10] The former image tends to appear fleetingly in pre-
seventeenth-century texts to produce worthy heirs or else to
lament the loss of a husband (examples are Iaroslavna in *Slovo o
polku Igoreve* (*Tale of Igor''s Campaign*)[11] and Evdokiia in *Slovo o
zhitii velikogo kniazia Dmitriia Ivanovicha* (*The Life and Death of Grand
Prince Dmitrii Donskoi*)[12]). The Virgin's literary counterpart
appears as the original sinning Eve figure, frequently portrayed
in dubious colours, leading her innocent male victims to ruin
and perdition. The Church, with its monopolistic hold on
literary activity, thus inspired a tradition of great distrust
towards women, which was to last for several centuries and
certainly did much to taint their depiction in literature.

A few notable exceptions to such images, however, may be
found in the wealth of oral and folkloric traditions. There was
no conscious effort to document works of folklore in Russia
until the seventeenth century; understandably, it was not in the
interests of ecclesiastical scribes and bookmen to record pre-
Christian pagan traditions. Scattered in part or whole among
longer devotional works and collections, though, we do find
some extraordinary portraits, such as Princess Ol'ga of Kievan
times who is remembered in the *Povest' vremennykh let* (*Primary
Chronicle*) as a larger-than-life legendary heroine with a predilection for using imaginatively gruesome tactics in the annihilation
of her enemies.[13] In the eyes of the Christian authorities,
Ol'ga's savage acts of vengeance (a most un-Christian quality)
were probably substantially redeemed by the fact that she
converted to Christianity long before Vladimir I brought
Orthodoxy to the nation as a whole, and thus 'cleansed' herself
of previous sin. International folkloric motifs abound in the
Povest' o Petre i Fevronii Muromskikh (*Tale of Petr and Fevroniia of
Murom*): Fevroniia, a sixteenth-century Christianized version of
the traditional folkloric Wise Maiden character, engagingly
leads her prince successfully through trial and tribulation by
dint of her superior wit and foresight.[14] Not all these exceptions

are agreeable images of woman, though: all the stereotypical and witch-like qualities of a harridan are applied to the widowed and terrifyingly masculine mother of St Feodosii of the Kievan Caves Monastery, who openly beats, bullies and verbally abuses her son in her attempt to prevent him taking the tonsure.[15] All these character portraits appear to be based upon clichés, however, with little or no opportunity for real character development.

Neither did hagiography, the stalwart and arguably most varied genre of medieval Russian literature, provide any outstanding female portraits. Among the myriad Byzantine saints' lives imported to Rus' during the tenth and eleventh centuries, only a small handful depicted female subjects of veneration; and this dearth appears to have been perpetuated by the *knizhniki* (bookmen) of Kiev. Although some rather conventional hagiographical works (such as the *Povest' o Evfrosinii Polotskoi* (*Tale of Evfrosiniia of Polotsk*)[16] do exist in extant form, their origins and date of composition are often dubious, and they cannot be counted for sure among native Russian hagiographies. It is very probable that many more women than we now know of were venerated on a local basis, but their lives were simply never recorded. The criteria for official canonization by the Orthodox Church were stringent, and one may speculate as to how the long traditions of a patriarchal – and misogynistic – establishment tended to be more hostile towards a female candidate. It is indeed remarkable to consider that no *zhitie* (saint's life) dedicated to Princess Ol'ga of Kiev, one of the very earliest Orthodox Christians in Rus', has come down to us, although we must again remember the wealth of medieval Russian literature which has not survived.

The conspicuous absence of focus upon a female protagonist up to this time makes the sudden appearance in the seventeenth century of two extraordinary hagiographical works all the more surprising. The *Povest' ob Ul'ianii Osor'inoi* (*Tale of Ul'ianiia Osor'ina*) [17] and the *Povest' o boiaryne Morozovoi* (*Tale of Boiarynia Morozova*)[18] contain so many features which are radically modern in comparison with the traditional canons of hagiography that several critics have insisted that they be classified as secular biographies rather than as hagiography.[19] These works were the first serious attempts in hagiography to portray a female subject, and the impact they made in terms of the evolution of the hagiographical genre is quite spectacular.

The *Povest' ob Ul'ianii Osor'inoi* was composed in honour of a woman who led a life of extreme charity and godliness, yet who never entered a church before she was married at sixteen years old, thereafter attended irregularly and, when widowed, chose to remain in the secular world rather than retreat to a convent, as was customary. Thus all her life she was a layperson, as was her bureaucrat son Kallistrat, the author of her *zhitie*. Although this attests to the fact that literacy had by now escaped the monastic monopoly and was apparent in administrative areas as well, it is still remarkable for a layperson to have composed a hagiographical work in the early seventeenth century.

Kallistrat's literary labour of love, however, was clearly intended to convey far more than traditional hagiographical accounts of devotion and piety. Throughout the *Povest' ob Ul'ianii Osor'inoi* we find a quite remarkable tone of anti-clerical sentiment which must be considered at best out of place in a work written with the express intention of having its subject approved for veneration or canonization. Kallistrat appears to have been putting forward the thesis that salvation could be won through diligence in following God's teaching in the secular world, as well as through retreat to a life of prayer and contemplation behind the cloistered walls. The black robes of monastic orders, Kallistrat reminded his audience, do not guarantee salvation, and it is often better to remain in the outside secular world where true and tangible deeds of charity can be realized.

While using his mother's life-story to illustrate this concept, the narrative also reflects Kallistrat's very real admiration and love for Ul'ianiia. She is bestowed with every quality a hagiographical heroine could aspire to, yet she has her feet firmly in the real world, bringing her family and household through the hardships of the Time of Troubles and the ravages of famine and plague. The extraordinary nature of her goodness – semi-saintly, semi-secular – is defended honestly and deliberately by a loyal son. Kallistrat, one feels, would not have allowed the fact that Ul'ianiia never took solemn vows to belittle the remarkable achievements of her life, in the eyes of either the reader or of God.

Kallistrat's notions of salvation attainable in the secular world strongly suggest that he sympathized with the religious trans-Volgan hermit movement, a large group of Orthodox believers more concerned with an individualized approach to religion and inner salvation than with the complex rituals and external signs of devotion so common in the traditional Orthodox services of the late fifteenth and early sixteenth centuries.[20] This is interesting, for it allows us to speculate that radical factions within the Orthodox faith were possibly more accommodating towards the literary depiction of woman than the established Church: as numbers in such factions were fewer, woman quite simply stood a better chance of relatively equal recognition.

This is certainly the case with the second of our saintly heroines in the *Povest' o boiaryne Morozovoi*. Feodosiia Morozova is the most famous female Old Believer, and her hagiographer offers us one of the most penetrating psychological character analyses of all medieval Russian literature. The author is believed to have been a high-ranking servant in her household; it is beyond question that whoever composed the work knew her well and was closely acquainted with her daily routines. This effectively forceful and emotive narrative describes another strong-willed and highly intelligent woman, resolute in her faith and prepared to undergo torture and finally pay the ultimate price of life in order not to compromise this faith. Feodosiia's skill in conversation and theological debate were widely admired, and learned men sought out her company. The emotional portrait is warm and loving: she emerges as a devoted wife, mother, sister and friend, even throughout the vilest torture heaped upon her. Thus she is seen to triumph morally and psychologically – if not ultimately physically – over the state institutions which relentlessly persecute her. This work was obviously intended as a testament of courage and inspiration for future generations of Old Believers, and Feodosiia was presented as a truly extraordinary martyr to the cause.

In the autobiographical *zhitie* of another Old Believer, the Archpriest Avvakum, we find his wife Markovna portrayed in gentle and loving terms.[21] Not only does Markovna fulfil the role of mother and loyal wife, following and supporting her husband through times of great trial and tribulation, prepared, as she admits, to keep struggling on through all adversity, until death itself if necessary, but her strength of conviction and persuasive powers keep her husband from giving up the fight in the face of great persecution. Avvakum seeks her opinion and advice on virtually all important issues, and, remarkably for such a strong central male protagonist, acts upon her suggestions. Although an underdeveloped secondary character in the work, Markovna commands admiration and respect, leaving a quiet but strong impression upon the reader.

Such innovative developments in the hagiographical depiction of women were, however, exceptions and could not possibly hope to alter definitively the literary attitudes and traditions of six centuries. Seventeenth-century Russian literature was for the most part still dominated by the prejudiced, misogynistic attitudes of works such as *Domostroi* (*Household Management*) a sixteenth-century manual describing the most effective methods of keeping one's wife under lock and key, beating her in a 'humane' manner and inspiring the fear of God, and husband, lest she overstep the gender barrier.[22]

Towards the end of the seventeenth century, however, the appearance of a new literary trend provided hagiography with the first serious challenge to its moral values: the semi-fictional secular *povest'* genre, a creative style of composition, often liberally sprinkled with thinly disguised historical and contemporary aristocratic figures.[23] The *povest'* appeared to have no aspirations to imitate the traditions of hagiography in structure or style; writers opted for a more liberal and imaginative approach to their work, beginning to espouse the concept that literature should provide entertainment as well as moralistic instruction.[24] Various tales recount incidents of contemporary everyday life, portraying interaction between the sexes as never previously seen in Russian literature: licentious behaviour, bawdiness and greed frequently add a colourful ingredient. Such a modern approach to both subject and style naturally also opened up a host of opportunities for the development of female characterization.

Some tales, however, still clung to an ultimately safe and religious didactic conclusion, hovering between total moral relaxation and the safety of the established ecclesiastical literary conventions. Returning to the timeworn pit or pedestal formula, for example, the *Povest' o Savve Grudtsyne* (*Tale of Savva Grudtsyn*) deals with the theme of good and evil in a very Christian context, yet includes some rather explicit raunchiness.[25] The innocent youth Savva is most horribly seduced by the serpent-like scheming of a young married woman, and is eventually driven to sign away his soul to the Devil in order further to satisfy his lust. It is only intercession at the eleventh hour by the Mother of God that redeems Savva's soul and succeeds in having his Faustian contract erased. Although he is depicted as the innocent victim of an Eve-figure temptress, Savva must, in return for the Mother of God's intervention, maintain his purified state, renounce the worldly pleasures he has come to know, and be tonsured.

However, with Savva thus safely ensconced in monastic repentance, we may now turn to the greater majority of late seventeenth-century *povesti* in which moralistic didacticism and biblical backdrops are all quite simply abandoned. Our heroines now find themselves fortuitously far from the constraints of ecclesiastical idealism imposed upon their earlier sisterly image. No longer are they expected to be superhuman paradigms of purity, humility and obedience, but rather they are conceived and portrayed as resourceful and intelligent human beings, with not a hint of hidden horns or cloven hoof. Such bold steps away from the idealized ecclesiastical female image were further accompanied by a general growing interest in more realistic psychological character analysis, involving an examination of motive and reasoning in the protagonists.

This is illustrated particularly well in two of the *povesti*: the *Povest' o Karpe Sutulove* (*Tale of Karp Sutulov*)[26] and the *Povest' o Frole*

Skobeeve (*Tale of Frol Skobeev*).[27] Interestingly, in the case of the *Povest' o Karpe Sutulove* we find an example of the increasing paradox concerning the title of such works. Although Tat'iana, Karp's wife, is the central character throughout the narrative, Karp himself being almost totally absent from the action, the author, almost certainly a man, awarded her no credit in the title. This appears suspiciously close to the notion, conscious or subconscious, that a woman – albeit the main protagonist – was still viewed as inferior to a man or perhaps even his property, her own identity ignored and ultimately lost.

The one indisputable fact is that Tat'iana takes centre stage in this tale of two thoroughly modern-minded business people. Left to manage the household and estate while Karp is absent on a three-year business trip, she is portrayed firstly as the obedient wife, turning, as instructed by Karp, to one of his merchant friends for temporary financial assistance. Finding herself having to promise to agree to the latter's demands to share her bed – or not receive the promised money – she turns, as every honest and pious person ought, to her Father Confessor and then the archbishop for help and advice, only to find eager offers of yet higher bids for her bed from these godly representatives, and a reassurance from the archbishop that he will personally absolve her of all sin! It is at this point, having exhausted the conventional options available to the usual character of the good wife, that the author begins to reveal the other qualities possessed by Tat'iana: quick-witted resourcefulness, intelligence and improvisation, not to mention great financial acumen. She is a character of true brains and brawn – and the liberal-minded author does not condemn her for using these faculties. Only one century previously a character such as Tat'iana would undoubtedly have been slandered by the author as cunning, sly, intent on leading the male characters into moral and monetary perdition, even enticing Church officials into depravity and sin.[28] Now, however, Tat'iana is praised for her cleverness and wit (not to mention fidelity to her husband) by the *voevoda* (provincial governor) to whom she turns for disposal of the three would-be bed-partners, and Karp upon his return admires and applauds her actions, feels no shame or anger towards her and appreciates the financial benefits.[29]

The author's jibes at the unscrupulous and ignoble behaviour of most of the male characters – he does not even hesitate to bring the corruptness of the clerical hierarchy into the open – also reflect favourably upon Tat'iana. Her status and credibility as a positive character to whom the reader reacts favourably are heightened by her adept and entertaining humiliation of three manipulative men, whilst rigorously maintaining her own blameless position. Tat'iana thus emerges as an important female protagonist: neither witch nor folkloric figure, she emulates the social misbehaviour of innumerable male protagonists over the centuries and exploits the situation to her own advantage; although, unlike many of her male counterparts, our heroine is gracefully carried through her trials by dint of wit and initiative.

The *Povest' o Frole Skobeeve* goes even further in exposing the frailty and vaunting bravado of male characters, ceding the traditionally stronger and positive character to the female. The first page of this *povest'* reveals the motive behind Frol's behaviour as his own insatiable greed and social ambition, and we are frequently reminded that Frol is, almost without exception, considered a good-for-nothing scoundrel and social parasite.[30] He is surrounded on all sides in the tale by a broad cross-section of female character-types: his own sister, an old-fashioned girl who seeks Frol's permission rather than taking her own decisions (although this could simply be a literary device, a necessary vehicle to bring together Frol and his sought-after bride); the old nurse, infinitely bribable and complicit; and finally our most extraordinary and adventurous heroine Annushka. She is portrayed from the start as a strong character who knows her own mind and, like Tat'iana, is not afraid to use it. Coping with Frol's forcible seduction in the most matter-of-fact way (telling her nurse that there is no point in bemoaning her lost virginity, as it cannot be restored[31]), she turns the situation to her own advantage. Understanding that Frol wants something from her, which puts him in the weaker position, she is fully determined to get something out of it for herself in return. Thus, after their first night of carnal pleasure instigated by Frol, it is *she* who detains *him* for another three days and nights of frolicking.[32] Whether or not this detail is simply the product of a male author's fantasy, we should note that the author is always sympathetic to Annushka, never reproaching her for lustful wantonness, as would earlier have been expected, but rather describing her instinctive feelings towards Frol – pity. This most persuasively posits Annushka as head and shoulders above Frol in terms of strength of character, both emotionally and in a practical sense. Annushka is furthermore sufficiently independent-minded to stand up to social mores and wilfully direct her own destiny: it is she who actively plots the elopement-escape from the parental home.[33]

Annushka's character has a strong flavour of the folkloric Wise Maiden, as indeed does Tat'iana, yet at the same time is also firmly rooted in real life. The author has achieved a previously impossible goal: a strong yet charismatic depiction of an intelligent female protagonist who, whilst carrying the weaker male character along with her, schemes and intrigues to get exactly what she wants, winning and maintaining a sympathetic – even admiring – slant from the author at the same time.

In conclusion, although this essay cannot even begin to approach the scope and nuance which appear in seventeenth-century literary works, it does go some way towards illustrating how far the image of woman progressed during this century. The traditional black-and-white stereotypical depictions of woman in medieval times were expanded into more realistic portrayals, and the art of characterization was greatly developed to reflect psychological reasoning and motive. The opening up of these broad new horizons in literary depiction meant that we finally began to be shown a fairer side of the fairer sex.

NOTES

1 For a general history of seventeenth-century Russia, see J. H. Billington, *The Icon and the Axe* (New York: Knopf, 1966), Chapter

3, and Paul Dukes, *The Making of Russian Absolutism 1613–1801* (London: Longman, 1982), Chapters 1–3.

2 See D. S. Likhachev, *Velikii put': stanovlenie russkoi literatury XI–XVII vekov* (Moscow, 1987), pp. 185–230, and V. Terras, *A History of Russian Literature* (New Haven: Yale University Press, 1991), pp. 85–114.

3 For a brief outline of foreign literature translated into Russian in the seventeenth century, see Dmitrij Cizevskij, *History of Russian Literature from the Eleventh Century to the End of the Baroque* (The Hague: Mouton, 1960), pp. 326–31 and pp. 382–7.

4 With the exception of Adele M. Barker's *The Mother Syndrome in the Russian Folk Imagination* (Columbus, OH: Slavica, 1986), no single work has concentrated wholly on the role of the female figure in folk and oral traditions. However, see also Linda J. Ivanits, *Russian Folk Belief* (Armonk, NY: M. E. Sharpe, 1989).

5 For an excellent socio-historical overview of the position of women in medieval Russia, see Barbara Evans Clements, Barbara Alpern Engel and Christine D. Worobec, eds., *Russia's Women: Accommodation, Resistance, Transformation* (Berkeley and Oxford: University of California Press, 1991). For specific comment on women's legal status, see N. Shields Kollmann, 'The seclusion of élite Muscovite women', *Russian History*, 10, 2 (1983), pp. 170–87; Eve Levin, 'Women and property in medieval Novgorod: dependence and independence', *Russian History*, 10, 2 (1983), pp. 154–69; S. Levy, 'Women and the control of property in sixteenth-century Muscovy', *Russian History*, 10, 2 (1983), pp. 201–12.

6 See M. A. Thomas, 'Muscovite convents in the seventeenth century', *Russian History*, 10, 2 (1983), p. 240.

7 See M. Ziolkowski, 'Women in Old Russian Literature', in Toby W. Clyman and Diana Greene, eds., *Women Writers in Russian Literature* (Westport, CT: Greenwood Press, 1994), p. 1.

8 See N. K. Gudzii, 'Molenie Daniila Zatochnika', *Khrestomatiia po drevnei russkoi literature XI–XVII vv.* (Moscow, 1962), p. 143.

9 T. V. Chertoritska, 'Slovo o zhenakh o dobrykh i o zlykh', *Krasnorechie drevnei Rusi (XI–XVIIvv.)* (Moscow, 1987), p. 312.

10 See E. Levin, *Sex and Society in the World of the Orthodox Slavs, 900–1700* (Ithaca, NY: Cornell University Press, 1989) and H. W. Dewey, 'Muted eulogy: women who inspired men in medieval Rus'', *Russian History*, 10, 2 (1983), p. 189.

11 O. V. Tvorogov, 'Slovo o polku Igoreve', *Pamiatniki literatury drevnei Rusi. XII vek* (Moscow: Khudozhestvennaia literatura, 1980), pp. 373–88.

12 M. A. Salmina, 'Slovo o zhitii velikogo kniazia Dmitriia Ivano-
    vicha', *Pamiatniki literatury drevnei Rusi. XIV–seredina XV veka*
    (Moscow: Khudozhestvennaia literatura, 1981), pp. 208–29.

13 See S. H. Cross, *The Russian Primary Chronicle* (Cambridge, MA:
    Harvard University Press, 1930), pp. 164–8.

14 L. A. Dmitriev, 'Povest' o Petre i Fevronii Muromskikh', *Pamiat-
    niki literatury drevnei Rusi. Konets XV-pervaia polovina XVI veka*
    (Moscow: Khudozhestvennaia literatura, 1984), pp. 626–47. For
    structural and thematic similarities to folklore traditions, see also
    R. P. Dmitrieva, 'O strukture povesti o Petre i Fevronii', *Povest' o
    Petre i Fevronii* (Leningrad, 1979), pp. 6–34, and M. O. Skripil',
    'Povest' o Petre i Fevronii Muromskikh v otnoshenii k russkoi
    skazke', *Trudy otdela drevne-russkoi literatury*, 7 (1949), pp. 131–67.

15 *Zhitie Feodosiia Pecherskogo (Life of Feodosii of the Cave Monastery)*; see
    M. Heppell, trans., *The Paterik of the Kievan Caves Monastery* (Cam-
    bridge, MA: Harvard University Press, 1989), pp. 28–31.

16 'Povest' o Evfrosinii Polotskoi', *Pamiatniki starinnoi literatury*, 4 (St
    Petersburg, 1860).

17 M. O. Skripil', 'Povest' ob Ul'ianii Osor'inoi', *Trudy otdela drevne-
    russkoi literatury*, 6 (1948), pp. 284–309.

18 A. I. Mazunin, 'Povest' o boiaryne Morozovoi', *Pamiatniki literatury
    drevnei Rusi. XVII vek. Kniga vtoraia* (Moscow: Khudozhestvennaia
    literatura, 1989), pp. 455–84.

19 For details of this polemic see, for example, J. Alissandratos,
    'New approaches to the problem of identifying the genre of the
    Life of Julijana Lazarevskaja', *Cyrillomethodianum*, 7 (1983),
    pp. 235–44; T. A. Greenan, 'Iulianiya Lazarevskaya', *Oxford
    Slavonic Papers*, 15 (1982), pp. 28–45; Skripil', 'Povest' ob Ul'ianii
    Osor'inoi', pp. 256–76.

20 For details of the trans-Volgan movement, see Billington, *The
    Icon and the Axe*, pp. 60–6, and Paul Bushkovitch, 'Orthodoxy in
    the sixteenth century', *Religion and Society in Russia: the Sixteenth and
    Seventeenth Century* (Oxford: Oxford University Press, 1992),
    pp. 10–31.

21 *Zhitie o protopope Avvakume, im samim napisannoe*; see K. N. Brostrom,
    ed. and trans., *Archpriest Avvakum. The Life Written by Himself* (Ann
    Arbor, MI: University of Michigan Press, 1979).

22 V. V. Kolesov, 'Domostroi', *Pamiatniki literatury drevnei Rusi.
    Seredina XVI veka* (Moscow: Khudozhestvennaia literatura, 1985),
    pp. 70–173.

23 See A. Stokes, 'Literature of the seventeenth century', in J.
    Fennell and A. Stokes, eds., *Early Russian Literature* (London:
    Faber and Faber, 1974), pp. 249–63; William E. Brown, *A History*

54 ROSALIND McKENZIE

of *Seventeenth-Century Russian Literature* (Ann Arbor: Ardis, 1980), especially pp. 37–74.

24 Terras, *A History of Russian Literature*, pp. 75–9, provides a good comparative outline of the 'fictional' literary material available in previous centuries.

25 A. M. Panchenko, 'Povest′ o Savve Grudtsyne', *Pamiatniki literatury drevnei Rusi. XVII vek. Kniga pervaia* (Moscow: Khudozhestvennaia literatura, 1988), pp. 39–54.

26 M. D. Kagan-Tarkovskaia, N. A. Kobiak, 'Povest′ o Karpe Sutulove', *Pamiatniki literatury drevnei Rusi. XVII vek. Kniga pervaia* (Moscow: Khudozhestvennaia literatura, 1988), pp. 65–70.

27 V. P. Budaragin, 'Povest′ o Frole Skobeeve', *Pamiatniki literatury drevnei Rusi. XVII vek. Kniga pervaia* (Moscow: Khudozhestvennaia literatura, 1988), pp. 55–64.

28 In the light of Chapter Six, 'Sex and the Clergy', of Eve Levin's *Sex and Society*, it could be argued that the clergy would have needed very little encitement. The author clearly intended these corrupt men of God to represent the darker realities of the Church, as opposed to its official image of purity.

29 Kagan-Tarkovskaia, *Pamiatniki*, p. 70.

30 Budaragin, *Pamiatniki*, p. 55.

31 *Ibid.*, p. 57.

32 *Ibid.*, p. 57.

33 *Ibid.*, p. 58–9.

CHAPTER 3

Conflicts over gender and status in early nineteenth-century Russian literature: the case of Anna Bunina and her poem Padenie Faetona

Wendy Rosslyn

As Judith Vowles has recently observed,[1] the history of the 'feminization' of Russian language and literature has been written almost entirely on the basis of what men wrote, and women's perception of their own relation to language and literature has received scant attention. The purpose of the present article is to illustrate the part of Vowles's argument dealing with women's resistance to the literary roles prescribed for them, by reference to *Padenie Faetona* (1811), the principal work of Anna Bunina, whom Vowles rightly identifies as one of the least conformist women writers of the period.[2] Bunina frequently discusses gender issues and women's status in the literary process, but since space precludes extensive analysis of her accommodations and challenges to current ideas, I here focus on the poem which aroused most controversy amongst contemporary readers and aim to show how the views about women and writing discussed by Vowles manifested themselves in actual behaviour in one (of the few) documentable case(s).[3]

Early nineteenth-century Russia was a particularly status-conscious society, in which the place of women was explicitly defined,[4] and I shall describe the latter in some detail. At this point the events of the French revolution and the part played in it by politically active females had discredited women's emancipation in Russia. Social stability was a prime concern,[5] and few disputed that women's place was in the family. The Sentimentalist definition of gender developed in the 1790s was based on Rousseau's view that women were naturally radically different from men, and that their function was as ornaments to men's existence, and instruments to men's well-being. The qualities required of them included, therefore, 'pleasantness, decorum, modesty, a mild temperament, meekness, discrimination in all goodness, refinement, propriety'.[6] Rousseau's doctrine of the different essences of men and women legitimated the confinement of women to the domestic arena, but within this sphere their status was high: women were supposed to be the embodiment of virtue and thus able to improve the moral state of the nation by their influence on husbands and children.

Their status in the literary process was, however, less exalted. Because women were to devote themselves to home and family, and were not to shine in their own right, creative writing was considered inappropriate. Women who engaged in it were thought by many to have 'fingers covered in ink, pedantry in the brain and a printing press in the heart'.[7] The unwomanliness associated with writing led both to the assumption that women writers were over-educated, unfeeling and sexually unattractive, and to suspicions that a woman capable of selling her sentiments in book form might also be capable of selling her body.[8] Ekaterina Sumarokova (1746–97), the first Russian woman poet to publish, was satirized by Ivan Krylov as a chatterbox barely able to write platitudes, but nonetheless vain and sexually brazen.[9]

The theories of the chief literary groupings, *Beseda liubitelei russkogo slova* (Society of Lovers of the Russian Word, 1811–16) and the followers of Nikolai Karamzin, which differed on almost all issues, were at one in asserting that the role of women in the literary process was not to write (Karamzin's 'Epistle to women' asserted that women could not express their own feelings), but to act as arbiters of good writing. In other words, the criterion of the language used by a woman of quality was invoked to cleanse literary language of pedantry.[10] Admiral Aleksandr Shishkov, the leader of *Beseda*, agreed with Karamzin that women were to listen, encourage, and refine:

Ladies, this most charming half of the human race, this soul of conversations, these kind teachers who inspire in us the language of affection and courtesy, the language of feelings and passion, ladies, I say, are those lofty inspirations which fire our spirit for song ... Industrious minds imagine, write, compose expressions, define words;

ladies, reading them, learn purity and correctness of language; but this language, when it passes through their lips, becomes more clear, smoother, pleasanter, more sweet.[11]

In practice, although the standard of 'what would not offend a lady' might act as an inner guide, refinement of poetic language was the function of the literary circle and the real critics were other practitioners. Just as assertions of the virtue and moral power of women served to keep them contentedly in the home, their literary status, when high, was also nominal.

Ideas that women could not and should not write were, however, outweighed by the principle of the instrumentality of women and in fact supporters of both groups helped women to publish – not, of course, for the authors' own satisfaction or glory, but for the sake of morality. It was claimed that if women took to literature, 'the golden ages when one look, one kiss of the hand rewarded a hero for decades of feats would return to Earth the good of humanity'.[12] But women were not expected to practise the serious didactic genres. Even pro-feminists such as the poet Milonov, who defended the propriety of women's writing, assumed that only unmarried women would have time to write, that their experience would limit them to the theme of love, that they would imitate the great male writers, and that their audience would be female;[13] and Zakharov, one of the principals of *Beseda*, whilst recognizing the distinction of Russia's women writers, thought them best equipped for depicting tender and charming love (in Sentimental taste) and for imaginative fiction.[14] As Vowles has demonstrated, the assumption that women would write artlessly in the light genres for a female audience was by this time of long standing.

In spite of the supposed grandeur of their vocation, as writers women characteristically had low status. Their literary ability was devalued, assumed to be merely the result of the spread of enlightenment, or as intrinsic to their nature, the result of the superior sensitivity which Sentimentalism attributed to women, rather than as technically skilled art. Most literary groups were (like other social institutions) exclusively male preserves. *Beseda* was an exception, specifying audiences of both sexes at its readings, and having three women (Bunina, Volkova and

Urusova) in its ranks, but they were only honorary members, and though one of the declared purposes of the society was to give public readings of members' works,[15] the women did not do so. Volkova's poem addressed to *Beseda*[16] makes a favourable comparison between the attitude to women here and the attitude of the Masons (who excluded women entirely); but the attitude she describes is condescending: women are 'allowed' to write, writing is 'the quiet entertainment of the mind', and the women writers are led to the abode of glory by the men, who give light to their ideas, correct their style, animate their imaginations and strengthen their spirits, for which the women are grateful. The poem was printed in the society's journal with a dismissive footnote saying that it was published to fulfil the author's wish that it should be. Volkova's poem suggests that, unlike Bunina, she did not find this condescension offensive. Women writers were also often artistically and/or financially dependent on patrons. One of the factors enabling the marked growth of women's writing at this time was the incentive to the male writer to take up the Sentimentalist stance of benevolence and act as patron of the arts, a philanthropic act which brought public attention and esteem. Many women writers of this period (Volkova, Pospelova, Kul'man, Iartsova, Ishimova) were less highly educated and socially privileged than such predecessors as Catherine II, Ekaterina Dashkova or Urusova, and they needed patronage.[17] It was common for women to begin as the literary apprentices of their male relatives, or of writers such as Derzhavin, who held literary evenings which attracted large numbers of women[18] and encouraged the establishment of a publishing house, which engaged several noblewomen as translators,[19] or Shishkov, who helped numerous women writers via the Russian Academy when he became its president.[20] Some editors of journals, such as N. Ostolopov of *Liubitel' slovesnosti*, issued invitations to women to publish.

The low status of women's writing was also evident from the critical reception of their writing. Ostolopov, inviting contributions from women, assumed that the standard would not be high, but guaranteed in advance an enthusiastic response.[21] The double moral standard which assumed women to be physically and mentally weak and therefore allowed them indulgence, also applied in literature, so that it was common for journals to greet women's writing with excessive praise. In 1805 the journal *Moskovskii Merkurii* assured women that they would make such speedy progress in literature that they would teach male writers, in gratitude for which the latter 'would erect altars to them and the word "adore" [*obozhat'*] would receive its natural meaning' – women would acquire god-like status. Such praise was intended as encouragement, but was also dismissive: 'the very exercise which frequently tyrannizes us with the sharpest of needles is for women simply roses without thorns, for what pedant, what barbarian, will have the temerity not to praise that which has been written by a soft, white, beautiful hand?'[22] And women's writing was to be approved for its instrumentality in improving writing by men, not for its own sake. As Ostolopov wrote, 'We know that a commonplace composition by a woman has more effect on our sex than a model work by a man, because when we read the former we imagine the lady writer herself, transport ourselves mentally into her study, see the beautiful one, kiss the hand which depicts her thoughts and feelings for us, and strive to imitate her ourselves.'[23] The polarization of attitudes to women's writing was underpinned by the social code of gallantry and flirtation, which meant that to address a woman as an equal was to imply a lack of respect and chivalry. The tacit assumption behind the welcome of women into literature was that the woman writer would flatteringly remain a pupil or protégée, and not strive to excel or become a rival. Women were invited to offer a service to the nation, but this was not licence to gratify their vanity or to be socially disruptive, as women writers had been in the West.[24]

Bunina's biography shows her resistance to these preconceptions about women and writing. Unmarried, she paid for her own advanced education and then devoted herself exclusively to her writing. Refusing to be financially dependent on her family, she needed patronage and was helped by Shishkov, who petitioned for annuities for her from the Court, but the annuities were insufficient and she lived also on the income from her numerous books. Her poetry and prose were not calculated for the female audience and dealt with love relatively rarely, and then as romantic passion. She knew that art was a learned skill, and she translated a manual of poetics for use by women.[25] Her poem 'Sumerki' ('Twilight'),[26] written in praise of Derzhavin, a reflection on the power and authority of the poet, constitutes an apotheosis of Derzhavin and in effect asserts that the poet is an immortal with god-like status. Her images for the woman writer, reflecting trepidation and tempered by modesty, were more humble and often self-mocking (the dragonfly learns to sing from the nightingale),[27] but precisely on account of ambitious aspirations to high achievement. Several poems described the literary process as the competitive (also hesitant and difficult) pursuit of renown.[28] One depicted it as a race run in China in which men run one distance, children a shorter one – and the sole woman contestant has to run against the children, because her feet have been bound. But even so, she wins the applause she seeks. Evidence of Bunina's ambitious pursuit of literary recognition includes her cultivation of the traditionally prestigious genres (the ode and didactic poetry), and her adherence to *Beseda*, whose province was public discourse, the high genres, and the Church Slavonic linguistic inheritance, while the Karamzin school cultivated the private sphere, the middle genres, the lyric, and gallicized syntax – in other words, the feminized segment of Russian writing.[29]

Bunina analysed literary activity in terms of hierarchy. She observed that male writers veered to extremes in evaluating the woman writer ('you begin arbitrarily at one moment to shower her with irrelevant praise and at the next to humiliate her with irrelevant domination'). But she acknowledged women's complicity: in conforming to the demand for modesty they encouraged men to assert their superiority ('meekness in women is not distasteful to men. Making use of it, they encroach on everything and make themselves into absolute rulers'). She perceived that men welcomed women's self-exclusion from competition ('meekness is still more useful to men when it is found in women who are in the same walk of life as they are'), and she expressed the wish as a woman writer to be treated on equal terms and to receive reasoned criticism of her work:

A male poet showers a woman writer with praise more willingly than he does his male fellows; for he is accustomed to think that he knows more than she does. He is ready to squander praise on her, even the most immoderate praise ... madrigals please frivolous women. The woman who has become accustomed to reason desires only that people should treat her worthily.

She drew analogies between the male writer and the landowner and between the woman writer and a serf: 'The landowner is not averse to having many servants. The more there are, the more profitable it is for him; but let us ask these servants whether they would wish to make an agreement with their landowner'.[30] The notion of contract suggested the desirability from the woman writer's point of view of a move away from hierarchical relations towards greater equality.

Bunina's mock epic *Padenie Faetona* can be read as an allegory of the woman writer's claim to the god-like status reserved in pre-Romantic (and still more so in Romantic) ideology for the male writer. The poem also deserves attention since it illuminates Bunina's perception of the situation of the woman writer. The history of the reception of the poem also shows what forms challenges to the establishment could take, what the results and costs were, and where the limits of the encouragement of women writers were drawn.

The poem tells the story of Phaethon, son of the god Helios and the mortal Clymene. Humiliated by mockery of his claim to divine descent, Phaethon asks Helios to confirm his parentage by allowing him to drive the chariot of the sun across the heavens. Helios agrees reluctantly, foreseeing the dangers, but Phaethon cannot control the horses, who desert their path and nearly set the earth on fire. Zeus has therefore to slay him to avert disaster. Because the controversy surrounding the poem did not focus on its interpretation, it is difficult to tell how contemporaries read the fable. *Padenie Faetona* could certainly have been seen as a playful retelling of a traditional narrative. But Phaethon's loss of direction probably reminded listeners of Derzhavin's use of the Phaethon image to symbolize Alexander I

losing control of the chariot of state as a result of imbibing the
ideas of his tutor La Harpe.[31] This interpretation would
certainly have appealed to the arch-nationalist Shishkov. But
although Bunina was brought up for a time by a gallophobic
relative[32] and may have approved anti-French sentiments, it is
unlikely that she would have risked offending Alexander, who
had recently cleared her debts and given her an annuity.[33] It
would seem that if her poem carried a political message, this
was read into it; if so, Bunina's political naivety may have been
exploited by Shishkov, who perhaps reasoned that his patronage deserved some return.

The poem can also be read as an allegory of the woman
writer, who, claiming the same exalted status as male writers,
meets with retribution for her challenge to hierarchy and order.
Bunina suggests that women's challenge to the hierarchy was
capable of destroying the social fabric and would be parried by
the establishment, especially when conservatism was in the
ascendant, as in 1811. It is unlikely that Bunina intended her
analysis of her own anxieties as a woman writer for public
consumption, but the classical myth would have provided cover
for the controversial theme of female aspiration.[34] This latter
interpretation explains, moreover, the substantial digression on
artistic motivation. In fact the poem was understood as a
self-portrait.[35]

The poem presents an ambivalent picture of the woman
writer. The cause of all Phaethon's psychological and social
problems is that he is descended from god and mortal, but
belongs in neither category. Similarly, the woman writer is an
ambiguous figure. She has the divine gift of poetry, but is
categorized by others as a mortal – as a physically weak and
socially limited woman.[36] The woman writer is, her critics
allege, neither real writer nor real woman. The poem is
essentially a dialogue about ambition and assertiveness, conducted by two opposing voices within Phaethon. One voice
applauds him for claiming the status of a god, for his daring, his
confidence, and for attempting a heroic feat. But the other
voice reproaches him for trying to be other than destined by
birth (god, rather than demi-god), for being presumptuous and

arrogant, for acting out of hurt pride, for having ambitions which exceed his capacities, and for being unable to retreat for fear of mockery. In this view he is not courageous but foolhardy, and must be punished severely. Phaethon's reactions on entering the palace of Helios (a witty reference to the luxurious setting in which the meetings of *Beseda* were conducted) symbolize those of a novice woman writer: he feels a mixture of desire, ambition, shame, timidity, and lack of self-confidence. The expressed moral of the poem is that 'it is senseless to hope for success in works to which your strength is unequal'. But although Phaethon fails to realize his ambitions and is destroyed,[37] he is immortalized in myth for making the attempt. It is remarkable that when the project of defining and depicting the woman writer in Russian literature was still in its very earliest stages, Bunina identified many of the characteristics which are now taken as axiomatic, including the internalization of masculine scorn, the divided self and conflicting rebellious and conformist urges.[38]

The circumstances of the poem's writing and publication well illustrate Bunina's increasingly confident assertion of her independence and worth. Firstly, she did not consult her patron about the poem.[39] (In fact she asked Shishkov for his observations, but he did not have time to make them.)[40] Secondly, although she modelled her poem on an episode from Ovid's *Metamorphoses*, she charged the myth with revisionary content. And thirdly, she submitted the poem under a male pseudonym, although this was not her custom, perhaps hoping that a male pseudonym would enhance the reception of her work, given the society's ambivalent attitude to women.

In a covering letter Bunina performed the ritual self-denigration and gave permission for corrections to be made if the poem could be read at *Beseda*.[41] This gave rise to a confrontation about literary authority in which Bunina was extraordinarily assertive. The circumstances were as follows. The poem was duly accepted but was then subjected to substantial editing, about which Bunina was not consulted, although Shishkov was aware that she was the author. The poem 'had the honour of being read', Bunina observed sardonically, 'cut by a whole half' on account of its averred flabbiness, low style, unnecessary witticisms and fecundity and because two works of allegedly much higher quality had to be read in the same session. Another complaint was that whereas in Ovid's version 'every personage of his story acts and speaks in accordance with his condition',[42] this did not happen in Bunina's (subversive) text. The effect of the cuts was to reduce the poem to its plot, decimating the lively digressions, and thus minimizing the role of the female author-narrator. Much of the imagery relating to the theme of status was also removed. The editor, in fact, acted in the same spirit as Zeus when he felled Phaethon.

The poem, given its public reading by Krylov, was well received. This approval mattered greatly to Bunina, who called it a 'priceless treasure', whilst tactically attributing it to indulgence rather than justice.[43] Further recognition came in the form of a gold and diamond brooch from Elizaveta Alekseevna, consort of Alexander I.[44] An entry made in Bunina's album at this point speaks of the swift upward flight of her fame,[45] but Bunina recorded that she felt 'complete satisfaction and involuntary embarrassment; I saw my goal both achieved and seriously set back'.[46] Set back, because of possible envy from other writers.[47] She therefore resorted again to the modesty strategy and promptly wrote a poem in which she tactfully attributed the success of the poem to Krylov.[48]

Success apparently gave her confidence, and enabled her to make a public challenge to literary authority. The abridged, edited, and still pseudonymous poem was published in the society's journal,[49] still without consultation, but Bunina immediately regained control of her text by re-publishing it (in her second volume of poems,[50] then going to press) in the original version. She also added a preface of no less than eighteen pages, in which she disparaged the emendations. Perhaps her anger had been further fired by the paper 'In praise of women' by Zakharov, one of the texts which had necessitated the cuts to her poem. In his paper Zakharov had listed eminent Russian women writers, including Urusova (one of the other honorary members of *Beseda*), but he had pointedly omitted Bunina and Volkova, no doubt because these two impoverished women could not occupy the same breath as the aristocratic Urusova. But Zakharov had not dealt justly with their respective literary merits.

In challenging the emendations Bunina had transgressed the requirement, re-stated in Zakharov's remarks about the ideal woman, that women conform malleably to the feelings and judgements of society. Bunina's reaction also contravened the convention that writers, however keenly injured, maintain their dignity and not reply to criticism: since the proclaimed aim of literature was to improve morals, quarrels were deemed inappropriate. Bunina could not therefore expect her reaction to endear her to *Beseda* (whose leader was her patron), and this was no small matter, for little solidarity was forthcoming from any other quarter.[51] Moreover, the society offered the only forum in which she could make direct contact with her audience and receive criticism, just or unjust: published criticism of literature was not yet common. She was thus taking the risk that henceforth response to her work would come in the form of scurrilous satire, casual remarks, or failure to notice its existence – and this was indeed the result.

Bunina's preface was a courageous, foolhardy, Phaethon-like assertion of equality with the editor, who was either Shishkov, a minister of State, or Zakharov, a senator.[52] Bunina therefore tactically blunted the most assertive statements with blander ones and provided passages which lent themselves to being read with or without irony. She began with a modest declaration of her inadequacy, but undermined it by pointing out the conventionality of such declarations. Instead of invoking Ovid in her defence, she emphasized the cultural gap between herself and her source, observing how much imagination (and independence) her poem had required. The amendments were firmly rejected on the grounds that accepting them would be theft. Cuts were restored because, she explained, she did not know which were on account of brevity, and which for stylistic reasons. And towards the end of the preface she argued line by line for the superiority of her own text. This assertiveness was again tactically softened by the claim that faults remained, so that she was in need of the public's condescension, and the preface concluded with her declared willingness to accept advice. But the last blow was a spirited footnote, in which she further justified her text. Bunina thus disputed the chairman's judgement, and in so doing laid claim to the role of critic, in what must be one of the earliest examples of published literary criticism by a Russian woman.

Bunina's defence of her poem itself evoked reactions which reflected on the question of status. Shishkov made some acrimonious entries in Bunina's album, presumably at this time. He complained that she had not acted as his Muse, praised meekness, modesty and self-control in women, reminded Bunina that praise from ignoramuses brings only dishonour, and warned her against criticizing intelligent men for fear of revealing her own ignorance. To these Bunina added her own forthright comments. Throughout this episode Bunina failed to act with the sycophancy which patrons required, and this seems to have led to a rift between the two, for Bunina's absence from the society's journal suggests that she did not contribute further works to the readings until 1815. Bunina found patronage constraining:

In all mutual relationships the more condescending one party is, the more cautious the other must be, the less he can permit himself, and the fear of using for ill the indulgence granted him must keep him within the tightest bounds.[53]

But it was not financially possible for her to exist permanently without it, and good relations with Shishkov were eventually restored, though Bunina humorously refused to forsake 'slanging matches'.[54]

The response to *Padenie Faetona* came in the form of an anonymous unpublished poem,[55] probably emanating from the Karamzinists, which satirized Bunina for her aspirations to the high calling of writer and therefore for her unwomanliness (in the poem she both cursed and used Church Slavonic lexis and syntax). Bunina's perceived presumption was caricatured by depicting her as Apollo in exile from the heavens and sent to earth as a shepherd. The ex-god, whose rapture has faded and whose song fails to scan, cannot ride Pegasus, the steed of the

Muses, because his foot gets entangled in his skirt and he falls off. He is advised to abandon art in favour of embroidery. In terms of status Apollo is demoted from god to mortal, from 'sire of verse' to incompetent performer, from male to a figure of ambiguous gender. He is also humiliated by having his errors condescendingly corrected. The import of the satire was that poetry is the preserve of the youthful male who can burn with divine inspiration, and engage rightfully in disputes about it.

The romantic view of the masculinity of the priest-like inspired poet was one of the factors which made it increasingly difficult for women to achieve recognition as writers. Only a few years earlier women's writing had been greeted with indiscriminate indulgence, but since then the political climate had become more conservative and anti-western. Bunina, particularly since she had previously earned praise as a writer, now had to contend with indiscriminate hostility which did not engage in specific discussion of her poems, but addressed itself, usually unprintably, to her gender and person. Attacks on her were made consistently by the Karamzinists (meeting latterly as the *Arzamas* circle) in the course of their onslaught on *Beseda*, and their reception of her writing demonstrates that although Karamzin valued women as ideal readers, encouraged them to read, and privileged personality traits conventionally identified as feminine, once women took up writing their reception by his followers was far from benevolent. Thus, for example, in his satire on Bunina of 1815 Uvarov ridiculed her for her aspirations, depicting her flying above the heights of Pindus in sacred rapture.[56] Pursuing the assumption that women could not and should not be writers, Uvarov implied that because Bunina wrote, she was not a (sexually effective) woman.[57] He lampooned her for her child-like chastity,[58] implied that in Shishkov she chose a preposterous object for her platonic love;[59] ridiculed her for producing poems rather than children; and fantasized that she eventually lost her faithless beloved to rivals of both sexes.[60]

Pushkin contributed to *Arzamas*'s mockery of *Beseda* and Bunina. His 'Ten' Fonvizina' ('Fonvizin's Shadow', 1815) continued the vertical imagery, and described Bunina as a pseudo-goddess, whose rightful position was both low and prostrate. And it was he who made the fatal comparison between Bunina and the universally despised incompetent Khvostov,[61] which relegated her to the lowest level of the Russian literary ranks and meant that few, apart from family and feminists, thought her worth reading thereafter.

One of the earliest forms in which the woman question arose in Russia was the debate about whether women should be creative writers, and what they could write. Bunina asserted that women could write, even for income, that women's writing was not mere spontaneity, that they could address the same audience as their male counterparts, could employ a wide range of genres and themes, and engage in literary criticism. She asserted that women could write not only for edification or pleasure, but even for fame, and was able to withstand the hostility which she provoked. She perceived that approval was men's to bestow and men's to withhold,[62] and that the task of the woman writer was to refuse undeservedly low status and falsely elevated status alike. Because she understood some of the mechanisms of discrimination against women and resisted them resourcefully, she is an important figure in the early stages of Russian feminism; her clear perception of gender issues was, sadly, lost to women of the following generations.

NOTES

1 Judith Vowles, 'The "feminization" of Russian literature: women, language, and literature in eighteenth-century Russia', in Toby W. Clyman and Diana Greene, eds., *Women Writers in Russian Literature* (Westport, CT and London: Greenwood Press, 1994), pp. 39–40.

2 For contemporary criticism on Bunina, see N. N. Golitsyn, *Bibliograficheskii slovar' russkikh pisatel'nits 1759–1859gg* (St Petersburg, 1889), pp. 32–5. Bunina's work has only returned to notice in the last twenty years, and recent interpretations of her work include: Rebecca Bowman, 'Bunina, Anna Petrovna', in M. Ledkovsky, C. Rosenthal and M. Zirin, eds., *Dictionary of Russian Women Writers* (Westport, CT and London: Greenwood Press, 1994), pp. 107–11; Frank Göpfert, 'Poniatie "remeslo" v traditsii russkoi

zhenskoi poezii', in Marianne Liljeström, Eila Mäntysaari and Arja Rosenholm, eds., *Gender Restructuring in Russian Studies* (Tampere: University of Tampere, 1993), pp. 65–72; Yael Harussi, 'Women's social roles as depicted by women writers in early nineteenth-century Russian fiction', in J. Douglas Clayton, ed., *Issues in Russian Literature before 1917* (Columbus, Ohio: Slavica, 1989), pp. 35–48; Barbara Heldt, *Terrible Perfection: Women and Russian Literature* (Bloomington and Indianapolis, IN: Indiana University Press, 1987), pp. 108–10; Catriona Kelly, *A History of Russian Women's Writing, 1820–1992* (Oxford: Clarendon Press, 1994), pp. 30–2; Giovanna Spendel de Varda, 'Anna Bunina – "Rossiiskaia Safo"', in Frank Göpfert, ed., *Russland aus der Feder seiner Frauen* (Munich: Sagner, 1992), pp. 197–205; Giovanna Spendel, *Il silenzio delle albe. Donne e scrittura nell'Ottocento russo* (Turin, 1993), pp. 1–32. My own monograph on Bunina is nearing completion.

3 Bunina is one of the few women of this period for whom it is possible to construct a detailed biography. This is because she was sufficiently well known and controversial in her own time to have been relatively well documented. Because no extensive biography has yet been published, my endnotes are sometimes particularly extensive.

4 Definition was largely connected with successive prescriptions for the curriculum in women's educational institutions. The course of the debate is examined in detail in E. Likhacheva, *Materialy dlia istorii zhenskogo obrazovaniia v Rossii 1086–1796* (St Petersburg, 1890) and *Materialy dlia istorii zhenskogo obrazovaniia v Rossii 1796–1828* (St Petersburg, 1890).

5 See, for example, N. M. Karamzin: 'Now all the best minds cluster round the banner of the rulers and are only prepared to aid the successes of the existing order of things, with no thought for innovations. Never has their consensus been so clear, sincere and dependable' ('Priiatnye vidy, nadezhdy i zhelaniia nyneshnego veka', in his *Izbrannye sochineniia v dvukh tomakh* (Moscow–Leningrad, 1964), p. 269).

6 Quoted in Likhacheva, *Materialy 1796–1828*, p. 287.

7 I. V. Kireevskii, 'O russkikh pisatel'nitsakh', *Polnoe sobranie sochinenii v 2-kh tomakh*, II (Moscow, 1911), p. 68. This view persisted into the 1830s.

8 *Patriot*, September 1804, quoted in Likhacheva, *Materialy 1796–1828*, p. 272.

9 In his play *Prokazniki* (1788).

10 Cf P. I. Makarov (1803): 'In order to eradicate pedantry, and, on

the contrary, to harmonize our bookish [literary] language with
the language of good society we would wish that Women took up
Literature; out of their subtle taste, their ardent imaginations,
their gentle souls we await good Authors' (quoted in B. A.
Uspenskii, *Iz istorii literaturnogo iazyka XVIII–nachala XIX veka.
Iazykovaia programma Karamzina i ee istoricheskie korni*, (Moscow,
1985), p. 59). On gender and the Karamzin school, see Gitta
Hammarberg, *From the Idyll to the Novel: Karamzin's Sentimentalist
Prose* (Cambridge: Cambridge University Press, 1991), pp. 95–7,
and her 'The feminine chronotope and Sentimentalist canon
formation', in A. G. Cross and G. S. Smith, eds., *Literature, Lives
and Legality in Catherine's Russia* (Cotgrave: Astra Press, 1994),
pp. 103–20. She rightly concludes that while the Sentimentalists
were male authors who strove to emulate female models, women
were models *in potentia* only, and real women were found wanting.
Real women were satisfactory only as readers and as future
writers. As I suggest here, they were not required as practitioners
of writing, still less as rivals.

11   A. Shishkov, 'Rech′ pri otkrytii Besedy liubitelei russkogo slova',
     in his *Sobranie sochinenii i perevodov*, 4 (St Petersburg, 1825), p. 143.

12   *Moskovskii Merkurii*, 1 (1805), quoted in Likhacheva, *Materialy 1796–
     1828*, pp. 269–70. The idea that the future of Russia was to be
     assured by virtuous women recurs in literary texts from this point
     onwards.

13   'K A. P. B-oi. O prilichii stikhotvorstva prekrasnomu polu', *Polnoe
     sobranie sochinenii russkikh avtorov. Sochineniia Milonova* (St Petersburg,
     1849), pp. 147–54.

14   'Pokhvala zhenam', *Chteniia v Besede*, 4 (1811), pp. 3–67.

15   On the formal organization of *Beseda*, see *Chteniia v Besede*, 1 (1811),
     pp. ii–iii. For an extensive discussion of the group, its aims, and
     its writings, see M. G. Al′tshuller, *Predtechi slavianofil′stva v russkoi
     literature* (Ann Arbor, MI: Ardis, 1984).

16   'Stikhi k *Besede liubitelei russkogo slova*', reprinted in M. G. Al′t-
     shuller and Iu. M. Lotman, *Poety 1790–1810 godov* (Leningrad,
     1971), pp. 495–6.

17   Volkova, like Bunina, benefited from the patronage of Shishkov
     and the Court (see the article on her by A. L. Zorin in P. A.
     Nikolaev, *Russkie pisateli: biobibliograficheskii slovar′ v dvukh chastiakh*
     (Moscow, 1990), 1, pp. 467–8). On Pospelova, see M. D.
     Khmyrov, 'Russkie pisatel′nitsy proshlogo vremeni', *Rassvet*, 12, 11
     (1861), 257–63. On Iartsova and Ishimova, see M. Sh. Fainshtein,
     Pisatel′nitsy pushkinskoi pory (Leningrad: Nauka, 1989).

18   Likhacheva, *Materialy 1086–1796*, p. 261.

19 *Sochineniia Derzhavina*, vi (St Petersburg, 1871), pp. 579–61.
20 Fainshtein, *Pisatel'nitsy pushkinskoi pory*, pp. 19, 46, 58.
21 *Liubitel' slovesnosti*, i (January 1806), pp. 2, 4–5.
22 *Moskovskii Merkurii*, i (1805), quoted in Likhacheva, *Materialy 1796–1828*, pp. 269–70.
23 *Liubitel' slovesnosti*, i (January 1806), pp. 2, 4–5.
24 See, for example, *Vestnik Evropy* (September 1811), quoted in Likhacheva, *Materialy 1796–1828*, p. 272.
25 *Pravila poezii, sokrashchenno-perevedennye iz abbata Batte, s prisovokupleniem rossiiskogo stoposlozheniia v pol'zu devits* (St Petersburg, 1808).
26 Reprinted in Al'tshuller and Lotman, *Poety 1790–1810 godov*, pp. 451–3.
27 'Ivanu Ivanovichu Dmitrievu', in her *Neoptynaia muza*, i (St Petersburg , 1809), pp. 57–8.
28 'Pekinskoe ristalishche', *Padenie Faetona*; 'Razgovor mezhdu mnoiu i zhenshchinami' (on which see Barbara Heldt, *Terrible Perfection*, pp. 110; Kelly, *A History of Russian Women's Writing*, pp. 30–2 and Vowles, 'The "feminization" of Russian literature', pp. 52–3). The text of 'Razgovor', with an English translation, is in Catriona Kelly, *An Anthology of Russian Women's Writing, 1777–1992* (Oxford: Oxford University Press, 1994), pp. 8–11 and 403–6. Bunina's contemporary Elizaveta Kul'man describes with confidence the triumph of Corinna over male poets, and the tribute paid to her by the ageing Pindar ('Korinna', in V. V. Uchenova (comp.), *Tsaritsy muz* (Moscow: Sovremennik, 1989), pp. 49–57). But Bunina was less optimistic about the ease of victory in literary competition. Not all women writers felt able to admit that they sought recognition for their work: see, for example, Volkova's poem 'Gimn slave', *Chteniia v Besede*, 14 (1815), pp. 67–74, in which she describes how fame can be won, but does not include herself amongst the seekers.
29 On the gender distinction between 'masculine' Church Slavonic and 'feminine' gallicized Russian, see Vowles, 'The "feminization" of Russian literature', pp. 36–7.
30 All these observations are from Bunina's album, described and quoted in K. Ia. Grot, 'Al'bom A. P. Buninoi', *Russkii arkhiv*, i (1902), pp. 500–6. The original album is in the Institute of Russian Literature, f. 88, No. 16012. It is not clear how Bunina arrived at these views. Texts such as A.-L. Thomas, *Essai sur le caractère, les moeurs et l'esprit des femmes dans les différents siècles* (1772) were known in her circle, but there is no record of her reading, and she may have drawn her conclusions from experience alone.
31 Derzhavin's poem is 'Kolesnitsa'. For the political interpretation

of Bunina's poem see Al'tshuller, *Predtechi*, pp. 231–6 (a republica-
tion of his 'Krylov v literaturnykh ob"edineniiakh 1800–1810-kh
godov', in I. Z. Serman, ed., *Ivan Andreevich Krylov. Problemy
tvorchestva* (Leningrad, 1975)). Both Derzhavin and Shishkov dis-
approved of the project of liberating the serfs which Alexander
had conceived under the influence of La Harpe, and feared the
contagion of revolution coming from the West.

32 Letter to S. R. Vorontsov, St Petersburg Branch of the Institute
    of Russian History, f. 36, op. 2, No. 1243, ll. 116–17.

33 Khvostov's diary, quoted in A. V. Zapadov, 'Iz arkhiva Khvos-
    tova', in S. D. Balukhatyi, ed., *Literaturnyi arkhiv*, 1 (Moscow–
    Leningrad, 1938), p. 366.

34 See Sandra M. Gilbert and Susan Gubar, *The Madwoman in the
    Attic. the Woman Writer and the Nineteenth-century Literary Imagination*
    (New Haven and London: Yale University Press, 1984), p. 72, on
    female artists who deal with central female experiences from a
    specifically female perspective which is ignored by critics because
    concealed behind more accessible 'public' content.

35 See the parody on the poem discussed below, and Shishkov's
    remark: 'I listen to you and converse with you in the fall of
    Phaethon ...' (letter to Bunina, May 1816, Manuscript Section of
    the Russian National Library, St Petersburg, f. 862, No. 7, ll.
    8–9).

36 The same mixed descent was specified a little later in Elizaveta
    Kul'man's myth of the origins of the woman poet, who is
    daughter of the goddess Diana and the mortal Endymion ('Nart-
    siss', in her *Polnoe sobranie russkikh, nemetskikh i ital'ianskikh stikhotvor-
    enii: Piiticheskie opyty*, 1 (St Petersburg, 1839), pp. 27–30).

37 Kul'man's myth of the woman poet arrived at similar conclusions
    about the cost of her enterprise: Nartsissa falls in love with the
    image of Apollo which she sees in the waters of a pool, plunges in
    to unite herself with him, dies in the attempt, and is mourned
    only by her mother.

38 See, for example, the characterization of the woman writer
    established by Gilbert and Gubar, *The Madwoman in the Attic* (New
    Haven and London: Yale University Press, 1979).

39 Bunina, Preface to *Padenie Faetona*, in her *Neopytnaia muza*, 2 (St
    Petersburg, 1812), p. 81.

40 Letter from Shishkov to Bunina (Manuscript Section, Russian
    National Library, f. 862, No. 7, l. 5).

41 Zapadov, 'Iz arkhiva Khvostova', p. 383.

42 Bunina, Preface to *Padenie Faetona*, p. 92.

43 Bunina, Preface to *Padenie Faetona*, p. 97. It was not Bunina's

custom to solicit public indulgence, although this was common literary etiquette.

44 Khmyrov, 'Russkie pisatel'nitsy', p. 224.

45 Entry by G. Kutaisov on 20 November, a week or so after the reading.

46 Bunina, Preface to *Padenie Faetona*, p. 96.

47 Her testament referred to the need to forgive 'those who envied me and obstructed my path', presumably those who resented competition. Part of the testament is in D. Mordovtsev, *Russkie zhenshchiny novogo vremeni. Biograficheskie ocherki iz russkoi istorii*, 3 (St Petersburg, 1874), pp. 47–58.

48 'I. A. Krylovu, chitavshemu *Padenie Faetona* v *Besede liubitelei russkogo slova*', reprinted in Al'tshuller and Lotman, *Poety 1790– 1810 godov*, p. 463.

49 *Chteniia v Besede*, 4 (1811), pp. 68-99.

50 *Neopytnaia muza*, 2 (St Petersburg, 1812).

51 I have found no record of contacts between the three women members of the society. Bunina's sole close literary ally, apart from Shishkov, was the writer Katerina Puchkova, who published an article entitled 'On women', which advanced the rationalist feminist argument that women's dependence on men made them sly, mean and selfish, and only development of their reason could counterbalance social conditioning and improve their morals (*Vestnik Evropy*, 4 (1810), 4, quoted in E. N. Shchepkina, *Iz istorii zhenskoi lichnosti v Rossii. Lektsii i stat'i* (St Petersburg, 1914), pp. 185 and 225). On Puchkova see also *Damskii zhurnal*, part 29, 14 (1830); M. Makarov, 'Materialy dlia istorii russkikh zhenshchin-avtorov', *Damskii zhurnal*, part 44, 51–2 (1833), pp. 147–8.

52 K. Ia. Grot identifies the editor as Shishkov ('Poetessa Anna Petrovna Bunina (k 100-letnei godovshchine ee smerti 4 dekabria 1829g)', Institute of Russian Literature, R.1, op. 5, d. 137, p. 29). Shchepkina, *Iz istorii zhenskoi lichnosti v Rossii*, p. 219, identifies Zakharov as the president of the section. I have found no conclusive evidence on this point.

53 Bunina, Preface to *Padenie Faetona*, p. 97.

54 'You write that you are glad to quarrel with me as before on occasion. Quarrel? No, my esteemed Aleksandr Semenovich, this you will not achieve. From now on you can speak boldly; I shall not engage in slanging matches with you. Oh, what am I saying! I promise more than I have the power to do. My spirit is not one to be silent! I shall, I shall engage in slanging matches just as before' (letter to Shishkov, February 1813, Institute of Russian Literature, f. 13842).

55 The text is in Zapadov, 'Iz arkhiva Khvostova', p. 383.

56 The custom was for new members of *Arzamas* to pronounce a
    funeral oration on a member of *Beseda*. At the time Bunina was
    seriously ill with breast cancer, and the oration was in poor taste.
    Uvarov's text is in M. Borovkova-Maikova, *Arzamas i arzamasskie
    protokoly* (Leningrad, 1933), pp. 119–25.

57 Kelly, *A History of Russian Women's Writing*, p. 42, outlines the
    views of critics who argued in reverse that women who wrote
    were women, but that their writing was not worthy of the name.

58 Uvarov states: 'in her cradle ... she trembled at the name of the
    Grey-haired Grandfather [Shishkov]. In winter's cold she
    warmed herself at the flame of his poetry ...'.

59 'Sappho and Phaon [Shishkov] lived as if they were one soul,
    were carried away by the same feelings, wrote with the same pen.
    It is even said that the eloquent patriarch who summoned nations
    and tsars to battle tenderly pressed the passionate Diva to his
    heart and – sometimes sharpened her quills.' Uvarov implies
    both role and sex reversals between Bunina and Shishkov.

60 'Bathyllus Sh. [Shirinskii-Shikhmatov] clanked on the patriarch's
    lyre and shared all the movements of his heart with the Diva.
    What a picture! The Grey-haired Grandfather, embracing the
    ardent maid with one arm, played with the hair of the singing
    youth with the other. Happy Phaon savoured all the delights of
    elegant luxury. The maid and the youth vied with one another,
    trying to pander to all the whims of his literary voluptuousness.
    They knew no jealousy of one other; and in this miraculous union
    she did not cease to be a maid, nor he a youth.
        What callous divinity broke these bonds of passion asunder?
    What foes tore the grey-haired Grandfather from the embraces
    of the tender maid and the sensitive youth? The Sarmatian
    Lovely and the intricate progenitor of the Cold Fur Coats
    [Shakhovskoi].'

61 A. S. Pushkin, 'Pervoe poslanie tsenzoru'.

62 A. S. Pushkin, 'Razgovor mezhdu mnoiu i zhenshchinami'.

CHAPTER 4

Reading the future: women and fortune-telling in Russia (1770–1840)

Faith Wigzell

Tat'iana, the heroine of Pushkin's *Evgenii Onegin*, treasures one book above all others. After purchasing Martyn Zadeka's dreambook from a passing pedlar, she keeps it by her bedside:

> Мартын Задека стал потом
> Любимец Тани ... Он отрады
> Во всех печалях ей дарит
> И безотлучно с ней спит.

(Martyn Zadeka then became | Tania's favourite ... He gave her comfort | In all her sorrows | And was her inseparable companion as she slept.)   (*Evgenii Onegin* V, xxiii)

Tat'iana's attachment to her dreambook was matched by Pushkin's own interest in fortune-telling. Apart from owning two fortune-telling books, he had, like Pechorin, the fictional hero of Lermontov's novel *Geroi nashego vremeni* (*Hero of Our Time*), consulted a professional fortune-teller. So popular were the fortune-telling books that appeared in Russia from the 1760s on (some ran to ten editions in the eighteenth century alone), and so well known were fortune-tellers, that Tat'iana's, Pushkin's and Pechorin's interest in prediction cannot be regarded as in any way unusual. But understanding the popularity of fortune-telling and the role played by women in what was an important, if largely unseen, sub-culture, is possible only in the broader Russian context, more particularly the oral divinatory traditions from which members of the Europeanized gentry had so recently been divorced. Peter's forcible westernization of his nobles inevitably took time to filter both into the consciousness of the upper nobility and to reach the lesser, mainly rural

country gentry.[1] In attempting an assessment of women's part
in the popularity of fortune-telling books and fortune-telling,
the roles played respectively by men and women in divination
as part of Russian traditional life are important both as context
and as contrast.[2]

Within the peasant community predicting the future was part
and parcel of the highly ritualized structure of life; behaviour
was ritually conventionalized and semiotic in character down to
the smallest details of everyday life. Hence correct behaviour or
interpretation of objects and events helped ward off and warn
of bad luck. Within this system, the past was significant as
memory, but since it was seen as unchanging and unchange-
able, it was not a matter of ongoing concern or discussion. The
lore of the past provided the traditional knowledge of the
present, but the concerns of Russian and other oral cultures
were focused on the future rather than the past: 'hence the
huge role played ... by predictions, fortune-telling and prog-
nostication'.[3] These were means of smoothing a path for self
and family through life, an attempt to deal with man's help-
lessness in the face of nature and fate. While folk belief and
magic practices varied in detail according to locality, the world-
view as well as the general categories and functions of divination as described below were common throughout Russia.

Within divination, as in many other spheres of life, gender
roles were often quite distinct, but in some areas were shared,
some type of everyday divination in the Russian village forming
part of both male and female culture. The commonest were
omens (*primety*), widely known still among Russians today.
These covered weather forecasting, calendar agricultural activity (when to sow, reap, and so on), domestic and personal
signs (for example, what it meant when the cat curled up in a
ball or your nose itched) and lucky and, particularly, unlucky
omens (such as seeing a hare crossing the road or a horned
moon on the left, to quote two familiar to Pushkin). However,
although the whole community concurred in beliefs in omens,
knowledge of particular signs reflected male and female spheres
of influence and activity. For women, this was the house and
the family. While men needed to know weather and agricultural

signs, and to be able to interpret ill omens in the environment at large, women were familiar with omens relating to domestic objects and happenings.[4]

They were also more keenly interested in questions of personal fate, playing the leading role in all forms of prediction about future prospects. Since they were generally in charge of rites of passage, especially birth and marriage, they were the bearers of tradition as far as the many associated forms of divinatory ritual were concerned. For example, they were the prime participants in the best-known type of calendar divination, which took place at Yuletide (*sviatki*). In the period up to 1840, come New Year's Eve, few girls spurned the chance of trying to determine their marital prospects: Zhukovskii's Svetlana and Pushkin's Tat'iana were following time-honoured practice when they tried to conjure up the image of their intended.[5] Older women often conducted the proceedings, while unmarried women and, to a lesser extent, men made up the participants.[6] Similar rituals were practised on St John's Eve (23–4 June), St Agrafena's day (23 June) and St Andrew's day (late November).[7]

Women were also the prime movers in a common form of everyday prediction, interpretation of dreams. Oneiromancy was directed towards the future, with dreams regarded as pointers to the personal fate of the dreamer and her or his family and friends. Chulkov noted that as many believed in dreams as in gypsy fortune-telling,[8] and I. P. Sakharov remarked in the 1830s that 'there is not a single woman or girl in our towns or villages who does not believe in dreams'.[9] With the house the women's sphere of activity, it was natural that dream divination, a morning activity, should have been largely the province of women, especially older women. Interpretation was iconic in character, being based upon the object seen in dreams, although some attention was paid to the time of night (evening, midnight or morning) when the dream occurred. It may be noted that, in S. T. Aksakov's lightly fictionalized autobiographical account *A Russian Gentleman*, his grandmother, an old-style Russian landowner, always asks her husband in the morning what dreams he has had.

Women also played the major role in other kinds of divination, such as Psalter divination, divining from the shape of an
egg white or two needles in water, or examining eggs broken
into a dish in order to determine the sex of an unborn child. In
these instances, older women mainly performed the rituals
while younger women took part, but in another important
aspect of village divination, detection of theft, women divined,
but all members of the community participated. Once an object
or an animal went missing, the fortune-teller was summoned
and all those who might be suspected of the deed assembled.
Using various methods involving water, or a black hen or the
use of a sieve, the fortune-teller or older female member of the
family claimed to reveal the guilty party.[10]

Folklorists commonly divide folk customs and beliefs into
'ritual' (*obriadovyi*), connected with the calendar (like Yuletide
divination), and 'non-ritual' (*neobriadovyi*), performed on any
appropriate occasion (such as crime detection or elucidation of
dreams and omens), but this distinction is less relevant in a
consideration of gender roles in divination than that between
specialist and non-specialist practitioners of magic and prediction. The dividing line was thin; some of the divinatory
methods already mentioned, such as oneiromancy or crime
detection, might be practised either by a knowledgeable older
woman from within the family, or by someone known in the
locality for their expertise and receiving, if not a living, at least
some means of support by the exercise of his or her craft.

In rural Russia, specialist practitioners of magic were of two
kinds: generally maleficent (the sorcerer and witch – usually
termed *koldun* and *ved'ma*) and beneficent (magic healers –
znakhar'/znakharka, who mixed herbal cures with magic charms)
and, very close to them, the *vorozheia/vorozheika*, who was both
healer and fortune-teller).[11] Sorcerers and witches were believed capable of affecting the fate of those who attracted their
disfavour (by putting the evil eye on them or 'spoiling' them),
but they did not indulge much in divination, which was
generally the province of benign magic practitioners.[12] It
should not be assumed, by analogy with western Europe, that
the power to cause harm or practise witchcraft was more the

province of women than men. Indeed the reverse may have
been the case.[13] On the other hand, the female *znakharka*
appears to have been nearly as familiar as the *znakhar'*.[14] Even
more than healing, divination was almost always a female skill.
According to Vladimir Dal', a word for a male fortune-teller
(*vorozhei*) existed, but it seems to have been very little used. The
word *vorozheia*, which he says applies to both sexes, is commonly
found, but very frequently refers to women. As early as the
1830s, it was beginning to be viewed as a feminine noun.[15] The
commonest word in this period is *vorozheika*, sometimes *voroz-
haika*, which applies exclusively to women, and is almost always
the word used by Sakharov.

Apart from the *vorozheiki*, some specialized kinds of traditional
healers, also all women, supported themselves through their
divinatory skills, especially dream interpretation. According to
Sakharov, who was referring to past rather than present
practice in this instance, 'dream interpretation among the
Russians was the occupation of gossips, elderly nursemaids, old
women in the neighbourhood, and a particular class of people –
healers (*lecheiki*) who wandered the streets of villages and towns
with bundles of herbs on their backs, and on Saturdays acted as
midwives in bath-houses'.[16] None of the above received
payment as such, but were rewarded with gifts.

The reasons for the male predilection for black magic and
the female mainly for healing and prediction are unclear, but
one may speculate that this may be partly because magic is
more obviously concerned with power, with controlling and
changing fate rather than merely interpreting it. While it would
appear that divination was part of the duties of the sorcerer in
medieval and Muscovite Russia, with time, some types of
fortune-telling may have become less respected or feared. Since
sorcerers and witches relied on fear for their power over other
members of the community, they would have distanced themselves from any activity that might undermine their position.
Even in the first part of the nineteenth century, as Sakharov
makes clear, some forms of divination were taken much more
seriously than others,[17] while others always contained an
element of fun (some of the Yuletide forms of divination fall

into this category). Both healing and divination were aspects of
the female role; the first helped an individual escape from his
current situation of ill-health towards a healthy future, the
second interpreted signs to help the individual cope with the
future. Furthermore, women's traditional role in the rituals of
birth and marriage would have naturally inclined them towards
prediction about these matters. Even if black magic practitioners were more involved in divination in sixteenth- and
seventeenth-century Muscovy, it is highly probable that women
were then, as later, extensively involved in personal and household divination.

Women thus played a significant role in divination either as
non-specialists or as 'professionals' (I use the term in quotation
marks, since they did not demand or receive payment as such).
Assuming that a world-view changes more slowly than individual circumstances or social situation, it would be expected that
in the new urban or westernized upper-class setting women
would continue to be attached to divination, albeit that traditional divinatory practices would be in some ways transmuted.
In general, this assumption is borne out by the evidence,
despite some important differences.

There had always been sorcerers and fortune-tellers in towns,
consulted by great and lowly alike, but it appears that sorcerers
gradually left the towns during the eighteenth century. Certainly, urban sorcerers do not feature in the admittedly scanty
sources for the period after 1740, such references as there are
being to their rural counterparts.[18] On the other hand, fortune-
tellers seem to have proliferated, as Nikolai Novikov's account
of readers of coffee grounds (1772) suggests: 'the whole bunch of
old women is nothing but an assemblage of vagabonds, who
can only be regarded as outcasts from the human race', he
declared in disgust.[19] Novikov was, nonetheless, forced to admit
that they were immensely popular. He personally knew large
numbers of people who consulted them, including one lady
whose daily expenditure on the services of a fortune-teller
should, he thought, have been written into the household
budget.[20]

Not only Novikov's account, but other references to fortune-tellers in both the eighteenth and early nineteenth centuries indicate that they were overwhelmingly female, elderly and of humble origin.[21] For example, the reader of coffee grounds (*kofeinitsa,* or *kofegadatel'nitsa*) seems always to have been a woman, in Novikov's derogatory description 'an elderly creature, who can no longer earn her living and does not wish to feed herself honestly'.[22] Ten years later, Krylov worked Novikov's information (and attitudes) into an early comic opera *Kofegadatel'nitsa* (1783), in which the elderly female fortune-teller summoned for the traditional purpose of discovering who had stolen some silver spoons is revealed as a complete charlatan. Such was Chulkov's view as well,[23] while Antonii Pogorel'skii's 'The poppy-seed cake seller of Lafertovo', written in 1825, but set in the last decade of the eighteenth century, depicts a sinister old woman who secretly practises fortune-telling. Pushkin's clairvoyant was female, which tallies with Sakharov's consistent assumption that they were female. Urban fortune-tellers, therefore, conformed to the pattern of gender roles (and age) among folk specialists in divination.

Although their success lay in supplying a group who had become detached physically but not psychologically from a traditional cultural environment, fortune-tellers' adaptability also contributed to their continuing success among the upper classes. For, apart from traditional methods (such as sieve divination), they also adopted some of the new foreign forms of fortune-telling fashionable in the eighteenth and early nineteenth centuries. Coffee-cup divination and cartomancy were both imported skills. Presumably, servants picked up these skills from their masters or, more likely, mistresses, or from other servants at home or abroad, before passing them on to others, including fortune-tellers. In this way, fortune-tellers were also acting as cultural intermediaries by transmitting new imported forms of fortune-telling to the urban populace at large, who had little or no access to printed information. Rural types of fortune-telling were, as a result, gradually squeezed out by divinatory methods popular with the upper classes, and, subsequently, with all urban classes. By the 1830s, and indeed throughout the nineteenth century, urban fortune-tellers specialized in reading coffee cups and cards, with sieve divination becoming a rural skill.[24] Dream diviners, according to Sakharov and later commentators, were a separate category of people.[25]

Throughout the period from 1770–1840, fortune-tellers continued to perform traditional functions, detecting thieves, and offering guidance on matters of the heart and material prospects. Novikov abhorred their detective role, since false accusations often led to the ruin of an innocent servant.[26] Sieve divination, as practised by Pogorel'skii's poppy-seed cake seller, was always directed towards crime detection.[27]

While it is impossible to define the gender of the clientele of urban fortune-tellers with any degree of accuracy, it would appear that they were largely, but not exclusively, female. In Novikov's account, as well as in Chulkov's dictionary and Krylov's play, much is made of the way fortune-tellers took care to know the servants of a house, suggesting that they were welcomed by many from the gentry. Some clients, it would appear, were men, and this situation seems not to have changed by 1840. In Dal''s story, 'The Clairvoyant' (1847–8), the narrator describes wealthy people leaving their carriages some distance away from the fortune-teller's house and, pulling down hats or veils, making their way discreetly to her house. His two male protagonists visit the fortune-teller in connection with a theft, a traditional male use of divination. If men's interest in fortune-tellers, including their role in crime detection, existed in the 1840s, it must have been at least as strong earlier, though it may be that the social stigma involved was somewhat less severe. It was precisely the element of social stigma that was new. With the emphasis on rational thought and rejection of popular superstition, fortune-telling became an art despised by the growing numbers of educated people. Whereas the village magic healer (*znakharka*) had enjoyed the respect of her community (and sometimes beyond), urban fortune-tellers were derided. It is no coincidence that the sources for professional urban fortune-tellers cited in this article were all critical and all penned by educated men. The abiding popularity of fortune-telling in the face of high-minded disapproval reflects its importance in women's culture.

Amateur fortune-telling did not lose its hold over gentle-women, but, as they lost touch with oral tradition, they turned to a useful substitute, the printed fortune-telling book. Such books were part of the wave of commercial literature which reached Russia in the late 1760s. Virtually without exception translated or adapted from French or German, they were produced for unashamedly commercial reasons by serious presses such as Moscow University or the cadet presses trying to make ends meet, and after 1790 also by commercial presses. They enjoyed enormous popularity, second only to songbooks, amongst the entire reading public.[28]

One of the distinctive features of Russian development lies in the appearance of popular printed books along with the inges-tion of Enlightenment attitudes. Only the literate, who in the main came from the nobility, could afford to buy or read books (though there is evidence of a small urban market from the 1790s).[29] These were exactly the same people expected to pour cold water on superstition and prejudice. In the light of this, and of the large role played by women in rural divination, one must ask for whom such books were intended, who used them and how seriously. Was it, as in villages, women, and did men turn up their noses?

Divination continued to be regarded as part of women's sphere in noble households, judging by N. P. Osipov's remark in the foreword of a book he had translated that '... fortune-telling for the most part belongs to women'.[30] Some books do recognize a female market, as is clear from the inclusion in fortune-telling manuals of sections detailing Yuletide divina-tory rituals, or onomantic texts enabling the user to discover the name of her future beau, rather than his sweetheart. A very few titles, such as *The Fortune-Teller for the Profit and Enjoyment of Young Ladies* (Moscow, 1795), clearly target women, while another adds men as an afterthought: *A Girlish Trinket, with which Men may also Play, or A Bouquet of Flowers not for the Corsage but the Heart* (St Petersburg, 1791). There are no books or sections of books specifically for men. At first sight, this

would appear to demonstrate conclusively that fortune-telling
books followed traditional practice in being a predominantly
female preserve. This would be a simplistic view. There was
no need to declare that such books were intended for men,
since publishing was in male hands.[31] This being so, did men
produce fortune-telling books for women or did they use them
themselves?

For the eighteenth century at least, the latter seems closer to
the truth, depending on class and educational level. Prior to the
1760s, literacy amongst the country nobility was still regarded
as a rarity; books were mainly religious and too much reading
was thought to drive you mad. Women, who were, in general,
more poorly educated than men, clung even more firmly to the
old ways. Both men and women were extremely superstitious,
'believing', in the words of Chechulin,[32] 'in all kinds of omens,
divination and dreams'. It took until the 1780s for the rural
nobility to acquire a respect for education, and adopt European
manners. Literacy among women continued to lag behind.

In this context, book-buying and book-owning were male
activities; outside Court circles, known libraries all belonged to
men. New male readers probably did not distinguish between a
pseudo-science like physiognomy and science proper, and many
continued to be superstitious themselves. Male *aficionados* of
divinatory pseudo-sciences were to be found even among the
educated élite of the early nineteenth century, if Nikolai Il'in's
comedy, *The Physiognomer and Chiromancer* (1816) reflects a
genuine phenomenon or at least the realistic possibility of one.
The play follows the Molière pattern of ridiculing one character
for his/her *idée fixe*, in this case a count whose obsession causes
him to rush up to strangers in the street to read their faces; at
the end, thanks to his wife and her friend, he is brought to his
senses. Here, unusually, it is the women who are sensible and
the man who is foolish.

As early as the 1770s, literate upper-class women from élite
families may have been persuading their husbands or fathers to
order fortune-telling books for them, but it is more likely that,
initially, men bought out of curiosity, with their womenfolk
taking them over only afterwards. As the titles mentioned above

suggest, it took until the 1790s for publishers to begin to cater overtly for a female market, and, presumably, for women to begin to purchase the books for themselves.

Out in the country, the situation changed more slowly, judging by two satirical portraits of landowners of the early decades of the nineteenth century. Izmailov's Nevezhin owns some popular novels, woodcut (*lubok*) editions of folk tales and a dreambook, while at Oblomovka the library at first sight looks more serious (volumes of Kheraskov, Sumarokov and Golikov with just one fortune-telling text, *The Newest Dreambook*). It might be thought that the dreambook was for the female members of the family, but Goncharov makes it clear that book-reading is entirely a male occupation, the womenfolk holding store by traditional omens and beliefs – Goncharov depicts them whiling away the time recounting their dreams and interpreting them not from the dreambook, but from oral tradition. Though the Oblomov family is a comic literary portrait, it is probably not far from the truth in its depiction of backward rural gentlefolk. Together the two sketches suggest that, in the early nineteenth century, rural male landowners bought and used fortune-telling books.

One may go even further – it is likely that urban men from lower social groups were purchasing books, including fortune-telling guides, before they became the favourite reading of rural noblewomen.[33] Two inscriptions in dreambooks add weight to this supposition: the 1807 edition of a dreambook which also included Martyn Zadeka's famous prophecy and a section on conjuring tricks (*Fokus-Pokus*) contains a note indicating that the owner is a clerk (*pisar'*), who had purchased the book from a merchant, while the inscription on a fortune-telling compendium published in 1817 reveals the owner to be a semi-literate young merchant: «Сия книга принадлежыт Московскому купецкому сыну Яково Кирилову» (sic!) ('this book belongs to the Moscow merchant's son Iakov Kirilov').

Romanticism seems to have given a temporary respite in fortune-telling's slide into disrepute. In the 1820s, the interest in the irrational, shown by educated young men such as Pushkin and his circle, extended briefly to fortune-telling books. Pushkin himself, however, despite his ownership of two texts, regarded them with a degree of irony, as his account of Tat'iana and her dreambook shows.

Pushkin and his friends apart, amateur fortune-telling was generally associated with women by this time – cartomancy was a standard occupation on country estates, for example, as Pushkin's poem 'Winter. What's to do in the country?' shows. With boredom commonplace, books like *Amusement for Times of Boredom, or A New, Diverting Method of Reading the Cards* would have caught the eye. By 1840, fortune-telling books had become almost exclusively part of women's world, viewed by educated men as symptomatic of their owners' frivolity and foolishness. The period of acceptability in educated society was over.

One important factor had served to make the purchase of fortune-telling books respectable. As already noted, traditional divination incorporated an element of fun, but in polite society much stronger emphasis was placed on divination as innocent enjoyment (*nevinnoe uveselenie*), since this was the obvious way of making it acceptable to enlightened society. As western attitudes spread, women were assigned the role of diverting society. The fad for fortune-telling was made to serve these ends. As Ivan Kurbatov remarked in his foreword to his fortune-telling manual published in 1808, *Soothsay, Do not Jest, Speak the Whole Truth that is in Your Heart* ..., his intention was not to reinforce superstitious belief but to provide entertainment and relaxation from wearisome duties or to promote lively conversation. He hoped that the book would commend itself to the fair sex, the guardians of the gentle art of conversation. Even Sumarokov, an established writer, devised a little divinatory volume, elucidating romantic prospects. It was composed of couplets drawn from his verse tragedies. In so doing, he was writing for women's entertainment, not pandering to superstition.[34] While eighteenth- and early nineteenth-century fortune-telling books are prefaced by declarations that they are not to be taken seriously, editors, who were of course all men, sometimes could not resist suggesting otherwise. This could be seen merely as evidence of commercial acumen (far better to promise your book will work), but it is equally likely that they knew that many readers regarded them as more than mere entertainment; it is highly unlikely that Pushkin's Tat'iana was the only one to treasure her dreambook or indulge in cartomancy.

Fortune-telling books thus received a considerable degree of acceptance among both sexes in the late eighteenth and early nineteenth centuries, but only through their classification as a harmless pastime. Given the popularity of fortune-tellers, and the seriousness with which their services were viewed, the assumption that many persisted in seeing them as serious guides to the future, regardless of disapproval from some quarters, would appear a reasonable one. Men's interest in both the books and professional fortune-tellers, already lessened by their adoption of western culture, gradually diminished. Whereas professional fortune-tellers were overwhelmingly women while their customers included men, fortune-telling books were produced by men while their users were largely women.

NOTES

1 Peter himself was hostile to magic and sorcery, but he still believed (as did many educated western Europeans) that his dreams could predict the future. For details see James Cracraft, 'Some dreams of Peter the Great: a biographical note', *Canadian-American Slavic Studies*, 8, 2 (1974) , pp. 173–97.

2 Evidence for oral divinatory practices is largely drawn from the best description of the period in *Skazaniia russkogo naroda, sobrannye I. P. Sakharovym* (Moscow, 1990) (hereafter Sakharov, *Skazaniia*). Sakharov collected his material in the 1830s in Russian towns and villages. Additional information is drawn from M. Chulkov, *Slovar' russkikh sueverii* (Moscow, 1782), or its 1786 edition, *Abevega russkikh sueverii, idolopoklonicheskikh zhertvoprinoshenii svadebnykh, prosto-narodnykh obriadov, koldovstva. shemanstva i proch.* (hereafter Chulkov, *Abevega*), as well as from a variety of references in memoirs and fictional sources (the last have to be used with care).

3 Iu. M. Lotman, 'Neskol'ko myslei o tipologii kul'tur', in B. A. Uspenskii, ed., *Iazyki kul'tury i problemy perevodimosti* (Moscow: Nauka, 1987), pp. 3–11.

4 For example, the womenfolk in the Oblomov family discuss omens in the famous 'dream chapter' in Goncharov's *Oblomov*.

5 For a detailed description of these practices and their reflection in *Evgenii Onegin*, and Zhukovskii's *Svetlana*, see W. F. Ryan and Faith Wigzell, 'Gullible girls and dreadful dreams: Zhukovskii, Pushkin and popular divination', *Slavonic and East European Review*, 70, 4 (1992), pp. 647–69.

6 Twentieth-century evidence of male participation is provided by the well-known Soviet foreign minister and diplomat, Andrei Gromyko, who relates how he took part in some of these rituals during his youth in a Belorussian village: see *Memories*, trans. by Harold Shukman (New York: Hutchinson, 1989), pp. 6–7. See also A. Makarenko, *Russkii narodnyi kalendar' v etnograficheskom otnoshenii. Vostochnaia Sibir'. Eniseiskaia guberniia*, Zapiski Imperatorskogo russkogo geograficheskogo obshchestva po otdelenii etnografii, 36 (St Petersburg, 1913); hereafter Makarenko, *Narodnyi kalendar'*.

7 See Makarenko, *Narodnyi kalendar'*.

8 Chulkov, *Abevega*, p. 295.

9 Sakharov, *Skazaniia*, p. 130. In the summer of 1994, I asked a group of Russian village women living in Karelia whether they believed in dreams predicting the future. Not merely did they all believe this to be the case, but several could cite examples of their own dreams, whose dire predictions had been fulfilled. This particular tradition dies very hard.

10 Sakharov, *Skazaniia*, pp. 118–19, 122–4.

11 There were other names. See, for example, the list offered by Linda J. Ivanits, *Russian Folk Belief* (Armonk, NY and London: M. E. Sharpe, 1989), p. 85; hereafter Ivanits, *Folk Belief*.

12 Ivanits suggests that the division of sorcerers from magic healers was probably not valid for the Kievan and Muscovite periods (Ivanits, *Folk Belief*, p. 90). She cites in support L.V. Cherepnin, 'Iz istorii drevne-russkogo koldovsva XVII v.', *Etnografiia*, 2 (1929), pp. 86–109. One may assume that his evidence included Tsar Aleksei Mikhailovich's *Ulozhenie* of 1648 which attacked popular entertainments and mentioned disapprovingly that 'they tell fortunes' (see D. Rovinskii, *Russkie narodnye kartinki*, 4 (St Petersburg, 1881), p. 210). However, those accused of sorcery in the eighteenth century were sometimes also said to tell fortunes with dice, the Psalter or beans and to interpret dreams. Equally it is probable that even in the Muscovite period beneficent healers did the bulk of divination. Unless something had gone seriously wrong, they were unlikely to be brought to trial. The role of sorcerers and witches and others deemed maleficent in divination may not have signifi-

cantly changed from the Muscovite period to the nineteenth century.

13 R. Zguta, 'Witchcraft trials in seventeenth-century Russia', *American Historical Review*, 82 (1977), p. 1196, cites ninety-nine cases of sorcery, of which fifty-nine involved men. W. Ryan, 'The witchcraft craze in Europe. Was Russia an exception?' (forthcoming), casts doubt on the usefulness of these figures by pointing out that seventeenth- and eighteenth-century court cases predominantly involve men because many of those accused were in State or Church employ. However, ethnographic accounts from the nineteenth century imply that sorcerers were at least as common as witches.

14 There are no reliable figures for gender representation. N. A. Kogan, 'O znakharstve v Novouzenskom uezde', *Vrachebnaia Khronika Samarskoi Gubernii*, 5, no. 7, 1989, pp. 1–11 found thirty-two *znakharki* to fifty-nine of their male equivalents. Not only, however, is the survey incomplete, but the interchangeability of functions and title between the usually female *vorozheia* and the *zhakharka* mean that some women folk healers may have described themselves as *vorozhei* and hence been excluded.

15 For example, *Kliuch k ob"iasneniiu snov, sostavlennyi po sochineniiam slavneishikh snotolkovatelei: Kaliastro, velikogo Alberta, Martyna Zadeka, Indeiskikh, Tsyganskikh i Afrikanskikh mudretsov, i poverennyi s iz"iasneniiami znamenitoi Chukhonskoi vorozhei* (Moscow, 1838). The noun *vorozheia* was masculine in the late eighteenth century: see, for example, the title of a fortune-telling book: *Nelozhnoi vorozheia*, (1787, 1792, 1793). By the twentieth century it was feminine, referring exclusively to female fortune-tellers and magic healers.

16 Sakharov, *Skazaniia*, pp. 130–1.

17 Sakharov reports that cartomancy was taken much less seriously than reading the coffee grounds. As imported types of divination, they were feared less than divining the future with a psalter, or trying to see the image of your intended in a mirror at midnight (*Skazaniia*, pp. 115–22)

18 In 1740, an old-style sorcerer, one Iakov Iarov, was accused of practising black magic and divination (Ryan,'Witchcraft craze'). Chulkov also refers to sorcerers, but without specifying whether they were urban or rural. It may be that they disappeared from the sources earlier than they did from towns, i.e. the westernized upper classes, who provided almost all the written sources, had stopped consulting sorcerers.

19 Novikov, *Zhivopisets*, Part 1 (1772), p. 348 in P. N. Berkov, ed., *Satiricheskie zhurnaly N. I. Novikova* (Moscow–Leningrad, 1950).

20 Novikov, *Zhivopisets*, pp. 349–50.

21 This situation remained unchanged throughout the century, judging by the survey of fortune-tellers in St Petersburg in 1894 published by an author who calls himself 'Otshel'nik' (*Peterburgskie gadalki, znakhari, iurodivye i pr. (Ocherki peterburgskoi zhizni)*).

22 Novikov, *Zhivopisets*, p. 348.

23 Chulkov, *Abevega*, p. 76.

24 See for example, Sakharov, *Skazaniia*, pp. 115–17, 118.

25 Sakharov, *Skazaniia*, pp. 130–1.

26 Novikov, *Zhivopisets*, pp. 349–50.

27 Sakharov, *Skazaniia*, p. 119. See also Vladimir Dal''s story 'The Clairvoyant' ('Vorozheia') of 1848, not to be confused with the better-known story 'The Fortune-teller' ('Vorozheika') of the same period.

28 Probable exceptions to this are the Old Believers, some of whom owned manuscript copies of certain divinatory texts of Byzantine provenance, but who, as is well known, were resistant to secular and contemporary culture. There is evidence for ownership of printed divinatory texts among priests, merchants and artisans, as well as among the gentry in this period.

29 V. Shklovskii, *Chulkov i Levshin* (Leningrad, 1933), pp. 32–7, quotes Novikov's view that there were humble readers (servants, artisans, etc.). He further argues that towns were booming in the late eighteenth century, with peasants doing well on the *obrok* (quit-rent) system. The commercial publishers, like Reshetnikov, who produced cheaper, cruder books, and the *lubok* (cheap popular literature) publishing industry, catered for the humble reader.

30 The book, *Liubopytnoi, zagadchivoi i predskazchivoi mesiatseslov na 1796 god i na sleduiushchiia. Dlia molodykh krasavits* (St Petersburg, 1796), was not a fortune-telling book but one which pretended to be one, while in fact offering moral advice to young girls. The foreword is the only part of the book that can be attributed to Osipov.

31 The exceptions, Catherine the Great and Princess Dashkova, were both wealthy, educated women who were essentially interested in publishing their own works. Neither was involved in commercial publishing.

32 N. Chechulin, *Russkoe provintsial'noe obshchestvo vo vtoroi polovine XVIII veka* (St Petersburg, 1889), p. 34.

33 According to Novikov, any printed book that ran to more than three to five editions included artisans among its readers: see Foreword to *Novyi zhivopisets*, cited by V. Shklovskii, *Chulkov i Levshin* (Leningrad, 1933). The most popular eighteenth-century

divinatory book on physiognomy and chiromancy ran to ten editions, and there were numerous slightly varying editions of dreambooks, geomantic, cartomantic and onomantic texts. By 1840, the only upper-class group that still widely valued fortune-telling books was countrywomen.

34 *Liubovnaia gadatel'naia kniga* (St Petersburg, 1774). One of the four editions is in Sumarokov's collected works.

CHAPTER 5

Russian women writers of the nineteenth century

Ol'ga Demidova

Women's writing began to flourish in the second third of the nineteenth century, influenced to some extent by the development of Romanticism in Russian literature.[1] From the 1830s to the 1860s, critics turned to the problem of women's writing after the publication of the well-known article by the critic Stepan Shevyrev, 'An observer's catalogue', which recognized women's right to engage in literature, and stated that the works of women writers introduced into literature an indispensable 'society' element and would contribute to 'a softening and improvement of social manners'.[2] In their response to Shevyrev, critics from the leading Russian journals eagerly debated the question of whether women should or should not take up the pen, and attempted to define the themes and specific nature of women's writing.

A growing interest in women's writing was also promoted by the emergence from the 1820s onwards of a significant number of works published under women's names. The appearance in those years of a number of bibliographic catalogues and materials relating to the biographies of Russian women writers attests to a sharp increase in the number of women writers.[3]

There are several reasons for this, which are for the most part similar to those which promoted the development of women's literature in Europe as a whole. Above all, the development of women's writing was connected with the general cultural upsurge of the age of Sentimentalism (c.1780–1810). One historian of women's literature, Ekaterina Shchepkina, has rightly pointed to the significance of the age of Sentimentalism for Russian women's development: 'Russian women were invited into the social arena, encouraged to educate themselves and have faith in their own powers. Their intellectual development was rapid, and they succeeded in exerting an influence on society and culture'.[4]

In the interests of historical accuracy, we should note that women writers had already emerged in the eighteenth century.[5] True, the eighteenth century had traditionally scoffed at educated women, but had also bestowed generous praise on the 'latter-day Minervas',[6] 'Russian Sapphos and de la Suzes'.[7] There were only very few of them, and, as they afforded no competition to their brother writers, the Russian Minervas embarked on a literary career with no particular fear, confident of the public's indulgence. One of the first women writers, Princess Ekaterina Urusova (1747–after 1816) wrote in 1774 in the preface to her epic *Pollion*: 'I cherish the hope that my readers, respecting my sex and my first experiments in this genre of poesy, may forgive the faults contained here, and may approve further exercises of my shy Muse'.[8] In the late eighteenth and early nineteenth century there was no lack of approval:[9] Russian journals were ready to praise not only the two Catherines,[10] but also Anna Bunina, Anna Volkova and Mariia Izvekova.

Moreover, in the first decades of the nineteenth century the publishers of special ladies' journals wrote enthusiastically about the role of women in education and literature, and included biographies of women writers.[11] In Moscow, for example, from 1823 to 1833 Prince P. Shalikov, in collaboration with the journalist, historian and memoirist M. Makarov, published the *Ladies' Journal* (*Damskii zhurnal*), whose aim was 'to acquaint women readers with the biographies and literary works of outstanding women'.[12] As a rule the central feature of every issue of the journal consisted of a story translated from German or French, although in those years publishers also began to publish the works of English and even American authors. Thus, along with the works of Washington Irving and Walter Scott, women's writings too were quite extensively represented: translations were published of Madame de Genlis,[13] Frau Pichler,[14] the Duchess Duras[15] and even a translation by the Hungarian writer Mrs Nitra: 'Lady Kalli-chado and Gottfried Oppel-Maier, or The letters of two lovers living in the Carpathian Mountains, on the banks of the Bystritsa River' – an obvious imitation of Goethe's *The Sufferings of Young Werther*. Russian imitations of the Gothic novelist Ann Radcliffe could also be found:[16] for example, 'Sof'ia and Aleksei, or The Beautiful Castle on the wild bank of the Kama' by a certain lady disguised under the pseudonym 'E.Ch.' Of considerable interest too are series of articles entitled 'Women who were practitioners of art and artists' patrons in Greece, Rome, Italy and France' and 'The Names of Esteemed Russian Ladies and Maidens' – a list of members of learned and charitable societies.

The publishers of journals exhorted Russian women to 'conquer the field of literature'; after they had occupied it, M. Makarov wrote, women would 'carry all before them and in a short while become our teachers', inasmuch as 'a mediocre work by a woman has more effect on our sex than a masterpiece by a man'.[17] True, even in those days not all Russian writers were so well-disposed towards women's writing: to some of them, such as the poet A. D. Il'ichevskii, the 'new Sapphos' seemed absurd.[18] But this was not because they regarded literature as an unsuitable occupation for a woman, but only because of the patronage extended to these 'Sapphos' by the 'Russian Slavs' from the 'Society of Lovers of the Russian Word'.[19]

Romanticism, which gained wide currency in Russian litera-ture in the 1820s and 1830s, promoted the further development of women's writing. The Romantic concept of the value of human individuality also led to an acknowledgement of the value of female individuality and the need for women's libera-tion. A significant role in this was played by the ideal of the 'superior woman' which emerged in the work of western European Romantics and quite rapidly became well known in Russia. Real women, 'exceptional personalities', who had risen to fame not so much for their creative work as for their role in the literary history of their country, became the focus of universal interest in Russia. Among them were the famous

Caroline Schlegel-Schelling, the inspiration for the entire German Romantic circle,[20] Rahel Levin (Varnhagen),[21] Goethe's disciple and the object of Heine's admiration, Bettina von Arnim,[22] and Charlotte Stieglitz,[23] whose suicide evoked a response in the work of Russian writers.[24]

Russia had its own 'exceptional women' who stood alongside Western Europeans at the source of women's literature of the years 1830–60. The most famous were Princess Zinaida Volkonskaia, 'the Queen of the Muses and of beauty',[25] the poet Elizaveta Kul'man[26] and the 'cavalry maiden' Nadezhda Durova. Durova's image excited her readers' imagination – and not only at the end of the 1830s.[27] Her legend still remained alive at a later date, when interest in women's emancipation had become universal. It is interesting that in 1874 D. Mordovtsev, a historian of Russian women, called Durova 'the precursor of all new Russian women, of that great multitude of women who sought knowledge and work, visited the public library, attended professors' lectures and medical courses, and longed to enter university ... Durova was the first Russian woman who proved in her own life that, with a strong will, everything is as attainable for a woman as for a man.'[28]

Following on from these outstanding women, the names of certain outstanding European women writers also became famous in Russia. These were writers whose work had been stimulated by Sentimentalism and, in particular, by the subsequent Romantic movement. English, French and German novelists affirmed the equality of the male and female personality and demanded equality with men in the realm of feelings. Ultimately, the theme of women's emancipation achieved its supreme expression in the work of George Sand.[29]

Although Western European Romanticism did not spread evenly on Russian soil, one point is indisputable: as in the West, women's names began to appear more and more often in journals and anthologies, and books written by women came to be published more frequently. It should, however, be noted that, in contrast to European literature, the novel had not yet become the leading genre in women's writing: Russian women writers mainly turned to stories and lyrical genres.

In comparison with the previous decade, benign responses from critics became rather rare in the 1830s. With only a few exceptions, Russian women writers of the 1830s encountered a derisive, unsympathetic attitude from Russian critics, who were still male (the age of women critics was yet to come; one of them, 'Evgeniia Tur', would begin writing in the next decade).[30]

If we examine women's writing in the second third of the century, numerous complaints about the fate of the woman writer become evident, while prejudice against women poets extended to all classes of educated society: from the salons of the capital to the provincial aristocracy and middle class. Thus, in Aleksandra Zrazhevskaia's 'Zhenshchina poet i avtor' ('The Woman Poet and Writer', 1842), the heroine encounters mistrust in the literary circles of the capital.[31] On the basis of her own sad experience, the acclaimed writer Elena Gan ('Zeneida R-va') states that for the public a Russian woman writer is 'a special creature, an ugly freak of nature, or rather, a freak of the female sex'.[32] In the opinion of Mar'ia Zhukova, 'a woman writer, a woman petitioner or a woman acting as a lawyer, even in her own affairs, will find no forgiveness in the eyes of society. Such women are said to be out of their mind'.[33] Even a member of the next generation of writers, Nadezhda Sokhanskaia ('Kokhanovskaia') came to the melancholy conclusion that 'Sometimes fluffy cats appear among grey cats: they are like writers among women'.[34]

It was not only in provincial living-rooms or the salons of the capital that Russian women writers of the 1830s and 1840s encountered a reception of this type. They fared no better on the pages of literary journals. One of the reasons for this may have been the competition which women's literature now began to afford men's. But for the most part, this critical attitude to Russian women writers represented a response of a kind to the appearance in Russia of the novels of George Sand, with their frank appeals for women's liberation.[35] It was from that time that the existence of women's literature began to be regarded as a threat to morals, and writing to be considered an unsuitable vocation for a woman.

It is interesting to note that, in their attitude to women writers, as in their view of George Sand, writers and critics of different tendencies, such as Faddei Bulgarin, Osip Senkovskii, Vissarion Belinskii, and even a woman writer, Mar'ia Korsini,[36] were initially in agreement. One story highly indicative of the mood of the time was 'Zhenshchina-pisatel'nitsa' ('The Lady Authoress') by N. N. Verevkin ('N. Rakhmannyi') in which an 'authoress' striving for 'equal rights' with men loses all her female qualities and virtues. In the author's opinion, the heroine's lot should serve as a warning to 'presumptuous' women writers. No less significant is the contrast drawn in the story between French and English women's literature: 'Only English women writers have made a correct choice, and write books on questions of children's education'.[37]

It is true that such rejection did not remain unanimous for long. If in 1835 the well known critic Vissarion Belinskii had spoken disparagingly of 'academicians in bonnets', by 1842 he became a vocal supporter of the rights of women writers.[38] Nor should we forget those writers – however few – who, irrespective of their views on George Sand, welcomed the first steps taken by Russian women writers in their literary profession and gave them all possible support.[39]

As in Europe, a very important factor motivating Russian women to take up the pen was their profound knowledge of literature, their great erudition in comparison with men. Confirmation of this can be found in the numerous memoirs, diaries and letters by Russian girls and women, and, not least, in their work. In Rostopchina's story 'Schastlivaia zhenshchina' ('A Happy Woman', 1851), for example, the heroine, the author's *alter ego*,

surrounded herself with geniuses and thinkers of all ages and nationalities – Goethe, Schiller, Jean-Paul [Johann Paul Friedrich Richter], Shakespeare, Dante ... Chénier, Zhukovskii, Pushkin, Thomas Moore, Hugo ... Balzac, George Sand, Edward Bulwer [Lord Lytton], Nodier – and everything that might elevate the soul, develop the imagination and touch the heart of the maturing recluse; all this she loved, knew and understood'.[40]

This extract suggests that the time for exclusively French books had passed: Russian literature had come to occupy an honourable place alongside French; and from the mid-1820s 'the fantasies of the British Muse'[41] also appeared in the libraries of young Russian ladies.

While waiting for marriage, a girl who, as a rule, had no occupation was transported into the distant fantasy world which books opened up for her. Evgeniia Tur said: 'I read a great deal, indiscriminately ... Novels, histories, poems, travel books – it was all the same to me. I read avidly.'[42] Avdot'ia Panaeva, writing under the pseudonym 'N. Stanitskii', commented: 'No other life could have promoted the enrichment of the mind more rapidly.'[43]

> В неволе жизни этой тесной
> Хоть взрыв мгновенной жизни ТОЙ

(In the close imprisonment of this life | Just a momentary flash of *that* life)

was what Karolina Pavlova sought in books.[44] Similar examples can be found in nearly every work by a woman writer in the 1830s and 1840s. Not surprisingly, the aspiration towards '*that* life' led to a protest against 'this life', a protest which allowed Russian women writers to reflect on typically 'George Sand-type' problems irrespective of George Sand's influence.

But even Sand's influence on Russian women's writing was not absolute. Those of Sand's novels which developed social theories, such as *Spiridion* (1838), *La Comtesse de Rudolstadt* (1843–4) and others, did not arouse any interest among Russian women writers.[45] It is possible to speak with confidence only of the influence of her novels concerned with the question of women's emancipation.[46] But Russian women writers became familiar with these works only after they had already addressed the problem of emancipation in one form or another, perhaps as a result of the general impact of the Romantic period, or of the influence of other writers.

An analysis of the factors influencing the development of Russian women's literature would be incomplete if we failed to point out that George Sand was by no means the only Western European woman writer whose works provoked such a lively response in Russia. The history of the translation of foreign literature affords evidence that Russian readers, both male and female, were very familiar with the novels of Maria Edgeworth, Frances Trollope, Ida von Hahn-Hahn and Fanny Lewald,[47] which were all translated at almost the same time as the novels of George Sand, or a little earlier. But probably only Charlotte Brontë can compete with George Sand as regards the significance she had for the development of women's literature in Russia.

The assimilation of their work on Russian soil occurred in a far from identical manner, which can be explained, first and foremost, by the situation in Russian literature, which had changed significantly between 1832, the year of the publication in Russia of the first novels of George Sand, and 1849, when the novel *Jane Eyre* was translated.[48]

George Sand's novels exerted a significant impact on Russian literature as a whole, both by men and women. By the beginning of the 1840s, a considerable number of stories about women's emancipation had already appeared, which, on the one hand, had been created under the influence of George Sand's novels, and, on the other hand, represented a response to the conditions of Russian life. But quite early on, Russian literature began to treat the theme differently from George Sand. Russian authors rejected the depiction of 'fatal' passions and turned to an exploration of typical real-life situations, the 'quiet terror of the everyday' which women suffered. A similar desire to overcome 'George-Sandism' characterized both male and female writers at the end of the 1830s and the beginning of the 1840s. The difference between their ideas and those of the French novelist was evident above all in the female characters. In the works of Russian male authors, such as Aleksandr Druzhinin's *Polin'ka Saks* (1847), Herzen's *Kto vinovat?* (*Who is to Blame?*, 1846–7) and *Soroka-vorovka* (*The Thieving Magpie*, 1848), the heroine is a creature who is 'humiliated and wronged', mutilated by life and worthy only of pity.

In women's writing of the 1830s, two basic types of heroines are depicted.[49] The first is an 'ideal' heroine who continues the series of ideal female images in male literature; the second is a 'superior' woman who fights for her happiness, an original corrective to the 'George Sand-type' images depicted by Russian male writers.

One example is Zeneida from Elena Gan's 'Society's Judgement' ('Sud sveta', 1839);[50] others are the heroines of Karolina Pavlova and Evdokiia Rostopchina. By the beginning of the 1840s, the second type underwent further modification as women writers began to master the realist manner of depicting life. Realist elements gradually transformed the artistic structure of their work; although feminine images still retained some features of the Romantic character, a 'deheroization' of Romantic heroines occurred, and authors began to treat the old Romantic stereotypes with irony.[51]

Hence the attempt by some researchers to interpret the work of Russian women writers from the 1830s to the 1850s exclusively as a demonstration of 'George-Sandism' on Russian soil is incorrect. Russian women's literature of this period was a completely independent phenomenon, although it developed under the influence of the French novelist.

Charlotte Brontë's work did not exert such an all-pervasive influence in Russia: her novels had virtually no impact on the development of men's literature. As regards women's literature, it is difficult to overestimate the significance of Brontë's work, especially *Jane Eyre*. In particular, the English novelist's work was drawn into the debate about Russian women's literature. The most significant articles were by Aleksandr Druzhinin[52] and Evgeniia Tur,[53] which can be regarded as an expression of male and female views on women's writing. Tur's articles are one of the very few attempts in the 1850s to affirm women's right to professional literary work.

The views expressed in the articles of both authors are pretty typical of their time and represent a fairly accurate reflection of attitudes towards women's writing. Druzhinin argues that its mission is purely educational; Tur suggests that the aim of women's literature is to alleviate personal sufferings and 'to recreate their dreams in the imaginary characters of their novels'. It should be noted that Tur's article 'Miss Brontë, her life and work' (1858) was virtually the first to state explicitly that a male pseudonym acts as a mask hiding a woman's face which allows her to think and feel in a way that she would not dare to do in real life.[54]

Furthermore, there is every reason to argue that Charlotte Brontë's novel *Jane Eyre* exerted an influence on the work of Russian women writers of the 1850s and 1860s. In the 1850s many stories appeared, anonymous for the most part, written in the genre of memoirs or biography, containing a detailed description of the heroine's childhood years and retaining the basic plot lines of the English novel.[55] Although these stories were frankly imitative, one relatively successful exception was Avdot′ia Panaeva's *Semeistvo Tal′nikovykh* (*The Tal′nikov Family*; completed in 1848).[56]

In the 1860s, Russian women writers began to pay attention to the 'adult' theme of *Jane Eyre*, not least because of the growing movement for women's emancipation – not so much in the realm of feelings, as had been the case in the 1830s, as in the social sphere. The works of Russian writers of this type shared similar attitudes towards problems of upbringing, education and the position of women in society, and treated similar themes, as is demonstrated by such titles as Apollinariia Suslova's *Svoei dorogoi* (*Her Own Way*, 1864), Iuliia Zhadovskaia's *Zhenskaia istoriia* (*A Woman's Story*, 1861) and Lidiia Kamskaia's *Moia sud′ba* (*My Fate*, 1863). In these years the typical image depicted in Brontë's novel became established: a plain, poor, but inwardly independent woman striving to live through her work.

Thus, notwithstanding all the differences between the work of George Sand and Charlotte Brontë and their assimilation on Russian soil, it is possible to argue that their novels exerted a similar influence on the development of Russian women's literature (and, indirectly, on men's). By the end of the 1860s, the image of the 'new woman' had become established in the work of Russian women writers, and became very popular in literature of the period of the *raznochintsy* (people of 'other ranks').[57]

Russian women's literature of the nineteenth century consists of more than a hundred names, many of whom are unjustly forgotten in Russia today. They constitute a significant part of the 'great' Russian literature of the nineteenth century (if it is valid to divide literature into 'great' and 'minor'). Unfortunately, Russian researchers into women's literature, even the most serious, have not made any attempt to regard it as a single whole, as a system in which every element has a specific place.[58] As a result, despite the many bibliographical works and research devoted to the work of individual women writers, in Russia to this day there persists an idea of women's literature as a chaotic assortment of disparate names with nothing to unite them. Nevertheless, for all the diversity of their social position, education, views and literary proclivities, it is quite simple to assign nineteenth-century women writers to one of four groups.

The first is composed of women writers who became famous not so much for their work as for their unusual lives: among them are Zinaida Volkonskaia, Elizaveta Kul'man and Nadezhda Durova. The appearance, in the words of the critic A. Beletskii, of such 'women of genius' paved the way for the emergence of the second group of writers, and the first signs of an interest in their work during the age of Pushkin and Zhukovskii. Women writers of both groups, with the exception of Durova, employed poetic genres; their work clearly demonstrates the influence of Sentimentalist poetics and the poetry of Zhukovskii. According to Beletskii's classification, the women poets of the first group 'stand at the threshold' of the second, which includes Marfa Lisitsyna, Nadezhda Teplova, Elizaveta Shakhova and Aleksandra Fuks.

The third, more numerous group of women writers can justifiably be called Romantic, because they are very closely associated with Western European and Russian Romanticism. They include Elena Gan ('Zeneida R-va'), Mari'a Zhukova, Elizaveta Kologrivova ('F. Fan-Dim'), Karolina Pavlova, L. Krichevskaia and Countess Evdokiia Rostopchina. The writers of this group wrote both poetry and prose; the so-called 'society tale' was the leading prose genre.[59] Pavlova's *A Double Life* represented the first attempt by a woman writer to synthesize the genres of poetry and prose. Both in their own consciousness and in the perception of contemporary critics, women writers of the 1830s and 1840s stood out from the general run of writers precisely because of the specifically female nature of their work: they all tried in one way or another to express their female identity in their work. It is interesting that all the writers of this group used female pseudonyms or signed their work with their own names, thereby emphasizing that they belonged to *women's* literature, as distinct from men's.

The fourth group of writers is the most numerous, and at the same time the most diverse. It is true, old-fashioned critics ascribed most of the writers belonging to it to the 'natural school', and the writers regarded themselves as belonging to this trend. Although much Romanticism still remains, both in their plots and characterization, their creative manner was developing towards a rejection of Romanticism. Unfortunately, while conquering Romanticism, these writers seemed at the same time to conquer their female identity, and by the beginning of the 1860s women's writing gradually lost its specifically female character. Another feature of this period was the appearance of a greater number of male pseudonyms: 'N. Stanitskii' (Avdot'ia Panaeva), 'V. Krestovskii' and 'V. Porechnikov' (Nadezhda Khvoshchinskaia), 'Ivan Vesen'ev' (Sof'ia Khvoshchinskaia), 'Marko Vovchok' (Mariia Markovich) and others. In my view, this phenomenon is related not only to the development of realism in Russian literature, but also with its increasingly ideological nature. The *raznochinets* period of Russian literature had begun; the question of the social equality of the sexes had turned into an affirmation of their psychological identity. Bowing to the demands of the time, women writers stopped speaking in their own names and aspired to become just writers. Those who were unable to do so fell silent. And only towards the end of the century, in the 1880s, did women poets again emerge in Russian literature, not just poets.

NOTES

Some of the notes were prepared by the editor in collaboration with the author.

1   Ed.: the influence of Romanticism on Russian women's writing is

a subject of some controversy. Catriona Kelly, *A History of Russian Women's Writing, 1820–1992* (Oxford: Clarendon Press, 1994), pp. 33–47, argues that Russian Romanticism, conventionally seen as the main literary movement in the period 1810–40, had a complex and ambiguous impact on women writers, since it was explicitly gendered, laying emphasis on the 'man of genius'.

2 S. P. Shevyrev, 'Perechen' nabliudatelia', *Moskovskii nabliudatel'*, 6 (1836), pp. 81–6.

3 S. V. Russov, *Bibliograficheskii katalog rossiiskikh pisatel'nits* (St Petersburg, 1826); M. N. Makarov, 'Materialy dlia istorii russkikh zhenshchin-avtorov', *Damskii zhurnal*, 29–30 (1830–1); 43 (1833); N. I. Vilevich, 'Russkie pisatel'nitsy XVIII i XIX vekov', *Moskovskii gorodskoi listok*, 78–80 (1847), pp. 108–14, 167–83.

4 E. Shchepkina, 'Zhenskaia lichnost' v staroi russkoi zhurnalistike', *Zhurnal Ministerstva Narodnogo Prosveshcheniia*, 7 (1912), p. 118.

5 Ed.: there is little hard evidence for the existence of any women writers before the eighteenth century. See Kelly, *A History of Russian Women's Writing*, p. 1, and McKenzie above, p. 42.

6 M. Mikhailov, 'Nemetskoe izvestie o russkikh pisateliakh', *Bibliograficheskie zapiski*, 3, 20 (1881), columns 809–33; M. V. Suslikova, 'Stansy na uchrezhdenie Rossiiskoi Akademii', *Sobesednik liubitelei rossiiskogo slova*, 9 (1783), p. 18.

7 This is a reference to 'Russia has Sapphos now, and de la Suzes ...', a line in Urusova's 'Invocation', the opening piece of her collection *Iroidy: Muzam posviashchennye* (*Heroic Verses Dedicated to the Muses*, St Petersburg, 1777). For a translation of Urusova's poem, see Catriona Kelly, ed., *An Anthology of Russian Women's Writing, 1777–1992* (Oxford: Oxford University Press, 1994), pp. 1–2.

8 E. Urusova, *Pollion, ili Prosveshchennyi neliudim* (*Pollion, or The Enlightened Misanthrope* (St Petersburg, 1774).

9 Ed.: some western feminist critics point to the implicit condescension of such ostensibly 'complimentary' criticism: see above, Rosslyn, pp. 57–9.

10 Ed.: Catherine the Great, Empress of Russia (reigned 1762–96) was the most prolific woman writer of eighteenth-century Russia, the author or co-author of twenty-five comedies and historical dramas, as well as many children's stories, a comparative dictionary of languages, a history of early Russia and a number of magazine articles. Princess Ekaterina Dashkova (1743–1810), who was closely associated with Catherine II until 1794, was a writer and journalist and the first woman in Europe to hold governmental office. In 1783 she was appointed director of the Russian Academy of Sciences, and the same year founded and became

president of the Russian Academy. She is best known for her autobiography, *Mon histoire*, written 1804–5 in French, usually translated as *Memoirs*. There were about a dozen other women writers between the mid-1770s, when Urusova published her earliest work, and the writing of Bunina (1774–1829), Volkova (1781–1834) and Izvekova (179?–1830) more than twenty years later. On Bunina, see Rosslyn, pp. 55–68.

11 Ed.: Earlier journals publishing women's writing in the 1790s included *Priiatnoe i poleznoe preprovozhdenie vremeni* and *Aonidy*, and in the 1880s, *Zhurnal dlia milykh* and *Vestnik Evropy*.

12 Ed.: this statement belongs to M. Makarov, *Damskii zhurnal*, pp. 51–2 (1830). The following information about publications in *Damskii zhurnal* is taken from *Biografiia A. I. Kosheleva*, 1 (Moscow, 1889), p. 570. The journal is now a bibliographical rarity.

13 Ed.: between 1780 and 1825, more than fifty books by the French novelist and educational writer Stéphanie-Félicité Ducrest, Comtesse de Genlis (1746–1830) appeared in Russian translation, and some of the writer's *nouvelles* appeared in French in Paris and St Petersburg simultaneously. See Kelly, *A History of Russian Women's Writing*, p. 28. On the influence of the French novelist and literary theorist Germaine de Staël (1766–1817) in Russia, see *ibid.*, pp. 35, 39, 56–7, 65.

14 Ed.: Karoline Pichler (1769–1843), an Austrian poet, novelist and dramatist, the hostess of a literary salon in Vienna, whose acclaimed novels included *Leonore* (1894) and *Frauenwürde* (*The Dignity of Women*, 1808).

15 Ed.: Claire Lechat de Kersaint, Duchesse de Duras (1778–1828) wrote two novels, *Ourika* (1823) and *Edouard* (1825), which advocated that passion rather than convention should serve as a guide to human conduct.

16 Ed.: Ann Radcliffe, author of the renowned Gothic novel *The Mysteries of Udolpho* (1794), enjoyed great popularity in Russia in the 1790s: see Kelly, *A History of Russian Women's Writing*, pp. 28–9.

17 Ed.: see the series of articles by Makarov under the general title 'Materialy dlia istorii russkikh zhenshchin-avtorov', in *Damskii zhurnal*, 1829–31; 1833.

18 See Il'ichevskii's poem 'Hail the new Sappho', 1827, cited in Kelly, *A History of Russian Women's Writing*, pp. 33–4. See also K. Batiushkov, 'Pevets, ili Pevtsy v Besede slaviano-rossov', in Batiushkov, *Sochineniia v dvukh tomakh*, 1 (Moscow, 1989), p. 393, which envisages 'ladies' as readers, rather than writers.

19 Ed.: the *Beseda liubitelei russkogo slova*, established by the conservative writer and statesman Admiral Aleksandr Shishkov,

attempted to defend the Russian literary language against what he regarded as unjustified Europeanization by Karamzin and his followers. His 'Discourse on the Old and New Style in the Russian Language' (1803) asserted that Old Church Slavonic was 'the root and source' of Russian, and recommended that Slavic roots be used for any new expressions. For Shishkov's patronage of Anna Bunina, see Rosslyn above, pp. 59, 66. In 1811, Urusova was made an honorary member of the Society.

20   Ed.: Caroline Schlegel-Schelling (1763–1909), a German writer and charismatic figure in the early German Romantic movement, inspired by the French revolution, who worked without acknowledgement with her husband August Schlegel on a translation of Shakespeare, and subsequently married the Romantic philosopher Friedrich Schelling.

21   Rahel Levin (1771–1833) was a German writer from a well-to-do Jewish family who married the diplomat K. A. Varnhagen von Ense. She was a prominent literary hostess in Berlin, attracting such luminaries as Hegel and Heine.

22   Ed.: Bettina von Arnim (1785–1859) was a German Romantic writer who advocated democracy and the rights of women.

23   Charlotte Stieglitz (née Willhöft, 1806–34) married the radical writer Heinrich Stieglitz in 1828. Her suicide by stabbing caused a public sensation – her declared motive was to give her husband a tragic experience which would release his creative powers (but he remained unproductive).

24   See, for example, A. V. Druzhinin, 'Sharlotta Shtiglits. Istinnoe proisshestvie', *Sochineniia*, 1 (St Petersburg, 1865); E. Rostopchina, 'Kak liubiat zhenshchiny. Predsmertnaia duma Sharlotty Shtiglits', *Stikhotvoreniia* (St Petersburg, 1857), 2, pp. 61–4.

25   A. Pushkin, 'Kniagine Z. A. Volkonskoi', 'Sredi rasseiannoi Moskvy ...' (1827). Ed.: Princess Zinaida Volkonskaia (1789–1862) was an aristocratic writer-dilettante and an intimate of Alexander I, best known as a salon hostess to Pushkin and other leading poets of the Russian Golden Age, who dedicated poems to her. After the accession of Nicholas I, she was exiled to Rome in 1829 for her Catholic sympathies.

26   Ed.: Elizaveta Kul'man (1808–25) was a child prodigy who died at seventeen.

27   Ed.: Nadezhda Durova spent nine years of service in the Russian military during the Napoleonic wars, dressed as a man. Her autobiography was published as *Kavalerist-devitsa* [1836]; *The Cavalry Maiden: Journals of a Russian Officer in the Napoleonic Wars*, translated by Mary Zirin (Bloomington, IN: Indiana University

Press, 1988). For a later, fictional treatment of her life, see Lidiia Charskaia, *Smelaia zhizn'* (1905); and the biography by Colonel A.Saks, *Kavalerist-devitsa. Shtabs-rotmistr A. A. Aleksandrov (Nadezhda Andreevna Durova)* (St Petersburg, 1912).

28 D. Mordovtsev, *Russkie zhenshchiny novogo vremeni* (St Petersburg, 1874), pp. 142–3.

29 The first publications in Russian of the novels and stories by George Sand which became most popular in Russia were: *Zhak*, trans. anon, *Otechestvennye zapiski*, 35–6, (1844), 4, pp. 189–328; 5, pp. 118–283; *Indiana*, trans. A. and I. Lazarev, Parts 1–4 (St Petersburg: K. Vingeber, 1883); *Konsuelo*, *Biblioteka dlia chteniia*, 158–9 (1880), Supplement.; *Leone Leoni*, trans. N. M. (Moscow: N. Stepanov, 1840); *Lucretia Floriani*, *Otechestvennye zapiski*, 42 (1845), pp. 65–234; for a review (most probably by Bulgarin), see *Syn otechestva*, 2 (February 1947), pp. 19–26; *Mel'nik [iz Anzhibo]*, trans. by P. Fuhrmann (St Petersburg: M. D. Ol'khin, 1845); for reviews by Belinskii, see his *Sobranie sochinenii*, ed. S. A. Vengerov (St Petersburg, 1914), x, pp. 122–4; *Morga*, *Moskovskii nabliudatel'* (1837), Part 13, 149–89, 131–75, 289–307; Part 14, 5–46, 127–62; reviewed by Belinskii, *Sobranie sochinenii*, vi, pp. 198–9, and most probably by Senkovskii, *Biblioteka dlia chteniia*, 37 (1839), pp. 28–31; *Oras*, *Otechestvennye zapiski* (1842), 23, 181–284, 45–173; *Uskok*, *Biblioteka dlia chteniia*, 29 (1838), pp. 113–204. George Sand's most complete collected works came out in St Petersburg in 1896–9, edited by G. F. Panteleev in eighteen volumes.

30 Ed.: 'Evgeniia Tur' (1815–92) was the lifelong pen name of Elizaveta Salias de Turnemir, a prose writer, children's writer, editor, publisher, literary critic and salon hostess, who began her literary career in 1849.

31 A. Zrazhevskaia, 'Zhenshchina poet i avtor', *Moskvitianin*, 5, 9 (1842).

32 E. A. Gan, 'Sud sveta', *Polnoe sobranie sochinenii* (St Petersburg, 1905), p. 303.

33 M. Zhukova, *Povesti*, II (St Petersburg, 1840), p. 209.

34 N. Platonova, *N.Kokhanovskaia. Biograficheskii ocherk* (St Petersburg, 1909), p. 54.

35 On George Sand's influence in nineteenth-century Russia, see V. S. Botsianovskii, 'Zhorzh Sand v Rossii. Istoriko-literaturnaia spravka', *Novyi zhurnal inostrannoi literatury*, 4 (1898), pp. 2–11; 'Zhorzh Sand i ee vliianie na russkuiu literaturu', *Vestnik inostrannoi literatury*, 6 (1901), pp. 306–14. [Ed.: as yet there is no full study of George Sand's reception in Russia, but Kelly, *A History of Russian Women's Writing*, pp. 60–1, suggests that *Jacques* (1834) was

most influential work for Russians; she also influenced the development of Russian regional prose through such works as *Le Meunier d'Angibault* (1845). Sand's denunciation of gender inequality and the oppressive institution of marriage influenced the development of the 'woman question' in Russia. In 1855, *Sovremennik* published George Sand's autobiography, 'Istoriia moei zhizni', translated by N. Chernyshevskii; in 1856, the publication continued under the title 'Zhizn' Zhorzh Sand'.]

36 Ed.: Mrs Korsini was one of the first women to attend lectures systematically at St Petersburg University; later she was married to N. I. Utin, a leader of the student movement in St Petersburg. For her comic treatment of Russian women writers, see M. Korsini, *Zhenshchina pisatel'nitsa*, vol. IX of her *Ocherki sovremennoi zhizni* (St Petersburg, 1848–51).

37 N. N. Verevkin ('N. Rakhmannyi'), 'Zhenshchina-pisatel'nitsa', *Biblioteka dlia chteniia*, 23, 5, part I (1837), pp. 33–4.

38 See V. Belinskii's article on the work of Elena Gan, 'Povesti Zeneidy R-voi', *Polnoe sobranie sochinenii*, 13 vols (Moscow, 1953–9), VII, pp. 648–78.

39 One such writer was Petr Pletnev: Evdokiia Rostopchina, Nadezhda Sokhanskaia and others had every reason to be grateful to him. See P. A. Pletnev, *Sochineniia i perepiska* (St Petersburg, 1885) containing Rostopchina's letters to Pletnev of 21 December 1838, 22 January 1840, 4 March 1852, etc.; Ia. K. Grot, ed., *Perepiska Ia. K. Grota s P. A. Pletnevym*, 3 vols. (St Petersburg, 1896): Pletnev's letters of 6 December 1840, 29 February 1841, 24 May 1841, 10 March 1842, etc. See also Pletnev's reviews in *Sovremennik*, 18 (1838); 29 (1841).

[Ed.: Sokhanskaia sent a couple of early stories to Pletnev, who had just stepped down as editor of the journal *Sovremennik*. He recognized her talent, but in an attempt to stop her using Sandian plots, set her the exercise of writing about her own life. As a result, she produced an excellent memoir of her childhood and youth (1847–8) which was first published posthumously in 1896.]

40 E. Rostopchina, 'Schastlivaia zhenshchina', *Moskvitianin*, 1, 6 (December 1851), p. 397.

41 Pushkin, *Evgenii Onegin*, Chapter 3, xii.

42 E. Tur, *Povesti*, 4 (Moscow, 1860), pp. 48–9.

43 'N. Stanitskii' (A. Panaeva), *Melochi zhizni. Roman* (St Petersburg, 1854), p. 231.

44 Ed.: K. Pavlova, *Dvoinaia zhizn'* (1844–7), in Pavlova, *Polnoe sobranie sochinenii* (Moscow–Leningrad, 1964), pp. 231–304; translated as

K. Pavlova, *A Double Life*, transl. and ed. by Barbara Heldt (Berkeley: Barbary Coast, 1986).

45 Sand's *La Comtesse de Rudolstadt* was translated into Russian much later than the period under discussion, and included in her *Sobranie sochinenii* (St Petersburg, 1896–9); *Spiridion* does not appear to have been translated, but was accessible to well-educated readers in the original.

46 Ed.: Sand's works focusing on 'feminist' themes are the early novels *Indiana* (1832); *Valentine* (1833); *Lélia* (1833) and *Jacques* (1834), which present marriage as 'one of the most barbaric institutions [society] has ever invented'.

47 Ed.: Maria Edgeworth (1768–1849) was an Irish novelist and educationalist, who defended women's education in *Letters to Literary Ladies* (1795). Frances Trollope (1779–1863) was an English novelist and travel writer, who, though politically conservative, displayed a concern for the poor and oppressed. Ida von Hahn-Hahn (1805–80) was a German poet, novelist and travel writer whose novels concerned aristocratic women of great beauty, moral strength and intelligence who yearn for emotional freedom. Fanny Lewald (1811–89) was a German novelist, author of *Clementine* (1842), *Jenny* (1843) and *A Question of Life* (1845), studies of women's social position, marriage and divorce.

48 For translations of *Jane Eyre* in Russia, see 'Dzhennyi Ir. Roman', trans. by I. Vvedenskii, *Otechestvennye zapiski*, 64–9 (1849), Section 1 (Literature), 175–250, 67–158, 65–132, 193–330; *Dzhenni Eir, ili Zapiski guvernantki. Soch[inenie] Kurrer-Bell'*, trans. by S. I. Koshlakova (St Petersburg, 1857).

49 This was first noted by A. I. Beletskii, the only scholar who analysed women's writing from a purely literary point of view and recognized the influence of women's writing on men's. [Ed.: see, for example, A. I. Beletskii, 'Turgenev i russkie pisatel'nitsy 30-kh–60-kh godov', in N. L. Brodskii, ed., *Tvorcheskii put' Turgeneva* (Petrograd, 1923), pp. 135–66; but for a critique of Beletskii's categorization of nineteenth-century Russian women writers into conscious 'groups', and of his view that it was 'natural' for women writers to flourish in an epoch of Romanticism, see Jane Costlow, 'Speaking the sorrow of women: Turgenev's 'Neschastnaia' and Evgeniia Tur's "Antonina"', *Slavic Review*, 50, 2 (1991), p. 329].

50 E. Gan, 'Sud sveta', in V. V. Uchenova, ed., *Dacha na Petergofskoi doroge: proza russkikh pisatel'nits pervoi poloviny XIX veka* (Moscow: Sovremennik, 1986).

51 See, for example, N. Khvoshchinskaia, *Anna Mikhailova, kto zhe dovolen?* (1853).

52 A. Druzhinin, 'Dzhen Eir, roman Korrer-Bellia', *Sovremennik*, 21, 6 (1858), pp. 64–9; 'Korrer-Bell' i ego dva romana "Shirley" i "Jean [sic!] Eyre"', *Biblioteka dlia chteniia*, 117, 1 (1852), pp. 17–40; 'Literaturnye besedy i paradoksy inogorodnego podpishchika. Po povodu Korrer Bellia i ego romana "Vil'et"', *Biblioteka dlia chteniia*, 140, 11 (1856), pp. 93–120.

53 E. Tur, 'Zhizn' Sharlotty Bronte (Korrer Bellia), avtora "Dzhein Eir", "Shirli" i "Vil'et"', *Russkii vestnik, Sovremmennaia letopis'*, 9 (1857), pp. 109–19; 'Miss Bronte, ee zhizn' i sochineniia', *Russkii vestnik, Sovremennaia letopis'*, 18 (1858), pp. 501–75.

54 Tur, 'Miss Bronte, ee zhizn' i sochineniia', pp. 549–50.

55 Ed.: the fact that these anonymous authors were female has been established by a study of reference books and the 'Gonorarnye vedomosti' of the journals.

56 A. Panaeva, 'Semeistvo Tal'nikovykh', *Illiustrirovannyi al'manakh* (St Petersburg, 1848; delayed for censorship reasons until 1866). Panaeva knew Brontë's novel before she started writing her own story, since her husband, the writer Ivan Panaev, read *Jane Eyre* to her, translating it from the English-language Tauchnitz edition which they obtained in Russia immediately after the book was published in England in 1847. Panaeva's novel should not be regarded as an imitation of *Jane Eyre*, but rather as a story suggested by the English novel, based on a Russian childhood experience of a similar nature. [Ed.: Another example of a relatively successful work influenced by *Jane Eyre* is E. Tur, 'Antonina', first published as a fragment in the almanac *Kometa* (Moscow, 1851), which became an inset text within her novel *Plemiannitsa* (*The Niece*, Moscow, 1851). It depicts an orphan and a jealous stepmother; for further discussion, see Costlow, '"Speaking the Sorrow of Women"', pp. 328–35.]

57 Ed.: this refers to the period beginning in the late 1850s, when Chernyshevskii and other intellectuals of non-noble birth congregated round the journal *Sovremennik*. They called themselves '*raznochintsy*', hence the term.

58 The only work of this kind known to the author is the master's dissertation by A. I. Beletskii, written in 1919 and *never* published. A typewritten copy is kept in the Manuscript Section of the Institute of Literature of the Ukrainian Academy of Sciences: Fond 162, Archive of A. I. Beletskii, files 44, 46, 64, 84. Ed: since this essay was written, a more integrated picture of nineteenth-century women's writing has also been established in works by western scholars such as Frank Göpfert, *Dichterinnen und Schriftsellerinnen in Russland von der Mitte des 18. bis zum Beginn des 20.*

Jahrhunderts: eine Problemskizze (Munich: Sagner, 1992); Catriona Kelly, *A History of Russian Women's Writing*; Marina Ledkovsky, Charlotte Rosenthal and Mary Zirin, eds., *Dictionary of Russian Women Writers* (Westport, CT: Greenwood Press, 1994); Toby W. Clyman and Diana Greene, eds., *Women Writers in Russian Literature* (Westport, CT: Greenwood Press, 1994).]

59 Ed.: the 'society tale', popular in the 1830s and 1840s, was a novella that portrayed amorous intrigue among the upper classes, usually from an ironic viewpoint. Prominent examples were Elena Gan, 'Sud sveta' ('Society's Judgement', 1839); Evdokiia Rostopchina, 'Chiny i den'gi' ('Rank and Money', 1839); M. Zhukova (as M. Zh-va), 'Moi znakomye v Kurske' ('My Acquaintances in Kursk'), *Povesti*, 2 vols. (St Petersburg, 1840), II, pp. 181–283.

CHAPTER 6

The 'woman question' of the 1860s and the ambiguity of the 'learned woman'

Arja Rosenholm

Пансионерка

Nikolai Shelgunov, one of the 'progressives' of the 1860s, wrote in his article 'The soullessness of women' (1870): 'Which of our women writers – and we have a fair number of them – has studied the woman question and written about it? Not one. Is this not grim evidence of women's lack of resolve, of women's hereditary passivity?'[1] This opinion seems strange, not least because its writer is known as a 'radical' literary critic who was able to monitor at first hand the history of the 'woman question' (*zhenskii vopros*).[2] It does, however, demonstrate the ambiguity of women's opportunities to participate in the discourse of the 'woman question'.

The contradictory nature of the 'woman question' of the 1860s becomes apparent through comparison with the opening decades of the century or with the *fin de siècle*. The paradigmatic breakthroughs of the 1820s and 1830s and also those of the turn of the century[3] are characterized by the gradual rise to prominence of women's culture, notably in the diversity of their literature. What, then, were the opportunities for women's writing in the 1860s, characterized as it was by a forceful discourse on gender equality, on the 'woman question'? Why did Shelgunov fail to acknowledge the contribution of women writers? I pose the question in order to challenge the assumption that establishing an egalitarian gender model[4] of the period enhanced women's ability to transfigure the visions of their knowledge in a manner adequate to their cultural experience.[5] Rather, I think that it is important to examine how binary notions of gender were inscribed in the egalitarian model. Was women's 'equality' achieved at the expense of women's knowledge? How does this manifest itself in women's literature? These questions also reveal the danger of super-imposing women's history on the periodization of male discourse. Even if writers treat the 'woman question' as an explicit theme, this is no guarantee of their feminism, and even less of a paradigm particularly kindly disposed towards women's psycho-sexual and cultural autonomy.

Just as the history of women's culture exceeds the bounds of the 'woman question' discourse of the 1860s, neither can it be reduced to a chronicle of female figures in fiction: the history of Tat'iana, Elena or Vera Pavlovna[6] is not one and the same as the history of Russian women. Images of women and concepts of femininity have a history of their own which must be kept apart from the existence of women's cultural history. Drawing this distinction leads to important methodological considerations emanating from 'femininity' (*zhenstvennost'*), from cultural stereotypes, and from the fact that these in turn influenced women's culture. The history of female imagery shows that *zhenstvennost'* acts functionally: it acquires its substance from the reality of the images and the expectations projected on to them. *Zhenstvennost'* commonly appears to work like some underlying principle supporting metaphysical hopes of harmony, which are realized in the Russian concept of *tsel'nost'* [completeness, or integrity] representing 'femininity'.[7] This on occasion assumes the nature of mythical, ideal and demonic *zhenstvennost'*, and operates both in the relations between the sexes and on women's own image. Between the cultural historical presentations of 'femininity' and women's own cultural presence there operates a relation of transformation.[8] This is a link between women's literature and the ideology of femininity corresponding to the appropriate paradigm. Images of women live a life of their own, but their socio-historical content has an effect on the self-image of the woman writer. In this essay I will try to establish to what extent the concept of the *emansipirovannaia zhenshchina* ('emancipated woman') in the 1860s provided women writers with space to express the world of their own experience.[9] I will then present one example of a text in which a woman writer contributed to the attempts to define the 'new woman'.

The '*emansipirovannaia*', or more precisely *uchenaia zhenshchina* ('learned woman') was a 'new' type of woman in the 1860s. The female cultural type of the *uchenaia* can be seen as a natural product of the *prosvetitel'stvo* (enlightenment ideology) which dominated philosophy and socio-political thought in this period.[10] It could be argued that the egalitarian concept of gender, thematized as the discourse of the 'woman question', and the rationalistic thinking promoting 'reasonable' equality among the 'people' were mutually supportive. The model of the 'learned woman' shows that gender equality functioned simultaneously in two orders, or as Joan Kelly writes: 'in any of the historical forms that patriarchal society takes (feudal, capitalist, socialist, etc.), a sex-gender system and a system of productive relations operate simultaneously ... to reproduce socioeconomic and male-dominant structures of that particular social order'.[11]

The concept of the superior reason of the 'new', or 'rational person', (*razumnyi chelovek*), as an ideal criterion of truth, was extended to women. The new epistemological values stressed in the 'progressive' discourses of the time were guided by the rationalistic ideal of an intellectual human being as lord of nature. Women also had greater opportunities: all at once, as thinking human beings, women became reasonable beings, whom the generation of 'new' and 'radical' *raznochintsy* [men of other, non-noble ranks] accepted as worthy of furthering 'the common cause' in the historical breakthrough of the new bourgeoisie. It was for reason, enlightenment and the natural sciences to smooth over social inequality. But above all, it was for scientific, 'correct' education to enable the men of the new élite of the non-landowner class not only to 'earn their living by their brains',[12] but to confirm their position of power, for as Michel Foucault posits, power's relation to knowledge is never separable. Every society has its 'regime of truth' with its own particular mechanisms for producing truth.[13]

Normative enlightenment thinking incorporated 'the woman question' into its pragmatic programme, within which the 'woman question' became above all a question of education.[14] This discourse on 'learning' among women, which became the hallmark of the 1860s *nigilistka* [woman nihilist], shows that the position assigned to women by the sex/gender system was not a separate sphere or domain of existence, but a position within the general reform of the social system. This is also recognized by E. Shchepkina, who states: 'Within powerful popular movements, when all energies are drawn upon for the struggle, when the solidarity of the common masses is vital, women appear among the champions as indispensable comrades: the appearance of equal rights is replaced by women's real call for a role in the common cause; interest is expressed in the enlightenment and instruction of women, they are flattered, they are promised much. This exhortation to unite emerged here in the 1860s.'[15]

Power is not only exercised through repression. There was acceptance of women's need for education because it could be integrated into a male-dominated social and political ideology – and conversely, women were able to legitimize their own demands through reference to the discourse, but only via the men who decreed what constituted women's education.[16] The journalistic debate was conducted almost exclusively by men. The situation is analogous to the enlightened dreams of the eighteenth century. The opening of the first state educational institution for girls in 1764 was connected with the wider project to 'civilize' society: 'to overcome centuries-old superstitions, to provide the people with a new education, and, so to speak, a new development'.[17]

This controlled education of the 'new' woman was also met with enthusiasm by the 'new' men who organized themselves around the journal *Sovremennik* (*The Contemporary*). The enlightenment thinking of Nikolai Chernyshevskii, Mikhail Mikhailov and Nikolai Dobroliubov resulted in a rational canon of rules. It gave rise to an ahistorical human image, for the 'rational person' is a ready-made reasonable being. This view included a denial of all that did not fit into the controlled world-view of a rational person. Visual thinking and fantasy had to defer to journalistic and political discourse; ambiguity, individuality, the condition of being different, the libido were rejected in favour of empiricism and science.[18] The dreams of Vera Pavlovna in Chernyshevskii's novel *What is to be Done?* were possible only because they were expressed in the language of programmatic reason. The denial of the 'old' values and 'superstitions' (*sueveriia*) proved to be a psychodynamic and cultural historical suppression. It affected the semantic field of the marginalized Other: not-male, not-reasonable, not-empirical. Women, nature, the subconscious, fantasy, dreams and desire were all to be controlled in order to support the superiority of the male, mind and spirit. This was also the objective of the education of girls. Dobroliubov wrote: 'It is well known that in children in general and girls in particular, emotion dominates over reason, and imagination constantly interferes with memory. Therefore the teacher must take care above all to ensure the correct development of the imagination of his female pupils and the healthy direction of their emotions: otherwise these faculties will constantly interfere with the correct performance of reason and memory.'[19] By analogy, the 'new' rationalist aesthetics, which subjugated the 'new' morality to utilitarian thinking,[20] also seems to reject female imagery, for the enigmatic, mysterious and irrational nature of the Other constituted a threat to the 'rational' man. As well as being solitary, Vera Pavlovna is a somewhat anaemic figure, for there was no positive descriptive source for the figure of the 'learned woman' for the literature to draw on. The 'learned woman' was a ready-made ideal born from the heads of men with little tolerance for any difference by reason of gender. The 'enlightened woman' had to be a 'person', but representative of female history, as encapsulated in Mikhailov's words: 'But in these times we are set the task of establishing the view that there may not be anything female about women except their sex. In fact, what is still called female essence is enslavement, with all its failings and unhappiness. Indeed, there is not and must not be anything female in woman except her sex. All the rest is to be neither female nor male but purely human.'[21]

It seems that the ideal 'learned woman' was not permitted to represent a different rationality, that is, a reality which did not conform to the determinism of the 'new' men. The 'woman question' raised by the young *Sovremennik* men was firmly harnessed to their own power struggle. Thus, learning in women was not a virtue in its own right, but rather was instrumental in character.[22] This is borne out by their deprecating attitude to women writers who failed to meet the criteria of the rationalist canon, such as Evdokiia Rostopchina, whose work both Chernyshevskii and Dobroliubov criticized with censorial irony. Her incontestable 'learning' was no guarantee of being the ideal 'enlightened woman', for in addition to representing the 'old' aristocratic power and romantic individualism, Rostopchina's female consciousness and her repudiation of asexual experience posit a 'second sex' alongside abstract gender.[23]

The 'women nihilists', with permission to operate under the protection of egalitarianism, were to be awakened to the 'light of reason'. This awakening was to be accomplished through men's discourse, at the expense of women's knowledge and women's history. This was metaphorically expressed on the front cover of the first issue of the publication *Rassvet* for 1859.[24] An allegory of Apollonic male knowledge, a genius of light and reason depicted as androgynous, is awakening a Russian girl from the obscurity of ignorance. His disembodied spirit is superior to her knowledge, which is symbolized by an abandoned book – a work of fiction – lying on the floor. There are two different ways of knowing and of being in the world: male-associated scientific knowing, disassociating the body from 'pure knowledge', and female-associated knowing with its predilection for fantasy and metaphorical thinking.[25] The metaphor of the 'Sleeping Beauty' reveals the relations between subject and object. The history of women is accorded an incomplete definition. Waking up to a 'new' consciousness signifies, as Judith Fetterley has put it, the 'immasculation of women by men',[26] while women's own experience and cultural history are in danger of remaining in the realm of unlegitimized darkness, of unarticulated dreams, prey to the 'powerlessness which results from the endless division of self against self, the consequence of the invocation to identify as male while being reminded that to be male – to be universal – is to be not female'.[27]

As an example of how women writers did participate in the

discourse of the 'woman question' – contrary to the assumptions of N. Shelgunov – I propose to analyse a *povest'* [novella] by the prose writer Nadezhda Dmitrievna Khvoshchinskaia, 'Pansionerka' ('The Boarding-School Girl'). One of the reasons why Shelgunov did not hear the voices of women writers is that at that time there were two different, gender-marked literary genres: journalism for men and *belles-lettres* for women. Women did not play a major part in the journalistic debate conducted by men. This was partly due to the socialization of women, which kept them in the home, left them without formal education and outside the social and professional societies of men. Shelgunov looked for women's voices within the journalistic debates of men which, in keeping with the gender-valued hierarchy, he preferred to women's literature.[28] But it was precisely *belles-lettres* which functioned as a channel for female intellectual expression and through which women joined the debate on the 'destiny' (*prednaznachenie*) of the 'new' woman.

'Pansionerka' appeared in 1861.[29] The ideological and philosophical ethos of the work will be examined in relation to the rationalist paradigm of equality. It is one of the most interesting texts of the period, in which a woman writer reflects on the relationship between the intellectual and physical identity of the female protagonist. It is the *Bildungsroman* of a young girl called Lelen'ka, who lives with her parents in a provincial town, which is visited by Veretitsyn, a former student critical of society. He awakens Lelen'ka to an awareness of the limitations of her surroundings, to the lack of substance in girls' education. When her parents arrange for Lelen'ka to be married to one of the municipal officials, she runs away to her aunt in St Petersburg. After eight years, Lelen'ka and Veretitsyn meet again at the Hermitage. Since their last meeting Lelen'ka has become an independent artist, an active and self-sufficient woman. The ways of Lelen'ka and Veretitsyn part for good: the 'new' Lelen'ka's independence is juxtaposed with Veretitsyn's melancholic scepticism.

The ideal of the 'learned woman' influences not only fact and fiction, but also leads to a rapprochement between the male and female *Bildungsroman*. The concept of equality brings

Lelen'ka's story of development closer to the male 'action-genre'. Her awakening is as much an awakening to the limitations of her gender as an awakening which marks a change in her outward 'art of living'.[30]

Lelen'ka becomes an artist who supports herself. She is a representative of the cultural type of 'learned woman' whose voice echoes the thrilling promises of education and independent work for the 'new' women – promises which were made by the 'new' men in the name of the 'new', progressive world.[31] This utilitarian ideology of enlightenment provides a shelter for the female writer. From this safe haven – the equality of all people in their human ability to reason – she overcomes the 'old' irreconcilability between reason and 'femininity', empowers woman to control her emotions by will-power and defies the tradition of self-denial as the preserve of women. But does the controlling will liberate Lelen'ka?

Through an empathetic narrator we are told of Lelen'ka's feelings throughout her process of development. The narrator describes empathetically the agony Lelen'ka experiences in her path towards emancipation and new anger. Different discourses – pedagogic, moral, political and economic – which construct the gendered progress of Lelen'ka demonstrate that the constitution and transformation of hierarchic relations cannot be positioned outside the individual, that power is not separable from the concrete social interactions of everyday life.

This process of development reaches its conclusion in the final chapter of the story: Lelen'ka is 'free', 'new' and 'learned':

'I vow that I will never again allow anyone to have power over me, that I will not serve this barbaric old law, either by example or in words ... On the contrary, I will say to everyone: do as I have, free yourselves, all of you who possess hands and a strong will! Live alone – that is life: work, knowledge and freedom.'[32]

The guarantor of her independence is a will which keeps her emotions under firm control. However, Lelen'ka remains a prisoner of binary values, in which desire and will repulse one another. The freedom afforded by rational individualism (*razumnyi egoizm*) is founded on negation, the object of which is the 'feminine' paradigm: Lelen'ka renounces woman's position as object, or, in her own words enslavement (*rabstvo*), family, marriage. This negation of marriage by an enlightened woman is a plot of autonomy which places her in a different position from the *Bildungsroman* of her male *sovremenniki*, the young men who, as Irina Paperno rightly states, 'sought a metaphysical release from the concerns of their era'.[33] They also sought it in marriage. If Chernyshevskii and his '*Sovremennik* brothers' are able to see marriage as 'a source of energy for activity', to implement the 'teacher scheme'[34] in their marriages, this was possible only because utilitarian and rational principles were also applied to marriage: it was to be seen as a functional relationship between two reasonable human beings.[35] The function of marriage was likewise the control of personal feelings. Into the game of repulsion came an expectation of harmony linked to *tsel'nost'*, femininity, a harmony which a man might employ for the 'salvage operation' entrusted to him. The ignorant 'people' (*narod*) are represented by the 'incomplete woman', the wife; by putting the finishing touches to her the 'new' man might fulfil his 'great' historical mission. Thus the transition was effected from collectivism to pseudo-individualism.

The concept of equality, however, only operated in one direction, namely with the man as 'teacher'. Marriage as a social salvage operation was out of the question for a 'free' and 'rational' woman: Lelen'ka was already a 'learned woman' and needed nobody to save her, still less a man posing as a representative of incompleteness for her to educate. The metaphysical combination of sense and sensibility in marriage does not work for Lelen'ka. Her 'new' independence guarantees a new kind of psychological preparedness for conflict which enables Lelen'ka to mobilize her will-power as a defence, to display an aggression which her girlhood socialization has not taught her. The model of her freedom is realized in a sphere commonly associated with men. Identifying with a masculine and public sphere, Lelen'ka regards herself as the opposite of her mother. She rejects the conventional society of women because of its claustrophobic domesticity. But at the same time her belief in sexual neutrality denies the specificity of women's collective history. Lelen'ka wants to regard life as a set of reasonable, possible choices. As she rejects the past and the psychological element, so also she rejects remembering and uncertainty, love and chaos, sensuality and desire, and indeed, the body itself. As a woman, she can achieve equality only by accepting the dominant male interpretation of rationality; she must be wary of 'sentimentality' so as not to relapse into the incompleteness of a feminine creature of feelings. Fearful of displaying the inadequacy commonly attributed to her sex, the 'new woman' in her thirst for reasonable knowledge must be superior to Veretitsyn, the man. She must believe in the enlightenment of sexual neutrality.[36]

The optimistic views of education and egalitarianism in the 1860s did not offer many alternatives to the 'learned woman'. Lelen'ka's markedly masculine quality suggests something of the ambivalence of denial strategy: denial may be seen as sexual resistance, but it also ignores positive utopias which Lelen'ka could adopt, from her as yet unarticulated women's history. Lelen'ka is 'learned'. She knows things which are unknown to the majority of women. But through her new androgynous identity, she becomes estranged from her body and its psycho-sexual mechanisms, from her uncontrolled desire. Lelen'ka's freedom is a lonely state. She has become an exception, 'the odd one out' in a male community.

The ambivalence of equality is reflected in the contradictory nature of the narrative strategies at the end of the story. Lelen'ka's new freedom provokes dissatisfaction, it is not enjoyable. Lelen'ka's lack of credibility manifests itself in the lack of congruence between her ideological and psychological levels. In the terms of the 'learned' discourse Lelen'ka makes ideologically 'correct' and 'healthy'[37] choices by defending study, work and reason at the expense of all that is not conscious or controlled. But the 'new' voice of freedom sounds programmatic, cold in its assuredness, and reminiscent of a manifesto in its clear-cut nature.

The aesthetic 'failure' of a coherent ending is to be explained through the relation of transformation between the woman writer and the predominant concept of 'reasonable' femininity. Leaning on the 'learned' discourse, the writer brings Lelen´ka to a triumphant conclusion, but at the same time Lelen´ka falls into the trap of male-associated development. Lelen´ka occupies a different position from the hero of the male *Bildungsroman*: her self-realization affords a more ambivalent perspective. After an initial separation from her society, she cannot be reintegrated into marriage *and* public life. The voyage of her self-realization will be unfinished, for to experience the beauty of the voyage out would depend upon a return journey, 'a reaffirming of connection'.[38] Lelen´ka's tragedy is that she can neither return to the (patriarchal) family, nor escape alienation in the male-dominated intelligentsia. Khvoshchinskaia deconstructs the workings of the gendered meanings and values which underlie the new 'purely human' equality: she resists the romance plot, but she cannot escape the normative masculinity still lurking behind the order of the new emancipation. The feminine still represents the negative: the 'old' and the non-rational. At the end of her development we can listen to the rationalist argumentation of the 'new' Lelen´ka who has become an unsexed *nigilistka*. The neglect of a female physical existence gives the 'learned woman' the right to make a speech, but it is marked by masculine semiotics: desire, fantasy, uncontrolled joy will be subordinated to the utilitarian systematization of life. Lelen´ka's 'art of living' is highly disciplined: 'This corner alone gave the impression of rest, everything else emphasized strenuous, uninterrupted labour calculated to the hour. Indeed, Lelen´ka glanced at her watch.'[39]

The writer comes up against the limitations of her own era, and this is reflected in the textual and narrative structure. Up to the final 'emancipation' chapter, the narrator follows Lelen´ka's process of development from Lelen´ka's own internal perspective, recording the development of her mind and body. Up to this point it is brought home to the reader how it feels – in her mind and body – to undergo a transformation. Throughout the initial narrative the narrator fixes on the object of description, focuses on Lelen´ka's emotions from the standpoint of her inner point of view. Each approaches not only the other, but also time and space, and this occurs, moreover, at the level of psychology and speech. The path of Lelen'ka's development is evoked through psychologically motivated realism, imbued with self-doubt, conflicts, reversals and despair. A radical change comes about in the 'emancipation' chapter: the narrator leaves Lelen'ka alone. The illusion of the authenticity of Lelen'ka's emotions, born when the narrator was 'living inside' Lelen'ka in the form of free indirect speech, is dispelled. Now Lelen'ka *herself* speaks: she expresses her opinions unequivocally, drawing support from rational, pragmatic argument. The narrator retires to a position of neutrality and listens like an outsider to the dialogue between the 'new' Lelen'ka and Veretitsyn. The narrator no longer narrates or comments on Lelen'ka's innermost feelings, but keeps a distance from the final result.

The voice of the woman writer's own experience 'disturbs' the ideologically 'correct' choice. The author's mistrust of Lelen'ka's consistent refusal to make sacrifices is reflected in the changing position of the narrator from an internal perspective of solidarity to a critical position of neutrality. The lack of congruence between the psychological and the ideological is proof that the emancipation conflict is not resolved. The position of the narrator is retiring and critical. The unresolved nature of the 'rational' choice is also, however, a non-neutral psychological stance on the part of the author. This is a documentation of the writer's understanding of self. In the struggle between desire and will one may sense the conflict within the woman writer of her own creativity and the denial it requires. Her desire to realize equality in a world of male writers and critics is forced to confront the painful condition of being solitary, and reminded of the loss of 'femininity'. However, it is just this quality of psychosexual conflict which makes Lelen'ka a realistic woman subject who assumes her place in the equality discourse of the 1860s.

This break in narrative strategy suggests that Lelen'ka's 'new' equality did not convince the writer, but she found for Lelen'ka no other model solution than a strategy of denial.[40] The 'new' freedom continues to be ambivalent. This ambivalence also concerns us as readers. At this point we are

conditioned by reading strategies which depend upon our
historical reality, and on our experience as female or male
readers, for, as P. Schweickart has said of a feminist reader-
response: 'If it is possible to formulate a basic conceptual
framework for disclosing the "difference" of women's writing,
surely it is no less possible to do so for women's reading.'[41]
How, then, can one read the open, decidedly problematic
ending of the story? What meanings can be ascribed to the
ambivalence of Lelen'ka's 'new' and 'enlightened' freedom?

Contemporary critics were displeased with the final chapter.
According to Dudyshkin, the conclusion requires further 'development', because 'everybody is praising "Pansionerka" but all
are very dissatisfied with its ending'.[42] Arsen'ev expressed the
view that Lelen'ka's independence is 'spiritless' and that the
'last lines are anything but a pleasure to read'.[43] Ostrogorskii
sees in Lelen'ka an 'egoistic woman activist with a will of her
own but with no heart'.[44] What is common to this criticism is
dissatisfaction that Lelen'ka's development lacks a happy
ending. This is due to the tendency to read Lelen'ka within the
paradigm of Russian female images of the androcentric canon,
against which Lelen'ka fails to function as a reflection of male
ideas and thus fails to represent the ideal woman figure
symbolizing the great future. Speaking of the difference
between men and women, of their different types of *Bildungsroman*, the story seems to be 'too' realistic: Lelen'ka, taking 'too'
seriously the challenges of the egalitarian paradigm, loses the
metaphysical enigma of 'eternal femininity' – and the status of
a canonized legend. But it is precisely the historical context and
the gender-biased realism of Lelen'ka's choice against which
the ambivalence can be given an interpretation, 'as a witness in
defence of the woman writer', according to Schweickart's
feminist reader-response criticism.[45] The story exposes the
limited nature of the vision of freedom; it is full of sadness
concerning Lelen'ka's lonely freedom, but the tale is not
without power in its ironic approach to the one-dimensional
egalitarianism of the time. This ambivalence implies a critique
of rationalism divorced from women's historical and cultural
knowledge. It challenges a theory of equality which destroys

difference in the name of a perfect but stalemated denouement to the plot. It is the open ambiguity of the emancipated but lonely Lelen'ka which lends realism to the story, and thus allows the difference to speak, thereby doing honour to female knowledge in the world.

NOTES

1 N. Shelgunov, 'Zhenskoe bezdushie', *Delo*, 9 (1870), pp. 1–34 (p. 11).

2 See Charles A. Moser, *Antinihilism in the Russian Novel of the 1860's* (London, the Hague and Paris: Mouton, 1964), pp. 119–20. See N. V. Shelgunov, L. P. Shelgunova and M. L. Mikhailov, *Vospominaniia*, 2 vols. (Moscow, 1967).

3 See, for instance, V. G. Belinskii, 'Sochineniia Zeneidy R-voi' (1843), *Polnoe sobranie sochinenii*, 13 vols. (Moscow, 1953–9), VII, pp. 648–78; M. Sh. Fainshtein, *Pisatel'nitsy pushkinskoi pory* (Leningrad: Nauka, 1989); Charlotte Rosenthal, 'The Silver Age: highpoint for women?', in Linda Edmondson, ed., *Women and Society in Russia and the Soviet Union* (Cambridge: Cambridge University Press, 1992), pp. 32–47.

4 The egalitarian gender paradigm should be distinguished from the supplementary gender theory, which aims to emphasize gender difference. See Silvia Bovenschen, *Die imaginierte Weiblichkeit. Exemplarische Untersuchungen zu kulturgeschichtlichen und literarischen Präsentationsformen des Weiblichen* (Frankfurt: Suhrkamp, 1979), pp. 80–150.

5 See, for example, G. A. Tishkin, *Zhenskii vopros v Rossii v 50–60 gg. XIX v.* (Leningrad: Izdatel'stvo Leningradskogo Universiteta, 1984).

6 The canonical female protagonists of nineteenth-century literature: Tat'iana Larina from *Evgenii Onegin* by Aleksandr Pushkin, Elena Stakhova from *Nakanune* (*On the Eve*) by Ivan Turgenev and Vera Pavlovna from *Chto delat'?* (*What is to be Done?*) by Nikolai Chernyshevskii.

7 See, for example, Vera Sandomirsky Dunham, 'The Strong-Woman Motif', in Cyril E. Black, ed., *The Transformation of Russian Society* (Cambridge, MA: Harvard University Press, 1960), pp. 459–83.

8 Bovenschen writes: 'For the image of the woman by the woman exists by no means independently of the gigantic portrait gallery of the feminine as it has gone on for centuries, the feminine

accompanied by objectivations and myths of triviality'. Bovenschen, *Die imaginierte Weiblichkeit*, pp. 57, also pp. 40–2.

9 These questions represent a preliminary discussion of issues
which I am examining in my more extensive work on women
writers in the middle of the century. See also Jane Costlow,
'Love, work and the woman question in mid nineteenth century
women's writing', in Toby W. Clyman and Diana Green, eds.,
Women Writers in Russian Literature (Westport, CT and London:
Greenwood Press, 1994), pp. 61–76.

10 See, for example, Irina Paperno, *Chernyshevsky and the Age of Realism*
(Stanford: Stanford University Press, 1988).

11 Joan Kelly, *Women, History, and Theory* (Chicago: University of
Chicago Press, 1984), p. 61.

12 Andrej Walicki, *A History of Russian Thought. From the Enlightenment
to Marxism* (Oxford: Clarendon Press, 1980), pp. 183–221 (p. 185).

13 Michel Foucault, *Power/Knowledge*, ed. by Colin Gordon (New
York: Pantheon, 1980), pp. 131–2.

14 See Richard Stites, *The Women's Liberation Movement in Russia*
(Princeton, NJ: Princeton University Press, 1978), p. 30, and pp.
29–63; Tishkin, *Zhenskii vopros v Rossii*, pp. 134–67.

15 E. Shchepkina, *Iz istorii zhenskoi lichnosti* (St Petersburg, 1914),
p. 270.

16 Later Shchepkina wrote: 'The question of reforming women's
education arises now out of the necessity for widespread educational reform'. Shchepkina, *Iz istorii zhenskoi lichnosti*, p. 274.

17 *Polnoe sobranie zakonov Rossiiskoi imperii*, 16, no. 12103 (St Petersburg,
1830).

18 Walicki, *A History of Russian Thought*, p. 184; Paperno, *Chernyshevsky
and the Age of Realism*, p. 10.

19 N. A. Dobroliubov, 'Mysli ob uchrezhdenii otkrytykh zhenskikh
shkol', *Sobranie sochinenii*, 11 (Moscow and Leningrad, 1962), pp.
360–73 (p. 365).

20 Charles A. Moser, *Esthetics as Nightmare. Russian Literary Theory,
1855–1879* (Princeton, NJ: Princeton University Press, 1989), pp.
150–217. See also Paperno, *Chernyshevsky and the Age of Realism*, p. 10.

21 M. L. Mikhailov, 'Uvazhenie k zhenshchinam', in M. L. Mikhailov, *Zhenshchiny, ikh vospitanie i znachenie v sem'e i obshchestve*. (St
Petersburg, 1903), p. 221.

22 See also Barbara Alpern Engel, *Mothers and Daughters. Women of the
Intelligentsia in Nineteenth-Century Russia* (Cambridge: Cambridge
University Press, 1986), pp. 125–6.

23 See, for example, Rostopchina's lyrics 'Kak dolzhny pisat'
zhenshchiny' (1840).

24 *Rassvet*, 1 (1859), see also the introduction, V. Krempin, 'Ot redaktsii', pp. 1–6.

25 On the difference between male- and female-associated ways of knowing, see Donna Wilshire, 'The uses of myth, image and the female body in re-visioning knowledge', in Alison M. Jaggar and Susan R. Bordo, eds., *Gender / Body / Knowledge. Feminist Reconstructions of Being and Knowing* (New Brunswick and London: Rutgers University Press, 1989), pp. 92–114.

26 Judith Fetterley writes that 'the cultural reality is not the emasculation of men by women, but the *immasculation* of women by men. As readers and teachers and scholars, women are taught to think as men, to identify with the male point of view, and to accept as normal and legitimate a male system of values, one of whose central principles is misogyny.' Judith Fetterley, *The Resisting Reader: A Feminist Approach to American Fiction* (Bloomington, IN: Indiana University Press, 1978), p. xx.

27 Fetterley, *The Resisting Reader*, p. xiii.

28 This is also apparent in his reading of the content of Nadezhda Khvoshchinskaia's literary work: 'All she writes about is inconsequentialities ... What is there for us in these observations describing all the pleats of a woman's dress and all the bagatelles of a woman's boudoir?' Shelgunov, 'Zhenskoe bezdushie', p. 11.

29 *Otechestvennye zapiski*, 135 (1861), p. 3. All quotations here will be taken from N. D. Khvoshchinskaia ('Krestovskii-psevdonim'), *Povesti i rasskazy* (Moscow, 1984), pp. 62–158.

30 Susan J. Rosowski writes about the female *Bildungsroman*: 'The protagonist's growth results typically not with "an art of living", as for her male counterpart, but instead with a realization that for a woman such an art of living is difficult or impossible: it is an awakening to limitations.' Susan J. Rosowski, 'The Novel of Awakening', in E. Abel, M. Hirsch and E. Langland, eds., *The Voyage In. Fictions of Female Development* (Hanover and London: University Press of New England, 1983), p. 49.

31 On the importance of education and economic independence for women, see Mikhailov, *Zhenshchiny*, pp. 3–72. See also Stites, *The Women's Liberation Movement*, pp. 33, 89; Elena Likhacheva, *Materialy dlia istorii zhenskogo obrazovaniia v Rossii*, 2 vols. (St Petersburg, 1890–1893), II, pp. 1–41, 453–92.

32 Khvoshchinskaia, *Povesti i rasskazy*, p. 157.

33 Paperno, *Chernyshevsky and the Age of Realism*, p. 109.

34 *Ibid.*, pp. 90, 91–112.

35 *Ibid.*, p. 107. The contemporary term *fiktivnyi brak* ('fictitious marriage') means literally 'reasonable, calculated marriage'.

36 Barbara Engel also stresses this characteristic of Russian women writers, who seemed to be afraid 'that to discuss sexual love in their writings was not only to be traditionally feminine, but also to equate personal life and social commitment, and this the women were scarcely prepared to do'. Engel, *Mothers and Daughters*, p. 114.

37 See Dobroliubov, *Sobranie sochinenii*, p. 365.

38 Carol Watts, 'Releasing possibility into form: cultural choice and the woman writer', in Isobel Armstrong, ed., *The Feminist Discourses* (London and New York: Routledge, 1992), pp. 83–102, 96.

39 Khvoshchinskaia, *Povesti i rasskazy*, p. 152.

40 This conflict between desire and will frequently recurs in Khvoshchinskaia's portraits of female protagonists in this period. Cf. 'Frazy. Derevenskaia povest'' (1855) or 'Za stenoiu' (1862). The writer also takes a stand on the *zhenskii vopros* in her literary critical articles. See 'V. Porechnikov' [pseudonym of N. Khvoshchinskaia], 'Provintsial'nye pis'ma o nashei literature', *Otechestvennye zapiski*, 1861–3.

41 Patrocinio P. Schweickart, 'Reading ourselves: toward a feminist theory of reading', in Elaine Showalter, ed., *Speaking of Gender* (New York and London: Routledge, 1989): pp. 17–44, 23.

42 Dudyshkin, cited in V. Semevskii, 'N. D. Khvoshchinskaia-Zaionchkovskaia. (V. Krestovskii-psevdonim)', *Russkaia mysl'*, 10 (1890), pp. 49–89 (p. 67).

43 K. K. Arsen'ev, *Kriticheskie etiudy po russkoi literature*, 1 (St Petersburg, 1888), p. 296.

44 V. Ostrogorskii, 'Etiudy o russkikh zhenshchinakh', *Zhenskoe obrazovanie*, 7 (1880), pp. 391–412 (p. 400).

45 Schweickart, 'Reading ourselves', p. 30.

CHAPTER 7

Carving out a career: women prose writers, 1885–1917, the biographical background

Charlotte Rosenthal

By the end of the nineteenth century, Russian women prose writers had established themselves in greater numbers than ever before.[1] There are several reasons for this greater participation. This was the first generation of women to come of age after the initial women's liberation movement of the 1860s; greater educational opportunities, including higher education, were becoming available to women, especially after 1894; after the emancipation of the serfs in 1861, the gradual breakdown of the gentry family structure, which could no longer provide for many of its unmarried young women, forced the latter to look for employment; while many other professions remained closed to women, as did jobs in the government bureaucracy until later in the twentieth century, writing remained an attractive possibility; finally, the advent of modernism in the 1890s, the period of the Silver Age, which promoted artistic creativity as a 'cause' worthy of the same degree of devotion as socio-political activity, attracted many women into literature despite the social opprobrium that still accompanied their transgressing traditional roles, as well as the poor pay and high degree of competition. In this essay I shall be exploring some of the conditions that favoured women's entry into literature as well as the obstacles that remained in their way.

The last factor mentioned above appears to have been crucial even for women writers who did not obviously subscribe to modernist aesthetics. The modernists' championing of individuality, their objection to all forms of determinism or obligation, and their 're-evaluation of all values' could not but affect the way that women thought about themselves and their roles.

For example, the young Liubov' Gurevich, the future publisher
and co-editor of the influential 'thick' journal *Northern Herald*
(*Severnyi vestnik*) wrote that she 'disdained ordinary life', by which
she meant conventional 'bourgeois' morality with its focus on
marriage as the goal of women's lives.[2] She emphasized the
notion of freedom from within the individual as the basis for all
fundamental change: 'I professed freedom of the spirit un-
hampered by vows of allegiance to any group' ('nikakimi
soiuznicheskimi obetami').[3]

The intelligentsia's traditional values of duty and self-
sacrifice had led women who were willing to risk society's
opprobrium by stepping outside the family not to art, but to
political and civic activities in which they subordinated an
exploration of personal identity.[4] Now modernist ideology
stressed self-expression and devotion to art, to the creation of
beauty. Art took precedence over social action. By endowing
art with such a metaphysical status, the modernists elevated a
sphere that had hitherto been justified mainly in terms of its
social utilitarian function. Women could now justify themselves
in terms of art. This is how Tat'iana Shchepkina-Kupernik
perceived the situation:

The nineties – a period of deaf-and-dumb reaction. A woman did not
have access to higher education: a majority of institutions of higher
education had been shut down. Because of this the best sort of girls
who in the sixties would have entered medical school, etc. in one way
or other threw themselves into art ... for a woman who thirsted for
freedom and independence had one remaining path: Art.[5]

Prejudices about women writers, however, persisted. They
touched on the nature of women's writing, generally regarded
as separate and inferior, and the nature of the woman writer
herself, still not quite considered a 'normal' phenomenon.[6]

By the end of the nineteenth century, critics commented on
the number of women writing prose fiction. Many issues of the
prestigious 'thick journals' such as *Severnyi vestnik* (*The Northern
Herald*), *Russkoe bogatstvo* (*Russian Wealth*), and *Russkaia mysl'*
(*Russian Thought*) contained work by or about women, although
this is not always evident because of the on-going use of non-
feminine pseudonyms. Their numbers and popularity had

grown with the increased number of newspapers and journals made possible by the new censorship laws under Alexander II and with the increasing size of the reading public. For example, women writers such as Ol'ga Bebutova, Vera Kryzhanovskaia ('Rochester'), 'Anna Mar' (Anna Lenshina), and 'Fortunato' (Evgeniia Vlasova) published in such popular newspapers as *Peterburgskii listok* (*The Petersburg Sheet*), *Moskovskii listok* (*The Moscow Sheet*), and *Svet* (*Light*). New journals aimed at a female audience such as *Zhenskoe delo* (*Women's Cause*, 1899–1900), *Zhenskii vestnik* (*Women's Herald*, 1904–16), *Sovremennaia zhenshchina* (*The Contemporary Woman*, 1907–16), *Damskii mir* (*Ladies' World*, 1907–16), *Mir zhenshchiny* (*Woman's World*, 1912–16), *Zhenskaia mysl'* (*Women's Thought*, 1909–10), *Zhenskaia zhizn'* (*Women's Life*, 1914-16), and *Zhurnal dlia zhenshchin* (*Journal for Women*, 1914–26) also provided additional opportunities for women to earn a living by writing. The popular fiction market grew, attracting women writers with its guarantee of more money and greater fame. The prose writer Anastasiia Verbitskaia, for example, exchanged the 'thick journals' in which she published earlier for the popular fiction market and became a best-selling author. This popular fiction was greatly influenced by the themes, character types, and forms of 'serious' literature, so that the boundary line between them is at times difficult to draw.

Pseudonym use indicates degrees of acceptance and an awareness of a separate set of expectations and demands on women writers. What is striking by the end of the nineteenth century is the increasing lack of pseudonym use, especially the lack of masculine pseudonyms. Russian critics for the most part had fairly exact notions of what constituted masculine and feminine writing. Women writers who were content or comfortable with that label tended to retain their real names or take on feminine pseudonyms (for example, Mariia Krestovskaia, Nadezhda Lukhmanova, Lidiia Avilova, Anastasiia Krandievskaia, Nina Annenkova-Bernar, Lidiia 'Charskaia'). Women such as 'Ol'nem' (Varvara Tsekhovskaia) and 'O. Mirtov' (Ol'ga Èmmanuilovna Kotyleva), whose prose seems consciously written against expectations of what 'ladies' would produce, took on masculine pseudonyms. To that end, Gippius signed her earliest prose simply with her initials or as 'Z. Gippius', which made deciphering her gender impossible. Masculine and neuter gender pseudonyms were used by others who were rather hesitant about their careers, such as Elena Shavrova ('E. Shavrov' and 'E. Shastunov') and Mariia Kiseleva ('Pince-nez' for fiction and 'Ègo' for translations and book reviews in the mystical journal *Rebus*, but under her real name for children's stories). Tèffi's pseudonym (Russian for 'Taffy') had an exotic ring to it, as did A. Mirè's (Aleksandra Moiseeva).

Most women writers in this period came from professional families: they were the daughters of lawyers, writers, publishers, bankers, professors, and employees of the civil or military service, particularly the latter. The fathers of Tèffi, Gippius and Shchepkina-Kupernik were lawyers. Mariètta Shaginian's father was a medical doctor. The fathers of Elena Shavrova, Anastasiia and Marina Tsvetaeva and Larisa Reisner were professors. The fathers of Annenkova-Bernar, Ekaterina 'Èk' (Kurch), and Mirè worked as civil servants; the fathers of Ol'ga Chiumina, Forsh, Guro, Vera Kryzhanovskaia ('Rochester'), Nadezhda Lappo-Danilevskaia, 'Ol'nem', and Verbitskaia were career military officers. Some had fathers who themselves were writers or publishers: Krestovskaia's father was the writer V. V. Krestovskii (1840–95), Nagrodskaia's father, Apollon Golovachev, was a journalist, and the fathers of Vera Inber and Anastasiia Krandievskaia were publishers. Almost none were of peasant or proletarian origin. Exceptions include Elizaveta Militsyna, 'M. Marich' (Mariia Chernysheva), and Nadezhda Sanzhar'. Some had mothers with professions, but this was unusual: Stefaniia Karaskevich's mother was a midwife, Shchepkina-Kupernik's mother was a semi-professional musician, and Nagrodskaia's mother was the writer Avdot'ia Panaeva.

Most women prose writers were born in, or eventually moved to, one of the two capital cities, St Petersburg or Moscow. Most had secondary-school education, a minority attended universities, while another minority attended art and music schools. Thus, in comparison with their male counterparts, women prose writers of the late nineteenth century received less formal education, though this gap was closing. As a group, women who chose to become literary critics and literary historians, such as Gurevich, Zinaida Vengerova, and Elena Koltonovskaia, received the best formal education available to them.[7]

Aside from parents involved in the cultural world, many had siblings and spouses who were also: Avilova's older brother was also a literary figure and her brother-in-law published her first stories in his newspaper, *Peterburgskaia gazeta* (*The Petersburg Gazette*). And it was in his home that she first met Chekhov; those with sisters who also wrote include Tèffi, Guro, A. Tsvetaeva, Verbitskaia (her sister wrote under the pseudonym 'Alekseeva'), and Kiseleva (the latter named N. V. Golubeva), and Gippius had sisters who were artists. Through both her parents Shchepkina-Kupernik was exposed to many people involved in the cultural world and had an aunt, R. L. Shchepkina, who was an actress.

Another critical factor appears to be the presence of a recognized male authority figure who encouraged women to take themselves seriously and helped them to get into print. E. M. Militsyna was encouraged by Korolenko and Gor'kii. Avilova's first mentor was the editor Viktor Gol'tsev, and she was given literary advice by Chekhov, who also helped Shavrova and Kiseleva, and encouraged Èk after reading her first story. Avilova was also praised by Bunin and Tolstoi; the latter also liked Ol'ga Runova's work. Briusov took an interest in the work of Anna Mar. Avgusta Damanskaia cited Viktor Miroliubov and Arkadii Gornfel'd as her mentors. 'Al. Altaev' (Margarita Iamshchikova) was encouraged by the writer Iakov Polonskii. Liubov' Gurevich gave credit to Akim Volynskii for helping her to 'refashion' herself both intellectually and psychologically.[8] The experience of the anonymous female author of the autobiographical memoir, 'Pervye shagi' ('First Steps', 1900),[9] though gained at a slightly earlier period, coincides in many details with that of Silver Age prose writers. She relates how the help of a sympathetic male editor of a 'thick' journal was critical to her in the early stages of her career. Marriages to literary and artistic figures were made by Guro (to the painter Matiushin), Gippius (to the writer Merezhkovskii), Zinov'eva-Annibal (to the writer V. Ivanov), and 'Ivan Strannik' (Anna Anichkova, who was married to the literary critic Evgenii Anichkov). There can be no question that these connections fostered their careers. Militsyna's second husband, who wrote fiction himself, strongly encouraged her.

Women's motives for becoming writers varied, from pure material need to a sense of a 'calling' and, in some cases, a combination of these motives. Most women began writing early, in childhood. Several who came to writing late did so out of necessity. Divorce forced Ariadna Tyrkova and Ekaterina Èk to take up writing;[10] widowhood did the same for Nadezhda Lukhmanova. Her father's early death created a need for Marietta Shaginian to earn a living by writing. Newspaper work opened the door to regular publication for Tyrkova, as well as others such as Verbitskaia and Ol'nem. Some upper-class women also became writers, despite the general opposition in their class to women's becoming professionals. N. A. Leikin's attitude was typical. After a visit to Lidiia Avilova, he wrote in his diary in 1897: 'A beautiful, simple woman – I like her, even though she's a writer'.[11]

According to available biographical information, almost all these prose writers married at least once, and among the married ones, over half had children, although none is known to have had a large family. Many who did not marry died young (such as Elizaveta D'iakonova and A. Mirè). Elena Guro never had any children, but so wanted to that she invented one.[12] But opposition from family members and family obligations appear to have been major obstacles for a number of women. Avilova's husband did not approve of her writing, partly out of jealousy and partly out of a sense of alienation from the world of culture which included Chekhov. Avilova herself complained that the quality of her writing suffered from her duties as a wife, mother of three children, and manager of a household. 'She wrote by fits and starts, often at night'.[13] Militsyna's first husband was strongly opposed to her literary ambitions.[14] One of the most bitter testimonies along these lines comes from Ol'ga Runova in an autobiography she wrote for S. A. Vengerov in 1913. The precocious Runova entered a female teachers' college at the age of fifteen while she lived with her uncle, Vissarion Komarov, the publisher of the newspaper *S.-Petersburgskie vedomosti* (*St Petersburg News*). Like many other women writers, Runova was attracted to writing in childhood and kept diaries and composed poems. But when these writings were discovered by her parents, she was sufficiently punished that for a long time she lost any inclination to write. She married first at the age of eighteen, and again at the age of twenty-five. 'Family life, the birth of children, the death of some of them, running a household, in general what is called "a woman's life" took from me a great deal of strength and occupied an enormous place in my life.' She published her first story in 1887 in the supplement to *Nedelia* (*Week*), encouraged by the actor and director Pavel Gaudeburov. Despite his high hopes for her, Runova says that the 'unfavourable' conditions of her personal life prevented her from fulfilling them: 'the children completely swallowed me up, ruined my health, pushed my psychological life in the direction of a slavish semi-mystical non-resistance to evil and deprived my work of any real content'.[15] She stopped writing for four or five years.

Several other women writers have left behind documents attesting to their struggle with parents, especially with their mothers, over their serious ambitions outside the roles of wife and mother. For some, just obtaining an education was a major victory. Elizaveta D'iakonova's posthumously published *Dnevnik russkoi zhenshchiny* (*Diary*, 1904) portrays a protracted struggle over five years with a domineering mother to obtain a university-level education. D'iakonova came from a tradition-bound merchant family. Even when she turned twenty-one and could enter university without parental consent, her mother was still able to block her acceptance temporarily.

Ekaterina Èk's autobiography echoes this story.[16] Like Gippius,[17] Èk records her closeness to her father, Mikhail Kurbanovskii: 'From the age of twelve I developed exclusively under the influence of my father, an exceptional person. He taught me to love literature and I am indebted to him for my very best and most joyous impressions.' Like many other women, Ek kept a diary and feared that her mother might discover it. Upon graduation from a gymnasium, Èk wanted to enter the university-level courses for women (*vysshie zhenskie kursy*), but her mother was opposed to this idea as well as to any specialized study of music or singing. The latter, Èk says, she was able to pursue only as a pleasant way to pass time. Èk's solution to her dilemma at home was to get married. She began her literary career only after she became divorced and moved to Moscow. The anonymous author of 'First Steps' also records that in childhood she wrote poetry and prose which her family made fun of and she singles out her mother as the one who took a novella she wrote and read it out loud to guests: 'The abundant laughter of these country bumpkins stopped me from any further attempts.'[18]

Verbitskaia also recorded a struggle with her mother to work in a professional capacity. In the second volume of her auto-biography, *Moi vospominaniia: Iunost'. Grezy* (*My Reminiscences: Youth. Daydreams*, 1911), she tells how her mother refused to allow her to accept a teaching job in their local town. Following this incident, Verbitskaia observes: 'One must know in what fear and dread before our mother we grew up in childhood, and how distant we were from her after completing our studies [at the institute].'[19]

Another obstacle that women faced besides societal and parental disapproval and discouragement was psychological: not only to write, but to seek publication, that is, to enter the public arena, required a certain amount of self-confidence and certainty about one's talent. Not surprisingly, self-doubt appears to have been a major obstacle that curtailed several careers. For example, Verbitskaia believed that her sister's writing career, and even her life, was curtailed by a loss of faith in her writing. Her sister, Aleksandra, secretly wrote a novella about four young women which she finally read to Verbitskaia. When the latter asked if she would read it to their mother, Aleksandra replied, 'Not for anything!'[20] However, she agreed to read it to their grandmother, a former actress, though anticipating that her effort would be greeted with laughter. When Verbitskaia tells their grandmother, the latter's response is: 'At first disbelief ... What can a mere schoolgirl [*devchonka*] write?'[21] Only seven years later, now a married woman, did Aleksandra send the manuscript off to a 'modest illustrated weekly',[22] *Svet i teni* (*Light and Shadows*). Though it was accepted and published, Aleksandra received no money for it, nor any offprints. By 1883 Aleksandra had published another novella in the prestigious 'thick' journal *Russian Thought*, which was praised by both Nikolai Mikhailovskii and Gleb Uspenskii. But Aleksandra's career was short-lived and she died rather young, in 1891. In her memoirs Verbitskaia blames the insensitivity of journal editors to new, young talents. She concludes: 'It is terrible to think that if she hadn't lost faith in her gift from continual failures and had she not lost the hope of feeding herself with her literary earnings, she might still be alive now!'[23] The lack of encouragement or acknowledgement may have also led to the abbreviated careers of such talented prose writers as Ol'nem and Ekaterina Èk.

Another very talented writer who suffered from lack of confidence was Mariia Kiseleva. She was much encouraged by Chekhov, who had a high opinion of her writing. He thought her work was noble in spirit and compared it favourably to that of Nadezhda Khvoshchinskaia, Smirnova and Tur. She, however, did not take herself seriously and stopped writing fiction completely after producing very little. Her low self-esteem is evident in a note to Chekhov which she attached to one of her stories: 'Taking heart from the words of a talented writer (An. Pav. Chekhov), that "in literature, as in the army, minor ranks are necessary" – I am allowing myself to proffer this writer my modest little work, counting on his indulgence of a minor children's writer. M. Kiseleva.' [24]

To sum up, then, becoming a woman writer usually involved being born into a professional family, getting oneself a secondary-school level education, taking up residence in one of the two capital cities, the acquisition of culture and connections through relatives or marriage, and enough of an ego to go public with one's writing and keep on writing in the face of adverse reviews or critics' silence. In the end few of the many who started out were able to sustain a career.

NOTES

Research for this article was supported in part by a grant from the International Research and Exchanges Board (IREX), with funds provided by the National Endowment for the Humanities, the United States Information Agency, and the US Department of State, which administers the Soviet and East European Training Act of 1983 (Title VIII).

1 See my article on these prose writers and their work, 'Achievement and obscurity: women's prose in the Silver Age (1885–1925)', in Toby W. Clyman and Diana Greene, eds., *Women Writers in Russian Literature* (Westport, CT: Greenwood Press, 1994), pp. 149–70. For background on the period and women writers' place in Russian culture, see also 'Configurations of authority: feminism, modernism, and mass culture, 1881–1917', Chapter 5 of Catriona Kelly's *A History of Russian Women's Writing, 1820–1992* (Oxford: Clarendon Press, 1994), pp. 121–80, and Jane A. Taubman, 'Women poets of the Silver Age', in Clyman and Greene, *Women Writers in Russian Literature* , pp. 171–3. For more information on the biography, career and bibliography of individual writers, see Marina Ledkovsky, Charlotte Rosenthal and Mary Zirin, eds., *Dictionary of Russian Women Writers* (Westport, CT: Greenwood Press, 1994).

2 L. Gurevich, 'Istoriia *Severnogo Vestnika*' in S. A. Vengerov, ed., *Russkaia literatura XX veka*, 1890–1900, I (Moscow: Mir, 1914), pp. 236, 237.

3 Gurevich, 'Istoriia', p. 246. In fact Gurevich never did marry, though she did have a child. In the aftermath of 1905, she became involved in politics, especially on behalf of the feminist movement. Her sister Anna (1878–1942), a Bolshevik, was deeply involved in the socialist women's movement. See Linda Edmondson, *Feminism in Russia, 1900–1917* (Stanford, CA: Stanford University Press, 1984), p. 34.

4 See Barbara Alpern Engel, *Mothers and Daughters: Women of the Intelligentsia in Nineteenth-Century Russia* (Cambridge: Cambridge University Press, 1983), pp. 4–5.

5 *Dni moei zhizni: teatr, literatura, obshchestvennaia zhizn'* (Moscow: Federatsiia, 1928), pp. 151, 152. In this quotation Shchepkina-Kupernik emphasizes the lack of other opportunities rather than

the attraction of art, though educational opportunities for women in the 1860s in Russia were severely limited. She may have felt the need for this revisionist version because she was writing in the later 1920s.

6 Though the most well-known female prose writers such as Gippius, Guro, Zinov′eva-Annibal, Tèffi and Verbitskaia are mentioned in this chapter, many of the women discussed are rather obscure. The reasons for this focus are an attempt to give an overall picture of the circumstances in which women attempted to establish careers, not just that of the few, sometimes exceptional cases, and the fact that it was often among the lesser-known writers that I was able to find the most revealing and conscious statements about the woman writer's predicament.

7 Prose writers who received a university-level education included Mariètta Shaginian, Vera Inber, Ol′ga Runova (a teachers' college), Shchepkina-Kupernik (who also studied for one year in Switzerland), Ariadna Tyrkova (a maths graduate), Anastasiia Krandievskaia, and Elizaveta D′iakonova. The latter studied at the Sorbonne after graduation from higher courses in St Petersburg. Women who attended a gymnasium include Èk, Mirè, the Tsvetaeva sisters, Annenkova-Bernar, Avilova, Tèffi, and Zinov′eva-Annibal; *institutki* ('boarding school girls') include Verbitskaia, Charskaia, Kiseleva and Forsh. Women who were educated at home by private tutors include Gippius and Chiumina, both in part because of poor health. Militsyna's only formal education was at the elementary level. Elena Guro and Ol′ga Forsh attended art schools; Verbitskaia, Shavrova and Zinov′eva-Annibal studied music.

8 Gurevich, 'Istoriia', p. 239.

9 'Pervye shagi: Iz vospominanii pisatel′nitsy. (1872–1892 gg.)', *Vestnik vsemirnoi istorii*, 9 (1900), 106–28.

10 The authoress of 'First Steps' was also forced into earning a living as the result of a divorce. One of her points is that the need to earn money by her writing compelled her to write a great deal without the luxury of considering the quality of this writing.

11 *Literaturnoe nasledstvo*, 68 (1960), p. 508.

12 Anna Ljunggren and Nils Ake Nilsson, eds., *Elena Guro: Selected Prose and Poetry* (Stockholm: Almqvist and Wiksell, 1988), p. 128, n.34.

13 Inna Goff, 'O Lidii Avilovoi', in L. A. Avilova, *Rasskazy; vospominaniia* (Moscow: Sovetskaia Rossiia, 1984), p. 7; Carolina de Maegd-Soëp, *Chekhov and Women: Women in the Life and Work of Chekhov* (Columbus, OH: Slavica, 1987), p. 192.

14 '[Her first husband] Kargin was decidedly opposed to her strivings for a literary career': M. Podobedov, 'E. M. Militsyna: Kritiko-biograficheskii ocherk', in E. M. Militsyna, *Izbrannye rasskazy* (Voronezh: Voronezhskoe oblastnoe knigoizdatel'stvo, 1949), p. 5.

15 Manuscript autobiography in the S. A. Vengerov archive, Pushkinskii dom, Rukopisnyi otdel, f. 377, No. 3104.

16 Dated 1913, it is to be found in S. A. Vengerov's archive, Pushkinskii dom, f. 377, No. 2023.

17 Gippius recorded her closeness to her father in the book *Dmitrii Merezhkovskii* (Paris, 1951); reprinted in D. S. Merezhkovskii, '14 dekabria', in Z. N. Gippius, *Dmitrii Merezhkovskii* (Moscow: Moskovskii rabochii, 1990), p. 289: 'When he was disssatisfied with something – he would stop paying attention to me, and I knew that I had to go and ask to be forgiven. Afterwards everything would get straightened out, and we would once more be friends. I mean exactly 'friends', because he would speak with me usually as with an 'equal', with an adult . . .'.

18 'Pervye shagi', p. 112.

19 Verbitskaia, *Moi vospominaniia*, p. 48.

20 *Ibid.*, p. 176. When their mother is informed about the novel, she reacts mockingly and asks 'Who needs it?' (p. 177). Ed.: for further discussion, see Marsh below, p. 191.

21 Verbitskaia, *Moi vospominaniia*, p. 176.

22 *Ibid.*, p. 178.

23 *Ibid.*, p. 179.

24 *Chekhov i ego sreda* (Leningrad: Akademiia, 1930), p. 241.

CHAPTER 8

The fate of women writers in literature at the beginning of the twentieth century: 'A. Mirè', Anna Mar, Lidiia Zinov'eva-Annibal

Mariia Mikhailova

In 1850 the prominent poet Fedor Tiutchev published lines which the critic Nikolai Dobroliubov characterized as 'desperately sad and heartrending':

> Вдали от солнца и природы,
> Вдали от света и искусства,
> Вдали от жизни и любви
> Мелькнут твои младые годы,
> Живые помертвеют чувства,
> Мечты развеются твои …
>
> И жизнь твоя пройдет незрима,
> В краю безлюдном, безымянном,
> На незамеченной земле, —
> Как исчезает облак дыма
> На небе тусклом и туманном,
> В осенней беспредельной мгле …

(Far from nature and the sun | Far from society and art | Far from life and love | Your young years will flash by | Your live feelings will die | Your dreams will be destroyed … | | Your life will pass unseen | In a lonely, nameless land | On undiscovered ground | As fades a cloud of smoke | In a dim, misty sky | In boundless autumn mists …)

The poem was entitled 'Russkoi zhenshchine' ('To a Russian Woman').

At the beginning of the twentieth century, it became obvious that Russian women had every intention of contradicting the poet's sorrowful 'forebodings'. They wanted to make their life *visible,* to bring *light* and *love* into it, to preserve their *dreams* and not to allow their *feelings* to be extinguished. Only one path led to this objective – creativity. There was an energetic influx of

141

women into all spheres of creative work. Acting, literature, journalism, translation and art were only a few of the professions that women pursued successfully. Moreover – and this should be particularly emphasized – social origin was not the decisive factor. Women from aristocratic or impoverished noble families, wives and sisters of officials, daughters of priests, even peasant girls, such as Nadezha Sanzhar', literally rushed to storm previously impregnable fortresses. Of course, many were motivated by the desire for autonomy and an independent salary. For some this became an exhausting daily grind. For example, the letters of A. Mirè (the pseudonym of Aleksandra Mikhailovna Moiseeva) are full of such confessions as: 'The whole time I'm struggling with life and tiredness ...';[1] 'I've got lots of trouble and worries now: I have to fix myself up with some work, but I don't know where yet.'[2] Even when she obtained an unexpected breathing-space, she was literally tormented by the idea of needing to earn money: 'Now I'm sitting over my translation for days on end'; 'I haven't finished it yet'; 'I'm finishing it, I'm very busy'; 'Could you please find out if my translation of Zola's *Germinal* has been printed? If not, when it will be; and if it has been, if they will send me some money as soon as possible.'[3] And even when she was completely broke and obliged to ask for credit (at that time she was in a psychiatric hospital and even wrote on squared paper to economize on postcards), she constantly referred to royalties which might help her pay her debts. Moreover, if we recall how she took the first steps on her literary career – she used the royalties she had earned the day before to buy vodka, cucumbers, bread and herring, locked herself in her hotel room for the night, and the next morning entered the editorial office of the *Nizhegorodskii listok* with a completed story – the way she filled her life will become obvious.

By no means all women managed to achieve independence; as often as not their success was very limited, but this did not diminish their eagerness to succeed, and, as a result, several outstanding names emerged in theatre and the arts, such as Vera Komissarzhevskaia, Anna Golubkina and Mariia Iakunchikova.[4]

This essay focuses on the creative destinies of three women writers who possessed different degrees of talent, and left varying marks on the history of Russian culture at the beginning of the twentieth century. They are Lidiia Zinov'eva-Annibal, a very interesting prose writer, the wife of the poet Viacheslav Ivanov; A. Mirè, a brilliant representative of the impressionist movement in Russian prose of that time; and Anna Mar (the pseudonym of Anna Iakovlevna Lenshina, the daughter of the well-known Petersburg artist Iakov Brovar), the writer of this period who produced perhaps the most accomplished version of women's popular fiction, looking 'at the world', as a contemporary critic said, 'through the prism of sexuality'.[5] This essay will focus on their work, not for its own sake, but for the light it sheds on their individual lives. The biographies of these writers are highly instructive in the sense that their lives ended at approximately the same time: Zinov'eva-Annibal died in 1907 at the age of forty-two; A. Mirè died in 1913 when she was thirty-nine; Anna Mar committed suicide in 1917 at the age of thirty.[6] But although the causes of their deaths were different – Zinov'eva-Annibal contracted galloping scarlet fever, Mirè died of an acute stomach infection, whereas Anna Mar decided to settle accounts with life – each of these deaths seems in its own way to be no accident; there is a certain logic in the fact that it was at that exact time, at precisely that point in their lives that fate, destiny or absurd chance placed a full stop. Some inner exhaustion, some sense of completeness in the face of destiny seems to push these women into the arms of death. And this occurs at a time when outwardly they feel that they are standing on the threshold of a new phase of life. In this context, Zinov'eva-Annibal's confession, made shortly before her death, is typical: 'I'm totally absorbed in life and some far-off, brilliant achievements. I can't calm down and grow old.'[7] Mirè has virtually the same feeling, despite the severe shocks she has experienced: 'My salvation is an infinite, unbounded love of life, and therefore of myself'; 'I have the feeling that my vitality will get the upper hand and conquer'.[8] And Mar, who conducted a dialogue with readers on the pages of the

Women's Journal, stated only a month before her fateful decision: 'Suicide is not the way out, even in the most desperate circumstances.'[9]

Thus, there can be no question of a loss of creative power. On the contrary, each of them was at perhaps the peak of her creativity. In 1907 Zinov'eva-Annibal published the collection *Tragicheskii zverinets* (*The Tragic Menagerie*),[10] about which Aleksandr Blok, who was very sparing in his praise, was to write that at last a book had appeared speaking 'of what is forgotten and terrible', extolling 'freedom, rebellion, intoxication, youth, physical love, animal pity and human criminality' – in short, everything that civilized human beings are afraid to admit to themselves, that they avoid or carefully conceal. It is this book which gave Blok the right to say after the writer's death: 'We cannot even imagine what contribution she might have made to Russian literature.'[11]

A year before her death A. Mirè published her best work – the story 'Stranitsy iz dnevnika' ('Pages from a Diary', 1912), in which she provided a sketch of her own character, dreams and aspirations through the portrait of Lara.[12] This story, written in the form of a provincial young lady's diary, depicted with subtle brushstrokes the vague spiritual longings of a charming young girl who aspired to break out of the confines of her everyday life, consisting of a cold, egoistic mother, a silent, nervous aunt and innumerable relatives – but no one who could warm her heart, no one to whom she could confide her hopes and secret plans, her ardent passion for the future, for life and the unknown.

Her one friend is Nature. She evokes a feeling of plenitude and the constant joy of life:

Томная прохлада под сенью ясных деревьев. Вот лес, не дрогнет — тихий, величавый. Важно поднимаются к высокому небу вершины старых деревьев. А вот вдруг — проталина — сколько золотого блеска неожиданно хлынет! И опять глухая, сумрачная, странно волнующая тишина. А вот что-то колыхнуло все деревья, ропот, проносится быстрый ветер, крупные капли дождя. Я прижимаюсь к стволу дерева и счастливо улыбаюсь.

(A languorous coolness under a canopy of clear trees. The quiet, majestic forest did not stir. The tops of the old trees rose importantly to the tall sky. And then suddenly a patch of thawed earth appeared – such an unexpected flash of shining gold! And again a dull, twilit, strangely disturbing silence. Then all the trees began to sway, there was a murmur, a swift wind blew, large raindrops fell. I pressed up against the tree trunk and smiled happily.)

This is the work in which she attains perfection in that 'quiet realism' which Blok referred to in his review of her first book, *Zhizn'* (*Life*), in 1904.[13] Even then, the poet and critic remarked that A. Mirè's works possess the appeal of 'quiet exhaustion, which does not impede freshness of perception'; there is 'nothing forced or artificial' in them, but a 'quiet simplicity'. Blok maintained that the writer's work was true literature, because she was able to perceive life's 'true essence' without chasing after 'truth to life'.

This assessment can be applied with even greater justice to her last works, particularly 'Pages from a Diary' and her story 'Na pchel'nike' ('In the Beehive'), a rich, powerfully written work in the style of Bunin which features characters who do not usually figure in Mirè's work, such as labourers, pilgrims and peasants, and expresses the ideal of an enlightened, regulated moral existence which would involve clarity of mind, an absence of nervous tension, inner calm, and confidence in the future.

Anna Mar's last work was the novel *Zhenshchina na kreste* (*Woman on the Cross*, 1916), which provoked an avalanche of responses, appearing the next year in a second edition[14] and a screenplay under the title 'Oskorblennaia Venera' ('Insulted Venus'). In the opinion of the critic Elena Koltonovskaia, it was written 'freely ... distinctively ... vividly'.[15] Of course, interest in it was whipped up by the sensational themes it treated: sadism, masochism, lesbian love. But, in my view, a more important factor was that it summed up in an original way her many years of searching for 'feeling, support, meaning and bread', it conveyed the endless torment of putting herself out for others and being crucified by the indifference of 'passers-by' (incidentally, this was the title of a story she published in

1913[16]), and depicted an 'abandoned, dissatisfied, infinitely lonely' woman[17] who had no way out except death. This novel treated all the main moral and religious problems in Mar's work, which she had also raised in earlier works such as the collection of stories *Nevozmozhnoe* (*The Impossible*, 1911), *Lampady nezazhennye* (*Unlit Lamps*, 1913) and the novel *Tebe odnomu sogreshila* (*For You Alone I Sinned*, 1914).[18] Anna Mar appeared in many guises, as a young Pole, 'spiritually alone, Catholic by religion, sensually aroused, socially gauche'.[19] She was practically the first to provide a frank revelation of the intimate sources of women's religious feelings (as a critic of her day commented, perhaps too explicitly: 'Religion for her is a form of eroticism'[20]).

The examples given above seem to afford indisputable proof of the feature which Zinaida Gippius regarded as typical of 'women's writing': its persistent, pronounced autobiographical character. In the opinion of Gippius, who was an aggressive opponent of almost all so-called 'women's literature', autobiographical writing is the main factor demonstrating women writers' narrowness of vision. She argues that it leads to confusion between the material of life and literature, and as a result 'a bad book emerges, which claims at the same time to be true to life and to be a work of art'.[21] Autobiography, she states, can produce only one book worthy of attention. Gippius poses the question: 'Who doesn't know that in actual fact any woman can write one good book, the book of her life? ... Because of her capacity to feel *her own* life and *her own* love deeply and be infinitely interested in it, a woman can speak about it particularly sincerely and accurately.' Such a book almost inevitably displays a 'pre-literary freshness' bordering on 'the highest artistic simplicity', which leads to the appearance of an 'organic, vivid and beautiful work'. But more often the reverse is true: after the first 'successful book the woman gets carried away' and begins 'to create'. And this results in a 'number of feeble works ... which cannot be called creations, but imitations', 'futile attempts at invention'.[22] With this last phrase Gippius denied any possibility of 'women's creativity'. The most women are capable of is to create sincere, emotional works, but creativity as a form of human activity is absolutely contrary to their nature.

In my opinion, the works of Zinov'eva-Annibal, Mirè and Mar discussed above demonstrate just the opposite. In their work autobiographical elements acquired a new character, coming to express features typical of women's behaviour, world-view and consciousness at the turn of the century. As Elena Koltonovskaia, a critic who followed the development of women's writing, aptly remarked, women writers at the turn of the century depicted 'the psychology of the new, or rather, the transitional woman in whom two women live and struggle: the new and the old. The former is bold and self-critical, fights conventions and traditions, strives for liberation; the latter is shy and submissive.'[23] The accuracy of this observation is attested by Nadezhda Tèffi's comic classification of women into categories, one of which she dubs 'the aspiring woman'.[24]

Nevertheless, in her reviews Gippius attempted to solve the problem of the woman writer's 'creativity and destiny', albeit in a negative sense. Koltonovskaia also identified this as a major problem in the foreword to her book *Feminine Silhouettes* (1912), entitled 'The Feminine'. After examining the biographies of brilliant women who had made a contribution to various fields of art and science, such as the mathematician and writer Sof'ia Kovalevskaia and the actresses Eleonora Duse and Vera Komissarzhevskaia, she came to the conclusion that for even the most gifted woman, more often than not creativity was not an aim in itself, but a refuge from the sufferings of unrequited love, from the failure to fulfil her feminine destiny, from the impossibility of drinking in 'the plenitude of existence' associated with the humane aspect of love. Koltonovskaia wrote: 'The stronger a woman's individuality, the more powerful the appeal creativity exerts on her, but also the more vividly her emotional nature is expressed.' Her talent does not eliminate the basic conflict, but aggravates it.[25]

In my view, it is no exaggeration to say that a woman finds fulfilment in love.[26] A man can be fully satisfied with creativity, which is an idiosyncratic form of solipsism. A woman's striving for love should be regarded not as a narrowing of her interests and demands, but as epitomizing life's supreme value, the concept of plenitude (*plerom*, as the Greeks would say), as endowing life with spirituality and meaning, and helping her to overcome the introversion and egoism of personal existence.

Flaubert's Madame Bovary could be interpreted as the most accurate embodiment of the feminine form of love. As often as not, man seeks his ideal; like Don Juan, he searches for his beautiful, perfect beloved. And, naturally, unable to find a real incarnation of the Eternal Feminine, he constantly moves from one object of affection to another. Woman searches not for a Beloved, but for Love, or a rapturous, elevated state which she associates with life itself. Therefore, when, as she thinks, she has found this Great Feeling, she can no longer see the real person. She is capable of romanticizing and idealizing him infinitely, putting him on a pedestal and bowing down to him. A woman's love is on the one hand more earthly – but, on the other hand, more elevated, since she longs to attain an ideal incarnation of life. This long digression on the metaphysics of love, which would appear to be only tenuously related to the main subject of this essay, was necessary in order to elucidate our main concern: the destinies these women writers achieved in love.

It is possible that this could be the reason why Mirè and Mar's creative talents were not completely fulfilled, why their creative potential seemed to hang in the air, finding no support in a successful personal life. It is true that their personal lives were monstrously absurd and disordered. But Mirè's life – which shifted from the stage of a provincial theatre to an underground conspiracy in the attics of Montmartre, to a brothel in Le Havre or Marseilles, until her random marriage to an agronomist from Perm', whom she fondly imagined to be like Glan, the hero of Knut Hamsun's novel *Pan* (1894),[27] which, not surprisingly, culminated in a psychiatric hospital and a lonely death in a hospital bed – was so 'macabre' and 'literary' that it served as the basis for a literary work,[28] Georgii Chulkov's story 'Shurochka and Venia' (1916), written three years after her death.[29]

Zinov'eva-Annibal's life seems to refute a similar interpretation. In her case everything is quite the reverse: she possessed

artistic achievements and a unique emotional and physical
relationship with the poet Viacheslav Ivanov. We recall Ivanov's confession: 'We each discovered ourselves through the
other ... And it was not only in me that the poet opened up
and became conscious of himself, freely and confidently, but in
her too.' The passion that united them 'was like a spring
thunderstorm, after which everything became new, green and
in bloom', and this feeling was 'destined only to grow and
become spiritually more profound'.[30] Nevertheless, even such a
rare union did not preclude a tragic denouement. After holding
views identical to those of her husband, becoming his 'colleague
in Bacchus and the Muses',[31] advocating, like him, ideas of life
and creativity, worshipping Dionysus, putting into practice the
concept of a new type of family embodying spiritual commu-
nion and allowing the idea of human commonality to be
realized, she did not find happiness. *Thirty-three Abominations*,[32]
which exposed the dangers of the dionysian experiments conducted by Ivanov in his 'Tower',[33] was an idiosyncratic prophecy of the end, a requiem for her life.

  Although the plot focuses on a love affair between two
women, it was dedicated to Viacheslav Ivanov, and was aimed
at him personally; it was an attempt to create a dialogue and
explain to him where the efforts to create a 'triple union' might
lead, regardless of whether a man or a woman formed one of
the angles of the triangle (in the Ivanovs' life, Sergei Gorodetskii
and Margarita Sabashnikova were destined to play this role in
turn). Zinov'eva-Annibal, who in life convinced herself that it
was her duty to 'give her beloved [Viacheslav Ivanov] to
everyone', resolved a similar love conflict differently in her art:
tragically. Vera, surrendering her beloved to 'others' – the
public, eager for aesthetic sensations – cannot endure the
ordeal and kills herself. I venture to suggest that there may be a
measure of truth in the idea that Zinov'eva-Annibal's galloping
scarlet fever was to some degree a disguised suicide. Not in the
sense that she infected herself on purpose, but in the sense that
she appeared to summon her own death. Some time later
Ivanov also acknowledged this, writing in his diary: 'Lidiia had
already "tasted death" beforehand, had crossed its threshold

... But then she lived on, already half-belonging to the other world ...'.[34] It is surely no coincidence that when she first entered the house in Zagor'e where she was fated to die, Zinov'eva-Annibal, who was always reserved, proud and majestic, burst out crying bitterly, as if she had some premonition. And while she was living there, she constantly longed to go away on a pilgrimage, as if in haste to set out on the distant road which awaited her.

In some strange sense, the works of each of the writers we have been considering possess a prophetic, premonitory significance. Anna Mar uses invented material to 'play through' the problems of her own life, and Zinov'eva-Annibal's forebodings have already been mentioned above. But perhaps A. Mirè's premonitions were the most striking. This is the conclusion to her story 'Dve iz mnogikh' ('Two of Many'):

Марианна наливает коньяк в свой стаканчик и в стаканчик Винченцы. Глаза ее смотрят спокойно и грустно.
— Ну, будет! Не порть себе крови, — говорит она ласково, — и в ее голосе проскальзывают теплые и мягкие, как бархат, ноты живого человеческого чувства. — Не перестроишь мир ... Пьяной почаще будь. А то одна у нас так *сдуру все читала.*
— И что же?
— *Сошла с ума.*[35]

(Marianne poured cognac into her own glass and Vincenza's. Her gaze was calm and sad.
'That's enough! Don't get annoyed', she said affectionately, and her voice was permeated with notes of keen human feeling, as warm and soft as velvet. 'You can't remake the world ... Get drunk more often.
As it is, one of us has *been stupid enough to read everything.*'
'What of it?'
'*She has gone mad.*')

In this extract the key words defining Mirè's way of life can be clearly distinguished: wine, books and madness.

In the story 'Belyi kliuch' ('The White Spring', 1910),[36] which she wrote shortly before her marriage, as if knowing everything in advance, she meticulously evoked her life on an abandoned estate, the monotony of her days, the sameness of country pursuits, the boredom of evenings all similar to one another –

in a word, everything that awaited her in the village of Chastye on the banks of the river Kama, where she settled with her husband. The heroine of the story, whose life is devoid of love, ceases feeling joy at 'the sparkling sky and the tree-tops streaming up into the height like silver tents'. She notes with satisfaction that her body is getting heavier, that she is turning into an old woman whom nobody needs, who is good for nothing and a nuisance to everyone. After the loss of love, which she considered a 'justification and culmination of everything that is and will be', she understood that 'what she needed to live for, what she had been born for – moments of happiness – had died for ever'. Perhaps it was because she was afraid of just such an outcome, and did not want to wait for a state when she would feel emotion at the disappearance of all ailments and sorrows, when she would feel joy simply because life was passing her by, imperceptibly, easily and forgettably, she fled from her Siberian backwoods, demanding from her husband intense emotion, a life that was not thawing, but burning.

And this was the bitter vision which pursued the prostitute who walked for hours along the embankment in search of clients. Observing a horse flailing about in its death throes, she painfully imagined how 'revolting, poor and wretched' her own death would be, how she would be taken into hospital on a limping nag, how her head would hit the side of the cart every time the wheels struck the carriageway, and how a policeman, picking up her lifeless corpse, which looked like a 'bundle of rags', would inevitably clutch at her limp hair.

It only remains to add that, after falling seriously ill, Aleksandra Mikhailovna Moiseeva was sent to a Moscow hospital in a state of semi-consciousness by the landlady of the flat she was renting, where she lay delirious for a week, without any visitors. Then, as was written in her death certificate, 'the unfortunate woman's body, clothed in a hospital shift, was left in the morgue to be identified'. But as the deceased was discovered to have no relatives, she was buried in a common grave in the Vagan'kovskoe cemetery. Her friends learned of her death only three months later. The basket of manuscripts and letters she left behind – her only possession – was lost.

152   MARIIA MIKHAILOVA

Only six people came to her funeral in St Petersburg's Kazan Cathedral.

One of the works dedicated to Zinov'eva-Annibal said: 'She sensed woman's body, soul and fate with great simplicity and vividness.'[37] Unquestionably, these words could aptly be applied to the work of any of the writers we have mentioned.

NOTES

Some of these notes have been prepared by the editor in consultation with the author.

1 RGALI, f. 548, op. 1, ed.khr.465, l.3.
2 *Ibid.*, l.4.
3 *Ibid.*, ll.13, 14, 16, 23.
4 Ed.: Vera Komissarzhevskaia (1864–1910) was a famous Russian actress, perhaps best known for her roles in Chekhov's *The Seagull* and Ibsen's *The Doll's House*; Anna Golubkina (1864–1927) was a famous sculptor, a pupil of Rodin; Mariia Iakunchikova-Veber (1870–1902) was an artist well known for her landscape painting, etchings and applied art.
5 B. Savinich, review of Anna Mar, *Zhenshchina na kreste*, *Utro Rossii*, 190 (19 July 1916).
6 Anna Mar poisoned herself at the Moscow hotel 'Madrid and Louvre' because of an unhappy love affair. She had a difficult life: after leaving home at age fifteen, moving to Kharkov and becoming attracted to Catholicism, she married at sixteen, but the marriage quickly broke up. For a long time she was unable to find work and lived in poverty until she received a grant from the St Petersburg Academy of Sciences in 1911. For further information on Mar's life and work, see Tat'iana Nikol'skaia, 'Mar, Anna', in Marina Ledkovsky, Charlotte Rosenthal and Mary Zirin, eds., *Dictionary of Russian Women Writers* (Westport, CT: Greenwood Press, 1994), pp. 406–8.
7 RGALI, f. 548, op. 1, ed.khr.336, l.2.
8 RGALI, f. 548, op. 1, ed.khr.465, ll.24, 30.
9 *Zhurnal dlia zhenshchin*, 2 (1917), p. 13. This statement was made in a popular column which Anna Mar wrote for the *Women's Journal* answering readers' questions about love and family matters under the pseudonym 'Princess Daydream' ('Printsessa Greza').
10 L. Zinov'eva-Annibal, *Tragicheskii zverinets. Rasskazy* (St Petersburg,

1907). For further discussion of this work, see Davidson below, pp. 155–75.

11 A. Blok, review of A. Mirè's collection *Zhizn'* (1904), in *Sobranie sochinenii v vos'mi tomakh*, v (Moscow–Leningrad, 1962), p. 226; first published in *Voprosy zhizni*, 7 (1905).

12 A. Mirè, 'Stranitsy iz dnevnika', *Zhatva*, 3 (1912), pp. 157–91.

13 A. Mirè, *Zhizn'* (Nizhnii Novgorod, 1904). For Blok's review, see note 11.

14 A. Mar, *Zhenshchina na kreste* (Moscow, 1916; 2nd edn, Moscow, 1917; 3rd edn, Moscow, 1918).

15 E. Koltonovskaia, 'Zhenshchina "na kreste"', *Rech'*, 167 (20 June 1916).

16 A. Mar, *Idushchie mimo* (Moscow, 1914; 2nd edn, Moscow, 1917).

17 A. Gornfel'd, *Russkoe bogatstvo*, 8–10 (1917), p. 319. This article is published without an author's name, but researchers have established that A. Gornfel'd, a permanent employee of the journal, was the author of the monthly reviews of literature.

18 The most accessible editions of these works are A. Mar, *Nevozmozhnoe* (Moscow, 1912); *Lampady nezazhennye* (Petrograd–Moscow, 1915) and 'Tebe odnomu sogreshila', in *My pomnim Pol'shu* (Petrograd, 1915).

19 Gornfel'd, *Russkoe bogatstvo*, 8–10 (1917), p. 319.

20 B. Savinich, *Utro Rossii*, 19 July 1916.

21 Z. Gippius, 'Zhurnal'naia belletristika (obzor)', *Russkaia mysl'*, 6 (1911), p. 18. Ed.: Jane A. Taubman, 'Women Poets of the Silver Age', in Toby W. Clyman and Diana Greene, eds., *Women Writers in Russian Literature* (Westport, CT: Greenwood Press, 1994), pp. 172–3, 186, n.7 attributes Gippius's denigration of women's literature to her realization that the female voice was not considered authoritative enough to treat serious philosophical and religious questions, and to her own confused sexual orientation.

22 *Ibid.*, p. 19.

23 E. Koltonovskaia, '"Mir" v mire (o sovremennoi zhenshchine)', *Den'*, 90 (2 April 1914). Ed.: For further information on Koltonovskaia, one of the most influential critics of the Silver Age, who was not much in demand after the Bolshevik Revolution, see Mariia Mikhailova, 'Koltonovskaia, Elena Aleksandrovna', in Ledkovsky, Rosenthal and Zirin, *Dictionary of Russian Women Writers*, pp. 310–13.

24 See Tèffi's story 'Tipy i gruppy'.

25 E. Koltonovskaia, *Zhenskie siluety* (St Petersburg, 1912), pp. xi–xii.

26 Ed.: the two paragraphs that follow express views influenced by

Elena Koltonovskaia and other Silver Age critics, which contemporary western feminists would find highly debatable.

27 Mirè's courtship was conducted by correspondence. Hamsun's novel *Pan* was apparently A. Mirè's favourite book, and the character of Glan is noteworthy for his almost boundless power over women.

28 Ed: Mariia Mikhailova provides a fuller account of A. Mirè's strange and tragic life in Ledkovsky, Rosenthal and Zirin, *Dictionary of Russian Women Writers*, pp. 427–30.

29 G. Chulkov, 'Shurochka i Venia', in *Liudi v tumane* (Moscow, 1916).

30 Entry in Viacheslav Ivanov's diary, in V. Ivanov, *Sobranie sochinenii*, II (Brussels: Foyer Oriental Chrétien, 1971–87), p. 20.

31 *Ezhegodnik rukopisnogo otdela Pushkinskogo Doma na 1980 god* (Leningrad, 1984), p. 183.

32 L.Zinov'eva-Annibal, *Tridtsat' tri uroda* (St Petersburg, 1907); translated by Samuel D.Cioran, in *The Silver Age of Russian Culture: an Anthology* (Ann Arbor, MI: Ardis, 1975).

33 The name of the famous literary salon hosted from 1905 by Lidiia Zinov'eva-Annibal and Viacheslav Ivanov, where the intellectual and artistic élite of Petersburg gathered on Wednesdays to discuss the latest literary, artistic, occult and philosophical trends. See also Davidson below, p. 161.

34 Ivanov, *Sobranie sochinenii*, II, p. 774.

35 A. Mirè, 'Dve iz mnogikh', in A. Mirè, *Zhizn'* (Nizhnii Novgorod). The italics are mine (M. M.).

36 A. Mirè, 'Belyi kliuch', *Novyi zhurnal dlia vsekh*, 23 (1910).

37 S. Gorodetskii, 'Ogon' za reshetkoi', *Zolotoe runo*, 3–4 (1908), p. 97.

CHAPTER 9

Lidiia *Zinov'eva-Annibal's* The Singing Ass: *a woman's view of men and Eros*

Pamela Davidson

Many of the most interesting women of the early twentieth century were and still are all too often perceived as the 'wives' or adjuncts of their famous literary spouses. One could cite several examples: Voloshin's wife, the artist Margarita Sabashnikova, Nadezhda Chulkova, or Liubov' Blok, the actress, are not so much remembered for their own achievements as for the roles they played in their husbands' lives. Lidiia Zinov'eva-Annibal (1866–1907) falls into a somewhat different category, in that she both was the wife of the well-known writer, Viacheslav Ivanov, and also nurtured literary ambitions of her own. In this sense the closest parallel to her example is the literary marriage of Gippius and Merezhkovskii. However, whereas the work of Gippius has received a fair amount of critical attention, that of Zinov'eva-Annibal is hardly ever considered in its own right outside the context of her husband's work.[1]

Zinov'eva-Annibal originally trained as an opera singer, but gradually joined Ivanov in moving towards literary pursuits some years after their first meeting in Italy in 1893. She wrote a number of strikingly original, if not always entirely successful works. Between 1904 and 1907, the year of her abrupt, premature death, she published two plays, *Kol'tsa* (*Rings*, 1904) and *Pevuchii osel* (*The Singing Ass*, 1907); a work of prose, *Tridtsat' tri uroda* (*Thirty-Three Abominations*, 1907) which achieved some notoriety for its treatment of lesbian love; and a collection of semi-autobiographical short stories, *Tragicheskii zverinets* (*The Tragic Menagerie*, 1907), as well as several essays of literary criticism and a few prose poems. A further collection of short

stories was published posthumously in 1918 under the title *Net!*
(*No!*), and an early novel, 'Plamenniki' ('Torches'), still remains
unpublished.

In seeking to establish her own voice as a writer, she had to
define her position with regard to a number of strong, pervasive
influences. One of these was endemic to the age, and derived
from the mystical view of women and of their role in love and
art which was widely held at the time. The second related to
her own specific circumstances: the fact that she was married to
Ivanov, a powerful personality and the chief ideologue of the
religious Symbolist movement which was instrumental in promoting this particular view of women.

This essay will argue that her literary development can best
be understood as a response to these pressures, gradually
shifting from initial acceptance to later strategies of ironic
subversion leading towards the discovery of her own independent voice. In order to demonstrate this, we shall first consider
the way in which the image and self-image of women and of
Zinov'eva-Annibal in particular were shaped by some of the
main ideological tenets of the period; then we shall look at her
writing in relation to these influences, focusing on one specific
late work of 1907, the satirical drama *The Singing Ass*, seen
within its biographical context.

THE SYMBOLIST IMAGE OF WOMEN AND ZINOV'EVA-
ANNIBAL'S RESPONSE

Mention must first be made of two principal ideas which were
in fashionable currency at the turn of the century, particularly
amongst Ivanov and his entourage. The following outline is
deliberately simplified and schematic in order to highlight those
features of Symbolist attitudes which – in distorted form – were
the target of Zinov'eva-Annibal's satire.

The first of these ideas was derived from Vladimir Solov'ev's
influential essay, 'Smysl liubvi' ('The Meaning of Love'), published in 1892–4 and regarded by the Symbolists as the most
important statement on love since Plato. This treatise advances
a justification of human, sexual love in terms of its mystical

dimension. Through sexual union with woman, man transcends his narrow individuality and comes closer to the mystical essence of the material world, referred to by Solov'ev as the 'eternal feminine' (*vechnaia zhenstvennost'*) and linked to the figure of Sophia or Wisdom.[2]

In theory, this view of love was applicable to either sex. Women could attain closer union with Sophia through union with men, just as men could aspire to the eternal feminine through contact with women. In practice, however, the ideology tended to place man as the subject and initiator of love, and woman as the object and medium of male aspirations, rather than the other way around. This was due to a variety of reasons. The language of the treatise, written by a man, implied a male perspective on love. Sophia, although not a woman, was closely related to the principle of the eternal feminine; she was often symbolically depicted as a female saint in the Russian iconographic tradition, and her cult was also associated with that of the Virgin Mary. Furthermore, most of Solov'ev's disciples who claimed to put his theory into practice were men, and to varying degrees tended to link their beloved woman with Sophia.

The second main idea, central to Ivanov's philosophy of love and aesthetics, derives from Nietzsche and relates to the cult of the Dionysian principle in life and art. Dionysus was a male God whose worship was best performed through sacrificial rites carried out by his female devotees, the Maenads. This practice tended to emphasize the ecstatic and sacrificial aspects of women as worshippers, an association which was reinforced by the tradition of female models of sacrificial love of Christ.

According to these two views of love, women were regarded either as passive objects to be loved as a means to a higher end, or as creatures capable of reaching or inducing Dionysiac transports of ecstasy – or sometimes even as both. In either case, their role in the experience of love was defined by men and in terms of male aspirations as a means to an end. This approach was also extended by the Symbolists into the realm of art and creativity. Following the Solov'evian model, the task of the artist is to 'bring Sophia down to earth' by creating beautiful forms in which to incarnate her essence.

The male-orientated view of love was carried over to art: the artist was usually regarded as male, and the woman as the inspiration or subject-matter of his art, leading him on to closer union with the eternal feminine. According to the Dionysian ideal, the sacrificial ecstatic character of woman can serve as a medium of inspiration, providing an essential preliminary stage of dark and sacred chaos through which man must pass to create Apollonian form.

This combination of ideas created a potentially problematic climate of opinion for women at the heart of the Symbolist circle who aspired to be creative figures in their own right. Critics at the time were well aware of these difficulties. In 1908 the anti-idealist Marxist critic Bazarov contributed an article to the anthology *Literaturnyi raspad (Literary Collapse)* in which he attacked Berdiaev's metaphysics of love and sex and its implications for women and creativity. Berdiaev's view of sex and love, like Ivanov's, was derived from Plato and Solov'ev. In the following extract Bazarov paraphrases and quotes from Berdiaev's definition of the distinction between the sexes:

Истинное назначение женской половины человеческой индивидуальности состоит вовсе не в том, чтобы что-нибудь творить, создавать, воплощать в жизнь. Творчество — удел мужчины. Женщине предопределено быть не творцом, а прекрасным творением, не художником, а «произведением искусства, примером творчества Божьего, силой, вдохновляющей творчество мужественное».

(The true calling of the female half of human individuality has nothing at all to do with creating, originating, embodying something in life. Creativity is the lot of man. Woman is predestined to be not a creator, but a beautiful creation, not an artist, but a 'work of art, an example of divine creativity, of the force which inspires male creativity.')

On this, Bazarov comments as follows:

Хотя г. Бердяев и старается уверить своих читательниц, что назначение их в качестве вдохновительниц творчества ничуть не ниже назначения мужчин-творцов, я не думаю, что метафизика его могла иметь значительный успех среди женских половин человечества. Даже дамы, всецело поглощенные «проблемой пола» — а таких в настоящее время

очень не мало — будут по всей вероятности несколько
шокированы той слишком уже примитивной ролью, которую
отводит им в жизни религиозно-эротический идеал вечной
женственности.[3]

(Although Mr Berdiaev does try to convince his female readers that
their calling as inspirers of creativity is no less worthy than the calling
of male creators, I do not think that his metaphysics can have had
much success among the female halves of humanity. Even those ladies
who are entirely engrossed in 'the sex question' – and in our time
there are more than a few such ladies – will in all probability be
somewhat shocked by the excessively primitive role which the religious erotic ideal of the eternal feminine assigns to them in life.)

This point should be borne in mind when considering the works
of women writers of the period, and, in particular, when we
come to look at Zinov'eva-Annibal's satirical play, published in
the same year as Berdiaev's essay.

Undeterred by critics like Bazarov, men of the Symbolist
persuasion went ahead and invested their womenfolk with these
ideals. Female responses varied from an enthusiastic embracing
of the ideal to bitter rejection. At one extreme is the case of
Anna Schmidt, a spinster from Nizhnii Novgorod, who presented herself to an astonished Vladimir Solov'ev and later to
his Symbolist disciples, announcing that she was none other
than Sophia incarnate. The role was played less willingly and
with increasing reluctance over the years by Blok's wife,
Liubov' Dmitrievna. In her youth she was inscribed into the
Solov'evian ideal, both in love and in art. Set up on a pedestal
as a passive object of worship, her image was linked to that of
the Beautiful Lady (*Prekrasnaia Dama*) and the eternal feminine,
and valued as a source of poetic inspiration. It was only many
years later that she was able to write frankly about the pain
which this caused her at the time. Her memoirs are a remarkable document, a woman's attempt to demythologize the
history of her relationship with her husband as reflected in his
poetry and canonized by subsequent generations of mainly
male critics.[4]

What of Zinov'eva-Annibal? What sort of an image did
Ivanov form of her, and how did she respond to this? She was

cast by her husband in both the Solov'evian and the Dionysiac moulds, as an ecstasy-inducing medium, leading towards spiritual renewal and poetic self-discovery.[5] Most of the poetry which Ivanov wrote about her both before and after her death presents her in this light.

Many memoirists and critics, whether consciously or not, echo this approach. For example, Pavel Florenskii, the religious philosopher, stressed the Solov'evian aspect. In his vast treatise of 1914, he interpreted one of Ivanov's poems on Lidiia as evidence of the poet's personal experience of Sophia.[6] Berdiaev tended to emphasize the Dionysian side of Ivanov's wife, presenting her in the light of his theory of women and creativity. In his description of Ivanov's salon, he portrays her as an elemental Dionysiac nature, an incarnation of 'talented femininity' (*darovitaia zhenstvennost'*), that is to say speaking little, presenting no grand ideas, and yet being the very soul of the company, inspiring *others* to be creative.[7] The male memoirists clearly could not imagine Zinov'eva-Annibal in any other way than in the light of the image which Ivanov had created for her. Modest Gofman's memoirs are typical in this respect; after describing the way Lidiia used to lie around at home in a loosely flapping Greek tunic, he adds a characteristic comment: «И я иначе ее — Диотиму Вячеслава Иванова, перед которой он благоговел, — и не представляю себе.»[8] ('And I simply cannot not imagine her – Viacheslav Ivanov's revered Diotima – in any other way.')

This was the 'canonical' image created by Ivanov and male memoirists. What of the women's view, however? Here it is interesting to note that the picture painted by female memoirists differs significantly. They do not take Ivanov's theoretical pronouncements as their starting-point, but rather their own personal observations of her as a woman and writer. Zinaida Gippius was in a good position to appreciate the pressures of being a woman writer married to a leading Symbolist. In a review article with the inauspicious title of 'The communal grave' ('Bratskaia mogila') written for *Vesy* in 1907, she condemned the current fashion for erotic or even pornographic literature, characterized in her opinion by a mania for 'laying bare' (*zagolenie*) and 'uncovering' (*obnazhenie*). She took the view that Zinov'eva-Annibal was a basically simple, 'innocent' woman who wrote her notorious but talentless work *Thirty-Three Abominations* in slavish imitation of this current fashion. According to Gippius, she was in fact capable of a much more talented, sincere type of writing as exemplified by the 'womanly warm' (*zhenski-teplye*) sections from her collection of autobiographical stories, *The Tragic Menagerie*.[9] The use of the word 'womanly' is significant here, implying that sincerity and innocence go with femaleness, and that the fashion for erotic decadence is more in line with the imitation of male models (the rest of the review was mainly devoted to works by Andreev and Kuz'min). As we shall see below, this point was also relevant to the portrayal of men and Eros in *The Singing Ass*.

Nadezhda Chulkova was a close friend of Zinov'eva-Annibal, and one of the few people to be present at her death-bed (summoned by a telegram from Ivanov). In her memoirs, she also takes the view that Zinov'eva-Annibal wrote decadent works in the spirit of Ivanov under his influence, but was herself a much simpler and deeper person, capable of a far better style of prose, as shown by *The Tragic Menagerie*.[10]

Another female memoirist, Ariadna Tyrkova-Vil'iams, follows a similar approach. In her opinion Zinov'eva-Annibal's love and blind adulation of her husband led her to imitate him in everything, even in her writing.

Она была им околдована ... Себя она беспощадно коверкала. Заразившись окружавшей ее поэтоманией, она тоже стала писательницей, хотя способностей к этому у нее было мало. Следуя общему духу Башни, отчасти и моде, она в писаньях своих старалась быть порочной ... Если ее муж жрец, она будет жрицей. Если он бог Дионис, она будет Менадой. На самом деле она была мать четырех детей и, вопреки всем своим стараньям, оставалась милой, добродушной русской барыней.[11]

(She was bewitched by him ... She distorted herself mercilessly. Infected by the poetomania which surrounded her, she also became a writer, despite the fact that she had little talent in this direction. Following the general spirit of the Tower,[12] and partly also fashion, she tried in her writings to be depraved ... If her husband was a priest, she would be a priestess. If he was the god Dionysus, she would be a Maenad. In actual fact she was the mother of four children and, despite all her efforts, remained a nice, kind-hearted Russian lady.)

One can therefore discern a certain clash of views: a canonical male view of Zinov'eva-Annibal as an erotic Diony-siac Maenad with touches of Sophia, and a directly opposed female view of her as a simple, 'nice Russian lady' whose susceptibility to her husband's influence had a generally detri-mental effect on her writing. The difficulty of reaching any final judgement on this matter lies in the inherent ambiguity of Zinov'eva-Annibal's own attitude to her husband's influence. At times she took on the role wholeheartedly, but at other times she adopted a more rebellious stance and seemed to wish to escape the image imposed upon her (this could, however, be construed as an extension of her role, as further evidence of her elemental Dionysiac nature).

This delicate balance between independence and influence was additionally complicated by the fact that Ivanov played a vital role in setting up his wife's literary career. He arranged through Briusov for her first works to be published by Skorpion and in the journal *Vesy*; later on, most of her main works were printed by his own publishing-house Ory. Their reviews and works regularly appeared side by side in the same journals and anthologies, reinforcing the impression of a close literary partnership. Even more pervasive than this type of technical assistance was the fact that Ivanov provided a theoretical frame-work within which his wife wrote and which he applied to her works. Her early play, *Rings*, incorporated into its text poems drawn from Ivanov's collection *Kormchie zvezdy* (*Pilot stars*), and was prefaced by an introduction by him entitled 'Novye maski' ('New Masks') which set the play firmly within his understanding of the theatre as a form of Dionysiac revival.[13]

Around 1906, however, this early type of dependence began to give way to a change of tone. This can be traced through the next two works which Zinov'eva-Annibal wrote – *Thirty-Three Abominations* and *The Tragic Menagerie*.[14] There is no space to dwell on these here, but it is worth making just one point: the choice of themes – lesbian love in the first work and autobiographical childhood reminiscences in the second – may well have been motivated by the desire to escape into a more autonomous female world, isolated from the sphere of male influence. In both works men are relegated to very much of a background role.[15]

The opening part of this essay has considered the Solov'evian and Dionysian ideas which shaped the Symbolist image of woman, their application to the case of Zinov'eva-Annibal and her ambiguous response to this image. It now remains to examine *The Singing Ass* in the light of these issues. This play is of particular interest when considering Zinov'eva-Annibal's development; it is one of her latest works, written hurriedly in the spring of 1907 and partly published in May, just a few months before her death. It returns to the drama form used three years earlier in *Rings*, but on this occasion the relationship to Ivanov's ideas is one of ironic satire and subversion rather than of supportive echo.

The play is not well known, and has received next to no critical attention.[16] And yet it is a fascinating document for at least two reasons. It provides an amusing and lively picture of the goings-on at the *bashnia* in 1906 (Ivanov's home and salon, known as the 'Tower', was in itself a microcosm of St Petersburg literary life). It is also remarkable as a rather daring piece of feminist rewriting of Shakespeare, adapted to satirize the Russian Symbolist canon.[17]

Biographical background

The polemic purpose of the play cannot be appreciated without a brief recapitulation of the main biographical events on which it is explicitly based.[18] The year 1906 at the *bashnia* was dominated by seemingly endless late-night discussions of the nature of Eros. Behind the public front of these debates, another more private and intimate one was also taking place within Ivanov's marriage. Both spouses were intensely preoccupied by the question of the ideal relationship between love (in its twin physical and spiritual dimensions) and marriage. According to the Solov'evian and Dionysian ideals discussed above, an individual's spiritual well-being depended on achieving self-transcendence through the love of another person. For a marriage to succeed, it was therefore essential for this mystic dimension to be preserved. And yet, as Vera, the heroine of *Thirty-Three Abominations* never tires of reiterating, the two greatest enemies of love are habit and fidelity. How, therefore, was one to maintain the ideal of Eros – love with a mystic dimension – in marriage?

A theoretical discussion of this question was provided by Ivanov in his essay of 1908, 'O dostoinstve zhenshchin' ('On the Dignity of Women').[19] Here he promotes the periodic separation of the sexes as a means of enabling each to fulfil its true spiritual potential by escaping the dulling routine of a closed marriage. This provided some sort of conceptual underpinning for experiments with homosexual love, and indeed, one finds that reflections on this theme become increasingly prevalent in Ivanov's diary of 1906, linked to a growing sense of loneliness and desire to prove that he is 'alive'. Around this time he was attending the meetings of the Hafiz circle, a mainly male group with homosexual overtones, described quite vividly by Kuz'min in his diary.[20] Parallel women-only meetings organized by Zinov'eva-Annibal were attended by Liubov' Blok, Nadezhda Chulkova and Margarita Sabashnikova.[21]

These issues were hotly debated by Ivanov and his wife in an atmosphere of some tension, and before the beginning of the summer of 1906 they reached a decision to introduce a third person into their marriage. This resolution led to two successive experiments. The first was with Sergei Gorodetskii and took place during Lidiia's absence in Switzerland from mid-June to mid-August 1906. Needful of a break, Lidiia left St Petersburg to spend the summer with her children, knowing before her departure that Ivanov was going to embark on an affair during her absence and apparently approving the choice of Gorodetskii for this purpose. Throughout her absence, Ivanov wrote her regular letters, chronicling the progression of his affair. He wanted to see Gorodetskii as a mask of Dionysus, but, ironically, complained that Gorodetskii did not want him to love him because he was a man. The affair received its literary embodiment in the poems of Ivanov's third collection, *Eros*, published in January 1907 and remarkable for their intensity of feeling. The second experiment involved Margarita Sabashnikova. She and her husband Voloshin had moved into the Tower in October 1906 and at some point from the end of 1906 and through the spring and summer of 1907, with Voloshin's consent and approval, she became enmeshed in an affair with Ivanov.[22]

Both experiments, while embarked on in good faith, evidently caused a certain amount of pain to Zinov'eva-Annibal and in the long term turned out to be failures.[23] *The Singing Ass* stands midway between the two episodes; it was written between March and April 1907[24] at a time when the second affair was in progress, and looks back from this standpoint at the first affair, quite possibly as a retrospective attempt to exorcize its memory through satirical parody.

The first act was printed in the anthology *Tsvetnik Or* (*The Flower-Bed of the Horae*), published by Ory in May 1907. Many of the works included in the anthology were by intimates of the *bashnia* and reflected events of the previous year. Zinov'eva-Annibal's contribution differed substantially from the other contributions through its satirical tone and humorous approach.[25] Three further acts of *The Singing Ass* survive in manuscript versions in Moscow and Rome. In 1993 the Moscow archive version of the three remaining acts was published in the journal *Teatr*.[26] The present discussion will, however, confine itself to the first act of the play which, through publication, acquired the status of a public statement and became a part of the literary culture of its time.

Relation to Shakespeare's original

Significantly, rather than composing an original work, Zinov'eva-Annibal chose to write a variation on an existing play, Shakespeare's *A Midsummer Night's Dream*. This is made plain on the opening page; the title *The Singing Ass* (a reference to Bottom with his ass's head) is followed by a subtitle «Вариации на тему из Шекспирова 'Сна в летнюю ночь'» ('Variations on a theme from Shakespeare's "A Midsummer Night's Dream"').

Shakespeare's play is a comedy of love, acted out between three different sets of characters (aristocrats, craftsmen and fairies), all of whom have one thing in common: the problems of love and its relationship to marriage. Theseus and Hippolyta are about to be wed and the planned marriage of Hermia and Lysander is under threat. The craftsmen face the problem of representing in art the tragedy of passionate yet unfulfilled love told in the story of Pyramus and Thisbe. Oberon and Titania are in a state of marital discord, and, through the juices of the magic flower procured by Puck, the fairy world represents the supernatural power which sets the forces of love in motion.

A Midsummer Night's Dream was almost certainly written as a wedding entertainment,[27] and its basic theme, the relationship of love to marriage, was, as we have seen, one which very much preoccupied Ivanov and Zinov'eva-Annibal at this time. In addition to the appeal of its subject-matter, the magical atmosphere of the play, together with its explicit theatricality (the play within a play prepared by the actors) made it an ideal source for the depiction of literary life at the *bashnia*, often described as a little theatre in itself.[28] The fact that Shakespeare's play is also well known in Russian under a title which carries a suggestive reference to Ivanov, *Son v Ivanovu noch'* or *Son v Ivanovskuiu noch'*, may also have been instrumental in this choice.[29]

Although *The Singing Ass* is a very free adaptation of Shakespeare (the title already indicates a substantial shift of emphasis in the play's centre of gravity), it relies on its original source and assumes a knowledge of it at all times. This device serves to add an extra implied layer of meaning to the work. The educated readership at which the play was aimed would inevitably focus its attention on the variations referred to in the subtitle: the areas in which the original plot was changed would stand out as the most significant.

What, then, were the principal changes made in the first act of the play? In terms of cuts, Zinov'eva-Annibal has made use of only part of Shakespeare's original and decreased the overall number of characters quite substantially. The actors have all been retained, but with new names and professions. Whereas Shakespeare's company have wonderfully homely names and down-to-earth occupations (Quince is a carpenter, Snug a joiner, Bottom a weaver, Flute a bellows-mender, Snout a tinker and Starveling a tailor), the members of Zinov'eva-Annibal's company carry fancy Greek-style names and have occupations to match.

Ligei is the chief poet of the group, and the author of the play to be performed. He corresponds to Bottom who effectively directs the play in Shakespeare's original, although Quince is its nominal director. Like Bottom he is turned into an ass; in Zinov'eva-Annibal's version this appears as an allegory of his true animal nature being revealed, reminding one of Shakespeare's description of Bottom as 'the shallowest thick-skin of that barren sort' (III. ii. 13). Other characters from the actors' group include Medon, described as a 'philosopher hymnosophist' (*filosof-gimnosofist*) and Baratron, a 'demagogue orator' (*demagog-orator*). The humbler professions are represented by Erast, a sculptor (*vaiatel'*), Leonid, a soldier, and Mormoliks, a 'master puncher' (*kulachnykh del master*). Unlike Shakespeare's engaging and unpretentious simpletons, Zinov'eva-Annibal's crew are represented as a loutish lot, who, despite their intellectual pretensions, spend most of their time conspiring to drag Hermia and Helena off into the bushes and arguing over who will have first go at them. From the last group, Oberon and Puck are present, but, Titania, significantly, is absent throughout the first act, having been advised by a female fairy acting on the instructions of Puck to visit her daughter Fida in order to escape her husband's bad temper.[30]

In terms of action, Zinov'eva-Annibal's play is much reduced in scope. The published first act of the play corresponds to the first scene of Shakespeare's Act II, and to the first and third scenes of his Act III, heavily adapted. There are several altera-tions, of which the major one is undoubtedly a mischievous piece of feminist rewriting of Shakespeare. Whereas in the original, Puck is the loyal servant of Oberon, always ready to do his bidding, in *The Singing Ass* he is fed up with his master's impossible requests and resolves to outwit him. This is made clear early on in the play when Puck refers to his master's 'insatiable spirit', feeding on illusions, and to the 'bitter poison' of his 'vain wishes'.[31] In Shakespeare's *Dream* Oberon asks Puck for the magic flower and applies its juices to Titania, causing her to fall in love with Bottom. In Zinov'eva-Annibal's version Puck denies having the flower and later sprinkles its juice on to his master's eyes while he is asleep, causing him, rather than Titania, to fall in love with the poet and playwright Ligei, dressed as an ass. In other words the magic forces governing love are no longer controlled by men, and Oberon falls victim to the plight originally assigned to Titania.

Relation to life

All these changes and variations were evidently designed to bring the plot of Shakespeare's original more closely in line with events as they were played out at the *bashnia* in 1906. These parallels were all perfectly obvious to initiated readers at the time. On 22 May 1907 Briusov wrote to Gippius drawing her attention to the play and commenting on its reflection of recent events: «А видели ли вы *Цветник Ор*? ... Г-жа Лидия Зиновьева и т.д. в драме, 'варьированной на тему из Шекспира' (так и сказано!), под прозрачными псевдонимами пересказывает недавние перипетии из жизни 'средового' кружка».[32] ('And have you seen *The Flower-Bed of the Horae*? ... Mme Lidiia Zinov'eva etc. in a drama based on "variations on a theme from Shakespeare" (so it says!), using transparent pseudonyms relates recent peripeteia from the life of the "Wednesday" circle.') It is clear from the language of the play that Oberon is Ivanov, and that the absent Titania visiting her daughter is Lidiia away in Switzerland for the summer, staying with her children. Oberon falling in love with a man disguised as an ass is a transparent allusion to the affair between Ivanov and Gorodetskii which took place during Lidiia's absence. His

effusive and rhetorical professions of love to Ligei, the ass,
parody Ivanov's attempts to invest love with mystical
significance; they are couched in language which directly
mimics the poetry addressed by Ivanov to Gorodetskii in *Eros*.[33]
The following extract describes Oberon's first glimpse of
Ligei in his new asinine guise. The characteristic Ivanovian
images of passion as a burning fire and of the beloved as a
divine creature or god are here addressed to an ass, traditionally regarded as an image of stupidity or lust; thus the language
of mystical eros is devalued and reduced to a meaningless
caricature.[34]

> ОБЕРОН
> Горит пожар любви без утоленья,
> Желаньем необъятным я палим . . .
>
>> *Лигей выбегает из-за кустов, на копытах,*
>> *с ослиным хвостом под короткой*
>> *туникой, в ослиной голове и с флейтой в*
>> *руках . . .*
>
> ОБЕРОН
>> *В экстатическом созерцании.*
> Прекрасный, кто ты? Дивного, как звать?
> Ты человек? иль бог? Мое желанье,
> Хватавшее весь мир, ты полонил.[35]

> (*OBERON*
> The fire of love burns unquenched,
> I am consumed by unbounded desire . . .
>
>> *Ligei runs out from behind the bushes on hooves,*
>> *with an ass's tail under a short tunic, wearing an*
>> *ass's head and with a flute in his hands . . .*
>
> *OBERON*
>> *In ecstatic contemplation*
> Beauty, who are you? Marvel, what is your name?
> Are you man? or god? My desire
> Which embraced the whole world has been captured by you.)

A later passage ridicules Ivanov's determined attempts to
overcome Gorodetskii's resistance to his advances, based on the
belief that Eros would lead them together to new mystical
heights.

ОБЕРОН
Цыпь, шут! Не зубоскалить зря! Молчи!
Эрот, приди, и сердце научи
Еще неведомым, сладчайшим ласкам.

ЛИГЕЙ
Ио! Ио! ... Нет!

ОБЕРОН
Что косных уст мне тайна изрекла?
Меня любя, ты станешь полубогом.
Два сильных выращу тебе крыла.[36]

(*OBERON*
Hush, fool! Don't bare your teeth for nothing! Be quiet!
Eros, come, and teach the heart
Caresses still unknown and sweetest.

LIGEI
Hee haw! Hee haw! ... No!

OBERON
What has the riddle of dull lips uttered to me?
By loving me you will become a demi-god.
I will grow you two strong wings.)

These general parallelisms are even extended down to small details. From Ivanov's letter to Lidiia in Switzerland we learn of his intense desire for her approval from afar of his affair with Gorodetskii: «Жажду твоей близости как жизнетворной силы ... Твое последнее слово необходимо мне, как творению слово Творца: 'хорошо', как утверждающая сила мирового Художника» ('I long for your closeness as a life-giving force ... I need your final word, just as the created world needs the word of the Creator: "good", as the sanctioning force of the universal Artist.')[37] This rather egocentric wish is parodied towards the end of the first act of *The Singing Ass*:

ОБЕРОН
Но где Титания?

ПОК
У милой Фиды.

ОБЕРОН
Хочу, чтобы любила нас царица.

ПОК
Желаешь вздора, — не слепа она.[38]

(*OBERON*
But where is Titania?

PUCK
At dear Fida's.

OBERON
I want the queen to love us.

PUCK
Your wish is foolish – she's not blind.)

Satirical intent

The Singing Ass was described by Zinov'eva-Annibal as a 'satirical drama'.[39] It is clear from the above comments that the main butt of her satire was the false pretensions surrounding the mystical cult of Eros, and in particular the tendency to substitute literary or metaphysical constructs for the reality of human experience. She questions the emphasis which the Solov'evian and Dionysian views of love placed on the attainment of self-transcendence through the ecstatic love of another being. The automatic assumption that physical love will always carry a mystical dimension is shown to be an illusion or pretence. Oberon's love for an ass demonstrates that the chosen object of love may be woefully at odds with the emotions invested in it, and the lecherous behaviour of the actors reveals the unvarnished cruder reality which underlay much of the philosophizing about mystical eros. Madness prevails, but in the form of human stupidity rather than of Dionysiac frenzy. The absence of Titania in the first act suggests that these features are characteristic of male rather than female attitudes to love.

How far did this satire in fact go? Mild satire can, after all, be an accepted part of any canon or tradition, only serving to bolster it within accepted limits. Blok's *Balaganchik* (*Puppet Booth*), first published and performed in 1906, not long before *The Singing Ass* was written, is a case in point; while outwardly satirizing the ideal of the Beautiful Lady (*Prekrasnaia Dama*), it in fact went some way towards reinforcing this tradition. The term 'mystical scepticism' which Chulkov used to characterize this work could perhaps also be applied to *The Singing Ass*, poised uncertainly between faith and irony.[40]

Ultimately, the problem of determining the limits of the satirical intent of *The Singing Ass* is bound up with the difficulty of evaluating the real extent of Zinov'eva-Annibal's emancipation from Ivanov's influence at this stage of her life. The biographical evidence presents a contradictory picture. On the one hand she appears to be playing a supportive role, echoing her husband's views. She begged him not to choose anyone other than Gorodetskii for his first experiment,[41] and later wrote to Mintslova with an ecstatic description of the mystical revelations brought about by his affair with Sabashnikova, duplicating his turn of phrase in every sentence.[42] And yet on the other hand, in a letter to Ivanov from Switzerland, she complained about his alienation from her and confessed to a feeling of envy;[43] when she returned to St Petersburg she evidently found Gorodetskii's presence distasteful. Later, during her husband's involvement with Sabashnikova, she confided to Chulkova that she found his coldness and insensitivity upsetting.[44] Voloshin's diary of the period reveals that she initially disliked Sabashnikova, and was quite desperate in March 1907 to get away from the mounting tension at home and to leave for Zagor'e.[45]

Zinov'eva-Annibal was clearly torn between conflicting needs and aspirations. This is confirmed by the revealing analysis of her character noted by Ivanov in his diary on 12 June 1906. After recording a recent day of emotional scenes between them, he comments on her insistence that she is not jealous but envious of him:

завидует же она всему и, больше всего, мужчине во мне, ее глубоко оскорбляет гордость мужской самовлюбленности, абстрактный нарцисизм моей чувственности ... Она горда и честолюбива, знает себя и все еще не нашла, величается и отчаивается. Замыкается и уединяется в мире своих идей и эмоций. Отчаянно борется за окончательную внутреннюю эмансипацию от моего идейного влияния. Сжигает то, чему поклонялась.[46]

> (she envies everything and most of all the man in me, she is deeply
> offended by the pride of male vanity, by the abstract narcissism of my
> sensuality ... She is proud and ambitious, knows herself and has still
> not found herself, glories in herself and despairs. Closes herself off
> and withdraws into the world of her own ideas and emotions.
> Struggles desperately for a final inner emancipation from my ideolo-
> gical influence. Burns what she used to worship.)

This characterization pinpoints a number of crucial details,
highly relevant to an understanding of *The Singing Ass*:
Zinov'eva-Annibal's struggle with her husband's influence, her
difficulty in resisting it without an alternative ideology, and her
resentment of aspects of his attitude to sensual love, regarded
by her as typically male. These features explain why she turned
to satire (the ideal genre for undermining without having to
present a positive alternative) and targeted it particularly at
male behaviour. Through her writing and the exercise of irony,
Zinov'eva-Annibal was evidently able to achieve a greater
measure of detachment from the circumstances of her life than
the contradictions of her temperament normally allowed her.
Although *The Singing Ass* was written for Ivanov's anthology and
with his active encouragement, it is nevertheless a surprisingly
sharp attack on various facets of life at the *bashnia*, and certainly
a far cry from the unquestioning parroting of *Rings*.

The extract cited above is also illuminating with regard to
the ultimate target of Zinov'eva-Annibal's satire in *The Singing
Ass*. She may well have written the play to provide an outlet for
the wounded feelings of bitterness and envy which the Gorodetskii episode had aroused, and which were revived by recent
developments in the affair with Sabashnikova at the time of
writing the play. On a deeper level, however, it is possible that
Zinov'eva-Annibal, who was a great advocate of passion and
physical beauty, was getting at something more fundamental –
at what she sensed was the essential *literariness* of Ivanov's
approach, the abstract nature of his feelings and his lack of real
passion or commitment. Her satirical portrayal of his feelings

for Gorodetskii may have been a vehicle for a more general
attack on his ability to relate to real people and emotions.

It is well known that the Symbolist ideal of incorporating
abstract ideas into life often resulted in the transformation of
life into a literary artefact, rather than in its desired intensification. In his memoirs Dobuzhinskii not only describes life at the
Tower as a 'theatre', but, more devastatingly, suggests that
Ivanov was a somewhat indifferent spectator of the performance.[47] Ivanov himself periodically expressed the fear that he
was 'dead',[48] and this accusation was also levelled at him in
various forms by others.[49] If this suggestion has any foundation,
it would go some way towards explaining Zinov'eva-Annibal's
choice of Shakespeare's play as a source, given its atmosphere
of magic and artificiality, and the extreme literariness of its
construction, comprising a play within a play. The device of
metatheatre traditionally suggests a view of the world as a stage
or of life as a dream. Shakespeare's humorous portrayal of the
craftsmen actors savaging Ovid's tragic tale of the noble love of
Pyramus and Thisbe was held up as a mirror image to the
actors of the *bashnia* acting out the Dionysiac mystery of Eros.

The satirical thrust of *The Singing Ass* is sharpened by the fact
that the play, while taking up many of the standard features of
Symbolist drama (written in verse form, replete with intertex-
tual, literary and mythological allusions, symbolic figures and
references to the cult of Eros), uses these to a very different end:
to point out the dangers of dogmatic assertions about the link
between this world and transcendent reality, thereby challenging the central claim of Ivanov's mysticism and aesthetics,
a realibus ad realiora. In this way Zinov'eva-Annibal has neatly
countered the claims which Ivanov had made for her play *Rings*
three years earlier, hailing it as a precursor of the new Symbolist drama of the future which would transform life through art.

Zinov'eva-Annibal's abrupt death in October 1907 makes it
impossible to know exactly what direction her writing would
have evolved in, had she lived longer. However, *The Singing Ass*
provides compelling evidence that she was beginning to detach
herself from her surroundings and to emancipate herself from
her husband's influence. It marks an important stage in the

development of her writing, considered as a response to some of the ideological pressures characteristic of the Symbolist ambience at the turn of the century.

NOTES

1 For a brief bibliography of works by Zinov'eva-Annibal and of early articles and reviews of her work, see K. D. Muratova, ed., *Istoriia russkoi literatury kontsa XIX–nachala XX veka: Bibliograficheskii ukazatel'* (Moscow and Leningrad, 1963), pp. 242–3. The fullest account of Zinov'eva-Annibal's literary achievement is by T. L. Nikol'skaia, 'Tvorcheskii put' L. D. Zinov'evoi-Annibal', in *Al. Blok i revoliutsiia 1905 goda: Blokovskii sbornik VIII* (Tartu, 1988), pp. 123–37. The first detailed encyclopaedia article on Zinov'eva-Annibal (by O. B. Kushlina) appeared in P. A. Nikolaev, ed., *Russkie pisateli 1800–1917. Biograficheskii slovar'*, II (Moscow, 1992), pp. 342–4. After work on this paper was completed, several English-language publications appeared with sections on Zinov'eva-Annibal. See Catriona Kelly, *A History of Russian Women's Writing 1820–1992* (Oxford: Clarendon Press, 1994), pp. 157–60; Charlotte Rosenthal's essay on women's prose in the Silver Age in Toby W. Clyman and Diana Greene, eds., *Women Writers in Russian Literature*, (Westport, CT: Greenwood Press, 1994), pp. 162–3; the entry on Zinov'eva-Annibal by Kristi A. Groberg in Marina Ledkovsky, Charlotte Rosenthal and Mary Zirin, eds., *Dictionary of Russian Women Writers*, (Westport, CT: Greenwood Press, 1994), pp. 752–4. In recent years a few of Zinov'eva-Annibal's stories have been reprinted in the Russian periodical press by Mariia Mikhailova.

2 For a fuller discussion of these ideas, see Pamela Davidson, *The Poetic Imagination of Vyacheslav Ivanov: a Russian Symbolist's Perception of Dante* (Cambridge: Cambridge University Press, 1989), pp. 53–62.

3 V. Bazarov, 'Lichnost' i liubov' v svete "novogo religioznogo soznaniia" ', in *Literaturnyi raspad: Kriticheskii sbornik* (St Petersburg, 1908), pp. 231–2. Bazarov is criticizing Berdiaev's essay 'Metafizika pola i liubvi', published in *Pereval*, 5 (1907), pp. 7–16, 6 (1907), pp. 24–36 and as a chapter in Berdiaev's second book, *Novoe russkoe soznanie i obshchestvennost'* (St Petersburg, 1907).

4 L. D. Blok, 'I byl' i nebylitsy o Bloke i o sebe', in V. Orlov, ed., *Aleksandr Blok v vospominaniiakh sovremennikov*, I (Moscow: Khudozhestvennaia literatura, 1980), pp. 134–87. Evidence of Zinov'eva-

Annibal's sense of 'earth-born' kinship with Liubov' Blok is provided by the inscription which she wrote for her on a copy of *Tragicheskii zverinets*: 'Sestre po Materi Demetre Liubovi Demetrievne ot Lidii Demetrievny' ('For Liubov' Demetrievna, my sister by Mother Demeter, from Lidiia Demetrievna'). See K. P. Lukirskaia, ed., *Biblioteka A. A. Bloka. Opisanie*, 1 (Leningrad: BAN, 1984), p. 285.

5 See Ivanov's description of Zinov'eva-Annibal's role in his life in his autobiographical letter of 1917, quoted in his *Sobranie sochinenii*, ed. by D. V. Ivanov and O. Deschartes (Brussels: Foyer Oriental Chrétien, 1971–87), II, p. 20.

6 Pavel Florenskii, *Stolp i utverzhdenie istiny: Opyt pravoslavnoi feoditsei v dvenadtsati pis'makh* (Moscow, 1914), pp. 570, 801. The poem under discussion is 'Pokrov' from the 'Povecherie' section of the first book of *Cor Ardens*.

7 Nikolai Berdiaev, '"Ivanovskie sredy"', in S. A. Vengerov, ed., *Russkaia literatura XX veka: 1890-1917*, III, Book 8 (Moscow, 1916), p. 98. Reprinted in Lidiia Ivanova, *Vospominaniia: Kniga ob ottse*, ed. by John Malmstad (Paris, 1990), pp. 320–1. A similar view was conveyed by Belyi: in his obituary of Zinov'eva-Annibal, *Pravda zhivaia*, 1 (26 October 1907), he describes her role as that of an inspirer in Ivanov's literary circle, rather than as that of a theoretician or writer in her own right.

8 Modest Gofman, 'Peterburgskie vospominaniia', *Novyi zhurnal*, 43 (1955), p. 123. Gofman was a regular visitor at the Tower in 1906 and 1907; he became the secretary of Ivanov's publishing-house Ory which printed Ivanov's *Eros*, Zinov'eva-Annibal's works *Tridtsat' tri uroda* and *Tragicheskii zverinets*, and the anthology *Tsvetnik Or* which included 'Pevuchii osel' amongst its contributions.

9 Anton Krainyi [Zinaida Gippius], 'Bratskaia mogila', *Vesy*, 7 (July 1907), p. 61.

10 N. G. Chulkova, '"Ty — pamiat' smolknuvshego slova ..."': Iz vospominanii o Georgii Chulkove', *Vestnik russkogo khristianskogo dvizheniia*, 157 (1989), p. 130.

11 Ariadna Tyrkova-Vil'iams, 'Teni minuvshego: Vokrug bashni', *Vozrozhdenie*, 41 (May 1955), pp. 80–1. See also the same author's earlier portrayal of Zinov'eva-Annibal at the *bashnia* as an actress, dressed up for a masquerade, whose natural character showed through this artificial mask as soon as she began to speak; Ariadna Tyrkova, 'Pamiati Al. Bloka: Beglye vstrechi', *Rul'*, 256 (1921), p. 4.

12 See p. 149, and p. 154, n. 33 above.

13 Ivanov's essay 'Novye maski' was published as the introduction to Lidiia Zinov'eva-Annibal, *Kol'tsa: Drama v 3-kh deistviiakh* (Moscow, 1904), pp. iii–xiv, and also separately in *Vesy*, 7 (1904), 1–10.

14 The first work was written in the summer of 1906 and published in March 1907. The second one was published in May 1907. See Nikol'skaia, 'Tvorcheskii put'', pp. 129–30.

15 Sergei Gorodetskii traces this tendency back to *Kol'tsa*; see his comment following his discussion of *Kol'tsa*, *Tridtsat' tri uroda* and *Tragicheskii zverinets* in his obituary article on Zinov'eva-Annibal, 'Ogon' za reshetkoi', *Zolotoe runo*, 3–4 (1908), p. 97: 'Vo vsekh trekh knigakh muzhskoe pochti neulovimo ... Stikhiia avtora — zhenskoe' ('In all three books the masculine is almost imperceptible ... The author's element is the feminine').

16 Surprisingly, contemporary reviewers of *Tsvetnik Or*, while discussing other contributions to the anthology, generally omitted all reference to 'Pevuchii osel'. Blok considered the anthology in his review of literary publications for 1907, but failed to mention the play (despite the fact that further on in the same essay he praised *Tragicheskii zverinets* extensively). See A. Blok, 'Literaturnye itogi 1907 goda', in Aleksandr Blok, *Sobranie sochinenii*, ed. by V. N. Orlov, v (Moscow and Leningrad, 1962), pp. 223, 226. Belyi's review of the anthology described it as a collection of aromatic flowers engulfed in nettles and also passed over Zinov'eva-Annibal's contribution in silence, presumably relegating it to the nettles; see Andrei Belyi, Review of *Tsvetnik Or: Koshnitsa pervaia*, *Vesy*, 6 (June 1907), 66–9. The obituaries of Zinov'eva-Annibal which appeared in 1907–8 only occasionally mentioned the play in passing; Sergei Gorodetskii's obituary article refers to 'Pevuchii osel' in a footnote ('Ogon' za reshetkoi', pp. 95–8). Sergei Auslender's obituary ('Iz Peterburga', *Zolotoe runo*, 10 (1907), pp. 76–7) likewise makes only passing mention of the play. A. Amfiteatrov was one of the few critics to comment on the play, albeit briefly, in the context of his general drive against writers he described as 'khudozhniki russkoi pornografii' ('artists of Russian pornography'). After some discussion of Kuz'min's 'Komediia o Evdokii iz Geliopolia', published in the same anthology, he condemned Zinov'eva-Annibal's play (without mentioning its author or title) as a travesty of Shakespeare, referring to it as 'sploshnoi lepet besstydnichaiushchei impotentsii' ('an unbroken babble of shameless impotence'); see A. Amfiteatrov, *Protiv techeniia* (St Petersburg, 1908) pp. 146–7.

Among more recent critics Temira Pachmuss includes a brief reference to Amfiteatrov's comment in her outline of Zinov'eva-

Annibal's work, but mistakenly attributes it to the wrong play, *Kol'tsa*; see Temira Pachmuss, ed. and trans., *Women Writers in Russian Modernism: An Anthology* (Urbana, ILL: University of Illinois Press, 1978), p. 195. Nikol'skaia devotes a paragraph to the play, contrasting its light humour with the more ponderous *Kol'tsa* ('Tvorcheskii put'', p. 147). Nikolai Bogomolov's recent publication of the full text of the play is prefaced by his introductory article, 'Na grani byta i bytiia', *Teatr*, 5 (May 1993), 159–91. Further comments on the play in relation to meetings of the Hafiz circle are also included in N. A. Bogomolov, 'Peterburgskie gafizity', in Viach. Vs. Ivanov, V. N. Toporov and T. V. Tsiv'ian, eds., *Serebrianyi vek v Rossii: Izbrannye stranitsy* (Moscow: Radiks, 1993), pp. 167–210.

17 Meierkhol'd praised the play both as a piece of drama, and for its revival of Shakespeare. In a letter of 17 July 1907 to the actress Vera Komissarzhevskaia he recommended it for staging, mentioning that although only the first act had been published, Zinov'eva-Annibal had read the full work to him; see V. E. Meierkhol'd, *Perepiska: 1896–1939* (Moscow, 1976), pp. 103, 373. In a later article dated 1911, 'Russkie dramaturgi (Opyt klassifikatsii, s prilozheniem skhemy razvitiia russkoi dramy)', he lists 'Pevuchii osel' among works of the 'New Theatre' (favourably contrasted with the theatre of the 'decadents') which attempt to revive aspects of an earlier genuinely theatrical epoch; Zinov'eva-Annibal's play is cited as a revival of the manner of Shakespearian comedies. See Vs. Meierkhol'd, *O teatre* (St Petersburg, 1913), p. 115.

18 For a fuller view of this period in Ivanov's life, see his diary for 1906 in V. Ivanov, *Sobranie sochinenii*, II, pp. 744–54, Ol'ga Deschartes's commentary on the diary (II, pp. 754–64) and her introduction to Ivanov's works (I, pp. 96–106). Aspects of the relationship between Ivanov's ideas and his life are also discussed in Davidson, *The Poetic Imagination of Vyacheslav Ivanov*, pp. 110–20.

19 First published in the newspaper *Slovo*, 650 (1908), p. 3; 652 (1908), p. 4; then in Viacheslav Ivanov, *Po zvezdam: Stat'i i aforizmy* (St Petersburg, 1909), pp. 377–92.

20 See the description of these evenings in Kuz'min's diary published with an introduction and notes in George Cheron, 'The diary of Mixail Kuzmin, 1905–1906', *Wiener Slawistischer Almanach*, 17 (1986), pp. 391–438.

21 See Chulkova, ' "Ty — pamiat' smolknuvshego slova ..." ', pp. 132–3.

22 A detailed account of the affair from March 1907 can be found in

Voloshin's diary entries for 1907; see M. Voloshin, 'Istoriia moei dushi', in Maksimilian Voloshin, *Avtobiograficheskaia proza. Dnevniki*, compiled and edited by Z. D. Davydov and V. P. Kupchenko (Moscow: Kniga, 1991), pp. 261–84.

23 Despite Zinov'eva-Annibal's official 'approval' of the two affairs, there is evidence which suggests that they involved her in a considerable amount of suffering. In her memoirs Lidiia Ivanova notes her mother's unusual sadness during her stay with her children in Switzerland at the time of Ivanov's affair with Gorodetskii: 'na etot raz chuvstvovalos' chto-to inoe, chto-to ochen' pechal'noe, kakoi-to solnechnyi zakat. Mama byla grustnaia, otiazhelevshaia ...' ('this time something different could be sensed, something very sad, some sort of sunset. Mother was sad, burdened ...'). (Ivanova, *Kniga ob ottse*, p. 23). Zinov'eva-Annibal recorded in her diary on 21 August 1906 her feeling of displeasure at Gorodetskii's presence when she returned from Switzerland and was met by Ivanov at the station (Ivanov, *Sobranie sochinenii*, II, p. 755). Chulkova also recalls Zinov'eva-Annibal's complaints and suffering at the time of Ivanov's affair with Sabashnikova (Chulkova, ' "Ty — pamiat' smolknuvshego slova ..." ', p. 134).

24 On 24 March 1907, Zinov'eva-Annibal wrote to her daughter Vera that the decision to publish the anthology had just been taken: 'I Viacheslav ochen' khochet, chtoby poshla moia satiricheskaia drama, kotoruiu teper' pishu v stikhakh i ne znaiu sekundy otdykha'('And Viacheslav very much wants to include my satirical drama which I am writing now in verse without a second's rest'). See *Literaturnoe nasledstvo*, 92, *Aleksandr Blok: Novye materialy i issledovaniia*, III (Moscow: Nauka, 1982), p. 274. This suggests that the first act of the play was written between March and April 1907, as *Tsvetnik Or* was printed in May 1907. For evidence that the rest of the play was completed by mid-July 1907 at the latest, see Meierkhol'd's letter, quoted above in note 17.

25 'Pevuchii osel', *Tsvetnik Or: Koshnitsa pervaia* (St Petersburg: Ory, 1907), pp. 121–69. On the opening pages of the anthology the play is listed as 'Komediia Lidii Zinov'evoi Annibal'. On p. 121 of the anthology a fuller description is given: L. Zinov'eva-Annibal, 'Pevuchii osel. Trilogii pervaia chast': "Altsvet". Variatsii na temu iz Shekspirova "Sna v letniuiu noch'"'.' Although the play is described here as a trilogy, four acts were in fact written. Other contributions included Maksimilian Voloshin, 'Kimmeriiskie sumerki', Sergei Gorodetskii, 'Alyi kitezh', M. Sabashnikova, 'Lesnaia svirel'', and Viacheslav Ivanov's cycle of seventeen sonnets, 'Zolotye zavesy', commemorating his affair with Sabash-

nikova. The arrangement of these items is significant; 'Pevuchii osel' immediately precedes the poems by Gorodetskii, and the last two items by Sabashnikova and Ivanov were published next to each other at the conclusion of the anthology.

26 A manuscript version of Acts II–IV is held in the Manuscripts Section of Rossiiskaia Gosudarstvennaia Biblioteka, fond 109, kart. 41, ed. khr.19–21. This version, together with the text of Act I printed in *Tsvetnik Or*, is published with an introduction by Nikolai Bogomolov in *Teatr*, 5 (May 1993), 159–91. Ivanov's archive in Rome contains the proofs of Act I, marked with corrections in the hand of Ivanov. It also contains the final typescript of Acts II, III and IV, with corrections (possibly in the hand of Zinov'eva-Annibal), representing the definitive text of the play (Box 8, containing 26, 20 and 14 large format sheets, corresponding respectively to Acts II–IV). This information has kindly been provided by Andrei Shishkin, who is currently preparing a full descriptive catalogue of Ivanov's Rome archive. For evidence of Ivanov's unrealized plan (1918–1921) to publish the entire play under the imprint of Alianskii's publishing-house Alkonost, see G. V. Obatnin, 'Viach. I. Ivanov. Predislovie k povesti L. D. Zinov'evoi-Annibal "Tridtsat' tri uroda"', *De Visu*, 9 (10) (1993), p. 25.

27 For a discussion of this point, see the introduction to the Arden edition of W. Shakespeare, *A Midsummer Night's Dream*, ed. by Harold F. Brooks (London: Methuen, 1979), pp. liii–lvii.

28 See, for example, M. Dobuzhinskii, 'Vstrechi s pisateliami i poetami', *Novyi zhurnal*, 11 (1945), p. 284. M. Dobuzhinskii designed symbolic covers for *Tsvetnik Or*, *Tridtsat' tri uroda*, *Tragicheskii zverinets* and Ivanov's *Po zvezdam*.

29 The title 'Son v Ivanovu noch'' derives from the link between Midsummer Day (24 June) and the feast of St John the Baptist ('Ivan Kupala'), known as 'Ivanov den'' and widely celebrated in traditional Russian folklore on 24 June. Midsummer Night was termed 'Ivanova noch'' or 'noch' na Ivana Kupalu' and was regarded as a time when lunacy was supposed to be prevalent. For a list of Russian translations and adaptations of *A Midsummer Night's Dream* (which omits reference to 'Pevuchii osel'), see *Shekspir: Bibliografiia russkikh perevodov i kriticheskoi literatury na russkom iazyke, 1748–1962* (Moscow, 1964), p. 615 and listed entries. Several versions of Shakespeare's play appeared during the 1880s, 1890s and 1900s; one of the most popular translations, by N. M. Satin (1851), was reissued in 1902 in the Brokgauz and Efron edition of Shakespeare with a preface by F. D. Batiushkov.

Apart from translations, there were also a few other free adaptations of Shakespeare's play which predated 'Pevuchii osel', including one by Kiukhel´beker and another by Vel´tman (1844).

30 For this purpose the play starts with an additional scene between Puck and a female fairy, 'Serdtse-rozy' (Rose-heart). In the remaining acts of the play, Titania returns and plays a prominent role.

31 *Tsvetnik Or*, pp. 126–7.

32 *Literaturnoe nasledstvo: Valerii Briusov*, 85 (Moscow, 1976), p. 696.

33 See, for example, the poems 'Vyzyvanie Vakkha', 'Zodchii', 'Khudozhnik' and 'Pozhar' in Ivanov, *Sobranie sochinenii*, II, pp. 368–9, 380–1. As well as echoing Ivanov's poetry in this way, 'Pevuchii osel' also incorporates two poems by him directly into its text (on pp. 123 and 131, ascribed to Ivanov in a note on p. 169).

34 In this context it is worth recalling that in Apuleius' *Golden Ass* (one of the sources for *A Midsummer Night's Dream*), the ass typifies lust, and Lucius' transformation into an ass is seen as a just punishment for his carnal sins and for meddling with the supernatural. See Lucius Apuleius, *The Transformations of Lucius, otherwise known as The Golden Ass*, translated by Robert Graves (London: Penguin, 1954) and the introductory comments by Robert Graves on pp. 12–13.

35 *Tsvetnik Or*, pp. 160–1.

36 *Ibid.*, pp. 164–5.

37 From letter of 11 August 1906, quoted in Ivanov, *Sobranie sochinenii*, II, p. 758.

38 *Tsvetnik Or*, p. 168. Other details parodied include the numerous references to the phases of the moon (a recurrent feature of Shakespeare's play and of Ivanov's own references to his affair with Gorodetskii) and the description of Oberon dozing all day in his bower (an allusion to Ivanov, who used to sleep for most of the morning in the *bashnia*).

39 See note 24 above.

40 'Balaganchik' was published in April 1906, in the first issue of the miscellany *Fakely*, which also carried contributions by Zinov´eva-Annibal and Ivanov. The opening performance, produced by Meierkhol´d, was held on 30 December 1906. Chulkov's comments on the play were published a few days earlier. See the notes on the play in Blok, *Sobranie sochinenii*, IV (Moscow and Leningrad, 1961), pp. 567–8. A similar strain of 'mystical scepticism' was reflected in Blok's projected play 'Dionis Giperboreiskii', drafted on 29 December 1906 on the eve of the premiere

of 'Balaganchik', evidently written with Ivanov in mind and intended as a humorous pastiche of the concept of mystical ascent. See Aleksandr Blok, *Zapisnye knizhki 1901–1920*, ed. by V. N. Orlov (Moscow, 1965), pp. 87–91. Further evidence of the close link between Blok and Zinov'eva-Annibal is provided by the story 'Golova Meduzy' in which Zinov'eva-Annibal portrays Blok as Neznakomov, drawing on his poem of 1906, 'Neznakomka'. For an analysis see A. V. Lavrov, 'Marginalii k Blokovskim tekstam', in Iu. K. Gerasimov, N. Iu. Griakalova and A. V. Lavrov, eds., *Aleksandr Blok. Issledovaniia i materialy* (Leningrad: Nauka, 1991), pp. 182–8. 'Golova Meduzy' can be compared to 'Pevuchii osel' in its self-conscious use of literary sources to achieve a stylized portrait of contemporary figures in the artistic world.

41 See the extract from Zinov'eva-Annibal's letter to Ivanov, dated 4 August 1906, quoted in N. A. Bogomolov, 'Epizod v peter-burgskoi kul'turnoi zhizni 1906–1907 gg.', in *Al. Blok i revoliutsiia 1905 goda: Blokovskii sbornik VIII* (Tartu: Tartuskii gosudarstvennyi universitet, 1988), p. 100. The same article includes a note on 'Pevuchii osel' on p. 110.

42 'Bolee istinnogo i bolee nastoiashchego v dukhe braka *troistvennogo* ia ne mogu sebe predstavit', potomu chto poslednii nash svet i posledniaia nasha volia — tozhdestvenny i ediny' ('I cannot imagine a *triple* marriage more true or genuine in spirit because our last light and our last wish are identical and one'). See letter of 2 March 1907, quoted in N. A. Bogomolov, ' "My — dva grozoi zazhzhennye stvola": Erotika v russkoi poezii — ot simvolistov do oberiutov', *Literaturnoe obozrenie*, 11 (1991), p. 60.

43 Noted by Ivanov in his diary, Ivanov, *Sobranie sochinenii*, ii, p. 753.

44 For sources, see note 23 above.

45 The last entry before the diary is resumed in September 1907 is dated 11 March 1907 and concludes with the following words: ' "Ia za kazhdyi novyi den' boius" ', — govorit Lidiia. U vsekh takoe zhe chuvstvo. Vse stremiatsia raz"ekhat'sia, otdokhnut', uspokoit'sia ot etoi nechelovecheskoi napriazhennoi atmosfery poslednikh dnei' (' "I'm fearful of each new day" ', says Lidiia. Everyone has just the same feeling. Everyone wants to get away from each other, to have a rest, to calm down from the inhuman tense atmosphere of these last days'). See Voloshin, *Avtobiografi-cheskaia proza*, p. 266. Lidiia's initial dislike of Sabashnikova is noted in the first entry for 1907, dated 1 March (p. 261).

46 Ivanov, *Sobranie sochinenii*, ii, pp. 747–8.

47 'K etomu "teatru" my ... otnosilis' ochen' ne vser'ez, no s

liubopytstvom. Ochevidno ko vsemu po-filosofski ravnodushno otnosilsia i sam khoziain' ('We regarded this "theatre" ... with very little seriousness but with curiosity. Evidently the host himself regarded everything with philosophical indifference'). See Dobuzhinskii, 'Vstrechi s pisateliami i poetami', p. 284.

48 'A vprochem — ne mertv li ia sam?' ('But come to think of it, am I not dead myself?'). Diary entry of 1 June 1906, Ivanov, *Sobranie sochinenii*, II, p. 744.

49 Berdiaev, for example, accused him of living his life at one remove, in a sphere of purely 'philological existence' (*filologicheskoe bytie*); Nikolai Berdiaev, 'Ocharovaniia otrazhennykh kul'tur', *Birzhevye vedomosti*, 15833 (30 September 1915), pp. 2–3.

CHAPTER 10

Anastasiia Verbitskaia reconsidered

Rosalind Marsh

At first sight, Anastasiia Verbitskaia (1861–1928) seems an unlikely candidate for rehabilitation. If she is mentioned at all in histories of Russian literature,[1] she usually receives a critical reference as an exponent of 'women's prose' (zhenskaia proza), which has been characterized by both contemporary and later critics, in Russia and the West, as a literature of trivial or sensational themes, obsessed by sentiment and romance, and couched in a weak or hysterical style.[2] In recent years, historians of Russian women's fiction have also generally accepted this view, arguing, for example, that 'The prose of Anastasiia Verbitskaia at the turn of the century made the term "women's prose" derogatory.'[3] Why is it worth revisiting such a seemingly unpromising subject?

There are several good reasons for taking a fresh look at Verbitskaia's work. The first, general point is that a reassessment of Verbitskaia will contribute to the valuable feminist project of rediscovering and reinterpreting the lives and work of neglected Russian women writers, which is still in its infancy in comparison with the reclamation of English and American women's fiction initiated during the early stages of the second-wave feminist movement in the 1960s and 1970s.[4] Like feminist writings in English from the 1880s onwards, Verbitskaia's novels played a progressive role in the Russian women's movement, even if they were not 'great art';[5] and her activities as writer and publisher rendered her an important role model for Russian women and an influential popularizer of contemporary feminist ideas. In the second place, it is necessary to put the record straight, because Verbitskaia has been partially misrepresented by other critics,[6] who have, with only a few recent exceptions,[7] simply accepted the opinions of the hostile critics of her own day, possibly without re-reading all her works, which only began to be reprinted in Russia in 1993, and are, admittedly, difficult to obtain. Thirdly, whatever view one takes of her writing, Verbitskaia deserves attention because she was such a phenomenon in her day. Her works were bestsellers, more sought-after in public lending libraries than those of Tolstoi;[8] and she herself can be seen as the Catherine Cookson, Danielle Steel or Jackie Collins of her day (or perhaps a more appropriate comparison might be with popular feminist novelists such as Marilyn French or Erica Jong).[9] It has been argued by social historians of Russia and other countries that a study of 'popular culture' can often be more revealing about contemporary social conditions, or social aspirations, than 'high culture'.[10] I hope to show that Verbitskaia's works, particularly her early novels, afford interesting insights into the lives and problems of Russian women at the beginning of the twentieth century, and could serve as a useful source for social historians. Finally, a study of Verbitskaia's work provides a fascinating case study, since it raises many historical, literary and theoretical questions of interest to historians and feminist critics today.

Women writers in many cultures have been disadvantaged, persecuted and marginalized,[11] and Anastasiia Verbitskaia is no exception.[12] She was the daughter of a prosperous colonel, a hereditary nobleman, and of a mother from a well-known family of actors, but her father subsequently lost most of his money and died when she was in her early teens. She rebelled against the conservative system of education at her Moscow girls' boarding school, and against her mother, who forbade her to go on the stage.[13] When she left school she found the life on her mother's country estate stifling, and left home in order to live an independent life. Her view of men cannot have been improved by losing a suitor on account of her sudden poverty, and by the humiliation she suffered when interviewed for a governess's post by ill-educated, insensitive prospective employers. She tried her hand at a number of teaching jobs, but failed to earn enough money to achieve her aims of becoming a singer (she had to abandon her studies in singing at the Moscow Conservatoire because of lack of means) or, alternatively, of studying medicine in Zurich. She experienced at first hand the conflict between love and work, since she was obliged by law to leave her job as a music teacher on her marriage to the engineer A. V. Verbitskii, with whom she had three sons. After a struggle to make her way in the literary world, she embarked on a full-time literary career in 1894. Her first works were well received, but her later bestsellers were lambasted for their artistic faults, over-simplified treatment of social problems and allegedly pornographic content.[14]

Verbitskaia suffered throughout her life for her unconventional opinions. Before the revolutions of 1917, as a feminist and an avowed Social Democrat (she allowed her flat to be used by Bolshevik activists during the 1905 Revolution), she experienced political hostility from the tsarist government[15] and patriarchal hostility from male critics. After the Revolution she fell into poverty and disgrace: she was doubly suspect both because of her upper-class background, and because she was stigmatized as a vulgar 'decadent', an advocate of sexual libertinism, the discredited ideas of so-called 'bourgeois feminism' and reactionary, anti-Semitic tendencies. At the end of July 1919, after complaints about her in the Soviet of Workers' Deputies, all her works were banned, and even condemned to be burnt. One work subjected to censorship was the third part of her novel *Igo liubvi* (*The Yoke of Love*, 1914–16), which was completed in 1920, but has never been published in Russia.[16] Although, after Verbitskaia appealed against her treatment, a commission eventually established that her works contained no harmful elements, and even called for the publication of new editions of individual novels, these recommendations were never put into practice, as the individual responsible for the 'Verbitskaia case' died shortly after the end of the proceedings. By 1924 Verbitskaia's situation had become critical, as her name was put on the Index of banned authors, and she was reduced to writing children's books under a pseudonym.[17] Only in 1926, shortly before her death, did the prominent Bolsheviks Lunacharskii,

Ol'minskii and Mitskevich make some attempt to 'rehabilitate' her, arguing that, although she was a writer of limited talents, her works had nevertheless played a progressive role in pre-revolutionary Russia.[18] However, all efforts to intervene on her behalf in the 1920s proved unsuccessful; subsequently Stalin's rise to supreme power and the insistence of successive Soviet leaders that the 'woman question' had been solved made her posthumous rehabilitation unthinkable throughout most of the Soviet period.[19]

Verbitskaia's work has received a hostile reception by critics, predominantly male, both in her own day, and in more recent times. The most damning criticism published in her lifetime was a witty article of 1910 by the well-known critic Kornei Chukovskii,[20] who at that time was a supporter of the liberal Kadet (Constitutional Democratic) party and hence could not be expected to be sympathetic to her revolutionary leanings.[21] Chukovskii focuses entirely on Verbitskaia's immensely popular blockbuster *Kliuchi schast'ia* (*The Keys to Happiness*, 1908–13),[22] discrediting the novel on aesthetic grounds by pointing to the number of times the author uses the words: 'she flushes', 'her eyes are sparkling', 'incrustation', 'abyss' and 'blood'. His criticism, which picks an easy target and says nothing about Verbitskaia's better earlier works, or about the feminist themes in *The Keys to Happiness*, has been more influential than Verbitskaia's writing itself, and bears considerable responsibility for the scorn with which the term 'women's prose' (*zhenskaia proza*) has subsequently been regarded in Russia. Arguments by western feminist critics that 'women's literature' should be interpreted as a popular artefact which does not automatically deserve a critical reception, since it may contain progressive elements or be of therapeutic value to women readers, would still fall on deaf ears in Russia.[23]

In recent years, a derogatory view of Verbitskaia has been perpetuated by historians of Russian popular culture and women's writing, who have tended to focus almost exclusively on Verbitskaia's enormously popular later works, *Dukh vremeni* (*The Spirit of the Time*, 1907),[24] *The Yoke of Love* and, especially, *The Keys to Happiness*,[25] emphasizing her infatuation with

Nietzsche and other fashionable thinkers of her day, her predilection for sexual adventures, luxurious interiors and exotic locations known only through guidebooks, as well as her dubious fascination with right-wing aristocrats and Jewish millionaires, and her superficial depiction of political events purely as a sensational backdrop to a melodramatic plot. However, even these works have evoked some sympathy from feminist critics, who point out that Verbitskaia's heroines are actresses and ballerinas making their own way in the world, and that she was only advocating a sexual freedom for women which men had enjoyed for centuries.[26]

Verbitskaia's bestselling later novels deserve a more detailed re-evaluation; but this essay will be primarily concerned with some of her more interesting early works published in the period 1887–1903, before her fiction began to display elements of decadence and Nietzschean pretentiousness. These early novels possess considerable interest as sharp-eyed observations of the social scene, and as honest, progressive investigations of the problems and preoccupations of Russian women at the end of the nineteenth century. At the time of their first publication they were acknowledged and praised as such by Social Democratic critics, including Gor'kii.[27] Subsequently Verbitskaia's early novels were generally ignored, since they were overshadowed by the *succès de scandale* of her phenomenally popular later works. Verbitskaia's early fiction fits into the tradition established by other women writers of her day,[28] but it is more tendentious than some other contemporary feminist fiction, providing a clear, frank treatment of conflicts between men and women at the turn of the century and between women's dreams and the reality of their lives. Her work provoked interesting literary and social discussions, although very few contemporary critics recognized the significance of Verbitskaia's themes for Russian women of her day, and indeed for women in general. One exception was a shrewd female critic, Elena Koltonovskaia, who pointed out that Verbitskaia is interested in the internal aspect of women's emancipation: 'Has woman really found within herself the strength and means of realizing her cherished ideal: how is she, while remaining a woman, without distorting her nature, to extend the confines of her existence and to participate in general human life on an equal footing with men?' She also correctly indicated the essence of the conflict presented in many of Verbitskaia's novels, while not necessarily agreeing with the solutions she offers: 'In this female capacity to love, becoming full of another person, partially lies the key to the difficult, sometimes tragic fate of the new intellectual woman. Mrs Verbitskaia's usual recipe: "Accord love a secondary place in life" cannot prove suitable for everyone.'[29]

The typical heroines of Verbitskaia's early works are writers, teachers and women on medical courses who are attempting to make independent lives for themselves, and to face the real problems inherent both in their gender and their society. These literary images reflect aspects of Verbitskaia's own biography and the social reality of the time, for, as in Victorian England, the first professional activities of Russian women 'were either based in the home or extensions of the traditional feminine role as teacher, helper or mother of mankind'.[30] Such heroines were acceptable to the Social Democratic critics of Verbitskaia's day, who regarded them as 'socially useful'. By contrast, her later heroines, who tended to be actresses, musicians or ballerinas seeking new forms of female fulfilment which became fashionable in the Silver Age – through the pursuit of art and beauty, or through sexual satisfaction[31] – were stigmatized by some radical critics as 'parasites'.[32]

Verbitskaia's early work fits firmly into the 'feminist' phase of literature which spread throughout Europe at the end of the nineteenth century, under the influence of Ibsen's *The Doll's House* (1879), with which she was very familiar.[33] Verbitskaia, along with other feminist writers of the late nineteenth century, began to confront masculine society and literature, which still perceived women in terms of the age-old stereotypes of Virgin, Madonna, Whore and Witch. They challenged the many restrictions on female self-expression, denounced the gospel of self-sacrifice, attacked patriarchal religion, and exposed different forms of female oppression, although their anger with society and need for self-affirmation sometimes led them from realism into over-simplification, emotionalism and fantasy.

Verbitskaia's concerns are by no means unique: she follows the tradition of Russian feminist writing initiated by Nikolai Chernyshevskii and women writers of the previous generation, such as 'Marko Vovchok' (Mariia Markovich), Ol'ga Shapir and Nadezhda Khvoshchinskaia. Like other Russian feminists, she emphasizes the value of employment and education as means of changing women's lives, and contributes to the debate about women's sexual and economic independence being conducted by other writers of her day, such as Evdokiia Nagrodskaia, Anastasiia Krandievskaia and Tat'iana Shchepkina-Kupernik. The distinctiveness of Verbitskaia's novels resides in her acute psychological analysis of her heroines, and her ability to put across feminist ideas in clear, simple, highly readable form.

One of Verbitskaia's most characteristic works is her early novel *Osvobodilas'! She was Liberated!* (1898),[34] which depicts Liza Mel'gunova, a woman who stands out in the conventional bourgeois society which surrounds her. Despite the comfortable circumstances she enjoys as the wife of a professor, she chooses to give lessons in order to be economically self-sufficient, since she is estranged from her husband who has two children by another woman, and does not wish to be dependent on him in any way. However, the radical student Klimenko, an outstanding personality in Liza's circle, reproaches her for taking bread out of the mouths of poor girls who need to give lessons simply to survive. Inspired by Klimenko's views, Liza gives up her lessons to a poor teacher whose need is greater than her own, but is then obliged to try to make a living through translating English articles for her husband. Torn between her husband and Klimenko, who becomes her lover, Liza wages a desperate struggle to retain her own human dignity; but eventually her conservative husband denounces Klimenko to the police, and he is driven into exile. After surrendering to her husband again in a moment of weakness, Liza finally frees herself through suicide. One contemporary Social Democratic critic regarded Liza's struggle as a petty domestic one, and her suicide as a symbol of 'the total defeat of woman's social interests in the face of personal interests';[35] while another regarded as most significant 'the economic question – the significance of competition for women's work in the lowering of payment for intellectual work'.[36] Verbitskaia's intention, however, is to depict a strong woman fighting for self-determination, who is ultimately crushed by the constraints of her society and the contradictions of her own personality. The figure of Mel′gunova resembles the image of the 'new woman' portrayed in an article of 1911 by the socialist feminist Aleksandra Kollontai, who referred to 'contemporary heroines' who 'have to fight a battle on two fronts, with the outside world and with the inclination of their forebears which is deep within them'.[37] The fact that Liza commits suicide, like so many conventional heroines of nine-teenth-century literature, is not merely a literary stereotype, but also reflects the very real difficulties facing women who aspired to economic independence in pre-revolutionary Russia,[38] and the eternal feminine conflict between love and work. Verbits-kaia would have been very aware of this problem, as her own elder sister Sasha (Aleksandra Sornevaia), who possessed con-siderable literary talent, winning praise from Mikhailovskii and Gleb Uspenskii, repeatedly threatened suicide, and actually killed herself in 1891.[39] Verbitskaia partially attributes her sister's premature death, and certainly the end of her literary career, to the 'cliquishness' of the literary journals, which awarded Sasha no royalties for her works published under the pseudonym 'Alekseeva', and returned her manuscripts because of a few minor mistakes.[40]

Another of Verbitskaia's interesting early novels is *Istoriia odnoi zhizni* (*History of a Life*, 1903),[41] which depicts a strong woman, Ol′ga Devich, whose cherished aim of attending the higher medical courses in St Petersburg is defeated by the feminine side of her nature. Devich retains her strength and independence through her lonely childhood and difficult youth spent with a mother she does not love; eventually she breaks with her mother (as Verbitskaia herself was obliged to in order to follow her vocation), works as a music teacher in order to save money to pursue her dream, and volunteers as a nurse in the Russo-Turkish war – but none of this work brings her total satisfaction. She is not even deflected from her purpose by the warnings of the medical student Semenova, who tells her that Russian women doctors sometimes die of hunger. However, she falters at her first real encounter with temptation, falling deeply in love with the charming, but worthless Charnetskii. Verbitskaia's portrait of Charnetskii (as of many of her heroes) is the weakest point in the novel: he seems to possess none of the qualities which would attract a complex woman like Ol'ga, although Verbitskaia is more convincing when she implies that such a woman could not love in any other way than passionately and whole-heartedly. Verbitskaia provides a realistic analysis of the failure of their marriage, and of Ol'ga's struggle to bring up her child alone in dire poverty. This novel is less didactic than many of her others; Verbitskaia provides no easy answers to the conflict between Ol'ga's passion and her ambition. Devich's struggle also ends in death, but she is allowed a more heroic death than Mel'gunova: she sacrifices herself in the revolutionary movement. However, as the critic Koltonovskaia wryly pointed out, this denouement in no way represents 'a solution to the woman question'. The critic suggested that Verbitskaia's novel posed an unanswerable question: 'How far this distinctive characteristic of the female organism [passionate love] will change in the future, in more favourable circumstances, is another question, but for the time being it frequently makes itself felt, and becomes an obstacle to the realization of the boldest plans.'[42]

The lone woman's struggle with recalcitrant Russian reality is also depicted in *Pervye lastochki* (*First Swallows*, 1900), another of Verbitskaia's works which evoked considerable praise and some controversy.[43] The heroine, Valentina Lebedeva, is a hard worker who labours alongside her doctor husband in a cholera epidemic,[44] then, after his death, is left alone with three children to bring up. She has an affair with the aristocrat Chagin, thinking that he shares her values, but he is used to 'clean, elegant women', whereas she pays no attention to her appearance. Lebedeva is a proud, fanatical woman who places social interests above personal ones, rejecting love and personal happiness as a luxury. Convinced that 'love is a cunning trap, an eternal illusion which makes woman weep and perish', she eventually overcomes her love for Chagin and goes off to Moscow to work as a journalist and translator. The best part of the novel, no doubt based on Verbitskaia's personal experience of the ten years of 'humiliations and searchings' and loss of self-confidence which accompanied her efforts to make her way in the Russian literary world,[45] depicts Lebedeva's arduous experiences in a succession of editorial offices, as she tries to make ends meet by securing the publication of her articles. The failure of the journal which has provided work for her leads to her final collapse. The most unconvincing aspect of the novel is her proud refusal to accept any money from Chagin, which dooms her children to sickness and herself to an untimely death from consumption. Despite this somewhat melodramatic conclusion, Lebedeva's experience nevertheless reflected the plight of many working women in Russia at the turn of the century, whose work was poorly paid and undervalued.[46] A contemporary critic perceived her as an example of the new type of woman who longed for freedom and sought that freedom in work. Lebedeva, who passes on her experience to a young governess, could indeed be seen as a 'swallow', if not the first, who was preparing the ground for other working women in Russia.

A new departure for Verbitskaia was the portrayal of an anti-heroine, the eponymous *Vavochka* (1898), who is presented as typical of her generation of young ladies.[47] Verbitskaia satirizes the egoistic, parasitical Vavochka, whose only interest in life is to find a rich man to marry; and implies that patriarchal society, based on the exclusive power of one sex, is responsible for creating slave women who are prepared to trade their freedom for a rich life. In this novel, as in many others, Verbitskaia argues that the education of women is vitally important, since women are responsible for the upringing of the new generation.

Another work that did not elicit universal admiration was *Ch'ia vina? (Whose Fault Is It?*, 1900),[48] which provides a new permutation on Verbitskaia's favourite theme of female independence, while also raising the perennial question of divorce and its effect on children. Verbitskaia depicts the upper-class Vera, who is initially impressed by the strong, original character of the student Stanskii. It is only after marrying him that she learns that Stanskii's originality lies in an unwavering adherence to clichés and dogmas. He is in favour of female emancipation if it takes the acceptable form of attending medical courses, but has no sympathy for Vera's desire to develop her talent as a singer. After the birth of her daughter Mania, Vera leaves home to go on the stage, only returning to Russia years later as a well-known opera singer, the 'famous Lola'. Stanskii, who has remarried, tries to prevent his earnest young daughter from seeing Lola, but she goes to the theatre by chance, and is stage-struck. Although Stanskii is still attracted to his former wife, he cannot go back to her because he disapproves of her life as a 'loose woman', but nevertheless is on the point of agreeing to give up his daughter to her. In the mean time, the impressionable Mania accidentally finds out that Lola is her mother, and dies of shock. Despite its melodramatic denouement, this novel does raise an interesting moral problem about who is to blame for Mania's death. A male critic usually sympathetic to Verbitskaia claimed that Vera is guilty, because her aspiration to be a singer is not 'socially useful';[49] but an afterword which Verbitskaia herself added to a new edition of the novel published in 1911 makes it clear that her sympathies lay with Vera,[50] perhaps because her own youthful dramatic talents had been frustrated; later her reading of Nietzsche convinced her that nothing, not even her children's welfare, should fetter a woman's freedom and creativity. Even today, this viewpoint might appear rather extreme.

Another work which provoked considerable criticism was *Po-novomu* (*In a New Way*, 1902),[51] which was regarded by some contemporary critics as overly abstract and schematic, an attempt to depict family life as it should be, rather than as it really is.[52] The heroine Mar'ia Vasil'evna has attended the Bestuzhev higher education courses, and has dedicated her whole life to her teaching career, shunning marriage and personal happiness. Nevertheless, she eventually falls in love

and agrees to marry a fellow teacher, the gentle Mikhail
Sobolev, on condition that he accepts her plan for a new type of
marriage. This is a theme reminiscent of Chernyshevskii's
influential novel *Chto delat'?* (*What is to be Done?*, 1863),[53] but the
main difference from Chernyshevskii's novel is that Mar'ia
chooses this path for herself, rather than having it dictated to
her by a man. Her main requirements are that she and her
husband should each have their own room, which the other
may not enter without permission, and should be able to live
their own personal life. Verbitskaia demonstrates that
Mar'ia's programme is untenable, partly because her husband
finds it intolerable, but primarily because her dream comes
into conflict with Russian reality. When she becomes
pregnant she is legally obliged to leave her teaching job, thus
forcing the couple into poverty and a more conventional
marriage, which culminates in her husband's infidelity and
desertion. Verbitskaia's novel does contain certain excesses: for
example, Mar'ia's status as a 'new woman' is emphasized by
her refusal to wear corsets and even to look at herself in a
mirror, and her insistence on getting married in an ordinary
blouse and woollen skirt. These episodes provoked considerable
mirth and hostility from contemporary critics,[54] much as the
propensity of second-wave feminists to burn their bras and
wear boiler-suits aroused the ire and scorn of male critics in the
1960s and 1970s, deflecting their attention from more important
issues. However, to a modern audience, Mar'ia's demand for a
room and life of her own does not sound at all outlandish.

Verbitskaia's work not only displayed the influence of the
Russian radical tradition, but also of European feminist writing
of her time, which ventured much further than *In a New Way*,
with its portraits of 'new women' such as H. G. Wells's heroine
Ann Veronica, a suffragette who demanded a new, freer
relationship with a man, and its pictures of a female Arcadia.
Such images were largely based on fantasy, and were ahead of
their time, but they did contain some truth about women's
needs. The ridicule to which Verbitskaia's novel was subjected
suggests that Russian men, like men of other ages and cultures,
were deeply anxious about female autonomy,[55] and regarded

as absurd Verbitskaia's attempt to create a female role model who failed to conform to male definitions of 'femininity', but instead legitimized the author's own rebellious endeavours. Verbitskaia was perceived as guilty of demonstrating 'presumption' – a criticism frequently levelled at women writers whose creativity and unconventionality have been perceived as inappropriate to the female sex.[56]

As Verbitskaia's ambitions grew, the faults of her fiction became more marked. She proved to be less successful at depicting the 'new man' and the philosophical ideas becoming current in the early twentieth century, in her novels *Zlaia rosa* (*Evil Dew*, 1904)[57] and *The Spirit of the Time*, than at painting realistic pictures of the lives of Russian professional women. Although Verbitskaia herself attached more significance to her later works, her real talent lay in portraying women trapped in unsatisfactory relationships or conventional family life, or in pointing to the conflict between love and work, between the desire for fulfilment and the oppressive, humdrum reality of Russian women's lives.

However, even her later potboilers, which correspond more to popular sentiment than feminist aspirations, could be interpreted not, to use George Eliot's term, as 'Silly Novels by Lady Novelists',[58] but as 'carrying out subversive politicization, drawing women into structures of consciousness-raising without their knowing it'.[59] Such novels as *The Keys to Happiness* did not merely, in the words of a critic of Verbitskaia's day, fulfil the function of creating 'rest' and 'cheerfulness' for ordinary people;[60] rather, Verbitskaia's depiction of women running their own lives, however extravagant and neurasthenic the heroines may be, could not but exert some influence on her numerous female readers.[61] Even though the heroines generally end up submitting to their men, it could be argued that Verbitskaia had to introduce an artificially 'happy ending' to please her readers, and that her heroines' subordination corresponds more closely to the reality of Russian life in her day, when very few Russian women had the opportunity of attaining complete economic independence from men. Contrary to the opinion of Jeffrey Brooks,[62] the denouement of Verbitskaia's

Keys to Happiness, which ends with the heroine's suicide, does not necessarily invalidate the feminist 'message' of much of the text,[63] which portrays a sexually liberated heroine, a ballerina, who is devoted to her work, but also loves two very different men and sleeps with both. Verbitskaia's *Keys to Happiness* possesses considerable interest as a striking illustration of the way in which Russian popular culture contributed to the first-wave feminist movement and to women's discovery of their own sexuality, although it also raises controversial questions about the conflict between popular taste and feminist ideas, and between sexual freedom and women's emancipation.

Many of Verbitskaia's ideas were ahead of their time; indeed, they are probably unacceptable in Russia even today, since many women struggling for their own and their family's survival may well perceive such issues as personal fulfilment and the notion of 'a room of one's own' as unattainable dreams, and the choice between love and work as a sophisticated dilemma of concern only to rich women in the USA and western Europe.[64]

CONCLUSION

A reappraisal of Verbitskaia's work, particularly her neglected early novels, will make a contribution to the rediscovery of the 'Feminist phase' of Russian women's literature from the 1880s to the 1920s, a tradition largely forgotten in Soviet Russia. Although Verbitskaia did not create any lasting aesthetic values, her unpretentious early works, with their gripping plots, lively dialogue, frequently subtle analysis of female psychology and sexual relationships and satirical presentation of the social milieu of pre-revolutionary Russia, deserve to be better known, and to occupy an honourable place in the history of Russian feminist writing. Only Kollontai in her fiction of the 1920s has gone as far as Verbitskaia in suggesting that the key to becoming truly liberated is a woman's own efforts to rid herself of excessive economic and emotional dependence on men, while recognizing that such a change of focus will be agonizingly difficult.[65]

Despite the persecution to which she was subjected, Verbitskaia, both through her fiction and her editorial work, played an important role in the formulation and popularization of feminist ideology in Russia. She possessed a highly developed sense of belonging to an international sisterhood of women writers,[66] and felt that she had a duty to use her novels to introduce a wide circle of Russian readers to progressive ideas about the liberation of women through education and employment, and to new approaches to sexual and family relationships. By establishing a women's publishing company with the profits from her novels, Verbitskaia demonstrated her genuine commitment to the European women's movement, and her desire to acquaint Russian women with the image of the 'new woman' which was being popularized in English, French and German fiction of her day.[67]

The neglect and hostility which Verbitskaia provoked in Russia cannot be entirely explained by critics' sensitivity to her artistic shortcomings; it also undoubtedly stemmed from the feminist themes in her work. Her passionate advocacy of equality, self-assertion and material independence for women, her exposure of the hypocritical 'double standard' in male morality, her revelation of women's sexual, emotional and intellectual capacities and her attempt to encourage them to develop their latent potential, were uncongenial to many of her male contemporaries. Because of the enormous popularity of Verbitskaia's fiction, male critics unsympathetic to women's liberation felt the need to undermine it; while even radical critics who were basically sympathetic to feminist ideas sometimes failed to understand what she was trying to say,[68] or declared that her works had only a transitional value, since they accepted the dubious Social Democratic view that women's issues would be automatically solved in the wake of political and economic reform.[69] Verbitskaia's emphasis on gender equality, coupled with her depiction of women's sexual and emotional difference from men, did not correspond to the predominantly male agenda of the Russian revolutionary movement, which stressed women's rationality and similarity to men, and concentrated on women's emancipation as part of a general political programme.[70]

Verbitskaia's fiction has also been able to transcend its own time, inasmuch as it explores themes which are still relevant to women of her own and other cultures in the late twentieth century. Although economic and political circumstances have changed, allowing women, at least in Western Europe and the USA, greater opportunities for paid work and self-fulfilment than existed in Verbitskaia's day, some of the psychological dilemmas she analyses, such as the conflict between work and love, or the problems attendant on divorce and single parenthood, are still experienced by many contemporary women.

NOTES

1 Verbitskaia is not mentioned, for example, in D. S. Mirsky, *A History of Russian Literature* (London: Routledge, 1949); Richard Freeborn, ed., *The Russian Revolutionary Novel: Turgenev to Pasternak* (Cambridge: Cambridge University Press, 1982); or in Charles Moser, ed., *The Cambridge History of Russian Literature* (Cambridge: Cambridge University Press, 1992), which includes only one female contributor.

2 See, for example, Mark Slonim, *From Chekhov to the Revolution: Russian Literature 1900–1917* (New York: Oxford University Press, 1962), p. 165; the short biography by Tomas Venclova in Victor Terras, ed., *Handbook of Russian Literature* (New Haven and London: Yale University Press, 1985), p. 503, concedes that Verbitskaia was immensely popular, while stating that 'most critics did recognize the vulgarity and pseudo-intellectualism of her work'.

3 Sigrid McLaughlin, *The Image of Women in Contemporary Soviet Fiction* (London and Basingstoke: Macmillan 1989), p. 9.

4 For a similar view, see Helena Goscilo, 'Introduction', in Goscilo, ed., *Fruits of her Plume: Essays on Russian Women's Culture* (Armonk, NY and London: M. E. Sharpe, 1993), p. xviii.

5 For discussion of the potential conflict between feminist ideas and commercial success, see Rebecca O'Rourke, 'Summer reading', *Feminist Review*, 2 (1979), p. 3; Rosalind Coward, 'Are women's novels feminist novels?', in Elaine Showalter, ed., *The New Feminist Criticism: Essays on Women, Literature and Theory* (London: Virago, 1986), pp. 225–39.

6 See, for example, Barbara Heldt, *Terrible Perfection* (Bloomington: Indiana University Press, 1987), pp. 59–60; X[enia] G[asior-

owska], 'Women and Russian Literature', in Terras, *Handbook of Russian Literature*, p. 521.

7   See, for example, Rosalind Marsh, 'The birth, death and rebirth of feminist writings in Russia', in Helena Forsås-Scott, ed., *European Feminist Writing in the Twentieth Century* (London and New York: Routledge, 1991), p. 133; Tatjana Antalovsky, *Der russische Frauenroman (1890–1912). Exemplarische Untersuchungen* (Munich: Sagner, 1987); Charlotte Rosenthal, 'Achievement and obscurity: women's prose in the Silver Age', in Toby W. Clyman and Diana Greene, eds., *Women Writers in Russian Literature* (Westport, CT: Greenwood Press, 1994), pp. 153, 157–8.

8   V. Kranikhfel'd, 'O novykh liudiakh A. Verbitskoi', *Sovremennyi mir*, 7 (1910), Part 2, p. 68; L. Kleinbort, 'Maksim Gor'kii i chitatel' nizov', *Vestnik Evropy*, 12 (1913), p. 171. Jeffrey Brooks, *When Russia Learned to Read: Literacy and Popular Literature* (Princeton, NJ: Princeton University Press, 1984), p. 154 suggests that 'Gorky sold better than Verbitskaia at the height of his success, but he enjoyed the respect of an audience that stretched from educated readers and their critics down to a much lower reading public.' In 1914 more than twenty of Verbitskaia's books had appeared in half a million copies: see Verbitskaia's list in her *Igo liubvi* (Moscow, 1914).

9   Brooks, *When Russia Learned to Read*, p. 154 compares her to the sensational English writers Elinor Glyn (1864–1943) and Marie Corelli (1855–1924).

10 Richard Stites, *Russian Popular Culture: Entertainment and Society since 1900* (Cambridge: Cambridge University Press, 1992), pp. 1–2 and *passim*; Catriona Kelly, *Petrushka, the Russian Carnival Puppet Theatre* (Cambridge: Cambridge University Press, 1990), p. 234, n.18; Vera Dunham, *In Stalin's Time: Middleclass Values in Soviet Fiction* (Cambridge: Cambridge University Press, 1976). Much research into 'popular culture' still remains to be done, but its value in understanding social history has been amply demonstrated in Peter Burke, *Popular Culture in Early Modern Europe* (London: Temple Smith, 1978); Keith Thomas, *Religion and the Decline of Magic: Studies in Belief in Sixteenth- and Seventeenth-Century England* (Harmondsworth: Penguin, 1978); *Man and the Natural World: Changing Attitudes in England 1500–1800* (Harmondsworth: Penguin, 1984).

11 Elaine Showalter, *A Literature of Their Own: from Charlotte Brontë to Doris Lessing*, revised edn (London: Virago, 1992); Sandra M. Gilbert and Susan Gubar, *The Madwoman in the Attic: The Woman Writer and the Nineteenth-century Literary Imagination* (New Haven and

London: Yale University Press, 1979), pp. 3–92; Dale Spender, *Women of Ideas and What Men have Done to Them* (London: Routledge, 1982).

12 For a useful biography of Verbitskaia, see Alla Gracheva's article in K. D. Muratova, ed., *Istoriia russkoi literatury kontsa XIX–nachala XX vv. Bibliograficheskii ukazatel'* (Moscow and Leningrad, 1963), pp. 418–20. Gracheva's entry, 'Verbitskaia, Anastasiia Alekseevna', in Marina Ledkovsky, Charlotte Rosenthal and Mary Zirin, eds., *The Dictionary of Russian Women Writers* (Westport, CT: Greenwood Press, 1994), pp. 703–5, does not add substantially to her earlier article.

13 Verbitskaia tells her own story in *Moemu chitateliu. Avtobiograficheskie ocherki s portretom avtora i semeinymi portretami* (Moscow, 1911). On the value and interest of this memoir, see Rosenthal, 'Achievement and obscurity', p. 158.

14 See, for example, 'Tan' (V. G. Bogoraz), 'Sanin v iubke', *Utro Rossii*, 93 (31 December 1909), p. 3, which compares Verbitskaia's work with Mikhail Artsybashev's notorious, but highly popular, novel *Sanin* (1907), much criticized for its justification of male lechery; for Verbitskaia's reply, see *Utro Rossii*, 99 (6 February 1910), p. 8; and Tan's response, *Utro Rossii*, 105 (13 February 1910), p. 2. Another fierce attack was A. Bartenev, 'Parazity literatury (A. Verbitskaia)', *Zhatva* (1912), Part 1, pp. 233–40.

15 From 1899 to 1901 she was a member of a Moscow mutual aid society for people from the intellectual professions, which was closed on account of its allegedly anti-government activity. In 1905 she became president of a Society for Improving the Lot of Women.

16 A. Verbitskaia, *Igo liubvi: Roman trilogiia*, Parts 1 and 2 (Moscow, 1914–16); the manuscript of Part 3, *Speshite zhit'* (1920), is in RGALI, f. 1042, op. 1, ed. khr. 8.

17 Verbitskaia speaks of her hardships in her letter to M. Ol'minskii (M. Aleksandrov) of 4 August 1926, reproduced in M. Ol'minskii, *Po literaturnym voprosam* (Moscow–Leningrad, 1932), pp. 55–7.

18 See *Na literaturnom postu*, 7-8 (1926), pp. 56–61; reprinted in Ol'minskii, *Po literaturnym voprosam*, pp. 52–5, 58–9.

19 There was no reprieve for her, for example, in S. V. Kastorskii, 'Proza burzhuaznoi epokhi', in *Istoriia russkoi literatury*, 10 (Moscow–Leningrad, 1954), p. 621.

20 K. Chukovskii, 'Verbitskaia (posviashchaetsia uchashcheisia molodezhi)', in *Kniga o sovremennykh pisateliakh* (St Petersburg, 1914), pp. 7–21 (first published under the title 'Intelligentnyi Pinkerton', *Rech'*, 105 (13 February 1910), p. 2).

21 The Social Democratic critic V. Dadonov, in *A.Verbitskaia i ee romany 'Kliuchi schast'ia' i 'Dukh vremeni'* (Moscow, 1911), pp. 70–4 discerns political motives for the criticism of Verbitskaia and other radical writers in Kadet publications such as *Rech'*, *Russkie vedomosti* and *Russkaia mysl'*.

22 A. Verbitskaia, *Kliuchi schast'ia*, 1 (Moscow, 1910); 2 (Moscow, 1912).

23 Gilbert and Gubar, *The Madwoman in the Attic*, p. 348; on popular women's literature and its relation to high culture, see Lillian Robinson, 'On reading trash', in her *Sex, Class and Culture* (Bloomington, IN: Indiana University Press, 1978), pp. 200–22. See also Janice A. Radway, *Reading the Romance* (Chapel Hill, NC: University of North Carolina, 1984), which discusses women's attitude to popular fiction in the USA, suggesting that this relationship is not necessarily 'apolitical'.

24 A. Verbitskaia, *Dukh vremeni* (Moscow, 1907).

25 See, for example, Heldt, *Terrible Perfection*, pp. 59–60; Laura Engelstein, *The Keys to Happiness: Sex and the Search for Modernity in Fin-de-Siècle Russia* (Ithaca, NY: Cornell University Press, 1992); Brooks, *When Russia Learned to Read*, pp. 153–60; Alla Gracheva, 'Russkoe nitssheanstvo i zhenskii roman nachala XX veka', in Liljeström, Mäntysaari and Rosenholm, *Gender Restructuring in Russian Studies*, Slavica Tamperensia, 11 (Tampere: University of Tampere, 1993), pp. 87–98. Antalovsky, *Der russische Frauenroman* discusses both *Kliuchi schast'ia* and *Po-novomu*; Catriona Kelly, *A History of Russian Women's Writing, 1820–1992* (Oxford: Clarendon Press, 1994) concentrates on *Kliuchi schast'ia*, but also refers to Verbitskaia's collection of short stories *Schast'e: novye rasskazy* (Moscow, 1905).

26 See, for example, Marsh, 'The birth, death and rebirth ...', pp. 132–3; Heldt, *Terrible Perfection*, pp. 59–60; Charlotte Rosenthal, 'Achievement and obscurity', p. 158.

27 M. Gor'kii, 'Ob A. Verbitskoi', *Nizhegorodskii listok*, 24 (25 January 1901), p. 4.

28 For further discussion of realist and feminist writings by Russian women in the period 1881–1917, see Kelly, *A History of Russian Women's Writing, 1820–1992*, pp. 135–49.

29 E. Koltonovskaia, 'A.Verbitskaia. Istoriia odnoi zhizni. Povest' v dvukh chastiakh', *Obrazovanie*, 1 (1903), Part 2, pp. 74, 76. For the most forceful expression of this 'recipe', see A. Verbitskaia, *Kliuchi schast'ia*, 1 (Moscow, 1910), p. 108. On Koltonovskaia, see above, p. 147.

30 Showalter, *A Literature of Their Own*, pp. 14–15.

31 See Rosenthal, 'Achievement and obscurity', p. 153; see also Davidson, and Mikhailova above, pp. 156–63 and 147–9.
32 See, for example, Bartenev, 'Parazity literatury'.
33 See the discussion about Ibsen's Nora in A. Verbitskaia, *Osvobodilas'!* (Moscow, 1902), pp. 6–10.
34 A. Verbitskaia, *Osvobodilas'!*, *Mir bozhii*, 8–12 (1898).
35 V. Chimishliiskii, *Zhenskie tipy v proizvedeniiakh Verbitskoi. Opyt kriticheskogo razbora ee proizvedenii* (St Petersburg, 1904), p. 19.
36 P. Krasnov, 'Ideinaia pisatel'nitsa (literaturnaia kharakteristika A. A. Verbitskoi', *Literaturnye vechera 'Novogo mira'*, 5 (May 1903), p. 239.
37 A. Kollontai, *Novaia moral' i rabochii klass* (Moscow, 1918), p. 35 (first published as 'Polovaia moral' i sotsial'naia bor'ba', *Novaia zhizn'*, 9 (1911), pp. 155–82).
38 For further discussion of the problems facing women writers in the 'Silver Age', which sometimes led them to suicide, see Mikhailova, and Rosenthal above, pp. 143 and 136–7. On the Russian literary stereotype of the female suicide, see, in particular, Karamzin's *Bednaia Liza* (discussed by Roberts below, p. 255), and Tolstoi's *Anna Karenina*.
39 See also Rosenthal above, p. 136; and Gracheva, 'Verbitskaia, Anastasiia Alekseevna', p. 703.
40 A. Verbitskaia, *Moemu chitateliu*, I: *Detstvo. Gody ucheniia* (Moscow, 1908), pp. 36–7; II: *Iunost', Grezy* (Moscow, 1911), pp. 10, 175–8.
41 A. Verbitskaia, *Istoriia odnoi zhizni* (Mosow, 1903); the depiction of the 'woman question' in this novel is praised in E. Koltonovskaia, 'A. Verbitskaia. *Istoriia odnoi zhizni. Povest' v dvukh chastiakh'*, *Obrazovanie*, I (1903), Part 2, pp. 74–7.
42 Koltonovskaia, 'A. Verbitskaia. *Istoriia odnoi zhizni'*, p. 77; cf. Chimishliiskii, *Zhenskie tipy*, p. 23, who praised Verbitskaia's portrait of Ol'ga as a female social activist.
43 A. Verbitskaia, *Pervye lastochki* (Moscow, 1900); earlier published as *Razlad, Russkaia mysl'*, 6 (1887). Its success with the Russian reading public was demonstrated by the fact that it was republished in a separate book edition six times between 1900 and 1917. The word *lastochki* ('swallows') in the title should be interpreted as 'first signs', or 'portents' of change, as in the proverb 'One swallow does not make a summer'.
44 Rosenthal, 'Achievement and obscurity', p. 153 correctly points to the depiction of Valentina's selfless aid to the peasantry in the first part of the novel as a feature typical of the Russian populist heroine, and to her subsequent metamorphosis into a writer as a feature more typical of the new Silver Age heroine.

45 A. Verbitskaia, *Moemu chitateliu*, II, p. 178.
46 Chimishliiskii, *Zhenskie tipy*, p. 24.
47 A. Verbitskaia, *Vavochka*, *Zhizn'*, 8–12 (1898); published by Verbitskaia herself, 1900.
48 A. Verbitskaia, *Ch'ia vina?* (Moscow, 1900).
49 Chimishliiskii, *Zhenskie tipy*, pp. 33–5.
50 A. Verbitskaia, 'Posleslovie', in *Ch'ia vina* (Moscow, 1911), pp. 172–9. In response to critics who argued that 'The only thing that can serve to justify her is her talent', Verbitskaia declares rhetorically: 'Is talent not everything?'
51 A. Verbitskaia, *Po-novomu: roman uchitel'nitsy* (Moscow, 1905); first published in *Obrazovanie*, 1902.
52 Chimishliiskii, *Zhenskie tipy*, p. 35.
53 Chernyshevskii's depiction of Vera Pavlovna's passionless marriage to the medical student Lopukhov inspired the fashion of the *fiktivnyi brak* (fictitious, or rational marriage) among Russian radicals. Vera and her first husband live in separate rooms, and their relationship is based on mutual respect and personal and economic autonomy. Her second marriage to Kirsanov allows her freedom to pursue her own work as the manager of a model sewing co-operative.
54 Chimishliiskii, *Zhenskie tipy*, p. 37; Kranikhfel'd, 'O novykh liudiakh A. Verbitskoi', p. 78.
55 Dorothy Dinnerstein, *The Mermaid and the Minotaur: Sexual Arrangements and Human Malaise* (New York: Harper and Row, 1976); Gilbert and Gubar, *The Madwoman in the Attic*, p. 28.
56 *Ibid.*, pp. 48–52. An early response to such a critique of women writers came in a poem by Anne Finch, Countess of Winchilsea (1661–1720), which ironically described 'a woman that attempts the pen' as 'a presumptuous creature': see Anne Finch, *Selected Poems*, ed. Denys Thompson (Manchester: Fyfield, 1987), p. 26. Similar arguments were frequently directed against nineteenth-century Russian women writers: see the attacks on Anna Bunina's presumption, discussed by Rosslyn above, pp. 66–8.
57 A. Verbitskaia, *Zlaia rosa* (Moscow, 1904).
58 George Eliot, 'Silly novels by lady novelists', *Westminster Review*, 46 (1856), reprinted in Thomas Pinney, ed., *Essays of George Eliot* (London, 1963).
59 Coward, 'Are women's novels . . .?', p. 226.
60 Dadonov, *A. Verbitskaia*, pp. 48–57.
61 For a similar view of women's fiction in the West, see Nancy K. Miller, 'Emphasis added: plots and plausibilities in women's fiction', in Showalter, *The New Feminist Criticism*, pp. 339–60.

62 Brooks, *When Russia Learned to Read*, pp. 159–60.
63 Gracheva, 'Russkoe nitssheanstvo i zhenskii roman nachala XX veka', pp. 94–5 interprets Mania's suicide as a gesture of Nietzschean self-assertion, an affirmation of her desire not to live without the man she loves.
64 Such views were expressed by women at the Second Independent Women's Forum, Dubna, November, 1992; and by Ol'ga Lipovskaia, 'Sisters and Cousins: How Close is Sisterhood?', unpublished paper at conference on 'Women in Russia and the Former USSR', Bath, 1993.
65 Alexandra Kollontai, *A Great Love*, transl. Cathy Porter (London: Virago, 1981); Kollontai, *Love of Worker Bees*, transl. Cathy Porter (London: Virago, 1988).
66 In her autobiography, *Moemu chitateliu*, she refers to the influence of George Sand, Charlotte Brontë, Ol'ga Shapir, 'V. Krestovskii' (the pseudonym of Nadezhda Khvoshchinskaia) and Sof'ia Smirnova.
67 The works she published and introduced ranged from translations of George Meredith's *The Tragic Comedians* (1898) and novels by George Moore and Mrs Humphry Ward to more commercial novels advocating free love, such as Grant Allen's popular novel, *The Woman Who Did* (1895).
68 See, for example, Chimishliiskii, *Zhenskie tipy*.
69 O. Mirtov, 'Apofeoz dogmatov', *Obrazovanie*, 1 (1907), Part 2, pp. 88–99; for a critique of this view, later advocated by the Soviet government, the dissidents of the Brezhnev era and the democrats of the perestroika and post-perestroika eras, see Rosalind Marsh, ' "From problems to strategy"?', *Rusistika*, 7 (1993), p. 17.
70 In her afterword to the 1911 edition of *Ch'ia vina?*, Verbitskaia claims that not one Russian party, including the socialist parties, has a genuine desire to liberate women from conventional sexual and family ties. For further discussion of the predominantly male agenda of the Russian radical movement, see Linda Edmondson, 'Women's emancipation and theories of sexual difference in Russia, 1850–1917', in Liljeström, Mäntysaari and Rosenholm, *Gender Restructuring in Russian Studies*, pp. 39–52; Edmondson, 'Women's equality or difference: where does Russia fit in?', in Rosalind Marsh, ed., *Women in Russia and Ukraine* (Cambridge: Cambridge University Press, 1996); and Rosenholm above, pp. 112–17.

CHAPTER 11

Soviet woman of the 1980s: self-portrait in poetry

Elena Trofimova

Every work of art, of whatever type or genre, undoubtedly contains features of its creator and represents a distinctive autobiography of the creative personality. At the same time, it is no literal, mirror image of its creator, but rather a self-portrait of some lyric hero or heroine who emerges in the process of the creative act, a *persona* based on the artist's personality, but not totally identical with it.

The correlation between the poet's personality and the literary image which emerges while reading poetic texts always arouses the interest of literary scholars. One or another solution to this question provides the key to an analysis of the work, an elucidation of its typical or specific nature and an introduction to a definite socio-cultural context, not to mention its gender-specific attributes, a subject which arouses controversy today. An artistic self-portrait makes it possible to study not only a specific creative personality, but also the sensual, emotional and psychological aspects of a society, which are so important to its spiritual history. This is what enables us to appreciate an era from within, to explore and evaluate it not on the basis of external facts and events, but through the existential experiences and feelings of human beings.

From the works of Soviet women poets I have selected poems by Tat'iana Bek, Nina Iskrenko and Tat'iana Smertina, since, in my opinion, they represent different types of poetic heroine, with different patterns of mentality, temperament and philosophy. An analysis of their work will provide three case studies illustrating the divergent ways in which women's poetry has developed in contemporary Russia.

Tat'iana Aleksandrovna Bek was born in 1949 in Moscow, and, as the daughter of the well-known writer Aleksandr Bek, found it easier than many others to pursue a literary career. She joined the Union of Soviet Writers at the age of thirty; has published four collections of poetry: *Skvoreshniki* (*Starlings*, 1974), *Snegir'* (*Bullfinch*, 1980), *Zamysel* (*Scheme*, 1987) and *Smeshannyi les* (*Mixed Forest*, 1993); and her poems have been and are frequently published in literary journals.[1]

One of Bek's poems in *Zamysel* contains notable lines, which, although perhaps not presenting a complete image of her lyric heroine, may nevertheless be regarded as a key to her self-portrait:

> И за то, что враждой с однолетками
> Заслоняла просторные дни, —
> Исхлещи меня ливнями, ветками
> И словами, но прочь — не гони![2]

(And because I concealed my spacious days | With enmity for my contemporaries, | Lash me with showers, branches | And words, but do not chase me away!)

Through this confession of a breach with her contemporaries, of some distance in time and spirit separating her from contemporary life, Tat'iana Bek helps us to formulate that aspect of her heroine's mentality which can be called poetic retrospection. It would seem that there are two basic factors determining the poet's persistent predilection for 'looking back'. One of these can conventionally be called the aesthetic and political factor. The crux of the matter is the poet's open acknowledgement that she is, if not a direct participant, then at least a direct successor of the artistic and social tendency which literary scholars call 'the 1960s generation'. Of course, this was largely related to the fact that since her earliest years she had had the opportunity to associate with many of those who had been the main heroes of the short-lived Soviet 'thaw', and, particularly, with her father, the author of the famous novel *The New Appointment*.[3] The theme of society's return to a more or less normal life, the liberation of the human being and the word from the real and poetic Gulag could not fail to move the poet.

In one of her poems, as if showing solidarity with the words of
the former Gulag prisoner, the poet Anatolii Zhigulin,[4]
Tat′iana Bek writes:

> Эту страшную, большую
> Стынущую Колыму
> Никогда не затушую,
> От себя не отниму.   (*Zamysel*, p. 62)

(This terrible, vast, | Frozen Kolyma | I will never extinguish, |
Never amputate from myself.)

But it is not her political or civic spirit which enable us to
characterize Bek as a direct successor of the '1960s generation'. She finds this era valuable and appealing primarily
because it was a time when the great Russian lyric poetry of
the beginning of the century was rehabilitated and returned
to the reader. Plundered by the censorship, cut and abridged
in parts, furnished with highly dubious commentaries and
prefaces, the lyric works of Bunin, Mandel′shtam, Tsvetaeva
and Akhmatova returned to their homeland. The last two
poets are particularly significant for Tat′iana Bek. This is not
only because they wrote highly cultured verse and demonstrated a deep knowledge and understanding of words, but
also because the acute sincerity and profoundly confessional
nature of lyrics by Russian women poets of the Silver Age
are very close and attractive to Bek. This intimacy can also
be explained by the revelation of naked feeling, the dramatic
nature of the experiences, that special element of female
tragedy in the metamorphoses of love relationships which we
find in Akhmatova and Tsvetaeva and which are so close to
the psychological mould and life experience of Bek's poetic
heroine.

> О, толпа разодетая, важная,
> Жадно жрущая на серебре, —
> Не по вкусу тебе эта страшная
> Ворожба? Или нет — рукопашная,
> Где точны, как удары, тире.
>
> Мерить верстами землю чужбинную,
> Столбенеть перед редкой рябиною,
> Принимая сиротство как честь . . .

Надо быть несравненной Мариною,
Чтобы быть лишь такою, как есть.   (*Zamysel*, p. 57)

(O, well-dressed, important crowd | Greedily guzzling on silver | Is it not to your taste, this terrible | Sorcery? Or rather – this hand-to hand fighting, | Where the dashes are as precise as blows. || To measure a foreign land in versts, | To be rooted to the spot before the rare rowan tree, | Accepting orphanhood as an honour ... You need to be the incomparable Marina | To be only such as you are.)

Я люблю этот холод осенний,
Я люблю этой жизни зигзаги ...
Чем обиженней —
            тем вдохновенней
Отражается жизнь на бумаге.   (p. 43)

(I love this autumn cold | I love the zigzags of this life ... | The greater the offence – the greater the inspiration | When life is reflected on paper).

Я то лягушкой, то царевной
Глядела из-под челки гневной
И миру:
    — Мучь! —
... Мне просто не вручили ключ
от ровной жизни ежедневной!   (p. 47)

(Now a frog, now a princess | I looked out from under an angry fringe | And said to the world: | 'Torment me!' | ... I simply have not been given the key | to an equable everyday life!)

Pursuing the idea of a return to the past by the poet's lyric heroine, we should also mention another source of her deliberate retrospection. It is a result of her strength of feeling, the intensity of her spiritual experience and corresponding psychological reaction. Glancing through Tat'iana Bek's poetry, the reader can quite clearly picture the image of a woman capable of surrendering unconditionally to her feeling of love, concentrating all her emotional power upon it:

Лучилась, обзывала «суженым»,
Зрачком испепеляла суженным ...

Любви без удержу синоним,
Вбегала как приказ «По коням!»   (p. 55)

(She sparkled, called him her 'intended', | Her narrowed pupils incinerated ... | | A synonym of immoderate love, | In she rushed as if on the order 'To your horses!'.)

Elsewhere we find an even franker evocation of her experience of love:

> Безудержная в ревности своей
> Я слабовольна и нетерпелива ...
> А жизнь благоуханней, чем крапива,
> И жжет сильней, и старится скорей.   (p. 113)

(Unrestrained in my jealousy | I am weak-willed and impatient ... | But life is more fragrant than nettles, | And stings more fiercely, and ages more swiftly.)

The last two lines speak of the reckoning which awaits the heroine every time the lofty incandescence of feeling is extinguished, when disillusionment, weariness and bitterness set in. Tat′iana Bek virtually never describes the lovers of her lyric heroine – we are more likely to discover their age, appearance or character obliquely than through a literal portrait. However, each time the take-off and soaring flight of love ends in drama:

> Это в духе
> Любви — синонима разрухи.

(This is in the spirit | Of love – the synonym of ruin.)

One characteristic feature of the psychological portrait of Tat′iana Bek's poetic heroine is that special sense of time, or more precisely, of stagnating time, which was very prevalent in the 1970s. The feelings and experiences of the separate, individual human being appeared insignificant in the face of the sinister power of the state ideology. It seemed as though nothing would change or could change. And it was only old age that appeared to offer some kind of salvation from the all-knowing and all-seeing eye of the regime – the age of retirement, when human beings ceased to interest the state and received a small, though illusory degree of freedom. This melancholy 'last hope' for old age as a time when it might at last be possible to realize one's best human qualities, is conveyed in one of Tat′iana Bek's poems:

> Я буду старой, буду белой,
> Глухой, нелепой, неумелой,

Дающей лишние советы, —
Ну, словом, брошка и штиблеты.

А все-таки я буду сильной!
Глухой к обидам и двужильной.
Не на трибуне тары-бары,
А на бумаге мемуары.

Да! Независимо от моды
Я воссоздам вот эти годы
Безжалостно, сердечно, сухо ...
Я буду честная старуха.   (p. 123)

(I will be old, I will be white, | Deaf, absurd, inept, | Giving unnecessary advice, | Well, in short, a brooch and gaiters. || But still I will be strong! | Deaf to insults and tough. | No tittle-tattle on the platform, | But memoirs on paper. || Yes! Irrespective of fashion | I will reconstruct these years | Pitilessly, warmly, drily ... I will be an honest old woman.)

To a mock questionnaire she composed herself, the Moscow poet Nina Iskrenko responded:

Любимое слово — НЕТ
Любимое занятие — ВЫСЛУШИВАНИЕ ПОЛЕЗНЫХ
  СОВЕТОВ
Любимое животное — ДИКООБРАЗ
Любимый ~~издевательский~~ [word crossed out] издательский
ответ — ЖДИТЕ ОТВЕТА

(Favourite word: NO | Favourite occupation: LISTENING TO USEFUL ADVICE | Favourite animal: PORCUPINE | Favourite ~~mocking~~ [word crossed out] publisher's response: AWAIT A REPLY[5])

In these phrases the experienced ear of the researcher into contemporary Soviet culture (specifically *Soviet* culture, because we are talking about the beginning of the 1980s) can easily detect and interpret the typical melody of the Moscow poetic avant-garde to which the poet belongs.

Nina Iskrenko, who was born in 1951, can be regarded as one of the outstanding figures of the Moscow underground in the notorious 'era of stagnation' (the Brezhnev period), which has now sunk into oblivion, when uncensored Russian literature, barred from access by the reader, made its way to the listener through meetings of various kinds, 'poetry evenings', the activities of semi-legal poetry associations and clubs. Nina Iskrenko joined one of them, the *Poeziia* ('Poetry') club, which is still in existence. It is only since 1988 that she has managed to publish in the journals *Avrora*, *Rabotnitsa* and *Iunost'*,[6] in almanacs and collections, such as *Den' poezii*, *Istoki*, *Molodaia poeziia* and *Transtaraskonshchina*;[7] and her books *Referendum* and *Ili (Or)* were published in 1991.[8]

Unquestionably, Nina Iskrenko has a completely different mentality from Tat'iana Bek. Describing herself in a short introduction to the poetry collection *Transtaraskonshchina* (which also includes poems by Iurii Arabov, Igor' Dudinskii, Konstantin Kedrov, Aleksei Khvostenko and others), Iskrenko writes: 'The author belongs to a generation which was born in the 1950s and became conscious of its creative aspirations in the period of our history which represented the epoch of developed absurdism and the meticulously preserved principles of high artistic stagnation' (p. 48). The world of her lyric heroine, like the heroine herself, is discrete and fragmented. It does not contain the cohesive inner unity which defines the portrait of the heroine of Tat'iana Bek's poems. The moral system of the '1960s generation' allows Bek to construct a logical system of relationships, moral and aesthetic passions and antipathies. We will not find this in Iskrenko's poetic heroine. In fact, there are no frank assessments and relationships in her poetry; instead we encounter the sum of certain fragments of poetic realia which attest to the absence of any acknowledged standard by which the heroine can measure, organize and introduce some order into the intellectual expanse of her images. In general, this is a world of transit, of transition from one scale of values to another, when the first has been almost completely devalued, and the next has not yet taken shape. The kingdom of order has given way to the power of anarchy, in which every phenomenon or image is both of identical value and devoid of all values. Hence that aesthetic position which Iskrenko proclaims as her creative method: that is, polystylistics. The poet formulates her ideas quite clearly in 'Hymn to Polystylistics':

Гимна полистилистике
Полистилистика
    это когда средневековый рыцарь
    в шортах
    штурмует винный отдел гастронома № 13
    на улице Декабристов
    и куртуазно ругаясь
    роняет на мраморный пол
    «Квантовую механику» Ландау и Лифшица

Полистилистика
    это когда одна часть платья
    из голландского полотна
    соединяется с двумя частями
    из пластилина
    А остальные части вообще отсутствуют ...
    или тащатся где-то в хвосте
    пока часы бьют и хрипят
    а мужики смотрят   (*Ili*, p. 28)

(*Hymn to Polystylistics.* Polystylistics | is when a medieval knight | in shorts | storms the wine department of Gastronom No. 13 | on Decembrists' Street | and swearing courteously | drops on the marble floor | *Quantum Mechanics* by Landau and Lifshits || Polystylistics | is when one part of a dress | of Dutch linen | joins with two parts | of plasticine | And the other parts are completely absent ... | or are dragged somewhere in the train | while the clock strikes and wheezes | and men look on)

Iskrenko's heroine is in a state of constant psychological tension because of her need to make constant inner choices, choices between numerous essences, phenomena and relationships. The collapse of a single integrated construct of the external world and of the society where the heroine lives leads to the constant degradation of once significant elements and facts of life, to an unexpected and unpredictable change of signs and a transposition of emphases. As the material of life currently unravels, the only stable factor is the fact of disintegration itself, the sign of an alternative. This has a direct effect on the poet's language: nouns, adjectives and verbs lose their absolute priority as main parts of speech, and the adversative conjunction 'or' comes into the foreground. The poet herself states this openly in her poem 'Ili' ('Or').

это связующее звено в цепи бинарных оппозиций
это пробный скачок сгусток напряжения триггер
это очередная попытка смоделировать и удержать
в экологическом равновесии
бесконечно презирающие друг друга края антиномий
　　　темперамент и воля
　　　летучая мышь и заурядная мистификация
　　　чистые души погибшие в борьбе за идеалы и
　　　идеалы погибшие в борьбе за власть ...
или что-то совсем другое.　　　　　　　　　　　　('Ili', p. 3)

(It is a connecting link in the chain of binary oppositions | it is an experimental leap a knot of tension a trigger | it is a regular attempt to model and hold | in ecological balance | the edges of antinomies which infinitely scorn each other | temperament and will | a bat and mediocre mystification | pure souls who have perished in the struggle for ideals and | ideals which have perished in the struggle for power ... | or something quite different.)

Her vision of life is not only a distorting mirror, but a mirror shattered into pieces. The poetic text appears to stick these fragments together, but the mirror is not restored; rather, a mosaic is formed in which uneven, badly fitting reflections of different sizes display an externally random sum of images of existence. The poet expresses these disconnected phenomena, the vagueness of their formal relationships and hierarchical co-ordination in grammatical terms, rejecting capital letters and punctuation marks; and in graphic terms, distributing words in columns or ladders of various kinds, deliberately leaving in the printed text discarded, crossed-out variants of words, as if giving the reader to understand that she herself is not sure which variant to select:

Граждане СССР обязаны заботиться о воспитании
　　　　　　　　　　　　　　　ДЕТЕЙ
... обеспечить их необходимыми санитар-
ными нормами барабанами и горнами
~~игорными~~ игральными автоматами положи-
тельными примерами ...

Граждане СССР ~~в цепях коммунистического~~
　　　　　　　　　　　　　　~~строительства~~
в целях коммунистического строительства

Soviet woman of the 1980s 215

имеют право ОБЪЕДИНЯТЬСЯ в коммуналь-
ные квартиры воинские подразделения и другие ...

('Proekt konstitutsii', p. 95)

(Citizens of the USSR are obliged to show concern about the upbringing | of CHILDREN | ... to provide them with the essential sanit- | ary norms drums and bugles | automatic ~~gaming~~ playing machines posit- | ive examples ... | Citizens of the USSR ~~in the chains of communist | construction~~ | in the aims of communist construction | have the right to UNITE in commun- | al flats military sub-units etc. ...)

Another example is:

> ... Эта поза вызывает желание
> создать композицию типа Адам и Гея
> ~~пытающие друг друга~~
> пытающиеся друг друга постичь ...   (p. 98)

(... This pose arouses the desire | to create a composition of the type of Adam and Geia | ~~torturing each other~~ | trying to understand each other ...)

The deconstruction of the world inevitably results in the deconstruction of human life, both external and internal. And Iskrenko's poetic *alter ego* not only records the fact of this discord analytically, but also experiences emotionally this tragedy of the destruction of the personality, of its ideal divine essence. It is probably no accident that in the poem-story 'Sreda' ('Milieu'), among a number of 'lacerated', eclectic texts in the spirit of post-modernism, the reader suddenly comes across a monologue which is absolutely grammatically correct:

Почему убирается однозначность, четкость определения понятий, недвусмысленная мотивировка действий? Почему что перестал интересовать отдельно взятый конкретный человек. Точнее — его нет, этого отдельного конкретного человека, он существует лишь как некое вероятностное распределение, он размазан с некоторой плотностью, подобно элементарной частице. То есть имеет смысл говорить лишь о наборе ситуаций и наборе поступков, в пределах которых будет действовать в данной ситуации то или иное конкретное лицо, практически любое.

('Sreda', p. 42)

(Why have monosemanticism [lack of ambiguity], clarity of definition of concepts and unambiguous motivation of actions been removed?

Because the concrete human being taken separately has ceased to be of interest. More precisely – he does not exist, this separate concrete human being, he exists only as some probable distribution, he is smeared with density, like an elementary particle. That is, there is only sense in speaking of a set of situations and a set of actions, within the bounds of which some or another concrete character, practically any, will act in a given situation.)

Iskrenko painfully perceives the increasing spiritual shallowness and standardization of human beings, not least because she herself feels an intensification of the stifling atmosphere in herself, in her own life. However, she has no intention of surrendering to hostile and destructive forces. Irony becomes her weapon; she uses it to remove, reduce and expose the pseudo-grandeur and pseudo-pathos of official values.

> Когда сидишь полдня в травмпункте, то хочется сидеть
>   в трактире
> ... Но посидев полдня в трактире
> уж хочется сидеть в Кремле ...
> А отсидишь полдня в Кремле
> в палате скажем депутатов
> ... и думаешь на сон грядущий
> Что день грядущий мне готовит?
> В Кремле сидим ведь елки-палки
> А где ж потом прикажете сидеть? ...
>
> ('Kogda sidish′ poldnia v travmpunkte ...', p. 109)

(When you sit for half a day in casualty, you want to sit in a pub | ... But after sitting half a day in a pub | then you want to sit in the Kremlin ... | But if you sit half a day in the Kremlin | let's say in the Chamber of Deputies | ... and you think before going to sleep | What does the coming day hold for me? | After all hell's bells we're sitting in the Kremlin | And after that where do you order me to sit? ...)

Such is the heroine's relationship to herself too, however difficult her existential situation, whatever despair she may feel:

> Другая женщина на моем месте смотрит в зеркало
> наклонив лицо так
> чтобы не было видно кругов под глазами ...
>
> ('Drugaia zhenshchina', p. 56)

(Another woman in my place looks in the mirror | Inclining her face | So that the shadows under her eyes cannot be seen ...)

She understands that she must not step over the line beyond which things are irreparable and destruction lies. And again Iskrenko finds salvation, the ability to preserve the stability of her personality, in irony, which she turns against herself too.

> Свет мой зеркальце скажи
> Да всю правду доложи
>
> Я ль на свете всех милее
> всех лояльней и левее
> всех богаче одеяньем
> и общественным призваньем
> и огнем своих побед ...   ('Svet moi zerkal'tse ...', p. 99)

(Mirror, my dear, tell me | And report the whole truth | | Am I the sweetest in the world | the most loyal and left of them all | richest of all in attire | and social mission | and the fire of my victories ...)

The character of Iskrenko's poetry, its direction outwards, its frequently frank épatage leaves no room for doubt that, to use Carl Jung's terminology, we have before us an extrovert type of personality which has no wish to be in a state of poetic introspection. An extrovert does not want to remain passively dependent on the external world, but feels a constant need to exert an active impact on it. But she does not need to restructure the world rationally, to bring it into some kind of order conceived a priori; for Iskrenko a similar dictatorship of the rational is only a superficial, apparent power. As she says ironically: 'I began to stick the pieces together – but there wasn't enough glue. God forgive me!' But it is possible to possess the form and essence of the surrounding world only by finding an adequate means of expressing it in art and words. Thus, polystylistics for Nina Iskrenko becomes not only a stylistic principle, but also acquires the attributes of verbal magic, of an incantation in verse, through which her heroine returns integrity and meaning to the chaos of life.

> ПОЛИСТИЛИСТИКА
> это слияние речной волны
> с волной акустической
> это выплескивание смыслового номинала
> через жест

и берестяную дудку
это состязание тысячи и одной идеи
с природной грацией ...   ('Polistilistika', p. 64)

(*Polystylistics.* It is the merging of the river's waves | with the acoustic wave | it is the splashing out of meaning's face-value | through gesture | and a pipe of birch-bark | it is a contest of a thousand and one ideas | with natural grace ...)

Tat'iana Ivanovna Smertina was born in 1948 in Sorvizhi, a village in the Kirov (now Viatsk) region. She has written poetry since childhood; her first publications appeared in a regional newspaper when she was thirteen or fourteen years old. Tat'iana Smertina graduated from the Gor'kii Literary Institute in Moscow in 1974, and in 1979 became a member of the Union of Soviet Writers. She has won a number of prizes for her work from journals and newspapers, including the journals *Smena* and *Sovetskaia zhenshchina*, the newspapers *Literaturnaia Rossiia* and *Literaturnaia gazeta*. She was awarded the Lenin Komsomol Prize and a diploma from the Ostrovskii competition. Smertina has published a number of books of poetry,[9] and her work has also appeared in various collections and anthologies, such as *Molodye golosa, Poeziia rossiiskikh dereven', Chas Rossii, Vodolei — znak Rossii*[10] and others.

Tat'iana Smertina's poetic heroine displays a type of female character and talent which are quite new in today's Russia. Her heroine is a Russian woman living at the end of the 1970s and the beginning of the 1980s. She is a person who has rejected all the myths of totalitarian ideology and acknowledged that the meaning of human life cannot be attained either through the philosophy inculcated by the authorities, or through political opposition to it: the true meaning of life is much more profound than any ideological dogma or political conception. The poet discovers for herself that the world and nature – in the widest sense of this word – is not simply a surface, a decoration serving only as a background to the human drama or comedy. The meaning of the universe revealed to our senses – the sky, earth, stones or plants – is far deeper than their direct, obvious function. Tat'iana Smertina's lyric heroine discovers that by penetrating beyond the surface of phenomena, deciphering their symbolic subtext encoded in the mysterious signs of nature, she finds first and foremost the key to her own soul, to the sources of her feelings, thoughts and experiences.

> Наша Душа — теремница.
> В клетке грудной томится —
> Вещая, нежная птица.
>
> Эту-то птицу беспечно
> Будем разглядывать вечно
> И убивать ярким светом!
> И воспевать многи лета!
>
> Но и поймав, как синицу,
> Мы не постигнем ту птицу.
> Пленную ангелицу . . .
> Нашу Сверхсуть!
> Ей — заоблачный путь . . .
>
> ('Trava-sinitsa', in *Travnik*, p. 49)

(Our Soul is a tower-chamber. | It languishes in the thorax – | A prophetic, tender bird. | | This bird we will carelessly | Examine eternally | And kill with bright light! | And hymn for many years! | | But even having caught it, like a blue-tit | We will not understand that bird. | A captive angel . . . | Our Superessence! | For her – a path beyond the clouds . . .)

When reading Smertina's poetry, one senses her involvement in history and her consciousness of herself as an actor in history – but not in the traditional, academic meaning of the word. History for her means above all the natural cycle, defined by the movement and rhythms of nature, which mankind sensed so organically and directly in its early phase of development, when the stone, concrete, steel and glass barriers of civilization had not yet been erected between human beings and the universe. And Smertina's interest in the Old Slavonic calendar is not accidental, since in it the life of man and the life of the human community – the family, race or tribe – seemed to be symbolically united with the rotation of the life of nature. In *Troezel'e*, the third part of her poetic collection *Travnik* (*Herbarium*, 1992), she attempts a poetic reconstruction of the Slavonic solar calendar of the pre-Christian era, the so-called 'Calendar of Twelve Fridays'.[11]

The poet undoubtedly made use of historical, ethnographic and archaeological research (in particular, B. A. Rybakov's *The Paganism of the Ancient Slavs*[12]), but the basic source of her poetic cycle was her subconscious, her own artistic intuition. Smertina writes: 'In *Travnik* I created it [the calendar] artistically according to my own instinct, and possibly "remembered" information a thousand years old, although at first sight this appears unlikely. I also "remembered" the potions magically connected with the Fridays' (p. 121). This sense of her existence as a simultaneous reflection of someone else who lived long ago, who has physically left the transitory world, but lives on in the spiritual substance of her successors, constitutes the basis of Smertina's poetics. For her poetic heroine, therefore, the return to the past, like the return to nature, becomes a return to herself and a quest for herself. Thus it is no accident that Smertina is philosophically and aesthetically oriented towards ancient Russian literature, whose pattern of imagery, lexis and poetic rhythms she borrows.

> Темный бор я пройду плавным соболем.
> В реку проскользну я плотвицею.
> Прочеркнусь россомахой я по полю,
> Сквозь забор я пронижусь куницею,
> Пред тобой я предстану — девицею.
> На скамейку присяду, вздыхая,
> «Диамат» мракобесный листая ...   (p. 110)

(I will pass through the dark forest like a smooth sable. | I will slip into the river like a roach. | I will streak through the field like a she-wolf, | I will penetrate through the fence like a marten, | I will appear before you as a girl. | I will sit on the bench, sighing, | leafing the obscurantist 'Diamat'[13]...)

Contemplation of the universe and each small part of it allows Smertina to commune with new knowledge inaccessible to the prosaic mind. She discovers that every particle of the universe contains some esoteric information, some primordial subject which can become a topic of artistic and poetic interpretation. Essentially, she arrives at that source of ancient mythology which nourishes and has nourished human culture over many centuries. In this connection, many of the poet's verses contained in the collection *Travnik* are significant. As a rule, in nearly every one of them, side by side with a description of one or another of the attributes of a herb, we also discover some primary subject which substantiated both the name of the plant and its medicinal properties. For example, in the poem 'Mar′in koren′' ('Mar′ia's Root'), the deep crimson colour of the petals of 'Mar′iushka's flower' becomes the sign and memento of a dramatic love affair which occurred a long time ago:

> Я узрела, словно сон:
> Ты себе над тем прудом
> Горло взрезала серпом
> За поруганну любовь ...
> Лепесток густо-багров ...
>
> (p. 97)

(I saw it, as if in a dream: | Above that pond you | Cut your throat with a sickle | For a desecrated love ... | The petal is a rich crimson ...)

The medicinal properties of 'Mar′ia's root' are a logical outcome of this tragic narrative:

> Марьин корень — от душевной,
> От горючей боли гневной
> И от ярости мгновенной,
> От бессониц можно пить ...

(Mar′ia's root can be drunk – for emotional pain | For burning anger, | Momentary fury | And insomnia ...)

And at the end of the poem we again find the motif of the timeless unity of myth and life, past and present, a living person's memory of a person who used to live. The motif of reflection here also seems to merge reality and fantasy, dream and true story, what is seen and what is sensed intuitively.

> Я, ладонь прогнув ковшом,
> Ключевую воду пью.
> Окати стынь-серебром
> Русу голову мою!
>
> ... А мое лицо — на дне,
> Растекается в волне.
> Там упал мне на висок
> Густо-алый лепесток.

(Cupping my palm like a ladle, | I drink spring water. | Pour frozen silver | Over my red head! || ... But my face – on the bottom, | Runs in the wave. | There on my temple fell | A rich crimson petal.)

Of course, the heroine of Smertina's poems, like every thinking and feeling person in the seventh and eighth decade of our century, faces the problem of how to overcome materialistic soullessness, the moral dead-end in which Russia found herself after deviating from the normal historical path. Smertina understands that in order to save her soul, to preserve her spiritual world and elevate the feminine principle in that spiritual, lofty sense in which Blok and the Russian Symbolists understood it, it is necessary for a radical change to take place in the scale of internal values, assessments and guidelines. And a new understanding of the essence of history, referred to earlier, comes to her aid. Not a political or aesthetic confrontation with the regime and its cultural dogmas, but a rethinking of her inner life, its moral and existential leitmotifs – this is how Smertina's lyric heroine sees the process of her transformation. It is necessary to reject the role of an actor in the 'human comedy', it is necessary to regard oneself as a part of nature, and to find the meaning of one's existence not in the context of transitory political and ideological myths, but in the profound, mysterious connections and analogies of human beings with the world of herbs, plants, earth, water and sky. According to Smertina's heroine, such self-awareness genuinely elevates human beings, for only in the spiritual structure of the world is every human being – as an incarnation of the fusion of matter and spirit, of the unity of past, present and future – unique and valuable.

> Вдруг и я,
>   словно свечки свеченье,
> Чьё-то в толще веков —
> Отраженье?   ('Molitvennaia trava', p. 16)

(What if I too | like the luminescence of a candle, | Am in the depth of the centuries – | Someone's reflection?)

Smertina's lyric poetry can be identified with a social trend we might call 'the return to roots'. Essentially this means the resurrection of national self-consciousness, whose basis the poet sees in the culture of ancient pagan Rus'. Hence her aspiration to imprint in her poetry's pattern of imagery the grammar and syntax of ancient pre-Christian Russian culture, in which human life was included in mythological life, along with wood goblins, house-spirits, Slavonic gods and goddesses,[14] mermaids and shore sprites. The traces of that life can still be detected in contemporary culture, particularly in rural culture – in the motifs of carvings around doors and windows, in the filigree patterns of lacquered paintings, in the traditional ornamental designs of embroidery. And, of course, in the lexis and even phonetics of the regional dialects which still exist in remote corners of Russia, or are conserved in the memory of people who grew up there.

> За наш погром, забвенье и насилье, —
> О колокольная,
>   прости, Россия!
> За мертвый лес, за пепел трав в горсти,
> И колокольчиковая —
>   прости!   (p. 277)

(For our pogrom, oblivion and violence – | O chime of bells, | forgive us, Russia! | For the dead forest, for the ash of herbs in cupped hands, | Chime of handbells too – | forgive us!)

I hope that this analysis of the poetic self-portraits of Tat'iana Bek, Nina Iskrenko and Tat'iana Smertina will give some idea of the development of women's poetry in Russia and provide a stimulus to further research. I should like to conclude my study of the work of three Russian women poets with the words of Simone de Beauvoir, who suggests that if an 'author depicts her heroine with such pleasure', this presupposes that the 'portrait is to some degree a self-portrait'.[15]

NOTES

These notes have been compiled by the editor with the assistance of the author.

1 See, for example, Tat'iana Bek, 'Vosem' stikhotvorenii', *Znamia*, 8 (1988), 44–7; 'Predvaritel'nye itogi: stikhi', *Novyi mir*, 3 (1992), 3–5.

2 T. Bek, *Zamysel* (Moscow: Sovetskii pisatel', 1987), p. 40. Sub-

sequent page references to this edition will be given in the text. Translations are by the editor.

3　Aleksandr Bek, *Novoe naznachenie*, posthumously published in *Znamia*, 10–11 (1986), was one of the first works published in the USSR to contain an extended portrait of Stalin; for the original publication in the West, see Aleksandr Bek, *Novoe naznachenie* (Frankfurt: Possev, 1971). For further discussion, see J. Woodhouse, 'Stalin's soldier: Aleksandr Bek's *Novoe naznachenie*', *Slavonic and East European Review*, 69 (1991) 4, pp. 601–20; Rosalind Marsh, *Soviet Fiction since Stalin: Science, Politics and Literature* (London and New York: Croom Helm, 1986), pp. 33, 44–5, 72; Rosalind Marsh, *Images of Dictatorship: Stalin in Literature* (London and New York: Routledge, 1989), pp. 76–7, 113–15. In the Gorbachev era, Tat'iana Bek was very concerned to defend her father's memory against his former enemies like Mikhail Alekseev, who gave false reasons for their failure to publish his novel earlier: see *Znamia*, 2 (1988), pp. 237–8.

4　Zhigulin is the author of poems about the Gulag, such as *Za rekoi chunoi: stikhi* (Irkutsk: Vostochno-Sibirskoe knizhnoe izdatel'stvo, 1988), and of 'Chernye kamni', *Znamia*, 7–8 (1988), a remarkable memoir about his experiences in an anti-Stalin opposition group in the years 1948–9, his torture in Voronezh prison and his life in the camps of Taishet and Kolyma in eastern Siberia. Kolyma had the reputation of being one of the worst prison camps in Stalin's Gulag system, famously depicted in Varlam Shalamov's *Kolyma Tales* (Harmondsworth: Penguin, 1990).

5　For a fuller quotation from this work entitled 'Certain Facts about the Author', see Elena Trofimova's entry on Nina Iskrenko in Marina Ledkovsky, Charlotte Rosenthal and Mary Zirin, eds., *Dictionary of Russian Women Writers* (Westport, CT: Greenwood Press, 1994), p. 264.

6　For the journal publication of Nina Iskrenko's poems, see 'Poezokontsert', *Avrora*, 7 (1988); *Rabotnitsa*, 8 (1990); *Iunost'*, 11 (1991).

7　See the almanacs *Den' poezii* (Moscow: Sovetskii pisatel' 1988); *Istoki* (Moscow: Molodaia gvardiia, 1989); *Molodaia poeziia — 89* (Mos- cow: Sovetskii pisatel', 1989); and the poetry collection *Transtaraskonshchina* (Moscow–Paris: Vivrism, 1989).

8　See Nina Iskrenko and Iurii Arabov, *Referendum: Stikhotvoreniia* (Moscow: Moskovskii rabochii, 1991). Her most notable collection to date is Nina Iskrenko, *Ili: Stikhi i teksty* (Moscow: Sovetskii pisatel', 1991); subsequent quotations from this edition will be included in the text. Some of her poems have appeared in translation in *Women's View* (Somerville, MA, 1992), pp. 151–61.

9 Tat'iana Smertina, *Iagodinochka* (Moscow, 1976); *Selo Sorvizhi* (Moscow, 1982); *Venets iz iarykh pechel* (Moscow, 1976); *Brusnichnyi ogon'* (Moscow, 1987); *Mar'ia – zazhgi snega* (Moscow, 1987); *Gusinoe pero* (Moscow, 1990); *Leto-Letechko* (Novosibirsk, 1990); *Chernichnaia tsaritsa* (Moscow, 1991); *Deva L'nianitsa* (Moscow, 1991); *Travnik* (Moscow: Sovetskii pisatel', 1992). All references in the text will be to this edition. Her most recent collection is *Russkii pogrebok: dlia boiarin'-krestianok i gorodskikh khoziaiushek* (Moscow: SPAS, 1994)

10 See the collections *Molodye golosa* (Moscow: Khudozhestvennaia literatura, 1981); *Poeziia rossiiskikh dereven'* (Moscow: Sovetskaia Rossiia, 1984); *Chas Rossii* (Moscow: Sovremennik, 1988); *Vodolei – znak Rossii* (Moscow: Sovetskii pisatel', 1992).

11 The 'Calendar of Twelve Fridays' was an ancient folk calendar preserved from Church censorship which existed parallel with the Church calendar and retained some pagan elements, frequently decreeing festivities on days of prayer. The year began and ended on days different from those laid down by the Church calendar. The number twelve implied distribution throughout the entire twelve months. See B. A. Rybakov, *Iazychestvo drevnikh slavian*, second edition (Moscow: Nauka, 1994), p. 389. The calendar was named after the half-Christian, half-pagan goddess Piatnitsa ('Friday') who watched over women's work, demanded their obedience and forbade them to work on a Friday. If her commandment was broken, she could punish the culprit by pricking her with a spindle or turning her into a frog.

12 B. A. Rybakov, *Iazychestvo drevnikh slavian*, first edition (Moscow: Nauka, 1991).

13 The acronym for 'Dialectical Materialism'.

14 The actual word used is *leliami*, which, as the author herself has explained, has a dual meaning. As a feminine proper noun, it refers to the ancient goddess Lelia, daughter of Lada, a goddess of plenty linked with the rebirth of nature in the spring, the beginning of work in the fields and the ripening harvest: see Rybakov, *Iazychestvo drevnikh slavian* (1994), p. 600. In its masculine, more common meaning, 'lel'' is associated with 'an ancient Russian god, comparable with Cupid, Eros': see V. I. Dal', *Tolkovyi slovar' zhivogo velikorusskogo iazyka* (Moscow: Russkii iazyk, 1979), II, p. 247.

15 Simone de Beauvoir, 'Nuzhno li szhech' markiza de Sada?', in Simone de Beauvoir, *Ochen' legkaia smert'* (Moscow: Respublika, 1992), pp. 366–7.

PART II

The perspective of literary criticism

CHAPTER 12

The silence of rebellion: women in the work of Leonid Andreev

Eva Buchwald

Russian writers of the turn of the century discussed the woman question with renewed urgency. The problem of woman's sexuality informed the discussion at all levels.[1] As a consequence of earlier trends in the liberal reassessment of woman's role, the main focus remained on the issues of education and employment. Although the subject of women's political representation was now addressed in journalistic debate, it received little attention from writers of *belles lettres*. The few observations that were made followed the lines of Tolstoi's comment that 'women's lack of rights has nothing to do with them not being allowed to vote or be judges'.[2]

In the general discussion on how best to channel woman's specific qualities for her own benefit as well as for the greater good of society, writers also sought to create an emotive, ideal imagery of socially and politically committed womanhood. Among the positive portraits of revolutionaries, the classic example of the period is probably the title heroine of Gor'kii's *Mat'* (1906–8; *Mother*, 1954), whose actions are rooted in a selfless, spiritual awakening motivated by her love for her son. Woman's promotion of her own separate interests was generally portrayed (largely by male writers) as at best misguided, at worst divisive. In Kuprin's novel *Iama* (1909–16; *The Pit*, 1924), for instance, there is a moral hierarchy in the various types of 'new women' represented: most negative is the portrait of the English feminist philanthropist who alienates the Russian prostitutes she hopes to liberate (and, significantly, she cannot even speak their language); more sympathetic is the singer-actress, an independent career-woman who is able to foster a certain camaraderie with the brothel's inmates as fellow wage-earners; and most positive of all is the noble undercover revolutionary posing as a prostitute, who disseminates propaganda to her male clients, but not to her enslaved colleagues.

In the portrayal of politically active women, it is a curious absence of voice which distinguishes them from their male counterparts in turn-of-the-century Russian literature.[3] Politically conscious women are driven by passionate conviction and an instinct for justice. If a woman possesses a voice of leadership at all, it is self-effacing, and the words are invariably adopted from a man. Women do not formulate or articulate their political views in the way men do in countless passages of argumentative dialogue, general debate or internal monologue. If women's experience is represented in the political forum, it is done through the mouths of men and manipulated for the sake of the cause. There is a thematic neglect of women's own experience in the vast body of this period's literature. Woman's communication of her own, either feminist or other political expression, is missing. Both these factors are related to one of the most dominant features of female portraits in literature: woman's intrinsic affinity for silence.

It is important to remember that the turn of the century was a time when women, struggling for political representation, were fighting to be heard. As a central motif in this period's literary characterization of women, silence becomes a striking metaphor. At its most straightforward, woman's silence reflects traditional concepts of woman's place. Numerous heroines stifle their own voice or have their voice directly suppressed as a result of parental intolerance, social norms, male oppression or ignorance of their own needs and rights. Examples of this can be found in the work of all writers who portray women in social or political situations. However, the theme of woman's silence is more complex and far-reaching than this. Its allegorical significance lies in the ambivalent relationship women characters seem to have towards their own silence. Although on a superficial level their silence may indeed mark an internal frustration, grief or dissatisfaction, at a deeper level it also appears, notably in the work of male writers, as a normal condition for women. In a period of increasingly vociferous agitation from oppositional movements, women breaking their silence emerges as a powerful metaphor for the noise of revolution.

It is in the work of Leonid Andreev, a writer torn by his ambivalent feelings towards revolutionary action, that the most explicit use of this metaphor can be observed. It has been suggested that Andreev 'created the drama of the great revolutionary rumbling'.[4] It is precisely in connection with the thunder of revolution that women's silence bears most significance in Andreev's work. Before examining the dimensions of this theme, it is important to emphasize that dialogue is a key feature of Andreev's narrative technique. Like many of his contemporaries, Andreev developed a philosophy of a 'new drama' as the future, liberating force of Russian literature. From 1905 onwards, Andreev concentrated on writing plays, and many of his stories are dramatic in form, particularly in their extensive use of dialogue. Andreev explored themes of subjectivism and solitude in his work, within which silence acts as an isolatory and introspective phenomenon influencing human behaviour. Andreev is unusually conscious of the existence of woman's silence as an element of human dialogue. Silence is indeed the defining motif of his female characterizations.

Andreev's understanding of the different nature of female dialogue must be distinguished, however, from the approach of a playwright like Chekhov.[5] In Chekhov's work, women's muted speech is integral to the conversation. It is often an act of communication on stage, and is part of Chekhov's development towards what has been described as the reduction of heroic voice in his plays.[6] To characterize the distinction between the two authors, it can be said that while subdued voice is simply a feature of verbal exchange – both male and female – in Chekhov's plays, by contrast in Andreev's work, the male characters make repeated, anguished reference to the disturbing fact that the women do not speak. In Andreev's drama, female silence frustrates the male interlocutor and imperils the stability of his world. Woman has the capacity for a silence

which 'is worse than any words',[7] and which has consequences
for man's relationship to his rational world. It becomes, in fact,
her voice, her unique form of expression.

Andreev's view of the special power of woman's silence/voice
can be traced in a number of his early stories. He creates a
fusion between the thunder of destruction and the silent aftermath, a fusion which was to provide the underlying dynamic
tension of many of his later plays. Woman's fundamental
affinity for silence bears the threat of an apocalyptic shriek
which results in the disruption of organized society, the world
of men. At its most extreme, the power of woman's silence
exists even in death, as in *Molchanie* (1900; *Silence*, 1916). Vera,
depressed and silent, will not communicate the reason for her
Angst to her parents. Her father, Ignatii, knows that 'nothing
will come of their conversation with Vera'.[8] Indeed, she does
not respond to her parents' questions. That she commits suicide
after their evening conversation indicates that her death is a
continuation of the silence that constituted her part in the
dialogue. Vera's mother, grief-stricken, is paralysed and struck
dumb. The singing canary, which Ignatii identifies with Vera's
soul, has been set free, completing the voiceless effect of the
feminine presence which surrounds and oppresses Ignatii. He
searches for rational arguments to explain his daughter's death,
making speeches to himself justifying his role as a father. He is
answered only by the stillness of his daughter's grave and his
wife's paralysis, from which he yearns to wrest one word of pity.

The special form of silence attributed to Andreev's female
characters jeopardizes the male definition of the world. In *Lozh'*
(1900; *The Lie*, 1916), the woman refutes the hero's 'lie', which is
his belief in her infidelity. Her refusal to define their relationship according to his lie drives him to murder her. He discovers
that her death is merely a continuation of her denial of the lie.
It is a deafening silence which denies him knowledge of the
truth forever, and leads him to despair. The impression of a
scream beneath the soundlessness is more deliberately evoked
in *Smekh* (1901; *Laughter*, 1916). In this story, the woman's final,
ringing peal of laughter is the climax of her indifference to her
admirer's declaration of love. She is so overcome with hysteria

that she cannot speak. The laughter, 'such a laugh as I had never yet heard ... a resounding cascade of laughter'[9] bursts forth directly after his romantic speech, in which he states pointedly that he 'had never spoken so well'.[10] The clamour of woman's speechlessness overwhelms the ordinary words of men.

Andreev's heroines thus possess a singular and mysterious power which stems directly from their identity in silence. The different relationship of men and women to words in Andreev's work stems essentially from a mystification of feminine qualities. James Woodward has remarked that, for Andreev, woman often represents a 'mystical-symbolic incarnation of the primitive moral bases of life'.[11] It becomes particularly apparent in Andreev's more realistic plays that women embody the symbolic content of the work. Andreev's vision of woman places her on a supra-real plane. Just as Gor'kii and Tolstoi bestow on woman her most complete identity in motherhood, Andreev sees woman as an absolute embodiment of intuitive forces. Woman's intuitive superiority places her in effortless contact with a greater universality which Andreev's male protagonists can only struggle to attain. For Andreev, this instinct for the universal means that women do not possess or require expression in the ordinary terms of men.

Andreev's female protagonists are often given oral identity through music. The musical motif is prominent in figures closely associated with the force of political revolution or of rebellion in general. Music held a central place amongst Symbolists, whose main purpose was the renewal of Russian culture, as the most irrational and therefore pure form of creative expression. In the story concerning the fate of a group revolutionaries, *Rasskaz o semi poveshennykh* (1908; *The Seven Who Were Hanged*, 1941), the theory behind revolutionary ideology is represented by the male hero Werner, while the young female martyr, Musia, symbolizes the muse or the very spirit of revolution. Her thoughts are dominated by musical sounds. She reinterprets the ordinary sounds of the prison cell in terms of their melodic resonance, and escapes, ecstatic, from the banal death sentence which faces her by immersing herself in her musical fantasy.

It is in his play *K zvezdam* (1905–6; *To the Stars*, 1921) that music is fused most completely with woman's role in a political context. The revolutionary Marusia, whose dialogue is dominated by song, is given voice as the sound of turmoil in the play. In Act Two her arrival is announced because 'she awakened the whole house with her singing'.[12] When she enters she does so singing and throughout the play she continues to break into song.

In *K zvezdam*, unusually for Andreev, man as well as woman is attuned to the universe. Like Marusia, the astronomer Ternovskii is guided by elemental forces. Ternovskii is also the father of Marusia's fiancé, Nikolai, who has been arrested during the revolutionary unrest. Ternovskii does not participate in revolutionary activity, distancing himself from local events in the tower of his observatory. Marusia by contrast is at ground level, devoted to the cause as well as to Nikolai. Ternovskii's and Marusia's different approaches to the contemporary drama have been interpreted as a difference not in the nature of their vision, but in its breadth.[13] Ternovskii's idealism is characterized by his scientific preoccupation with the stars and is of a monumental, epic stature. Marusia, on the other hand, rejects Ternovskii's self-absorbed devotion to science because she is involved with the immediacy of genuine human suffering. The separate motifs of astronomy and music, associated with Ternovskii and Marusia respectively, are not so much indications of the relative breadth of their vision as aspects of their symbolic role in the scheme of things. Ternovskii, with his wisdom of the cosmic configurations of life, is sensitive to the 'music' in the stars, while Marusia's very being embodies music. Marusia is the spirit of revolutionary change, while Ternovskii represents the hope for future rationality, for the restoration to the eternal course of the stars. These two expressions of ontological reality reflect Andreev's uneasy reaction to the reverberations of revolution. His feelings were divided between an essential enthusiasm for the radical force of change, and a horror of the inevitable violence that change would bring with it.[14] This dual reaction is increasingly discernible in Andreev's attitude to the potential of female expression. Woman's voice is in harmony with life's natural rhythm, yet simultaneously presents a danger to the established order.

In Marusia's self-sacrificial idealism, as in Musia's impassioned martyrdom in *Rasskaz o semi*, the musical element still suggests a hopeful message of positive change. As Russia progressed towards its second revolution, Andreev's optimism diminished. His later plays reveal a sense of man's increasing inability to control and nurture the musical spirit of the universe. As man's ambitions grow more worldly, more self-interested, he forces woman towards a self-destruction which will ultimately act as a form of judgement upon him. Already in the story 'T'ma' (1907; 'Darkness'), Andreev hints at the personal price of revolutionary action too rooted in theory instead of compassion. The main protagonist, the revolutionary, is gradually forced to acknowledge his moral antagonist, the prostitute, as she passes judgement on the way he leads his life. Initially it is her silence which condemns him, but his endeavours to manipulate her voice only fuel its explosive anger:

But the girl was silent and, evidently, was altogether unwilling to converse.
— Liuba, let's talk calmly, one must ...
— I do not want to talk calmly'.[15]

Man's illusory faith in his own empirical authority is undermined by woman's unwillingness either to give up her silence to his cause or to talk calmly. The play *Anfisa* (1909) is considered to be one of the few works which deals directly with the nature of male–female antagonism, or 'the conflict between the sexes'.[16] It examines the love of three sisters for the same man. Married to the eldest, Aleksandra, Kostomarov seduces Anfisa and plans to seduce the youngest, Ninochka, during the course of the play. All three sisters are in some way associated with a lack of voice in direct relation to Kostomarov. Aleksandra, who knows her husband has already been unfaithful to her, never communicates with him directly. Soon after seducing Anfisa, Kostomarov remarks: 'What is she playing? Without words, without words, she is always without words. (*Gloomily*) Do you know she has not said a single word all day?'[17] To the younger sister Ninochka, in the first stages of his desire for her, he says: 'You have eyes like those of the silence in the forest.'[18]

The dialogue of the three sisters abounds with unspoken longings and secret experiences. It is above all the presence of the deaf grandmother which imposes a pervading hush over the action. Despite the fact that she cannot hear, conversation is difficult in her presence. Kostomarov draws constant attention to her peculiar, soundless existence which he cannot comprehend. He fears the riddle of her identity. Even as a child he feared her knitting, symbol of the thread of life. He states that he does not believe she can be creating so innocent an object as a simple sock.

Kostomarov's awareness of the sisters' silence, and his constant unease in the presence of the deaf grandmother are not coincidental. They mark the sharp difference which exists in Andreev's view of male and female contact with the environment. The absence of voice is an inherent quality in woman which defines her position not only in society, but also in the natural order. For the two women revolutionaries in *Rasskaz o semi*, the isolation of the prison cell presents no conflict. The description of their mental processes places their own expression at a remove. The maternal Tat'iana thinks only of the others. Musia, in the classical mould of the willing sacrificial virgin, expresses an intuitive affinity with death through her thoughts of music. Their peaceful, introspective consolations contrast with the stress caused in the male characters by the inability to communicate with the outside world. Silence robs them of their virility, of their masculine identity. It is this absence of masculine subjectivity which Kostomarov fears. Silence is woman's precious but unfathomable identity. In *Anfisa*, the grandmother's silence leads Kostomarov to question: 'Who is she? ... She is a woman – what does that mean? She is an old woman – what does that mean? What images are preserved in that worn out, decrepit memory?'[19]

In *Anfisa*, Kostomarov senses the threat of silence to his well-being from the beginning of the play. In Act One he says of the grandmother: 'I am afraid of her deafness, in which there is so much discernment. I am afraid of this silence in which there is so much unreckoned, but resounding falsehood.'[20] His fear of the sound behind the silence predicts the events of Act Three when Anfisa is driven to make a public declaration of the relationship between herself and Kostomarov, which forces him into a decision to leave with her. By Act Four the full impact of Anfisa's outburst is felt. It is at this point that Anfisa's music disturbs Kostomarov with its wordlessness. Silence begins to erase identities:

к: You are always in black. Who are you, Anfisa?
а: (*smiling*) Who are you, Fedor Ivanovich?
(*Both start laughing strangely and stop at once*)
к: A strange game. But I want to talk seriously. Today you haven't said one word all day, Anfisa. Maybe you haven't noticed, but you haven't said one word all day, Anfisa.[21]

The ensuing dialogue is built around the subject of her silence, which Kostomarov states he finds 'unbearable'. Anfisa explains: 'Did I not scream yesterday? Well I can still hear that scream, it still rings in my ears. But it was someone else who screamed, whereas I – fell silent.'[22] Anfisa poisons Kostomarov. The grandmother, symbol of the inevitable course of life, places the final seal on the dialogue. Repeating her words from Act One to indicate that the drama has come full circle, she speaks the final line of the play: 'There is nothing to be done. Everything is done.' And she adds: 'Be silent.'[23]

With the death of Kostomarov, the grandmother's words seem to imply that the remaining female world may retreat into its private silent solace. Man cannot share woman's special connection with silence, but he should know how to appreciate it. As in *Anfisa*, male rejection of the music played by women is a sign of men's failure to cherish properly feminine expression. In Act One of *Mysl'* (1915; *Thought*),[24] Tat'iana is urged to play the piano by her husband. For the dissatisfied Savelov, the tune proves no less unsettling than his wife's voice:

SAVELOV: Tania, go and play something for me. I need it. Don't talk
now – I need it. Go ahead ... Enough, Tania, Don't. Come
here! ... Talk to me rather ... but perhaps you don't feel like
talking to me...[25]

In Act Two of *Ekaterina Ivanovna* (1912; *Katerina*, 1923) the title
heroine begs her husband, Stibelev, five times to listen to her
play, but the latter neglects to grant her music the attention it
deserves, and this marks the decline of their marital
reconciliation.

To some extent, woman's apparent absence of voice in these
plays is a predictable condition of the social situation. Quite
frequently, women are unable to penetrate the intellectual
debate. Such is the case with Tatiana's exclusion from the
conversation conducted between the two male protagonists in
Act Three of *Mysl'*. The exchange concerns the possible
existence of a super-human 'thought' or idea, also the central
theme of the play. The conversation takes place between the
scientist Kerzhentsev, who expresses his faith in the theory, and
the writer Savelov, who opposes the theoretical premise in
favour of 'real life' (*nastoiashchaia zhizn'*). Savelov's wife,
Tat'iana, is meanwhile relegated to the children's nursery
against her wishes. A similar pattern occurs in *Ekaterina Ivanovna*
when the theory of art is discussed in the final act by the male
protagonists, while the two women present are silent onlookers.

In both plays, Andreev astutely portrays the psychological
stress women experience at being denied expression by male
force. Tat'iana tries to persuade her husband that Kerzhentsev
is dangerous (which she senses, of course, intuitively). Her
attempts to intervene in the escalating verbal conflict dwindle
to cries of her husband's name. Tat'iana's pleas of 'Alesha ...'
can be compared with Ekaterina's frequent interjections, in Act
Two of the play, of 'let me go ...' ('pusti ...'). This cry
represents Ekaterina's defeated efforts to interrupt her husband
as he holds her forcibly in his grasp. In both cases the heroine's
failure to be heard stems from the fact that she is powerless to
control both the situation in general and her actions in
particular.

As women are robbed of the ability to control events, the

collusion of men in the process is apparent. Male conflict in Andreev's work possesses the bonding quality that is popularly associated with the duel as a sport: the equal partnership of fair enemies. It is a battle of wits or love, in which the object of the conflict unites the contestants, invariably to the exclusion of women. Before Tat'iana is completely silenced by the theoretical fencing between the two men, she tries to separate them because she fears for her husband's safety. Far from succeeding, it is she who is sent from the room by her husband. Immediately before he does this, Savelov makes several references to the times when he and Kerzhentsev were students together, before he had met Tat'iana, underlining the stronger relationship between the two men. In *Ekaterina Ivanovna*, various pairs of men, and eventually all the men, are united by solid social bonds which contrast with the title heroine's increasing isolation. This bond is sealed on several occasions by an exchange of cigarettes, often while Ekaterina is playing music, and always once she has been excluded from the scene. The men belittle Ekaterina's art by indulging companionably in the banal, worldly preoccupation of smoking. Throughout the play, Ekaterina also fails to assert her version of the drama of infidelity which provides the plot-thread of the play. It was, in fact, Stibelev's obsessive conviction of her infidelity which propelled her towards her first seduction. Ultimately, it is a conspiracy of masculine interests, and masculine definitions of events, which lead her to self-destruction.

Andreev is sensitive to the sheer force of a male conspiracy which annihilates woman's presence by refusing to acknowledge her version of life's experience. In *Ekaterina Ivanovna*, Stibelev attempts to silence his wife literally and irrevocably by shooting at her three times in the opening scene, but he misses each time. The subsequent discussion of male 'sportsmanship' in the play implies the sexual violence inherent in these men's attitude towards women. Stibelev is ashamed of his poor marksmanship. His brother's remark that only men who know how to use a gun are entitled to shoot is a reflection on his virility. When the question is raised: 'And perhaps, there is no need to shoot at all?', Stibelev answers: 'So what are revolvers made for, then?'.[26] By the end of the play, Stibelev will encourage his wife's sexual exploitation by the other men in his social circle. If she survived his physical assault, she is destroyed psychologically and spiritually by the band of men in the final scene who encourage her to perform the naked dance of Salome.

Andreev's depiction of male abuse of women is skilfully convincing. It does not however represent a tendentious criticism in his work. Rather it is a descriptive motif in a broader, increasingly pessimistic picture of society. He does not suggest that male bonding itself, which requires a female victim to seal it, is the element which destroys human relationships and individual personalities. In both *Mysl'* and *Ekaterina Ivanovna*, the target of his criticism is man's divorce from genuine truth in favour of a false reality. Kerzhentsev is cut off from life by his faith in pure theory. Stibelev and his colleagues are cut off from humanity by their patronage of sophisticated society. Women appear as victims not so much because they are manipulated by men, but because they represent objectified facets of the 'living life' with which the men around them fail to connect. Woman's own subjective identity is not at issue here, or even represented. The choice between natural life and artificial reality remains a uniquely male conflict in Andreev's work.

Although *Ekaterina Ivanovna* and *Mysl'*, as indeed *Anfisa*, no longer seem to be directly concerned with the subject of revolutionary change, their underlying tensions constitute Andreev's commentary on contemporary social, political and aesthetic values. As men have lost the ability to conjure up or be inspired by woman's mystical voice, the pure muse of revolution has lost her capacity for restraint. Just as silence is woman's unique form of expression in Andreev, so woman's scream is her most penetrating silence. To force the expression of her despair is to invite irrevocable disaster. The power of the scream/silence engulfs the protagonists of the drama which provoked it. In the final act of *Mysl'*, Kerzhentsev, losing his mind, tries to understand why his superior rational idea proved inadequate. He struggles to reason with the servant girl, Masha, who repeatedly replies that she knows nothing, that she simply lives. Kerzhentsev cannot accept this.

He feels that her ignorance of culture (the theatre, the Bible, science) conceals a deeper knowledge:

You know something, Masha, you know something valuable, Masha, unique, which offers salvation, but what? But what? ... No, Masha, it is not true that you know nothing, that is a lie, and I cling to you on purpose ... No, you know something that you don't want to tell. Why did God give voice only to his devils, while his angels are without words?[27]

In the final encounter between Tat'iana and Kerzhentsev, there is a symbolic equation between woman and the exceptional 'thought' as the agent of Kerzhentsev's downfall. He states: 'I was basely betrayed, as only women, slaves and thoughts betray.'[28] He feels he was tricked by his scientific faith in the purity of his thought. Tat'iana, by contrast, feels she alone is to blame, that Kerzhentsev's love for her had driven him insane. It is precisely Tat'iana's conviction and statement of his insanity which the scientist finds insupportable. He struggles to prevent her from leaving until she categorically declares that she knows he is sane: 'Tell me! Gather all your intelligence and tell me calmly, I trust you, tell me, that I am not mad!'[29] Tat'iana's emphatic refusal, followed by the silence of her absence, is Kerzhentsev's final defeat, and unleashes a despair which destroys his rational world.

In Andreev's work, women's silence is a condition which is natural to them because of their greater affinity with the unspoken mysteries of the universe. But in the lives of men it plays a paradoxical role, one which often reflects the boundaries of revolutionary aspirations and social change. Women, attuned to the elemental life force, have no need for voice in worldly affairs. Men need to protect woman's uniquely melodic silence in order to preserve their earthly world. If they abuse it, they lose touch with 'living life', by favouring theory which is devoid of inspiration, by cultivating social reality which is without spirit. At this point woman's silence, like nature betrayed, takes its revenge. Man struggles to control it but only succeeds in forcing the scream which announces the irrevocable silence of destruction. Woman's voice released marks the onset of oblivion, often in death, but always in absolute discord between man and ontological reality.

NOTES

1 Ed: for further discussion, see Peter Ulf Møller, *Postlude to the Kreutzer Sonata: Tolstoy and the Debate on Sexual Morality in Russian Literature in the 1890s*, trans. John Kendal (Leiden and New York: E. J. Brill, 1989); Laura Engelstein, *The Keys to Happiness: Sex and the Search for Modernity in fin-de-siècle Russia* (Ithaca, NY: Cornell University Press, 1992).

2 L. N. Tolstoi, 'Kreitserova Sonata', in Tolstoi, *Sobranie sochinenii v dvadtsati dvukh tomakh*, XII (Moscow, 1983), p. 142.

3 For a detailed assessment of how writers in this period addressed the main issues of the woman question, and for an analysis of the literary images of politically active women, see chapters 1 and 2 of Eva Buchwald, 'Ideals of Womanhood in the Prose and Drama of Finland and Russia 1894–1917' (unpublished Ph.D. thesis, London, 1990), pp. 47–126.

4 Iu. N. Chirva, 'O p'esakh Leonida Andreeva', in L. N. Andreev, *Dramaticheskie proizvedeniia v dvukh tomakh*, I (Leningrad, 1989), p. 9.

5 For an examination of women in Chekhov's dialogue, see Buchwald, 'Ideals of Womanhood', pp. 175–80.

6 See, for example, Donald Rayfield, *Chekhov: The Evolution of his Art* (London: Elek, 1975).

7 Leonid Andreev, 'Ekaterina Ivanovna', in *Polnoe sobranie sochinenii*, 8 vols. (St Petersburg, 1913), VIII, p. 203.

8 Andreev, 'Molchanie', in *Polnoe sobranie*, I, p. 87.

9 Andreev, 'Smekh', in *Polnoe sobranie*, I, p. 138.

10 Andreev, 'Smekh', p. 137.

11 James B. Woodward, *Leonid Andreev: a Study* (Oxford: Clarendon Press, 1969), p. 237.

12 Andreev, 'K zvezdam', in *Polnoe sobranie*, IV, p. 206.

13 Woodward, *Leonid Andreev*, p. 138.

14 *Ibid.*, pp. 131–2.

15 Andreev, 'T'ma', in *Polnoe sobranie*, II, p. 157.

16 Woodward, *Leonid Andreev*, pp. 230–3.

17 Andreev, 'Anfisa', in *Polnoe sobranie*, VII, p. 303.

18 *Ibid.*, p. 282.

19 *Ibid.*, p. 268.

20 *Ibid.*, p. 269.

21 *Ibid.*, p. 310.

22 *Ibid.*, p. 311.
23 *Ibid.*, p. 319.
24 The subject of the play was first used for a short story of 1902 by the same name, written in the form of a diary. I will concentrate on the play version since I am concerned with dialogue.
25 Andreev, *Mysl'* (Berlin, no date), p. 13–14.
26 Andreev, *Ekaterina Ivanovna*, p. 193.
27 Andreev, *Mysl'*, pp. 57–8.
28 Andreev, *Mysl'*, p. 59.
29 Andreev, *Mysl'*, p. 63.

CHAPTER 13

Poor Liza: the sexual politics of Elizaveta Bam by Daniil Kharms

Graham Roberts

In her book, *The Originality of the Avant-Garde and Other Modernist Myths*, Rosalind Krauss argues that innovation in the arts is frequently anything but; apparently new trends, she suggests, may amount to nothing more than the repetition of old trends.[1] Although Krauss restricts herself by and large to the visual avant-garde, what she says may also be said to apply to much avant-garde writing. One text for which her argument seems particularly appropriate, at least in its sexual politics, is Daniil Kharms's 1927 play *Elizaveta Bam*.

Daniil Kharms (1905–42) was arguably one of the most important and influential literary figures of 1920s and 1930s Leningrad.[2] Although his writing ran from approximately 1925 to his death in 1942, he is perhaps best remembered as a founder member of the outlandish group of Leningrad writers known generally as *Oberiu* (a distorted acronym of 'Ob"edinenie real'nogo iskusstva', or 'The Association of Real Art'), in existence during the comparatively brief period 1927–30.[3] It was during the first public performance of *Oberiu*, on 24 January 1928, at the Leningrad Press Club, that Kharms's play *Elizaveta Bam* was premièred.[4] The declaration of the group's aesthetic principles, which was also part of the show, might be said to bear out Krauss's thesis concerning the avant-garde and its ambiguous attitude towards convention: on the one hand, 'Oberiu' was utterly dismissive of what it called 'art of the old schools'; on the other hand, it identified the *balagan*, or medieval Russian folk theatre, as the art form on which any genuine theatre should be based: '*balagan* is theatre', it proclaimed.[5] Kharms's play *Elizaveta Bam* is itself full of such ambiguities, and never more so than in its sexual politics, as we shall see. For when viewed from one perspective the work appears to be progressive in the images of women which it offers, while from another angle it can be read as far more reactionary.

Although female characters appear in a number of works by Kharms (prose, poetry and drama), the writer's representation of women is an area which has so far attracted very little critical attention.[6] The only scholar to have raised this question in any sustained way is Jean-Philippe Jaccard, although he has restricted himself to those examples of Kharms's verse and prose which contain an explicit element of sexuality.[7] In the texts which Jaccard discusses, sexuality – and in particular female sexuality – is depicted with a voyeurism verging on the pornographic (many of Kharms's women appear totally naked, with their odours and secretions described in lurid detail).[8] Jaccard, however, gives a primarily metaphysical reading of Kharms's interest in the corporeal (not to say the corpulent). Supporting his interpretation with references to the views on sex and women held by two of Kharms's close associates, namely Aleksandr Vvedenskii and Leonid Lipavskii, Jaccard maintains that for Kharms sex was ultimately linked to the question of temporality, and thereby death.[9]

Jaccard has nothing, however, to say about sexuality in *Elizaveta Bam*, a text where a woman, by giving herself (up) to two men, as good as lets herself die. The 'plot' (if that is the right word) of the play, which is split into nineteen sections or 'bits' (*kuski*) of varying length, concerns the arrest of Elizaveta by two men, Ivan Ivanovich and Petr Nikolaevich.[10] She is originally told that the reason for her arrest is, simply, the fact that she has no voice, a state which Petr Nikolaevich declares to be a 'heinous crime' deserving of 'severe punishment'. By the end of the play, however, she stands accused (and is even denounced by her mother) of perhaps an even more absurd 'crime', namely the murder of Petr Nikolaevich, the same Petr Nikolaevich, in fact, who has come to arrest her.

In a sense, Jaccard's omission of this play in his article on Kharms and sexuality is understandable. After all, although Elizaveta is the object of male desire, there appears to be nothing explicitly sexual about this desire, and little if anything sexual about Elizaveta herself. What Jaccard, and others, have instead focused on in their accounts of *Elizaveta Bam* is the fact that communication in the play constantly breaks down, in ways which look forward, so we are told, to the Theatre of the Absurd.[11] Yet, and this is what we shall be trying to show, issues of language in *Elizaveta Bam* are directly relevant to those of sex, and sexual politics.

To suggest that language is deeply political is, of course, to rehearse what is by now a familiar argument. One thinker who has made a particularly eloquent contribution to the debate is the French philosopher Jean-François Lyotard. In his provocative study of postmodernity, Lyotard has argued, echoing both Wittgenstein and Foucault, that societies and their élites use language and 'language games' to legitimate themselves and perpetuate their own power. In particular, Lyotard defines 'terror' as 'the efficiency gained by eliminating, or threatening to eliminate, a player from the language game one shares with him'.[12] *Elizaveta Bam* contains a particularly graphic example of such state-sponsored terror, and one could be forgiven for reading the play as a chilling prophecy of the Stalinist nightmare to come.[13] Yet in *Elizaveta Bam* the line between oppressor and oppressed, between those who speak and those who have no right to speak is clearly and explicitly gender-determined. Petr and Ivan both impose on Elizaveta from the outset the language game that she is guilty, and simultaneously deny her a voice, thereby excluding her from playing that game. In this way, Kharms's play shows male, patriarchal discourse manipulating language and language games to legitimate its power, to marginalize and ultimately suppress the female.[14]

Yet for much of the play, Elizaveta refuses to be silenced by the men. By continuing to speak she rejects their Freudian logic, which seeks to define her in terms of a 'lack', denying her not just a voice but a subjectivity. She uses her voice to turn the tables on her oppressors, imposing her own, alternative language games. If the men's game appears to be based on the desire to deny her the right to use any word, any signifier, Elizaveta seeks, on the contrary, to liberate the linguistic signifier (and thereby herself) as much as possible. Accordingly, she proceeds to invent new language games, where words do not have their usual meaning, where words and the world go their separate ways. The first time she does this explicitly occurs at the end of the second section of the play, and is all the more important since it concerns Elizaveta's response to the men's (criminalizing) charge of voicelessness:

ЕЛ.Б: Почему я преступница?
П.Н.: Потому, что Вы лишены всякого голоса.
И.И.: Лишены всякого голоса.
ЕЛ.Б: А я не лишена. Вы можете проверить по часам.[15]

(EL. BAM: Why am I a criminal?
PETR. NIK.: Because you have lost the right to speak.
IVAN IV.: Lost the right to speak.
EL. BAM: No I haven't. You can check by the clock.)

Once this desemanticizing pattern has been established by Elizaveta, Ivan and Petr (and, indeed, all the other characters) go along with her game(s) for much of the play. For example, Ivan calls Elizaveta a 'forget-me-not' (p. 225), and later refers to her by using a series of different patronymics (p. 226); Petr and Ivan use the same 'I' (p. 229); her 'daddy' (*papasha*) asks whether Ivan's children named Dar'ia, Mar'ia and Nina are boys (p. 232); and he declares that his right arm and leg are the same as his left arm and ear (p. 232).

In the play's eighth section, Elizaveta begins to howl like a wolf. Next, she utters a word irrelevant to the context ('prunes'), and finally she produces an irrelevant phrase ('A horse as black as a crow, and on the horse a soldier!'). Ivan Ivanovich seems to have no choice but to follow suit:

ЕЛ.Б.: Ууууу-у-у-у-у-у-у-у.
И.И.: Во-о-о-о-о-лчица.
ЕЛ.Б.: (*дрожит*): У-у-у-у-у — черносливы.
И.И.: Пр-р-р-рабабушка. *руку.*
ЕЛ.Б: Ликование!
И.И.: Погублена навеки! *палец.*
ЕЛ.Б.: Вороной конь, а на коне солдат!

(EL. BAM: Ooh-oo-oo-oo.
IVAN IV.: She-ee-ee-wolf.

EL. BAM (*shaking*): Oo-oo-oo-prunes.
IVAN IV.: Gr-r-r-r-eat grandmother. (*lowers his arm*)
EL. BAM: Triumph!
IVAN IV.: You're destroyed for ever! (*lowers his finger*)
EL. BAM: A horse as black as a crow, and on the horse a soldier!)

(p. 230)

Whole sections of the play are in fact constructed like language games, based on a split between signifier and signified. In the ninth, 'pastoral' (*peizazhnyi*) part, Ivan tells a story which appears to have nothing to do with the rest of the action, about a very brief meeting he has had with a certain Kol'ka. The next section of the play is made up of a monologue by Elizaveta's daddy about a group of girls and their bizarre need for a hot iron. Section Twelve features another apparently spontaneous language game, this time based on semantic substitution rather than isolation, and played while the characters run around the stage:

МАМАША (*бежит за Ел.Б.*): Хлеб ешь?
ЕЛ.Б.: Суп ешь?
ПАПАША: Мясо ешь? (*бежит*).
МАМАША: Муку ешь? [...]
МАМАША: Ой, ноги устали!
И.И.: Ой, руки устали!
ЕЛ.Б.: Ой, ножницы устали!
ПАПАША: Ой, пружины устали!

(MUMMY (*running after El. Bam*): Have some bread?
EL. BAM: Have some soup?
DADDY: Have some meat? (*running*).
MUMMY: Have some flour? [...]
MUMMY: Oh, my legs are tired!
IVAN IV.: Oh, my arms are tired!
EL. BAM: Oh, my scissors are tired!
DADDY: Oh, my springs are tired!)

(p. 232)

In the sixteenth section, entitled 'Chimes' ('Kuranty'), the characters suddenly play another spontaneous language game, one, moreover, clearly initiated by Elizaveta. This time, the basic syntactical structures, and rhythm, are maintained while the words themselves are switched around, forming sentences which are grammatically correct, but semantically 'nonsensical':

ЕЛ.Б.: Иван Иванович, сходите в полпивную и принесите нам бутылку пива и горох.

И.И.: Ага, горох и полбутылки пива, сходить в пивную, а оттудова   сюда.

ЕЛ.Б.: Не полбутылки, а бутылку пива, и не в пивную, а в горох идти!

И.И.: Сейчас, я шубу в полпивную спрячу, а сам на голову надену полгорох.

(EL. BAM: Ivan Ivanovich, go down to the halfbar and bring us a bottle of beer and some peas.

IVAN IV.: Aha! peas and a half bottle of beer, go down to the bar, and from there, back here.

EL. BAM: Not a half bottle, but a bottle of beer, and don't go to the bar, go to the peas!

IVAN IV.: Right away I'll hide my fur coat in the halfbar and I'll put halfpeas on my head.)   (p. 239)

Elizaveta clearly uses language to resist and subvert the patriarchal discourse of Petr and Ivan. In this way, Elizaveta's words and word games function rather like Julia Kristeva's semiotic chora, since by their 'revolutionary' resistance to meaning in any conventional sense they constitute (unconscious?) ruptures in the fixed, stable, centralizing language of the symbolic order.[16] To take this analogy further, it is surely the revolutionary nature of Elizaveta's voice which explains the men's desire to deprive her of that voice. For, as Toril Moi eloquently puts it, 'the symbolic order is a patriarchal order, and any subject who tries to disrupt it, who lets unconscious forces slip through the symbolic repression, puts her or himself in a position of revolt against this regime'.[17] Elizaveta resembles the Kristevan *sujet-en-procès* both as an unfixed, subversive subject-in-process, and as a subject-on-trial.

Although the analogy with Kristevan linguistics has its attractions, it should be noted that Kristeva avoids any essentialist position which might view the semiotic as biologically determined; much of *Revolution in Poetic Language* is concerned with finding traces of the chora in the work of the male poets

Lautréamont and Mallarmé. It is simply that for Kristeva, as Toril Moi observes, the semiotic and the feminine are linked by their marginality *vis-à-vis* patriarchal discourse.[18] In *Elizaveta Bam*, on the other hand, the line dividing oppressor and oppressed is clearly gender-specific.[19] For much of the play, Elizaveta is successful in her attempts to subvert her (male) oppressors' speech and thought. This is shown as early as section three, when Ivan explicitly subjugates himself to her:

Если позволите, Елизавета Таракановна, я пойду лучше домой. Меня ждет жена дома. У меня много ребят, Елизавета Таракановна. Простите, что я так надоел Вам. Не забывайте меня. Такой уж я человек, что все меня гоняют. За что, спрашивается? Украл я, что ли? Ведь нет! Елизавета Эдуардовна, я честный человек [...] Вы уж простите меня. Я, Елизавета Михайловна, домой пойду.

(If you will allow me, Elizaveta Cockroachovna, I had better be going home. My wife's waiting for me at home. I have lots of children, Elizaveta Cockroachovna. Forgive me for being so boring. Don't forget me. I'm the sort of person everyone sends on errands. Why, one wonders? Am I a thief or something? Of course not! Elizaveta Edwardovna, I'm an honest man [...] Please forgive me. I'm going home, Elizaveta Mikhailovna.)   (p. 226)

Elizaveta uses language as an epistemological tool, in order to come to terms with, to make public and thereby 'domesticate' a new and very threatening reality. Yet language in *Elizaveta Bam* also has an ontological function. For words appear actually to make things happen – and this apparently irrespective of the psychology, or volition, of the characters involved. As Jenny Stelleman has observed, 'the characters create a new situation, a different reality, by their speech'.[20] In Kharms's play, anyone's utterances have the potential to add new streets to what Wittgenstein termed the 'city' of language, thereby constructing new realities. Or almost anyone's.

For it is masculine discourse, however flawed, however 'absurd', which eventually wins the day. *Elizaveta Bam* draws a clear distinction between those who can articulate new worlds (men) and those who cannot (women). What the men say, even if it is as bizarre as the charge laid against Elizaveta, appears to become reality, as they eventually succeed in arresting Elizaveta and take her away. Their version of reality comes, moreover, complete with an 'official' seal of approval – as is implied by the title of the play's penultimate section, 'Realistic dry-official' ('Realisticheskii sukho-ofitsial'nyi', p. 240).[21] All women can do, it would appear, is accept this reality or perish, which is precisely perhaps why Elizaveta's 'mummy' (*mamasha*) eventually complies with the men's version of events – despite the fact that what they say is patently untrue – and denounces her daughter. Given what Kharms's play has to say about the primacy of (patriarchal) language, it is perhaps little wonder that Ivan Ivanovich declares (twice), 'I speak so as to exist' ('Ia govoriu, chtoby byt''), and, moreover, that Elizaveta's only reaction on hearing him is to foreground the issue of speech herself by asking, 'What are you saying?' ('Chto Vy govorite?', p. 230). In *Elizaveta Bam* it is one's gender which determines the status of one's language, and one's language which determines one's very existence as a human being – hence the tragic irony of Elizaveta's exultant, 'Hurray! I haven't said a thing!' ('Ura! Ia nichego ne govorila', p. 230).[22] This fact about gender and language is ultimately the reason why Elizaveta is persecuted, victimized and defeated by all of the other characters (including, significantly, her mummy who eventually denounces her, and her daddy, who appears unable and ultimately unwilling to help her).[23]

Elizaveta's struggle, and eventual alienation, are primarily linguistic. Her oppressors seek to deny her a voice, yet throughout the play she not only speaks, but speaks in a way which threatens the men and their status as oppressors. The real tragedy for Elizaveta, however, is that the 'alternative' discourse which she articulates, her disruptive, semiotic language, can never overcome the orthodox symbolic language of the patriarchy. For the cruel irony at the heart of *Elizaveta Bam* is that in seeking to play her own game, by splitting words and things, Elizaveta is in fact playing the men's game, speaking their language.[24] This is because the men's discourse is based on precisely the kind of 'rupture' between signifier and signified which Elizaveta appeals to throughout the play in her struggle with the men. It is only at the end of the play (in the eighteenth section) that this becomes clear, however, when Ivan Ivanovich and Petr Nikolaevich explicitly accuse Elizaveta of having murdered Petr Nikolaevich. It is perhaps the realization of the futility of her own, semiotic struggle, not to say of her connivance in her own destruction, that prompts Elizaveta to capitulate, once her mummy's denunciation deprives her of any female solidarity.[25] Yet whatever she does, Elizaveta stands to lose her own voice, her own language, and therefore her own world, her own reality, her own self. Oblivion at the hands – or rather in the mouths – of the public patriarchy and its official henchmen would seem to be her inevitable fate.

In *Elizaveta Bam* language, then, is no longer primarily a means of referring to objects in the real world, or even of making true or false statements about them; rather it is a tool by which the ruling élite of a given community exclude others from that community (more specifically, men, with the collaboration of some women, exclude women from the patriarchy). What Kharms's play seems to suggest is the idea, most forcefully argued by Dale Spender, that 'males, as the dominant group, have produced language, thought and reality'.[26] Ultimately, Elizaveta is marginalized by the patriarchy in much the same way as the 'non-referential' modes of discourse and 'popular' forms of literature which she embodies (examples of which also abound in the play) are excluded from the cultural canon. In an important sense then, Elizaveta stands as a reminder of the (Derridean) 'absent centre' of the predominantly male discourse of any patriarchal society. Indeed, that critical accounts of *Elizaveta Bam* have so far ignored the gender of the victim and her victimizers, suggests that patriarchal values are as much a part of the world outside the text as the world depicted within it.[27] (Mikhail Meilakh, for one, has suggested that the real-life inspiration for Elizaveta's abduction may have been the arrest of a man, Georgii Katsman, who had previously collaborated with Kharms on theatre projects.)[28] By her socially transgressive behaviour and discourse, by her refusal to bow to the men's will, to accept either the words they speak or the world they attempt to construct, Elizaveta represents in miniature the subversive, carnivalesque ideology of popular festive modes of literature.[29] Her 'dialogic' language – and the language games which for a time she succeeds in getting the men to speak – are profoundly carnivalesque in the Bakhtinian sense.[30] It is in vain that Petr Nikolaevich asks her 'to listen properly to my words' (p. 229). Mocking and inverting forms of 'high' culture and 'official' discourse, Elizaveta is reminiscent of the Freudian 'hysteric'. Yet it is arguably in Elizaveta's carnivalesque, hysterical nature that the problem lies. For as Bakhtin's accounts of Rabelais and Dostoevskii make clear, carnival is politically ambivalent, since it represents only the temporary inversion of existing power structures, structures which it ultimately re-establishes and reinforces. As Bakhtin puts it, 'the primary carnivalistic act is the mock crowning and subsequent decrowning of the carnival king . . . through [which] *a new crowning already glimmers*'.[31] An analogous pattern occurs in *Elizaveta Bam*, where Elizaveta's revolt is framed by the affirmation, and subsequent reaffirmation of patriarchal rule. Her subversive activity is itself limited, for, as Clair Wills notes, the hysteric's 'capacity for turning things "upside down" is contained within the family'.[32] Tragically for Elizaveta, it is indeed only 'within the family' that she represents a subversive, carnivalizing force to counterbalance the masculine, patriarchal discourse of the two henchmen. For it is her mummy who finally denounces her as a murderess (while her daddy declares, unsympathetically, that 'women understand nothing'), thereby precipitating the tragic denouement.

Mention of the carnivalesque underlines the fact that the sexual politics of *Elizaveta Bam* are a good deal more ambivalent and less progressive than our reading of the text first suggests. In a sense this should not surprise us, given the ways in which women are depicted elsewhere in Kharms's opus. To return for a moment to Jaccard and his article, most of the texts discussed are profoundly misogynistic, a point which Jaccard surprisingly overlooks. Women are mostly naked, unclean (these two ideas appear to be fundamentally linked by Kharms), and, most importantly, voiceless. One of the best examples of this is contained in the prose piece involving an artist's model who sits naked while a group of artists attempt to paint her. The only male in the group finds the woman seductive, while two female artists find the sight of the woman, the smell, and the secretions emanating from between her legs, quite disgusting. We never hear a single word from the model herself, however, who remains entirely passive throughout. The woman's status here is entirely determined by the male 'artist', whether Kharms's character or Kharms himself.[33] (This text offers a typical example of Kharms's tendency to dehumanize in one way or another virtually all his female characters.)[34]

It may well have been texts such as this which prompted one reviewer recently to argue that Kharms himself belonged 'entirely within the Russian patriarchal tradition'.[35] Whatever the truth of this statement, this brings us back to *Elizaveta Bam* in which, ironically, one could argue that Kharms himself eventually silences the main female character by having her suddenly and unexpectedly accept the fate imposed upon her by the patriarchy. Like any carnivalesque text, Kharms's play looks forward to the recrowning of the decrowned authority, in this case the reimposition of men's power over women, depicting such power as inevitable, natural, and supported by the very circular logic which ensnares Elizaveta.

That male power over women is natural is a message, moreover, which is ultimately reinforced by the stereotypical images of women which Kharms presents us with in *Elizaveta Bam*. Of the eleven major stereotypes of femininity which Mary Ellmann identifies, Elizaveta conforms at one time or another to at least six; trapped in her small room, uttering 'nonsensical' language and repeatedly changing her attitude to the other characters, Elizaveta is the embodiment of formlessness, passivity, instability, confinement, irrationality and compliancy.[36] In the final stages of the play Elizaveta appears suddenly and unexpectedly to have no choice but to revert to a sexual stereotype; passive, and apparently helpless now her wicked mother (stepmother?) has condemned her, she merely submits to the end of the 'game', resigned, so it would seem, to the inevitability of her destruction. What Kharms ultimately presents us with, in fact, in this supposedly 'avant-garde' text is nothing more than two –

perhaps *the* two – archetypal images of 'women'; the maiden who has committed no sin, and the wicked stepmother/witch. This is perhaps the most interesting, not to say the most unsettling, aspect of Kharms's supposedly 'new' world-view, 'a new sense of life and its objects', so vaunted in the 'Oberiu' declaration.

Little, in fact, seems to have changed since the demise of Karamzin's heroine 'poor Liza', Elizaveta's namesake and role model, the innocent flower-seller who is seduced by the rake Erast and who eventually commits suicide when he betrays her love.[37] Like her eighteenth-century predecessor, Elizaveta ultimately has no control over her destiny, for, as is also the case with Liza, males compete over her virtue, (her daddy and Petr Nikolaevich clash (s)words in the mock-epic scene of the 'battle of the two heroes' in section fifteen) while she herself remains 'voiceless', and off stage altogether.[38] In terms of her relationships with other women, however, things are even worse for Kharms's heroine. For if, as Joe Andrew has pointed out, Liza's mother passively connives at her seduction, Elizaveta's mummy actually precipitates her daughter's destruction. Both cases, however, are in fact typical of those texts, generally written by men, in which, to quote Elaine Showalter, 'the feminine heroine grows up in a world without female solidarity, where women in fact police each other on behalf of patriarchal tyranny'.[39] With no males capable of defending her, and with other women conniving with her male enemies, Elizaveta's surrender in the final scene of the play means that she is in effect allowing herself to die. Her self-destruction is functionally indistinguishable from the suicide committed by Liza – and countless other heroines of male literature. In each case it appears, ironically, to be the only self-determining act the heroine is allowed, symbolizing as it does her acceptance of her exclusion from the patriarchy. That such passive consent is truly absurd is underscored in *Elizaveta Bam*, however ironically and unintentionally, by the fact that Kharms's heroine is survived by all the male characters, even those who are supposed to be dead.

Elizaveta Bam, then, is a play whose sexual politics are

profoundly ambivalent. On the one hand, Kharms shows how the patriarchy uses language and language games to terrorize those (women) whom it seeks to exclude, either imposing on them an alien discourse, or condemning them to silence.[40] At the same time, however, the play suggests that such a situation is natural, since all women are either pure, guiltless and capable of only limited resistance, or wicked, conniving creatures who betray their defenceless daughters/sisters. Patriarchal language and the power that lies behind it is challenged, but only temporarily, and in a way which ultimately reinforces it.

Viewed in this light, *Elizaveta Bam* is far less progressive than might first appear to be the case. But perhaps we should not be too surprised by this. For critics such as Barbara Heldt argue that writing conventionally termed 'avant-garde' tends to be not less sexually repressive than that which precedes it, but more so: 'in non-realist works, as the text fragments, as interest in word-formation and word-arrangement increases, there seems to be an increase among male authors in abuse of women'.[41] More generally, Naomi Segal maintains that when male discourse 'abjures the erotics of virtue, it tends to replace it by the erotics of rape or captivity'.[42] One could argue that in *Elizaveta Bam* something slightly different occurs, as Kharms retains the former only to subsume it within the latter. Kharms's inevitably male language is, like that of his characters, a typically patriarchal discourse, in which 'what is female is kept back, silenced and undervalued'.[43] Poor Liza; and poor Elizaveta Bam.

NOTES

1 Rosalind Krauss, *The Originality of the Avant-Garde and Other Modernist Myths* (Cambridge, MA: MIT Press, 1985).
2 One of the fullest summaries of Kharms's life and works is contained in Anatolii Aleksandrov, 'Chudodei: lichnost' i tvorchestvo Daniila Kharmsa', in Daniil Kharms, *Polet v nebesa: Stikhi. Proza. Dramy. Pis'ma* (Moscow: Sovetskii pisatel', 1989), ed. by A. Aleksandrov, pp. 7–48. See also A. Aleksandrov, 'A Kharms chronology', trans. by Neil Cornwell, in Neil Cornwell, ed.,

Daniil Kharms and the Poetics of the Absurd: Essays and Materials (London: Macmillan, 1991), pp. 32–46.

3 The poet Igor′ Bakhterev is the only surviving member of this group, which also contained Nikolai Zabolotskii, Aleksandr Vvedenskii and Konstantin Vaginov: see Bakhterev's reminiscences on *Oberiu*, 'Kogda my byli molodymi (nevydumannyi rasskaz)', in A. V. Zabolotskaia, A. V. Makedonov and N. N. Zabolotskii, eds., *Vospominaniia o N. Zabolotskom*, second edition (Moscow: Sovetskii pisatel′, 1984), pp. 57–100. By far the most detailed historical account of *Oberiu* in English is contained in Nikita Zabolotskii, *The Life of Zabolotsky*, ed. by R. R. Milner-Gulland, trans. by R. R. Milner-Gulland and C. G. Bearne (Cardiff: University of Wales Press, 1994), ch. 2.

4 See Bakhterev, 'Kogda my byli molodymi', pp. 86–98.

5 The Russian text can be found, preceded by an excellent introduction, in R. R. Milner-Gulland, ' "Left Art" in Leningrad: the OBERIU Declaration', *Oxford Slavonic Papers*, 3 (1970), 65–74. An English translation of the declaration has also been published: George Gibian, ed. and trans., *The Man in [with] the Black Coat – Russia's Literature of the Absurd: Selected Works of Daniil Kharms and Alexander Vvedensky*, (Evanston: Northwestern University Press, 1987), pp. 245–54.

6 See, for example, his novella 'The Old Woman' ('Starukha'), in *Polet v nebesa*, pp. 399–430; English translation contained in Daniil Kharms, *Incidences*, ed. and trans. by Neil Cornwell (London: Serpent's Tail, 1993), pp. 17–46.

7 Jean-Philippe Jaccard, 'L'impossible éternité. Réflexions sur le problème de la sexualité dans l'œuvre de Daniil Harms', in Leonid Heller, ed., *Amour et érotisme dans la littérature russe du XXe siècle: Actes du Colloque de juin 1989 organisé par l'Université de Lausanne, avec le concours de la Fondation du 450ème anniversaire* (Bern: Peter Lang, 1992), pp. 213–47.

8 Many of these texts can be found in English translation, grouped under the heading 'Erotica', in Kharms, *Incidences*, pp. 216–25.

9 Jaccard, 'L'impossible éternité', pp. 215–20. Vvedenskii (1904–41) and Lipavskii (1904–41) were very close to Kharms; together with the philosopher and mathematician Iakov Druskin (1902–80) and others, they formed a group called the 'Chinari', which held regular discussions of a broadly philosophical nature from 1922 until the mid 1930s. The best accounts of the group and their meetings are given in Iakov Druskin, ' "Chinari" ', *Avrora*, 6 (1989), 103–15, and T. Lipavskaia, 'Vstrechi s Nikolaem

Alekseevichem i ego druz'iami', in Zabolotskaia, Makedonov and Zabolotskii, eds., *Vospominaniia o N. Zabolotskom*, pp. 47–56.

10   The play, preceded by a lengthy introduction, is published, in both its 'standard' and 'scenic' versions, in Mikhail Meilakh, 'O "Elizavete Bam" Daniila Kharmsa (predystoriia, istoriia postanovki, p'esa, tekst)', *Stanford Slavic Studies*, 1 (1987), 163–246. All quotations from the play will be taken from this edition. A revised version of Meilakh's introduction to the play has been published in English translation: 'Kharms's play *Elizaveta Bam*', trans. by Ann Shukman, in Cornwell, *Daniil Kharms and the Poetics of the Absurd*, pp. 200–19. An English translation of the full 'scenic' version of *Elizaveta Bam* can be found in Kharms, *Incidences*, pp. 153–84.

11   Jaccard compares the play to Ionesco's *The Bald Prima Donna*: 'Daniil Kharms: teatr absurda – real'nyi teatr', *Russian Literature*, 27 (1990), 21–40. See also Jenny Stelleman, 'The transitional position of *Elizaveta Bam* between avant-garde and neo-avant-garde', in Jan van der Eng and Willem G. Weststeijn, eds., *Avant Garde 5/6, USSR* (Amsterdam and Atlanta: Rodöpi, 1991), pp. 207–29. An updated version of the latter has since been published: Jenny Stelleman, *Aspects of Dramatic Communication: Action, Non-action, Interaction: (A. P. Cechov, A. Blok, D. Charms)* (Amsterdam and Atlanta: Rodöpi, 1992), ch. 6.

12   Jean-François Lyotard, *The Postmodern Condition: a Report on Knowledge*, trans. by Geoff Bennington and Brian Massumi (Manchester: Manchester University Press, 1984), p. 63. For a reading of *Elizaveta Bam* based primarily on Wittgenstein's notion of 'language games', see Graham Roberts, 'Of words and worlds: language games in *Elizaveta Bam* by Daniil Kharms', *Slavonic and East European Review*, 72, 1 (1994), 38–59.

13   Kharms, who eventually fell victim to the purges in 1942, was himself first arrested less than four years after *Elizaveta Bam* was written, along with a number of other writers involved in children's literature: see A. Ustinov, 'Delo detskogo sektora Gosizdata 1932g.: predvaritel'naia spravka', in G. A. Morev, ed., *Mikhail Kuz'min i russkaia kul'tura XX veka: tezisy i materialy konferentsii 15-17 maia 1990g.* (Leningrad: Sovet po istorii mirovoi kul'tury AN SSSR, 1990), pp. 125–36.

14   For an example of Wittgenstein's notion of 'language games' used in feminist criticism, see Elizabeth Meehan, 'Women's studies and political studies', in Judith Evans *et al.*, *Feminism and Political Theory* (London: Sage Publications, 1986), pp. 120–38.

15   Meilakh, 'O "Elizavete Bam"', pp. 224–5. Subsequent page

references to this edition will be given in the text. All English translations of the play are my own.

16 For a useful introduction to Kristeva, see Toril Moi, *Sexual/ Textual Politics: Feminist Literary Theory* (London: Methuen, 1985), ch. 8. Kristeva's most sustained discussion of the semiotic comes in her *Revolution in Poetic Language*, trans. by Margaret Waller (New York: Columbia University Press, 1984). Extracts from this work can be found in Julia Kristeva, *The Kristeva Reader*, ed. by Toril Moi (Oxford: Basil Blackwell, 1986), ch. 5.

17 Moi, *Sexual/Textual Politics*, pp. 11–12.

18 *Ibid.*, pp. 165–6. Moi has herself criticized Kristeva's refusal to state what is specific about woman's marginalization in the patriarchy: Toril Moi, 'Feminism, postmodernism, and style', *Cultural Critique*, 9 (1988), 3–22.

19 The gender-specific nature of the power struggle is underlined in the seventh section of the play, when the two men, Petr and Ivan, appropriate the same 'I' while telling a story (p. 229).

20 Jenny Stelleman, 'An analysis of *Elizaveta Bam*', *Russian Literature*, 17 (1985), 319–52 (p. 343). (This is an earlier version of Stelleman, 'The Transitional Position.')

21 This section, the eighteenth, is the penultimate section of the play, but the final section included in the 'scenic' version as published by Meilakh. The nineteenth, and final section of *Elizaveta Bam* is, however, included in the 'standard' version; see Meilakh, 'O "Elizavete Bam" ', p. 221.

22 The use of the imperfective verb 'govorila' underlines the tragic nature of Elizaveta's 'silence', since it implies that Elizaveta never intended to say anything, rather than that she was prevented from doing so.

23 Many would argue that the absence of any effective solidarity between Elizaveta and her parents reflects the fact that the family is itself a patriarchal structure. See, for example, R. D. Laing, *The Politics of the Family* (New York: Random House, 1969), quoted in the introduction to Barbara Hill Rigney, *Madness and Sexual Politics in the Feminist Novel: Studies in Brontë, Woolf, Lessing, and Atwood* (Madison, WI: University of Wisconsin Press, 1978), p. 9.

24 To paraphrase Luce Irigaray, whose feminist linguistics have much in common with Kristeva's, Elizaveta might be said to react against the 'specular' logic of patriarchal discourse by producing her own, alternative, 'hysterical' discourse, only to find, at the end of the play, that by her discourse she has merely been enacting the specular representation of herself as a lesser male. See Luce Irigaray, *Speculum of the Other Woman*,

trans. by Catherine Porter (Ithaca, NY: Cornell University Press, 1985).

25 For Kristeva, the semiotic chora is linked to the pre-Oedipal mother. According to this logic, one might argue that Elizaveta has no choice, once her mother denounces her, but to abandon herself to the symbolic Law of the Father.

26 Dale Spender, *Man Made Language* (London: Routledge and Kegan Paul, 1980), p. 143. This statement is quoted by Alison Assiter in her more moderate account of patriarchal language: 'Did man make language?', in Roy Edgley and Richard Osborne, eds., *Radical Philosophy Reader* (London: Verso, 1985), pp. 310–21 (p. 310).

27 In a curious way, the reception of *Elizaveta Bam* echoes that of another text depicting a voiceless woman and her destruction by patriarchal forces, namely Balzac's story 'Adieu'. For a discussion of this aspect of the French work, see Shoshana Felman, 'Women and madness: the critical phallacy', in Catherine Belsey and Jane Moore, eds., *The Feminist Reader: Essays in Gender and the Politics of Literary Criticism* (London: Macmillan, 1989), pp. 133–53, and 231–3. I am grateful to Dr. Catherine Grant of the University of Strathclyde for bringing this article to my attention.

28 'Kharms's play *Elizaveta Bam*', p. 212. This view has been rejected by L. Druskina, who maintains that Kharms refused to allow any politics into his art: see her introduction to Iakov Druskin, 'Kommunikativnost′ v tvorchestve Aleksandra Vvedenskogo', *Teatr*, 11 (1991), 80–94 (p. 81).

29 For a discussion of the politically subversive nature of carnival, see Peter Stallybrass and Allon White, *The Politics and Poetics of Transgression* (London: Methuen, 1986).

30 It is important to emphasize that by 'dialogic' language we do not mean simply 'dialogue'. The model of dialogism elaborated by Bakhtin/Voloshinov/Medvedev implies a particular kind of dialogue, one in which each word does not belong exclusively to one party, but instead is 'a territory shared by both addresser and addressee': see V. N. Volshinov, *Marxism and the Philosophy of Language*, trans. by L. Matejka and I. R. Titunik (Cambridge, MA: Harvard University Press, 1986), p. 86. Whether as a normative, or prescriptive principle, dialogism implies struggle, a struggle, crucially, over the sign itself. Bakhtin's concept of dialogism has recently begun to be applied to feminist criticism. See, for example: Dale Bauer, *Feminist Dialogics* (Albany, NY: State University of New York Press, 1988); and Peter Hitchcock, *Dialogics of the Oppressed* (Minneapolis, MN and London:

University of Minnesota Press, 1993). Mention of Bakhtin also takes us back to Kristeva, since Elizaveta's language contains many of the figures which Kristeva specifically identifies as germane to carnival: *The Kristeva Reader*, pp. 48–51.

31 Mikhail Bakhtin, *Problems of Dostoevsky's Poetics*, ed. and trans. by Caryl Emerson (Manchester: Manchester University Press, 1984), pp. 124–5 (my emphasis).

32 Clair Wills, 'Upsetting the public: carnival, hysteria and women's texts', in Ken Hirschkop and David Shepherd, eds., *Bakhtin and Cultural Theory* (Manchester: Manchester University Press, 1989), pp. 130–51 (p. 133).

33 The full text is published in Jaccard, 'L'impossible éternité', pp. 240–1.

34 See, for example, 'Vyvalyvaiushchiesia starukhi', in *Polet v nebesa*, p. 356; English translation, 'The Plummeting Old Women', in Kharms, *Incidences*, p. 50.

35 G. S. Smith, 'Luminous fragments of the avant-garde' (review of Cornwell, *Daniil Kharms and the Poetics of the Absurd*), *Times Literary Supplement*, 1 May 1992, p. 23.

36 Mary Ellmann, *Thinking About Women* (London: Virago, 1979), ch. 3.

37 My reading of Karamzin's *Poor Liza* (*Bednaia Liza*) is taken from Joe Andrew, 'Radical sentimentalism or sentimental radicalism? A feminist approach to eighteenth-century Russian literature', in Catriona Kelly, Michael Makin and David Shepherd, eds., *Discontinuous Discourses in Modern Russian Literature* (London: Macmillan, 1989), pp. 136–56 (esp. 148–53). As Tat'iana Mamonova reveals, patriarchal values go much further back than this in Russian culture: 'Matriarchal [sic] roots in Russian culture', in Tatyana Mamonova, *Russian Women's Studies: Essays on Sexism in Soviet Culture* (Oxford: Pergamon Press, 1989), pp. 3–8.

38 As one anonymous reader has pointed out, something else which may unite Kharms's and Karamzin's heroines is their representative status; just as Elizaveta can be read as a metaphor for political oppression by the Bolsheviks, so Liza functions as a symbol of exploitation of the peasants under serfdom. For a discussion of how images of femininity have been used in Russian culture as metaphors for the state of the Russian nation, see Joanna Hubbs, *Mother Russia: the Feminine Myth in Russian Culture* (Bloomington, IN: University of Indiana Press, 1988).

39 Elaine Showalter, *A Literature of Their Own: British Women Novelists from Brontë to Lessing* (Princeton, NJ: Princeton University Press, 1977), p. 117; quoted in Andrew, 'Radical sentimentalism', p. 152.

40 In this sense, *Elizaveta Bam* calls to mind not *The Bald Prima Donna*, but another play by Ionesco, *The Lesson*, in which, after a series of language games played by the male teacher and his female pupil, he kills her with the word 'knife'.

41 Barbara Heldt, 'Men who give birth: a feminist perspective on Russian literature', in Kelly, Makin and Shepherd, *Discontinuous Discourses*, pp. 157–67 (p. 158).

42 Naomi Segal, 'Sexual politics and the avant-garde: from Apollinaire to Woolf', in Edward Timms and Peter Collier, eds., *Visions and Blueprints: Avant-Garde Culture and Radical Politics in Early Twentieth-Century Europe* (Manchester: Manchester University Press, 1988), pp. 235–49 (p. 235).

43 *Ibid.*

CHAPTER 14

The crafting of a self: Lidiia Ginzburg's early journal

Jane Gary Harris

From the perspective of the 1980s, when Lidiia Ginzburg's remarkable achievement as a scholar and writer finally received public recognition,[1] she could refer back to her student years as being in tune with history: 'The 1920s were for me the Institute of the History of the Arts,[2] and my introduction to the cultural-historical currents, which simultaneously both confronted the epoch and were spawned by the epoch ... It seemed to us – and so it was for a short time – that we were the principal actors in a segment of culture which had just begun.'[3] As a participant in the 'young Formalist' collective and hence part of the dynamic rethinking of the educational system, Ginzburg did not regard her professional life as marginalized until the Institute was forcibly closed down in 1930. Her involvement in the struggle by and for the thinking woman in the Soviet Union of the 1920s might be characterized as that of a first generation egalitarian or 'existential feminist' in Julia Kristeva's definition,[4] as one of those 'women in the socialist countries of Eastern Europe' who demanded equal rights with men, and whose demands for economic, political and professional equality 'have, to a great extent, been met'.

On the other hand, Ginzburg was hardly unaware of what Kristeva termed 'the fourth equality' – 'sexual equality, imply-ing permissiveness in sexual relations (including homosexual relations)' which was 'stricken by taboo in Marxian ethics as well as for reasons of state'.[5] As a lesbian living in such an environment of ethical and political 'taboos', Ginzburg was forced to conceal her sexual orientation while seeking out explanations for her sexuality in the limited sources available – in literature.[6]

I would like to suggest that the duality of Ginzburg's personal life, perhaps more than her purely intellectual struggle, may have inspired her profoundly analytical self-consciousness and redirected her aesthetic consciousness. I hope to show in the limited confines of this essay how in her early journal (1925–30) Ginzburg's interrogation of issues pertaining to self-definition and the formation of both personal and professional character traits results in the crafting of a self, a personality with which she could ultimately live and work. Moreover, the journal entries evolve into a 'literary genre' – a literary creation of self – which by the 1930s she regarded as the 'most suitable form' for her writing, but as 'unpublishable'. Only between 1982 and 1993 were large parts of the journal made available by Ginzburg and, subsequently, by her literary executor. Nevertheless, conclusions drawn here must be regarded as tentative, because according to her wishes the most private materials remain closed to the public for the next quarter of a century. This essay is limited, therefore, to available publications.[7] Paradoxically, in 1932 when her professional career was also marginalized, Ginzburg published a novel for adolescents, *The Pinkerton Agency* (*Agentstvo Pinkertona*), dedicated to her lesbian partner, Rina [Ekaterina Vasilevna] Zelenaia; but she dismissed it as 'not my own novel' and 'a conscious literary falsification'.[8]

Because Ginzburg never considered herself a 'feminist', it is difficult to place her in the current feminist theoretical debates. Nevertheless, in seeking a framework beyond Kristeva's to assess Ginzburg's social position as presented in her journal, I found a useful starting point in Edwin Ardener's theory of 'muted' and 'dominant' groups.[9] According to Ardener, whereas both 'muted' and 'dominant' groups generate beliefs of social reality at the unconscious level through different orders of perception, the dominant ones control the structures in which consciousness can be articulated. Women as a muted group must thus mediate their beliefs through the allowable forms of the dominant structures. This thesis seems to corroborate Ginzburg's interpretation of her own personality *vis-à-vis* her professional life, as she articulates it in the course of her early journal. On the other hand, consciousness of her marginalized sexual orientation seems to serve as the stimulus behind her literary efforts to overturn the 'dominant–mute' dichotomy by re-evaluating her male mentors and re-formulating her aesthetic consciousness.[10]

In the 1920s successful women students like Ginzburg were very few in number; unaware that they were accepting male definitions of gendered endeavours and values, they often echoed their male associates.[11] Encouraged to enter a formerly all-male discipline, Ginzburg was simultaneously urged to adhere to the language, gender roles and customs maintained by the culture of that discipline, and to model herself on the male faculty.

In 1922 Ginzburg enrolled as a student in the newly established Literary Section of the Institute of the History of the Arts and by the latter half of the 1920s was appointed to the staff; she taught and published under the Institute's auspices.[12] Nevertheless, while the Formalist movement, centred at the Institute after 1920, endeavoured to establish intellectual inquiry that would be 'neutral' and 'value-free', Ginzburg gradually came to question the epistemological viability of many of its basic tenets. She came to recognize that her interests in problems of literary and social behaviour and the study of personality, first initiated in 1925 in her seminar essay on Viazemskii and in her own journal, could not be conceived as purely 'literary' or as 'neutral'. By 1927, she no longer sought to study literature as an 'autonomous' phenomenon, or to maintain rigid distinctions between literature and life:

[Наука о литературе] не могла развиваться сама из себя, требовались внешние толчки и скрещивания с другими рядами. Боюсь, что мы паразиты, которым для того, чтобы не умереть от недостатка пищи (или от скуки), необходимо питаться либо социологией (эйхенбаумовский «литературный быт» и пр.), либо лингвистикой (Виноградов и пр.), либо текущей литературой. Для тех, кто ощущает себя не историками или теоретиками литературы по преимуществу, но шире того — литераторами, профессионалами слова, —

отсутствие последнего рода связей и импульсов — губительно.[13]

([Literary science] could not develop out of itself alone, external stimuli and association with other realms of thought were required. I am afraid that we are parasites who, in order not to die from a lack of food (or boredom) need to feed either on sociology (Eikhenbaum's 'literary life' etc.), or on linguistics (Vinogradov, etc.), or on current literature. For those who do not view themselves primarily as literary historians or literary theorists, but have a broader understanding of themselves as literary professionals, professionals of the word – such lack of nourishment is fatal.)

In examining the early journal entries in which Ginzburg interprets characteristics of her own personality, seeks models for her role as a literary professional, and establishes a rationale for writing, we find a striking correlation between her journal and her scholarship. It was Ginzburg, after all, who would define the role and function of what she came to call the 'intermediary genres' – journals, letters and autobiographical texts – in the history of Russian literature and culture, and who would develop new principles of literary and cultural analysis to reassess the aesthetic value of such materials hitherto not considered 'literature'.[14] Thus, I would also suggest that the interpretation of personality developed in her early journal played a significant role in the formulation of Ginzburg's theory of psychological prose, in which she develops her concepts of historical and empirical personality, and in her theory of the non-canonical genres.[15]

Ginzburg began keeping a journal in 1925–6 while writing a seminar essay, 'Viazemskii-literator',[16] on Prince Petr A. Via-zemskii and his *Staraia zapisnaia knizhka* (*The Old Notebook*). It was published in 1926 in *Russkaia proza*,[17] the 'young Formalist' anthology edited by Boris Eikhenbaum and Iurii Tynianov, the instructors of the now famous special seminar in Russian prose in which Ginzburg and other select Institute students partici-pated, beginning in the autumn of 1924. By 1929, Ginzburg's edition of *The Old Notebook* appeared.[18] However, her best known work, *On Psychological Prose*, which develops her theories of psychological prose and of personality formation, was not published until 1971.

Generally speaking, Ginzburg's empirical personality as it emerges in the journal is that of an intellectual, a thinking reader and scholar, and a would-be literary professional. Her emphasis is on rational behaviour. She perceives herself as a positivist, as a highly rational individual, who values logic, clarity and wit above all else, applying them even to the most irrational problems or situations. This trait often leads to theoretical interpretations of personal attitudes, but also to impassioned discussions of abstract issues.

Turning to two of Ginzburg's earliest entries, we note that one treats the fate of the literary professional and the other, the theme of homosexuality. In the first one (1925),[19] the twenty-three-year old student posed the problem of the potential conflict between the traits in her own personality she most valued and the requirements of the literary profession. She is responding to Kornei Chukovskii's invitation to write a review of Ermakov's books on Pushkin and Gogol', and to Veniamin Kaverin's comments on one of her first public appearances as a young scholar. She concludes by wondering whether either of her Institute teachers, Zhirmunskii or Tynianov, could serve as a model.

The opening phrase – 'Now more about me' – is followed by quoted advice from two successful literary professionals, both of whom recognize her superior intelligence, honesty and conscientiousness. Though their remarks must have first touched her pride, she ends up by asserting that her finest *personal* attributes are 'flaws' in a *literary professional* and by disclaiming the validity of honesty and conscientiousness as professional goals.

Typical of many entries for the 1920s, this one not only exemplifies Ginzburg's self-awareness and capacity for analysing the disjuncture between personal and professional goals, but serves as an example of the high value she placed on *writing* – on literary style, structure, and strategy – an indication that for her the journal was not merely a psychological outlet but a means of aesthetic cognition, a means of giving structure to her mental processes. In addition, writing may also have begun to serve as a strategy of 'defiance' opposing social, political, cultural or sexual limitations.

Теперь еще обо мне (впрочем, не без Чуковского), когда рецензия была наконец принята, он сказал мне на прощание: «Главное, не будь такой умной; я вам советую поглупеть немножко.»

Вениамин Каверин, выслушав мой отзыв о *Городах и Годах*, сказал мне: «Вы слишком честно работаете — так нельзя!»

Привожу эти отзывы отнюдь не из кокетства — все это подлинные недостатки для литератора, а может быть, и для ученого — особенно наивная честность (которой я страдаю). Пожалуй, честная семинарная работа еще допустима. Но во всякой *готовой вещи,* в особенности в статье, должна быть некая недобросовестная пружина, иначе не выйдет конструкции.

Жирмунский — честный человек, но на то он и классификатор. (Тынянов — мошенник).

(Now some more about me ... After the review was finally accepted, and we were saying goodbye, [Chukovskii] said to me: 'Above all, don't be so clever; my advice to you is to become a little stupid.'

Veniamin Kaverin, having listened to my critique of Fedin's *Cities and Years*, told me: 'You're over-conscientious – you can't go on that way!'

I cite these remarks not to show off, but because they indicate actual flaws in a literary professional, and perhaps even in a scholar, especially naive honesty (my problem). It may be that conscientious seminar work is still permissible. However, in any *formal text*, especially in an article, there must be some springboard of disingenuousness, otherwise the principal idea will not surface.

Zhirmunskii's an honest man, but he remains a classifier. (Tynianov's a scoundrel).)

While these remarks could be read, on the one hand, as a young woman's response to male authorities essentially asking her to downplay her best qualities, it seems that, on the contrary, Ginzburg is actually heeding their advice as spokesmen of the dominant literary establishment. Thus, in her professional life Ginzburg does not choose to make obvious distinctions with regard to whether her critics are male or female. The choice of professional models being limited, she must merely decide which to follow.

On the other hand, many entries express a kind of 'double-voiced discourse'. Hence, the highly structured nature of this one, with its carefully designed parallelisms, juxtapositions and paradoxes, and its concluding *pointe*, is deceptive; it suggests that Ginzburg is deliberately displacing her psychological and indeed, moral distress by aesthetic distance; that writing has become her means for such displacement. Moreover, the act of writing helps her to reinterpret her personality within the given social and cultural boundaries. Writing offers not only clarification, but articulation, if only for herself.

In the first half of this entry, Ginzburg's pride emerges both in the citations of advice and in her recognition of the irony of her critics' advice. In the second half, the first thing that appears is self-conscious fear of her own superciliousness and egotism (female self-consciousness, perhaps unrecognized as such). The formula – 'I cite these remarks not to show off, but...' – allows her to re-examine what could and should have been compliments, and to reappraise them as 'flaws in a literary professional'.

Hence, the entry concludes by posing the problem of the ambiguity of her intellectual and professional dilemma (not perceived specifically as a woman's dilemma). To become a 'literary professional', must she give up what has thus far been considered her greatest strength: her intelligence, honesty and conscientiousness? Must she be disingenuous so that the 'principal idea will surface'? The paradoxical concluding paragraph ends on a *pointe*, juxtaposing the models for professional behaviour offered by her Institute teachers: Zhirmunskii or Tynianov?

As is typical of the genre of the journal entry, this one raises several questions but draws no conclusions. However, its balanced structure reinforces the intellectual paradox: first, as expressed in the ironic questioning of fundamental values – the reversal of values presented in the first and second halves of the entry; and second, as the choice represented by the juxtaposition of her teachers. Ginzburg's attentiveness to literary composition is certainly not typical of the journal; it should thus alert us to her efforts to seek a literary or aesthetic solution to a problem she is not otherwise equipped to resolve.

As for the topic itself, particularly in the years 1925–7, Ginzburg viewed herself not simply as an individual scholar but as part of a collective intellectual project. In fact, frequently interspersed among the entries treating her own personality and professional concerns are efforts to define the character traits and behavioural patterns of her colleagues, to describe how they look, talk, dress and act, even how they perform in official debates.

In an entry from 1926 Ginzburg attempts to characterize the 'young Formalist' as a social type, including herself under that rubric. An objective general statement – 'The young Formalists, with the blessings and the example of their elders, have worked out their norms for social behaviour [*bytovye normy*]' – is followed by astute portraiture, as if she were depicting the hero of a realist novel. Ginzburg stands back and regards herself and her associates from a novelist's remove, with an equal share of irony and understanding. In fact, her depiction becomes another form of self-evaluation, an effort to look at her own socio-cultural type or historical personality objectively, as part of a 'tradition'.

In enumerating the characteristics of the 'young Formalist', Ginzburg carefully mentions that each trait is also typical of, and shared with, the older generation: taste, disposition, values, and even excesses. Her sociological portrait gradually reveals a rumbustious, rebellious student who is 'by nature' a 'literary professional' [*literator*] and a sceptic, up on contemporary literature and in tune with history, a contemporary phenomenon. Simultaneously, she inscribes herself into the portrait through the plural pronoun 'we': 'Our teachers also did not love science; they loved discoveries'; 'we know the taste both of piecework and of hackwork – the taste of our trade'; 'It seems that we all link scepticism with decency – also part of the tradition'.

The entry concludes on a *pointe* which again illustrates Ginzburg's keen sensitivity to the irony and paradox of human behaviour, and her literary strategy. The ironic restraint of the overall description, emphasizing feistiness as an essential *Opoiaz*[20] trait, climaxes in the shocking conclusion which suggests the total breakdown of the Formalist collective and the pain it has wrought on the younger disciples, herself included. The last line reads: 'In only one thing do the young Formalists deviate from the worldly traditions of their elders – they do not poison each other.'[21]

The personal pain Ginzburg experienced as she observed the disintegration of relations among the Formalists emerges frequently between 1927 and 1930, as the Institute was being forcibly closed. Reflected as profound personal loss and, perhaps, the end of innocence, it is captured in the elegiac tone determining a significant 1928 effort at personal stocktaking: 'Our love affair with our maîtres is coming to an end ... If not for Eikhenbaum and Tynianov, my life would have been completely different, that is, I would have been a different person, with different capabilities and a different potential for thinking, feeling, working, relating to people, seeing things.'[22]

The journal entries also indicate just how much Ginzburg tended to identify with her reading. While she tried to displace her problems through writing, she clearly relied on reading to comprehend life. Thus, another significant part of Ginzburg's journal in the 1920s was devoted to highly subjective comments on her current reading and on conversations not associated with her professional life. Here her views on women's issues and sexuality emerge most directly.

For example, reflections on a conversation with her former fellow Institute student, Tat'iana Roboli, serve as the impulse for the consideration of a whole set of women's issues beginning with the male-inspired images of women's role and family life accepted by women as the norm, but which evoke Ginzburg's personal disdain. 'T. A. R[oboli] told me that for her there was nothing more appealing or desirable in life than a family, *un homme*, and children, and a hot bubbling samovar on a table covered with a white cloth. What can you do if the family of her imagination was, and could be, imagined only from a "male perspective"?' The 'male perspective' is then defined: 'The desire to have children, but not bear them; the desire to drink tea at one's own table, but not pour it into tea glasses. For a man, the conception of the family is of a place to which he joyously returns after work; while for a woman, the way things stand, the family must be a place of work, a calling.'[23]

Although Ginzburg never refers to herself as a 'feminist', and writes infrequently on women's issues *per se*, when depicting women's lives all aspects are taken into consideration at once – sex, maternity, work, love, domesticity, passion, reason – and viewed as intricately interconnected. She raises questions about the image of the woman's role in society, the problem of the creation and acceptance of male images of women, and the absence of positive images of older women as opposed to those of older men: as opposed to the difficulty of imagining 'a good old age' for women, 'we can always imagine a handsome boy as a man'. Instead of perceiving a lined face and grey hair in women, as in men, to connote experience, character, staying power, sexual self-knowledge, she points out 'There are women for whom even the mention of old age is a criminal indelicacy – a rather terrifying thought'. Hence, Ginzburg's recognition of the need for an 'aesthetic of age (and probably, an aesthetic of gender)'.[24]

In addition, Ginzburg's general awareness of contemporary life provides sociological information about the status of women, including the problematic reliance on abortions, the fact that equal opportunity in the workplace fails to bring about equal work responsibilities on the domestic front, and the issue of young girls growing up too quickly.

Ginzburg's fluency in French allowed her to keep abreast of the current literary and cultural scene in the Soviet Union as well as abroad. She avidly read such *causes célèbres* as André Gide's *Corydon*,[25] published in 1924, and Marcel Proust's *A la recherche du temps perdu*, as each volume appeared, completing it in 1927.[26] In her comments on Gide, she also mentions parenthetically her admiration for Otto Weininger's *Geschlecht und Charakter* (*Sex and Character*), undoubtedly because of his frank discussions of homosexuality, in particular, female single-sex relations, and 'emancipated women',[27] obviously reflecting the dearth of information on the subject.

In this amazing early journal entry, beginning 'I was reading [Gide's] *Corydon* (Paris 1924)',[28] Ginzburg expresses a very definite attitude toward the subject of homosexuality, with respect to how it should be discussed and defended. Moreover, her defence is based on her female perspective. While praising Gide for his 'brilliance and wide-ranging unconventionality', she judges his book 'a flop' because of 'invalid methods', a false assumption that 'everything natural is good', and failure to discuss female as well as male homosexuality.

Not only does Ginzburg censure Gide's methodology as absurd, claiming: 'indeed, it is hardly in canine practices that we should be seeking the boundaries of human behaviour',[29] but she offers a vituperative and ironic critique of his 'zoo-logical perspective' and consequent misuse of the word 'natural'.

Естественность — это едва ли не самое пустое из всех слов, придуманных лицемерами.

В сущности, все хорошие вещи не естественны: искусство не естественно, умываться не естественно, не естественно есть вилкой и сморкаться в платок, не естественно уступить место женщине с ребенком ...

Нужно ли уничтожить ватерклозеты, потому, что собаки гадят на улице?

(The word 'natural' – isn't this the most vacuous of all the attributes hypocrites have invented?

In fact, all good things are not natural: art is not natural, washing is not natural; nor is it natural to eat with a fork or to blow one's nose in a handkerchief; nor to give up your seat to a woman and child ...

Must we do away with water-closets because dogs defecate in the street?)

Second, Ginzburg indicates her own preference for 'single-sex love' and 'lesbian love'. While her argument is based on elaborating 'the facts', she also invokes her considerable literary prowess to ridicule views she perceives as lacking in common sense.

Third, in condemning Gide for not considering lesbianism,

she accuses him of being sexist in promoting the traditional view of women's 'natural roles', and narrow-minded in his conception of the erotic ideal. In this context, she also points out a fundamental aesthetic as well as a psychological problem – that, in general, 'male love' has been the only category considered 'worthy of literature'.

У Жида, по обыкновению, почти не затронут вопрос о женском извращении, оно, вероятно, не удовлетворяет его требованию высшей эротики (Платон!) ...

(Еще Вейнингер в своей неповторимой, вдохновенной, не выдерживающей никакой критики книге очень тонко учел это.)

Плохо ли, хорошо ли, но несомненно, что до сих пор женщина в своем умственном росте равняется на мужчину.

И вот иногда доравнивается до непреодолимой не столько физической, сколько психической потребности в мужской любви, единственно ценной, полной, литературной.

(As usual, André Gide has hardly touched on the issue of female deviation; the topic probably failed to satisfy his demands for the highest form of erotic love (Plato!) ...

(Even Weininger in his unique, inspiring book, which would not stand up to critical scrutiny, treated this topic very subtly.)

For good or for ill, there is no doubt that to this day women's mental development is equal to men's.

And sometimes women are even equal to the insuperable demands of male love, demands which are as much psychological as physical, male love being the only love which is valued, considered complete, and worthy of literature.)

Finally, in 1927, with the publication of *Le temps retrouvé*, the concluding volume of *A la recherche du temps perdu*, and its revelations about the narrator, Marcel Proust becomes the central focus of Ginzburg's contemplation. The fact that until 1994 no Russian translation of the last three books of the novel existed suggests the unique quality of her views at the time.

Ginzburg's defence of homosexuality as an intellectual and psychological issue, so clearly delineated in her reaction to Gide's book, emerges again in her apologia for Proust's master-piece. However, here her response moves beyond the social, psychological, and even political to focus on the aesthetic realm. Ginzburg justifies Proust's aesthetic vision against charges of 'pornography',[30] and defends his aesthetic decision to 'give pre-eminence to a person's solitary inner life', which is 'unacceptable to [Russians] today'.[31] To suggest the general tenor of conservative Russian attitudes towards Proust's subject-matter, Ginzburg cites an anecdote attributed to Pasternak: 'Pasternak is alleged to have said: "I bought Proust, but I haven't brought myself to open it".'[32]

Over the course of several journal entries written between 1927 and 1930, Proust becomes Ginzburg's model for reformulating and transforming her life image both as a writer and as a human being – as one who shares the complex layers of her individual consciousness as well as her need to give it expression in prose. In this way, Ginzburg gradually develops a method, as well as an explanation and defence of her method, for coping with the problems arising from her marginal social status. At least in part, she attributes her method to her affinity with Proust and his mode of writing: his 'monologized view of the world'. She comes to recognize that for herself, as for Proust, writing is life; writing is a means of apprehending the self and the world. Proust provides the entry into her particular interpretation of her own personality, and offers the aesthetic solution to her understanding of life.

Что касается меня, то я буду писать, вероятно, до последнего издыхания ... потому, что для меня писать — значит жить, переживая жизнь. Мне дороги не вещи, а концепции вещей, процессы осознания (вот почему для меня самый важный писатель — Пруст). Все неосознанное для меня бессмысленно ... Отсюда прямой ход: от вещи к мысли, от мысли к слову, от слова внутреннего или устного к письменному, закрепленному, материализованному слову как крайней в этом ряду конкретности.

(I will probably write until I take my last breath ... because for me to write means to live, to experience life. I not only cherish things *per se*, but conceptions of things, processes of perception (that is why Proust is the most significant writer for me). Whatever cannot be understood is meaningless for me ... Hence, the unmediated course of action: from thing to thought, thought to word, inner word or oral word to written word, the reinforced, materialized word which is the end in this series of concrete acts).[33]

Moreover, in 1927 and 1928 Ginzburg not only lauds Proust as a writer, but counterposes him to her earlier mentor, Tynianov. In 1927, in a discussion of their 'erotic scenes',[34] she praises Proust but condemns Tynianov. In 1928, she judges Tynianov as 'wrong [in] substituting an historical hero for an autobiographical one'. In contrast, she expresses admiration for Proust's method of writing about the self 'with total indirection, using other people and things such as they appear before [him]. Here is where the element of literary contemplation begins, the monologized view of the world (Proust)' which, she says, 'seems to have the greatest appeal for me'.[35] Significantly, it is in this context that Ginzburg evaluates her own writing – her journal – recognizing it for the first time as her own mode of literary expression, as the most 'appropriate form for [her own] inclinations', even though she is 'bothered by its being unprintable' and is concerned that 'it is too easy for me to write'.[36]

Finally, in 1930, it becomes absolutely clear how profound an impact Proust had on Ginzburg personally and professionally. Never before had she devoted 'so much energy, will, and personal interest' to writing any piece of scholarship as she claims she expended on her article on Proust. However, in her efforts to come to terms with the fact that her article could never be published, she wistfully remarks on its personal significance despite its lack of public value: 'for me its significance is that to an extraordinary degree it is completely oriented within me; it is totally oriented toward my special writer's (though I'm not a writer) ideas about the need to write a novel; moreover, it is generally oriented toward things which remain unarticulated for the outsider'.[37]

It was ultimately Proust,[38] then, who provided Ginzburg with the unique entry into her own personality which she had long been seeking, who offered her an ideal psychological and aesthetic solution to cope with her sexuality and simulta- neously articulate her creative energy. Ginzburg's journal thus became equally significant for her theory of literature and her philosophy of life. It validated her scholarly interest in the non-canonical genres as well as her literary, psychological and philosophical endeavours. And it served as a means of defying the dominant culture in which she lived.

To return to Ardener's theory of 'muted' and 'dominant' groups – if women must mediate their beliefs through allowable forms of the dominant structures, Ginzburg's models were all male, in particular, her scholar-mentors, Tynianov and Eikhenbaum, and her writer-mentor, Proust. Nevertheless, instead of deferring to the male hierarchy or emphasizing her own masculinity, she transforms those models in her journal by depicting and analysing them all as atypical males. Although she at first admires Tynianov, she is also wary of everything he does; she endeavours to see through him, to move beyond him, to counter him. Eventually, she grows highly critical[39] of his ideas, values, methods, focusing her criticism not on his theory, but on his narrative prose. Between 1927 and 1930, Proust clearly replaces Tynianov in Ginzburg's affections and as a mentor. As for Eikhenbaum, instead of expressing negative feelings towards him, she concludes that his personality does not typify the traditional male; she explains it as the result of his 'feminine' nature.[40] Ultimately, she is drawn to Proust, but hardly because of his masculinity. Rather, she finds an affinity with his mental processes and mode of writing, as well as shared images of the world, a marginalized life, sexuality, and literature: because Proust «с его гегемонией единичного, внутренного человека, неприемлем, в какой-то мере для человека современного (я подуразумеваю русского человека» ('gives pre-eminence to a person's solitary inner life unacceptable to Russians today').[41]

NOTES

1 Ginzburg's reputation as a literary theorist and scholar increased enormously in the post-Stalinist years with the publication of *O lirike* in 1964 by the Leningrad branch of Sovetskii pisatel', her publisher for the next two decades: see *O psikhologicheskoi proze* and *O literaturnom geroe* (1971, 1977, 1979); collections of essays,

memoirs, and excerpts from her journal: *O starom i novom, Literatura v poiskakh real'nosti*, and *Chelovek za pis'mennym stolom* (1982, 1987, 1988). However, not until 1988, at the age of 86, did she receive long overdue public recognition with the award of the State Prize for Literature. See Sarah Pratt, 'Lydia Ginzburg and the Fluidity of Genre', in J. G. Harris, ed., *Autobiographical Statements in Twentieth Century Russian Literature* (Princeton, NJ: Princeton University Press, 1990), pp. 207–16.

2 The Petrograd/Leningrad State Institute for the History of the Arts (GIII), a primary centre of Leningrad cultural life in the 1920s, whose faculty included the foremost literary and linguistic scholars, Tynianov and Eikhenbaum, Zhirmunskii, Tomashevskii and Vinogradov. Students included Veniamin Kaverin, Grigorii Gukovskii, Boris Bukhshtab. Associated with the Formalist movement, GIII was attacked in the official press in the second half of the 1920s and fully closed down by the authorities in 1930.

3 Ginzburg, *Chelovek za pis'mennym stolom*, pp. 305–19.

4 Julia Kristeva, 'Women's time', in Toril Moi, ed., *The Julia Kristeva Reader* (Oxford: Blackwell, 1986), pp. 187–213.

5 Kristeva, 'Women's time', p. 196.

6 In the 1920s, Ginzburg's sense of her marginalization did not include her Jewish identity. Indeed, among the Formalist 'brotherhood', most of her teachers and colleagues were Jewish, and anti-Semitism was 'one' of many issues discussed. The publication by Aleksandr Kushner, ed., 'Iz dnevnikov Lidii Ginzburg', *Literaturnaia gazeta*, 41 (5469), 13 October 1993, contains a remarkable entry pertaining to Ginzburg's views on anti-Semitism, her defence of her Jewish identity, and family pride. See my comments in 'Lidiia Ginzburg's Journal as a Contemporary Literary Genre', paper to be presented in September, 1995 at the 25th Anniversary Conference of the Neo-Formalist Circle. On the other hand, Ginzburg claimed that her most painful and frightening experience of anti-Semitism came during her interrogation in 1952 in an effort to force her to collaborate in building a case against Boris Eikhenbaum. See L. Ginzburg, 'Dve vstrechi', in her *Pretvorenie opyta* (Leningrad: Assotsiatsiia 'Novaia Literatura', 1991).

7 Ginzburg, *Chelovek za pis'mennym stolom*; L. Ginzburg, *Zapisi 20–30-kh godov* (*Iz neopublikovannogo*), Introduction by A. Kushner, Commentary by A. Chudakov, *Novyi mir*, 6 (1992); 'Iz dnevnikov Lidii Ginzburg', ed. A. Kushner, *Literaturnaia gazeta*, 13 October 1993, p. 6.

8 Ginzburg, *Chelovek za pis'mennym stolom*, p. 131: 'Ia napisala ne

svoiu knigu (*Agenstvo Pinkertona*). Kak kto-to skazal: soznatel'nyi literaturnyi fal'sifikat'.

9 See Shirley Ardener's Introduction to Edward Ardener's theory in Shirley Ardener, ed., *Perceiving Women* (London: Malaby Press, 1977), pp. 3–4, and Edward Ardener's 'Belief and the problem of women', in *ibid.*, pp. 5–19.

10 Due to the scarcity of primary sources, this hypothesis remains highly speculative. Moreover, the secondary literature on Ginzburg is not large, and does not treat questions of her sexuality. Rather, her interest in abstract questions and theory has been emphasized: see Pratt, 'Lidiia Ginzburg and the fluidity of genre'; Beth Holmgren, 'Russian women's autobiography', in Toby W. Clyman and Diana Greene, eds., *Women Writers in Russian Literature* (Westport, CT: Greenwood Press, 1994), pp. 138–40; and Catriona Kelly, *A History of Russian Women's Writing, 1820–1992* (Oxford: Clarendon Press, 1994), pp. 370–1. On the other hand, Ginzburg's wit, conversational skills, and personal life have been little discussed to date: see Patricia Carden, 'Wit and understanding: the voices of Lidiia Ginzburg' or my 'Biographical introduction', both in Jane G. Harris, ed., *In Memoriam: Lidiia Ginzburg, Canadian-American Slavic Studies*, Special Issue, 28, 2 (Summer 1994). See also: Irina Paperno, 'Beyond literary criticism' and Victor Erlich, 'Two conversations with Lidiia Ginzburg', in Sarah Pratt, ed., *Lidiia Ginzburg's Contribution to Literary Criticism, Canadian-American Slavic Studies*, Special Issue, 19, 2 (Summer 1985); Boris Gasparov, Alexander Kushner *et al.*, 'Tvorcheskii portret L. Ia. Ginzburg', in *Literaturnoe obozrenie*, 10 (1989), 78–86; and Elena Nevzgliadova, 'Na samom dele, mysl' kak gost'... O proze Lidii Ginzburg', *Avrora*, 4 (1989).

11 See Lynne Attwood, *The New Soviet Man and Woman* (Bloomington, IN: Indiana University Press, 1990); Richard Stites, *The Women's Liberation Movement in Russia: Feminism, Nihilism, and Bolshevism, 1860–1930* (Princeton, NJ: Princeton University Press, 1978).

12 Ginzburg never again held a post in an institution of higher learning except during the period 1947–50, at Petrozavodsk University.

13 Ginzburg, *Chelovek za pis'mennym stolom*, p. 35.

14 Ginzburg, *O psikhologicheskoi proze*. Ginzburg's lifelong study of the non-canonical genres is a major contribution to literary history and theory. That this contribution was made by a woman has never been appreciated. On women as critics, see Susan Lanser and Evelyn Torton Beck, '[Why] are there no great women critics? And what difference does it make?', in Evelyn Torton

Beck and Julia A. Sherman, eds., *The Prism of Sex: Essays in the Sociology of Knowledge* (Madison, WI: University of Wisconsin Press, 1979), pp. 79–91. In feminist critical theory, the relationship of women's writing to the non-canonical genres has been discussed in both negative and positive terms: whereas these genres provide a major outlet for women's writing, they have also been said to have marginalized women. See, among others, Celeste Schenck, 'All of a piece: women's poetry and autobiography', in Celeste Schenck and Bella Brodzki, eds., *Life/lines: Theorizing Women's Autobiography* (Ithaca, NY: Cornell University Press, 1988), p. 286. She claims that women have been 'edged into marginalized, non-canonical genres as a result of their exclusion from central cultural concerns.' Moreover, while a certain formalist emphasis had been used to suggest that women's writing is 'shapeless and indeterminate', Ginzburg defined the formal characteristics of the intermediary genres and assessed their prominent role and function in the history of literature. (Could this be interpreted as unconscious feminist work?)

15 See *O psikhologicheskoi proze* or *O literaturnom geroe*. On Ginzburg's contribution to autobiographical theory, see Jane Gary Harris, 'Diversity of discourse: autobiographical statements in theory and praxis', in Harris, *Autobiographical Statements in Twentieth Century Russian Literature*, pp. 3–35

16 See Jane Gary Harris, 'Lidiia Ginzburg, the "Young Formalists"', and *Russkaia proza*', in *Lidiia Ginzburg: In Memoriam*.

17 L. Ginzburg, 'Viazemskii-literator', in B. M. Eikhenbaum and Iu. N. Tynianov, eds., *Russkaia proza* (Leningrad: 'Akademiia', 1926), pp. 102–34; English translation by Ray Parrott, *Russian Prose* (Ann Arbor, MI: Ardis, 1985).

18 Petr A. Viazemskii, *Staraia zapisnaia knizhka*, ed. by Lidiia Ginzburg (Leningrad: Izd. pisatelei v Leningrade, 1929).

19 *Novyi mir*, 6 (1992), p. 146.

20 Editor's note: *Opoiaz* was an acronym of *Obshchestvo izucheniia poeticheskogo iazyka* ('Society for the study of poetic language'), a loosely structured scholarly society whose members were students of St Petersburg University. The group gained official recognition as a learned society in 1919, but was dissolved in 1923.

21 Ginzburg, *Chelovek za pis'mennym stolom*, pp. 22–3.

22 *Ibid.*, pp. 61–2.

23 *Novyi mir*, 6 (1992) p. 161.

24 *Ibid.*

25 André Gide, *Corydon* (Paris: Nouvelle Revue Française, 1924); English translation and 'Comments on the second dialogue in

Corydon' by Frank Beach (New York: Farrar, Straus and Giroux, 1950; reprint, New York: Octagon Books, 1977). Gide's defence of homosexuality, presented in four Socratic dialogues, was never translated into Russian. An anonymous edition of the first two dialogues appeared in Bruges in twelve copies in 1911, and in twenty-one copies in 1920. In May 1924, 5,500 copies bearing Gide's name went on sale.

26 The last three volumes of *A la recherche du temps perdu* were finally translated into Russian in 1994. The early volumes were translated and published by Akademiia between 1925 and 1928.

27 Otto Weininger, *Geschlecht und Charakter*, seventh edn (Vienna and Leipzig: Wilhelm Braumüller, 1905). Published in numerous Russian editions in the first decade of the twentieth century in Moscow and Petersburg, then relegated to 'special collections' (*spetskhrany*). Reprints in editions of 100,000 appeared in Moscow in 1991 and 1992. The English translation, *Sex and Character* (London: Heinemann, 1975) is a reprint of the German sixth edition (1906). Whereas Weininger is condemned and dismissed today in the West for being hopelessly sexist, anti-feminist, and anti-Semitic, his book remains extremely popular in Russia. Ginzburg's ambiguous admiration for his work undoubtedly reflects the extremely limited resources explaining homosexuality, and especially lesbianism, available to her. Moreover, he emphasized lesbianism as the prerogative of intellectually superior, 'masculine' women, which was certainly acceptable to Ginzburg's self-description. And having no other precedents, she must have been impressed, like Gertrude Stein before her, by Weininger's frank discussion and defence of female homosexuality. In the chapter 'Emancipated women', he writes: 'Those so-called "women" who have been held up to admiration in the past and present, by the advocates of women's rights, as examples of what women can do, have almost invariably been what I have described as sexually intermediate forms ... Sappho was only the forerunner of a long line of famous women who were either homosexually or bisexually inclined. Classical scholars have defended Sappho warmly against the implication that there was anything more than mere friendship in her relations with her own sex, as if the accusation were necessarily degrading ... For the present, it is enough to say that homosexuality in a woman is the outcome of her masculinity and presupposes a higher degree of development. Catherine II of Russia, and Queen Christina of Sweden, the highly gifted although deaf, dumb and blind Laura Bridgman, George Sand, and a very large number of highly

gifted women and girls concerning whom I myself have been able to collect information, were partly bisexual, partly homosexual' (pp. 65–6). On Weininger's reception in Russia, see Laura Engelstein, *The Keys to Happiness: Sex and the Search for Modernity in Fin-de-Siècle Russia* (Ithaca, NY: Cornell University Press, 1992).

28 *Novyi mir*, 6 (1992) pp. 148–9.
29 See Gide, 'The Second Dialogue', Part 6: the discussion focuses on the attraction of male dogs to female dogs.
30 *Novyi mir*, 6 (1992), p. 157.
31 Ginzburg, *O starom i novom*, p. 371.
32 *Ibid.*, p. 373.
33 *Novyi mir*, 6 (1992), p. 173.
34 *Ibid.*, p. 157.
35 *Ibid.*, p. 165.
36 *Ibid.*
37 *Novyi mir*, 6 (1992), p. 174.
38 On Proust in Ginzburg's studies of the novel, see Patricia Carden, 'Ginzburg on Proust', *Canadian-American Slavic Studies*, 19, 2 (Summer 1985), pp. 166–77.
39 Severe criticism emerges in a journal entry following the 6 March 1927 public debate at Tiuz: 'Chto kasaetsia T., to ia nakhozhus' v sostoianii permanentnogo razdrazheniia; do takoi stepeni, chto mne trudno govorit' s nim ... No togda on byl geroi, simvol, a glavnoe vozhd', a ia cherv'!' ('As far as T. is concerned, I am in a state of permanent irritation; so much so that I find it difficult to speak to him ... But at that time he was a hero, a symbol, and, what was most important, a leader, and I was a worm!') *Novyi mir*, 6 (1992), p. 154.
40 Ginzburg almost employs Weininger's concept of 'the feminine principle' to assess Eikhenbaum's dominant personality trait. See a 1927 entry, *Novyi mir*, 6 (1992), pp. 162–3: 'as soon as you expose the authentic actor, that is, the woman, indeed, the charming woman within, you can breathe freely because everything falls into place: biographical reminiscences, the feminine art of maintaining obligations to others (and simultaneously, others' obligations to herself) and not fulfilling those obligations; ingenuous female disregard for people who love her, while loathing the bitterness accumulated by that love ... B. M. ages like a woman, he admires himself like a woman, and like a woman loves others (Tynianov)'.
41 Ginzburg, *Chelovek za pis'mennym stolom*, p. 44.

CHAPTER 15

Voyeurism and ventriloquism: Aleksandr Velichanskii's Podzemnaia nimfa

Gerald S. Smith

The work of the Moscow poet Aleksandr Velichanskii (1940–90) has hardly been publicly discussed at all, either inside or outside Russia.[1] This is not surprising, because after the poet's remarkable début in 1969[2] there was no further substantial publication in the USSR until 1988.[3] Velichanskii did not take part in official literary life during the 1970s and 1980s. In the year before his death, Velichanskii's friends took advantage of the new situation in publishing in the USSR and sponsored a series of collections, each with a print run of 3000. These books are as follows: *Udel. Izbrannye stikhotvoreniia 1966–1973* (*Portion. Selected Poems 1966–1973*, 1989); *Basta. Rechitativ. 1973–1975* (*Basta. Recitative. 1973–1975*, 1989); *Pomolvka (nesostoiavshiisia roman). 1976–1977* (*Betrothal (A Love Affair that Didn't Work). 1976–1977*, 1990); *Podzemnaia nimfa. 1976–1977* (*The Underground Nymph. 1976–1977*, 1990); *Bezdonnyi cheln. 1982–1983* (*The Bottomless Boat. 1982–1983*, 1990); *Kakhetinskie stikhi. 1985–1986* (*Poems from Kakhetia. 1985–1986*, 1990); and *Vplot' (Right up to*, 1991), which collects lyrics from the last period of Velichanskii's life, 1983–9. All these books were published in Moscow by Prometei, the house attached to the Moscow State Pedagogical University; they all include a statement indicating that private sponsorship was involved. There is only one book published by a major Moscow house, *Vremeni nevidimaia tverd'. Stikhotvoreniia (The Invisible Firmament of Time. Poems*, Moscow: Sovremennik, 1990), a selection which includes items from almost all the books mentioned earlier.[4] It will be seen from their titles that the seven Prometei books are chronological collections, with a suggestion of thematic concentration. It is with the fourth of these collections, *Podzemnaia nimfa*, that we will be concerned here.

The reason for singling out *Podzemnaia nimfa* in the present context is that this book, by a male poet, is concerned almost entirely with the portrayal of women. It would seem to be the only book-length work in verse in post-revolutionary Russian literature of which this can be said.[5] An examination of this text should yield some further insights into that literary construction of women's identity by Russian males which was first subjected to a modern feminist critique by Barbara Heldt,[6] and also offer some interesting illustrations of the ways in which various literary techniques may be used for this purpose. In particular, Velichanskii employs two principal devices in presenting his female characters. In some poems he adopts an omniscient point of view which is not explicitly gendered, but which is implicitly male. In other poems, Velichanskii chooses to narrate using *skaz*, the notional speaker being female.

As an introduction to some of Velichanskii's procedures in *Podzemnaia nimfa*, the third poem in the book will be cited and discussed:

Девочка
Подростки: в очках он, а девочка в юбке короткой
На летней скамейке, обнявшись невинно и робко,
Сидят в ожиданьи дневного сеанса кино
И жадно глотают одно на двоих эскимо.

Но мальчик в очках и с пушком на губе — только мальчик:
и лакомство сладко и фильм предстоящий заманчив,
а девочка чувствует только объятия миг.

И жадно глядит на нее проходящий старик.   (pp. 3–4)

(*The Girl*. Adolescents, he in glasses, the girl in a short skirt. | On the summer bench, embracing innocently and timidly, | as they wait for the afternoon movie | and greedily swallow a shared choc-ice. || But the boy in glasses and with down on his lip is only a boy: | the treat is sweet and the forthcoming film beckoning, | but the girl feels only the moment of embrace. || And an old man passing looks at her greedily.)

Here we have a vignette in which an adolescent couple is observed by an impersonal narrator who is not identified in terms of gender, but in whom we inevitably postulate the male author of the book. This narrator witnesses and reports an intimate moment involving a young couple. The narrator empowers himself to represent and interpret not only certain physical aspects of the young couple, but also their unspoken thoughts and feelings, especially those of the female. However, there is no interaction between the observer and the observed. The observer is a voyeur.

The poem implies a difference between male and female perception: the female is entirely absorbed in the present, participating in a shared act (the embrace), while the male has his mind on other gratifications that concern only himself – he savours the ice cream and not the sharing of it that we have been told about in the last line of the first stanza, and he is also living outside the present moment, anticipating a visit to the cinema later on that day. And there is a difference between the two in the way they are perceived by the voyeur: the physical details of the male youth that are selected for comment speak of conventionally unattractive weakness (the spectacles – twice – and the immature moustache; he is 'only a boy'), while the only such detail we are offered about the young woman, her short skirt, implies the opposite by directing prurient attention to her legs. The poem is very effectively lifted into a different dimension in its last line when the narrator reports the presence of another voyeur besides himself, an old man who has eyes only for the young woman, with the implication that with male ageing comes a more threatening and ugly attitude than that of the youth sitting 'innocent and timid' with the young woman on the bench.

Certain aspects of this poem are typical of *Podzemnaia nimfa* as a whole. The emphasis is on reporting; the observer offers no explicit interpretation or judgement, moral or otherwise, on what he observes. There is little information about the socio-political context: Soviet urban life in the 1970s seems to be the assumed background culture for the vast majority of the poems. Stylistically, the book is consistent in its unassuming unpretentiousness; in this respect again, 'Devochka' may stand as a representative sample. The linguistic pitch ranges from middle to low; some poems have a folkloristic tinge. There is a general avoidance of figurative language – here as elsewhere in the collection.

The voyeuristic point of view adopted in 'Devochka' is to a certain extent characteristic of the book as a whole, but it is by no means universal. As an example of the principal alternative narrative procedure, we may take the tenth poem in the book:

> *Недоуменье*
> Бледнеет и скалится, грозно трясет бородою —
> ревнует — ни за что ни про что, ревнует, ну стоит
> мне с кем-нибудь слово сказать, улыбнуться кому,
> ревнует и стало быть любит, одно не пойму:
>
> ведь ежевечерне так просто дается ему же
> из бездны своей коммуналки вести меня к мужу —
> вести к мужу, о, Господи, прямо в кровать,
> прощаться у бензоколонки и не ревновать. (p. 8)

(*Incomprehension.* He goes pale, pulls a face, his beard wags threateningly | he's jealous – for no reason at all, he's jealous, I just | say a word to someone, smile at someone, | he's jealous and so he must love me, just one thing I can't understand: || after all, every evening it doesn't trouble him, | from the depths of his communal flat to take me back to my husband – | he takes me back to my husband, O, Lord, straight into his bed, | says goodbye at the petrol pump and isn't jealous.)

Here, the male poet permits himself to narrate from within a female persona, a procedure that has recently been termed 'female *skaz*',[7] an act of ventriloquism. The highly asyndetic structure that is generally characteristic of *skaz*[8] is here taken to the limit: the poem consists of a single sentence that literally represents a stream of consciousness. The impression of spontaneity is fostered by the extraordinarily high degree of disjuncture between syntactic and verse units; two of the lines (2 and 5) feature harsh enjambement, and there are many syntactic breaks within the line throughout the poem. The triple repetition of the key verb 'revnuet' in the first stanza effectively lays the ground for the concluding 'ne revnovat''. Stylistically, in this poem, as in 'Devochka', we observe prosaic colloquialism and a practically complete absence of figurative language. As in *Podzemnaia nimfa* generally, the versification is conventional.[9]

The poem is concerned with male double standards: the heroine cannot reconcile her lover's demonstrative jealousy, when he observes her paying even the most casual attention to another man in his presence, with his apparent lack of jealousy towards the unseen husband with whom he shares her sexually. If jealousy is a token of love, as she asserts, she therefore feels both loved and not loved. In this respect, 'Nedoumen'e' shares the concern simply to report that we have seen in 'Devochka'. The poet is not condemning his heroine, nor inviting us to condemn her; if anything, it is the man who provides the negative image. And the inability to communicate is striking: the man expresses himself in gesture, the woman cannot speak to him about her feelings.

Podzemnaia nimfa contains a total of fifty-seven poems, which range in length from 156 lines down to 6, running the gamut between extended narrative and the briefest of lyrical impressions. The balance between the two modes of narration that have just been illustrated and discussed is not even: thirty-nine of the poems can be provisionally assigned to the omniscient mode of 'Devochka', and seventeen to the 'female *skaz*' mode of 'Nedoumen'e'.[10] This leaves only one poem that clearly adopts a different procedure: poem 52, 'Ballada' (pp. 42–4), is male *skaz*, a narration by a dissident painter about how he is denounced by his fiancée, a Party member, and her sinister look-alike mother; he does a spell in the camps, and after his return, now old, has his only public exhibition, which is closed after one hour, but not before two old women have appeared:

> Их сходство в старости дошло
> До некого предела. Еле
> плелись, дышали тяжело.
> Но не стеснялись, не робели.
> «А неплохие акварели
> писал он … этот богомаз», —
> сказала мать … И в самом деле,
> кто будет отвечать за нас?   (p. 44)

(Their alikeness in old age reached | some sort of limit. Barely |

dragging themselves along, breathing hard. | But they weren't shy, weren't timid. | 'Not bad, those watercolours | he used to do ... that old dauber', | said the mother ... And indeed | who is going to answer for us?)

Here, exceptionally in the book, the women are malign; the mother and daughter act in concert to destroy the man's life. The last line just cited concludes every one of the poem's eleven stanzas; the first person plural identifies the male narrator and the two women with a larger social body, the whole nation.

The vast majority of the poems in the collection are self-contained, presenting women who are seen once only. But two women occur more than once. The first of them is the principal heroine of the five poems that bear the same title as the book, *Podzemnaia nimfa;* the first of them opens the book and the last one closes it, and the other three are placed at 11 (p. 8), 34 (p. 24), and 48 (p. 35). These five poems employ the same type of voyeur narrator as we have seen in 'Devochka'. He watches a woman in the Moscow underground as she rides the train, reading a newspaper (poem 1, p. 3), the trivial contents of which are mentioned (2, p. 8); he wonders about her ultimate fate (3, p. 24); and finally (5, p. 47) imagines her getting off the train and going home:

> Подземная нимфа, газету сложи:
> пора подниматься — сначала на землю,
> затем по ступенькам в автобус, где зело
> толкают, затем уже — на этажи —
> все выше — пусть лифт отказался от роли —
> а там еще выше: встав на табурет,
> возвысить газетою гору газет,
> растущую на антресоли.   (p. 47)

(Underground nymph, fold your newspaper: | it's time to get up, first to ground level, | then up the steps to the bus, where exceedingly | they jostle you, and then again – floor after floor – | ever higher, the lift has refused its part – | and then ever higher: standing on a stool, | to raise by one newspaper the mountain of newspapers | that's grown on the shelf over the door.)

The consistent upward movement of the poem is thus given a bathetic conclusion; this creature that the voyeur has fantasized into a 'nymph' ends up making a monumental gesture that sums up the banality of her 'days'.

These and other poems bring together the everyday life of women in contemporary Moscow with mythological females, a combination that is announced in the book's title. This association is most explicit in poem 13, 'Sestry' ('Sisters'), where two contemporary Soviet women are aligned with wronged and vengeful sisters from Greek mythology and made to relish male misfortune:

> В угловую толпу протолкавшись —
> и поближе, поближе бы каждой —
> раскрывая глаза на призыв
> и про тяжесть авосек забыв,
> под дождем накренившимся мокнут,
> но не прячут от ливня лицо,
> нет — глядят Филомела и Прокна
> на попавшего под колесо.   (p. 9)

(Shoving their way into the crowd on the corner – | and each of them trying to get as close as possible – | their eyes opening wide at the challenge | and forgetting the weight of their shopping bags, | getting soaked by the slanting rain, | but they don't hide their faces from the downpour, | no – Philomela and Procne gaze | at a man who's been run over.)

Besides the 'nymphs' in the Moscow underground and these sisters, Velichanskii introduces several other female figures from biblical and classical mythology. The figure of Eve appears several times. The postlapsarian world is taken up in poem 39, 'Izgnanie' ('Exile'), and here the male and female predicament is shared:

> ... не ведали они,
> что ждет и их изгнанье,
> за пропитанье
> кровавая борьба —
> силки, стрельба.   (p. 27)

(... they knew not, | that exile awaited them too, | and for sustenance | a bloody struggle – | snares, shooting.)

In a few cases, a mythological heroine is accorded no explicit contemporary parallel. The most extended example of female *skaz* in the book is Rachel's justification to 'the God of Abraham' of her actions (pp. 6–8): an oppressive and vindictive patriarchy is confronted with increasing desperation by a woman alone. Mary Magdalen is linked with Eve in poem 5:

> Магдалина, не ломай
> столь умелых рук —
> заповедный древний рай
> явится вокруг —
> без усилия извне
> ты войдешь туда
> новой Евой, ибо не
> ведала стыда.   (pp. 4–5)

(Magdalen, do not wring | those so-able hands of yours – | that promised ancient paradise | will be made manifest around — | without effort from outside | you will enter into there | as a new Eve, for you have not | known shame.)

And Rebecca is glimpsed as the salvation of Isaac in the highly atmospheric poem 41 'Vo sreten'e' ('Towards encounter', p. 29), the only case in the book where male–female relations appear to promise harmony.

Notwithstanding these assertions of sisterhood with women of other times and spaces, the book is dominated by the unambiguously portrayed women of contemporary Soviet Russia. There are about fifty of them. They range in terms of age from the young woman we have encountered in 'Devochka' to an old, ill woman staying at a dacha with her dying husband in 'Stariki' (pp. 45–6); the latter poem is narrated in female *skaz* by a younger woman who plays the couple an old romance on her guitar on the day she has received a 'sad letter' from her lover, and is touched when they supply the words that she has never heard. There is the horror-inspiring old woman glimpsed through the windows of a decrepit house in Telavi (poem 53, pp. 44–5). None of the women in the book are defined in terms of their work; there is practically no information at all about this aspect of their existence. Sociologically, almost all these women come from strata below the intelligentsia. There is only one educated woman in the book; she is retired, and is cruelly portrayed in *skaz* through her own words as obsessed with the well-being of her cat (poem 42, pp. 30–1).

Between these extremes of age we find a predominant population of women who are mature and sexually active – heterosexually active exclusively, it should be added. What is the nature of their experience? First and foremost, they are victimized. One young woman and her sister are gang raped[11] by six young soldiers disguised in gas masks (poem 4, p. 4). Another is subjected to persistent physical harassment by a former lover (poem 20, pp. 15–16). Yet another, a seventeen-year-old, is inveigled into a sexual relationship with a soldier by her drunken father and murdered by her lover when she becomes pregnant, as a result of which the lover is executed (poem 45, pp. 32–3, related in female *skaz* from beyond the grave). The most numerous cohort in the book is made up of women who are abandoned by their lovers and husbands for various reasons (poems 8, p. 5; 23, pp. 18–19; 30, p. 21; 31, p. 22; 32, pp. 22–3; 46, pp. 33–4). The reaction to being abandoned is summed up in one case as follows:

> Успокоилась работой.
> Верой в Божьи чудеса.
> Ненавистью. Верой в Бога —
> больше в Сына, чем в Отца.   (p. 22)

(She calmed herself with work. | And belief in the Lord's miracles. | With hatred. And belief in God – | more in the Son than the Father.)

In another poem, the male narrator wonders about the source of this 'faith in miracles':

> Откуда эта вера, вера в чудо,
> когда уже ни юных сил, ни чувства,
> казалось бы, остаться не должно
> у них — обманутых, растраченных давно
> на чьи-то прихоти, измаянных работой
> и одиноких ...   (p. 24)

(Where does this faith come from, this faith in miracles, | when neither youthful strength, nor feeling, | it would seem, should remain | with them – deceived, long since wasted | on someone's whim, worn out by work | and lonely ...)

This ability is attributed by the author to an atavistic memory women are said to have about a heroic age of personal relations during which they 'gave birth to giants'; but it is notable that while the male narrator empowers himself to name this dimension that transcends the immediate, the women themselves, in their various pieces of *skaz*, are on the whole denied this ennobling insight. The most they are allowed is a vague occasional reference to Christian mythology. In poem 49, 'Byt′ mozhet, tam' ('On the other side, perhaps', pp. 37–41), the longest text in the book, which switches between voyeur and female *skaz* narrative modes, a woman rejects her fiancé when he confesses that he is an NKVD executioner; he leaves the service for her, and is immediately arrested; she is sure he has been executed; in her dreams she sees him dead, and in her self-reproach she introduces the only mention in the book of the ultimate female vicarious sufferer. It is noteworthy that this woman does not identify herself with the Virgin Mary, but sees her as a compassionate presence:

> Она увидела кровавые тела
> им убиенных, и средь них — он — милый.
> Ведь это я сама его убила.
> Мне нужно было грех его вобрать
> в себя — терпеть, молиться — Божья Мать
> услышала б меня во что б ни стало.   (pp. 39–40)

(She saw the bloody bodies | of those he had killed, and among them there was he, her sweet man. | It was I who killed him, she thought. | I needed to take his sin | into myself – to endure, to pray – the Mother of God | would have heard me no matter what.)

What is the reaction of these women to this victimization? It is predominantly one of fatalistic acceptance. The victim of the gang rape 'submits' to the assault:

> ... Ну, я далась
> легко, чтоб не прибили часом!
> Ну и страшон противогаз!   (p. 4)

(... Well, I gave in | easily, so they wouldn't spend an hour beating me up! | And the gas mask was scary, too!)

This woman and her sister accept a bribe from the military

authorities not to press charges, and the speaker ends up as the complacent girl friend of one of the six rapists:

> За групповуху — к ногтю б их,
> да мы, однако, деньги взяли
> хоть покуражились вначале:
> начальству не с руки ЧП.
> Папаша дом сестрице справил.
> А с Мишкой ходим мы теперь. (p. 4)

(For gang rape they should have copped it, | but we accepted money | although I showed off at first: | an incident would have been bad for the commanders. | Dad fixed up somewhere to live for my sister. | And I'm going with Misha now.)

One woman calculatedly exploits her sexual relationship with another woman's husband for no other reason than to get herself a pair of boots (poem 33, p. 23). In the most physiologically gross of the male voyeur poems (35, p. 24), a scantily clad young woman is observed on the beach caressing her non-Russian lover, who is old enough to be her grandfather. The abandoned women as a rule look upon their situation and their victimizers with resignation or that incomprehension we have seen in 'Nedoumen'e'. The self-reproaching lover of the NKVD killer 'grew older proudly, as if she'd been his wife', and devotes her life to caring for the children of her friends in order to assuage her sense of guilt.

In all these cases, women are made to define their identities through relationships with men, and this is overwhelmingly the predominant mode of definition in *Podzemnaia nimfa*. However, there are three poems in which there is a heroinic refusal of such definition and an assertion of female autonomy. One woman (poem 38, pp. 25–7), now old, is observed doing her daily shopping in the middle of Moscow, and is seen as a figure to be scorned, by the male narrator and, through him – significantly – by other women too, but she is not daunted:

> ... Она всегда считала, что мужчины
> бесмомощны, смешны, каким бы чином
> их не венчали, бедных. Суть не в том.
> И думают, как дети, об одном.
>
> А женские презрительные взгляды

она не замечает. Их наряды
внушают отвращенье ей. И яд
их взглядов отражал бесстрастный взгляд —

им с юности она владела грозно.   (p. 26)

(... she had always thought that men | were helpless, ridiculous, no
matter what rank | they were crowned with, poor things. That's not
the point. | And like children they only think of one thing. || And the
contemptuous looks of women | she does not notice. Their get-ups |
revolt her. And the poison | of their looks she meets with her
dispassionate look – || since youth she'd learned to look menacing.)

A second old woman, whose children have grown up and
left, is approached by an old widower; he is a drinker, and she
works in the alcohol department of a food store. She is
tempted by the idea of a double pension and the man's larger
living space, where a portrait of his dead wife hangs, but she
refuses him:

Оглядела койку, подоконник,
стол, обоев рвань, в окошке — дворик,
и портрет старинный заприметив,
долго на него глядела бабка ...
Наглядевшись, деду отказала
наотрез: уж больно пьешь нетрезво.   (p. 29)

(She inspected the bed, the window ledge, | the table, the ripped
wallpaper, the courtyard through the window, | and noticing an old
portrait, | the old woman looked long at it ... | Having looked her
fill, she refused the old man, | once and for all, saying 'You really are
an awful drunk.')

The third of these women repudiates men in general and her
husband in particular, in the most startling example of female
skaz in the book:

Ненавижу мужиков.
Всех. Тебя вот, скажем. Мужа.
Всех. Живете вы легко.
И молоденьких подружек

ваших тоже не терплю—
Им-то, правда, отрыгнется
скоро, скоро — к октябрю,
к осени. Потянет в гнезда —

всем захочется тюрьмы.
Вы становитесь умнее,
интереснее, а мы —
мы рожаем и дурнеем.

Вам, подонкам, невдомек,
что мы чувствуем не хуже
вас ... Летит, как мотылек,
на любую юбку ... Ну же.   (pp. 20–1)

(I hate men. | All of them. You, for example. My husband. | All of
them. You have an easy life. | And those pretty young girl friends ||
of yours I can't stand. | True, they'll get spat out | soon, soon – by
October, | by autumn. The nest will call || and you'll all start
wanting your prison. | You grow more intelligent, | more interesting
with age, but we | we give birth and lose our looks. || You can't
understand, you scum, | that we have feelings | as much as you ...
Men flit, like a butterfly, | to any skirt ... Sod it. ||)

This woman is made to express contempt for the male
promiscuity that is endemic in *Podzemnaia nimfa*. But here we
meet perhaps the most remarkable aspect of *Podzemnaia nimfa* as
a male-authored work of Russian literature: there is no countering condemnation of female promiscuity, implicitly or explicitly. We have already seen in 'Nedoumen′e', the second
poem we examined, the way that female promiscuity is taken
for granted. This lack of condemnation goes against one of the
most consistent strands in the way male Russian writers have
attempted to define their women, to the extent that for a
woman who is even unfaithful once to one man to go unpun-
ished, let alone uncensured, is practically unknown in the
classic tradition. In this respect, if 'female *skaz* is used by most
male authors morally to damn the speaker: her otherness is a
reprehensible one',[12] then this seems not to be the case with
Velichanskii. He even permits one of his women to boast of the
extent of her sexual experience, in a way that has usually been
reserved for males; the poem's title is a male locker-room pun,
'Chlenstvo' ('Membership'):

Нет, что ты, я переспала
со всеми нациями нашей
империи, а как иначе
узнать, какая удала?   (p. 9)

(No, come off it, I've had one-night stands | with every single nationality in our | empire, how else | could I find out what I'm up to?)

This toleration and objectivity, limited though it is, is not the only remarkable and refreshing aspect of Velichanskii's construction of female identity in this book. Several other standard and persistent tendencies in male-authored Russian literature are remarkable for their absence in *Podzemnaia nimfa*. None of the women here are legitimized and celebrated as mothers. None of them are legitimized as servants; they are never observed cooking, for example. And they get as good (or as bad) as they give in marital sexual relations. The most we can say, perhaps, is that the conventional roles are assumed by the author to be too self-evident in terms of cultural norms to require mention or discussion; but at least he does not make them the most prominent aspects and goals of his definition, as has so often been the case. The mothering and serving roles are touched on in one of the most intriguing poems in the book, 'Roman' ('Love Affair', pp. 10–11). Here, a woman thinks back ten years to the time she was working as a physical training instructor in a Pioneer camp. She falls in love with one of her charges, a boy who is not yet thirteen years old:

> Два слова друг другу сказали едва ли
> за лето — все бегали да приседали.
> Была я — что надо: стройна.
> Но знал он, что я влюблена.   (p. 10)

(Hardly two words we spoke to each other | during the summer – it was all running about and knee-bends. | I was what was required – good figure. | But he knew I was in love.)

Her pseudo-maternal feelings do not prevent her from using this boy in her relations with another object of her affections:

> Я с Толькой спала, с баянистом, но это
> совсем не вязалось с моим шпингалетом,
> и он не сердился на нас,
> и даже помог нам не раз —
> как там говорили, стоял на атасе,
> ну, словом, стерег затаившихся нас он
> в орешнике за костровой
> поляной, как впрямь часовой.   (pp. 10–11)

(I was sleeping with Tolia, the accordion player, but this was nothing to do | with my pretty young man | and he didn't get angry with us | and even helped us more than once, | as they used to say there, he 'kept watch', | he was lookout, in short, for us when we hid away | in the hazel-grove behind the camp-fire | clearing, like a real sentry.)

The boy sprains his arm doing the long jump, and for three nights the woman goes from her bed with Tolia the accordionist to sit in silence with him:

> Раз только сказал, что со мною не больно.
> Я шопотом этим была так довольна,
> так счастлива — ну и дела —
> что после сама не спала. (p. 11)

(Just once he said that when he was with me there was no pain. | I was so happy with this whisper, | so happy – that's how it goes — | that afterwards I couldn't sleep.)

This is the only time in the book that a woman uses the word 'happy' of herself; as we have seen, this state is achieved by mentally separating her sexual relationship with the man from her caring relationship with the boy. The implications are bleak, but consistent throughout *Podzemnaia nimfa*.

Perhaps the most remarkable respect in which Velichanskii avoids received notions in the male construction of female identity is that there is almost no trace in this book of the supreme male hypostasis of woman as Russia; his women stand for themselves, with the mythological parallels serving to align them with other women in other cultures whose roles are not necessarily nation-defining or nation-embodying. But at the same time they do exhibit several of the principal characteristics of male-defined femaleness in Russian culture: constructed almost exclusively as victims, as more sinned against than sinning, they are by implication morally superior to the men, if only by omission rather than commission. They are also on the whole more articulate than the men, and emotionally more sensitive and responsive. Whether or not these myths are best read in psychological terms, as a displacement of some sort of atavistic male guilt, is a matter for speculation.

These general characteristics of the women in this book transcend the particularities deriving from the two major narrative techniques; they are consistent whether the women are being made to tell or being told about. Whatever may be the case, *Podzemnaia nimfa* is full of interest for the student of Russian gender relations. The author offers a series of sometimes brutal cameos that confront the reader with uncomfortable issues. Velichanskii does not formulate moral and ethical responses to these issues; in particular, he does not condemn many aspects of these relationships that are increasingly felt now to be worthy only of condemnation, in siding with which the reader could be offered the comfort of rectitude. But the book is a remarkable achievement, one that certainly deserves recognition – something that the author neither sought nor received during his lifetime.

NOTES

1 The only substantial statement published about Velichanskii during his lifetime appears to be the following: 'In the late 1960s, in one of the last issues of *Novyi mir* that he edited, Tvardovsky published poems by a young poet, then in his late twenties. His name was Aleksandr Velichanskii. Now Tvardovsky wasn't exactly generous towards poets – he had a kind of peasant complex towards some of them, I think. But now, in the Indian summer of *Novyi mir*, he didn't just give this poet a bit of space – he published, I think, 20 of his poems! As if he wanted to attract readers' attention to the fact that someone was writing good poetry. And indeed, this Velichanskii looked to me to be a very promising poet. But what happened to him? He simply disappeared. Only once afterwards did I ever see a poem of his – in a Moscow youth magazine'. Igor' Pomerantsev, 'Out of step', *Index on Censorship*, 3 (1986), pp. 15–18 (p. 16). There is a review of *Vremeni nevidimaia tverd'* by Svetlana Solozhenkina, '"Pod muzyku Vival'di ..."', *Literaturnoe obozrenie*, 8 (1990), pp. 60–2; and Velichanskii gets one paragraph in Mikhail Aizenberg's indispensable guide to poets repressed or ignored during the last twenty years of Soviet power, 'Nekotorye drugie ...', *Teatr*, 4 (1991), pp. 98–118.

2 See *Novyi mir*, 12 (1969), pp. 25–8.

3 *Oktiabr'*, 7 (1988), pp. 74–7. There had been two publications in the émigré press, both in *Neue russische Literatur: Almanach* 1 (1978),

4 (one poem); and Almanach 2–3 (1979–80), pp. 77–107; the latter selection gives a very fair impression of Velichanskii's work as a whole up to that date.

4 I am very grateful to Ol'ga Sventsitskaia for providing me with copies of these publications, and also for a copy of what appears to be the only obituary of the poet: L. Litinskii, 'Poet Aleksandr Velichanskii, 8-08-1940–10-08-1990', *Troitskii Variant*, 15, 29 August 1990, p. 16. We learn from this account that Velichanskii, in addition to his original poetry, translated a substantial number of literary works. They include: the poetry of Cavafy; Natalie Zemon Davis, *The Return of Martin Guerre*; Dee Brown, *Bury my Heart at Wounded Knee*; thirteen short stories by I. B. Singer; a collection of lyrics by Emily Dickinson; and Shakespeare's *Julius Caesar*. Litinskii's statement that Joseph Brodskii named Velichanskii as 'the second most interesting poet in Russia (after Evgenii Rein)', is inaccurate; in answer to a question about current Soviet poetry, Brodskii, after due reservation, states: 'I can only name Kushner, Rein, Elena Shvarts, who else ... Velichanskii, Eremin, Krivulin ...': 'Cheloveka mozhno vsegda spasti', *Ogonek*, 31 (1988), p. 29.

5 The principal predecessor, obviously, is Nikolai Nekrasov's cycle about the Decembrist wives, *Russkie zhenshchiny* (1871–2), a work utterly different from *Podzemnaia nimfa* in all important respects.

6 Barbara Heldt, *Terrible Perfection. Women and Russian Literature* (Bloomington, IN: Indiana University Press, 1987).

7 Barbara Heldt, 'Female *skaz* in Sasha Sokolov's *Between Dog and Wolf*', *Canadian-American Slavic Studies*, 22, 1–2 (1988), pp. 279–86; here, several earlier works are referred to in which this narrative procedure is adopted. In addition to those listed by Heldt, one may note: Remizov's first publication, *Epitalam* (1902), the lament of a young woman before her marriage; Shmelev's novel *Niania iz Moskvy* (1936), written entirely in *skaz* (as told to another woman, incidentally) from the point of view of an old Moscow nanny who has found herself in emigration; and perhaps the most ambitious example of female *skaz* so far published in Russian, Viktor Erofeev's *Russkaia krasavitsa* (1990); translated by Andrew Reynolds as *Russian Beauty* (London: Hamish Hamilton, 1992). In verse, Lermontov's 'Kazach'ia kolybel'naia pesnia' and Kol'tsov's famous song 'Okh, zachem menia/Siloi vydali' are textbook examples of female *skaz* written by a man. There are, of course, innumerable single male-authored works in verse in the Soviet period with central female figures; it is tempting to identify as particularly cognate with those of Velichanskii the women in the

songs of Aleksandr Galich and the early Vladimir Vysotskii, which make liberal use of *skaz*. Poem 47, 'Posvyashchaetsia vsem im' ('Dedicated to all of them', p. 35) is particularly reminiscent of Galich; 'Zhestokii romans' ('Cruel romance', poem 19, pp. 14–15, is particularly reminiscent of Vysotskii. Some remarkable examples of the device in verse have recently been published, the most assured of them being Oleg Chukhontsev's poem 'Iz odnoi zhizni. Probuzhdenie', a four-part work in which a family wakes up in their Moscow apartment one Sunday morning: the four parts are narrated in *skaz* in turn by the husband, the wife, their daughter, and the wife's mother; see Oleg Chukhontsev, *Stikhotvoreniia* (Moscow, 1989), pp. 206–10. It would clearly be interesting to compare the use of female *skaz* by male Russian poets with the practice of male poets in other national traditions, and to come to some estimate of whether the device is more or less common than it is in Russian.

8   Useful recent work on *skaz* includes E. G. Lushchenko, V. P. Skobelev, L. E. Kroichik, *Poetika skaza* (Voronezh, 1978), and I. A. Kargashin, 'O sovremennykh formakh skaza', in E. A. Toddes, ed., *5-ye Tynianovskie chteniia* (Riga, 1990), pp. 42–4; neither of these works, like the classic studies by the Russian Formalists that preceded them, pays any attention to the factor of gender.

9   The metrical typology of *Podzemnaia nimfa* is as follows: Iambic dimeter, 1 poem; trimeter, 2; tetrameter, 11; pentameter, 14; mixed iambic, 5; free iambic, 2. Trochaic tetrameter, 8; pentameter, 1; mixed, 1. Dactylic dimeter, 1; pentameter, 1. amphibrachic trimeter, 1; tetrameter, 1; pentameter, 3; mixed, 1. anapaestic dimeter, 1; trimeter, 1. Mixed ternary, 1; 3-ictus dolnik, 1. This distribution yields: Iambic, 61.5%; Trochaic, 17.5%; Ternary, 17.5%; Other, 3.5%, which represents an extraordinarily high proportion in the iambic group, and an almost complete absence of anisosyllabic metres, that is, a metrical typology characteristic of Russian poetry before the modernist period (except in respect of the prominence of iambic pentameter). The prominence of trochaic tetrameter is one of the strongest folkloric elements in the book. All poems are rhymed using standard schemes and contemporaneously accepted standards of exactness.

10 The 'female *skaz*' poems are as follows: 4, 'Pastushka' ('The Shepherdess', p. 4); 6, 'Vse normal'no' ('All in Order', p. 5); 8, 'Golosok' ('A Small Voice', p. 5); 9, 'Molitva Rakhili' ('The Prayer of Rachel', pp. 6–8); 10, 'Nedoumen'e' ('Incomprehension', p. 8); 14, 'Chlenstvo' ('Membership', p. 9); 15, 'Roman'

('Love Affair', pp. 10–11); 20, 'Pro movo' ('About my …', pp. 15–16); 21, 'Plyasovaia' ('Dance', pp. 16–17); 26, 'Rai' ('Paradise', p. 20); 28, 'Nenavizhu' ('I hate', pp. 20–1); 31, 'Lamentatsiia' ('Lamentation', p. 22); 33, 'Vidit Bog' ('As God Sees', p. 23); 42, 'Dlia kota' ('For the Cat', pp. 30–1); 45, 'Sredi liudei' ('Among People', pp. 32–3); and 54, 'Stariki' ('Old People', pp. 45–6).

11 Dr Lynne Attwood has reported that currently in Russia, one in four rapes is a gang rape, a phenomenon ascribed by Russian women to the historical tradition of collective action by Russian men – 'The Post-Soviet Woman', paper delivered at St Antony's College, Oxford, 16 November 1992.

12 Barbara Heldt, 'Female *skaz*', p. 279.

CHAPTER 16

Thinking self in the poetry of Ol'ga Sedakova

Stephanie Sandler

Among Russia's contemporary poets, two young women have drawn the attention of critics: Ol'ga Sedakova and Elena Shvarts. This essay, while it will draw some comparisons between the two, will concentrate on Sedakova, whose work has been somewhat less accessible.[1] Sedakova's poetry, admirable for its beautiful formal complexity and for its intricate thought patterns, often resists other characterizations: she is not a poet for whom closure, or certainty, has much appeal. She has disparaged those 'who would like a guaranteed and perfect organization of everything on earth', preferring 'the eternal freedom of the most important things in the world (which extends even to their names)'.[2] When she views naming as an act that liberates meaning, rather than pinning it down, Sedakova is exemplifying for us one verbal process that produces endless chains of signification in her poetry rather than fixable entities with which to build. The same structure emerges in her work at the level of ideas. Sedakova writes about processes of thought, about the emotions that surge when one turns an idea over in the mind, rather than the discoveries that thinking can yield. She is a meditative poet whose lyrics circle the eddying currents of mental change.

Even in her shorter poems, Sedakova does little to ease our entry into her ways of thinking about the world. Her poems frequently omit the familiarizing first moves that teach readers how to proceed, which is to say that for those who come for the first time to Sedakova's poetry, the experience can be frustrating and unsettling. Though her images and ideas give enormous pleasure, the poems themselves are splendidly difficult. Her poems are nearly always hard to figure out; densely and multiply allusive, they rarely tell anything resembling a story or present speakers more than fleetingly. Sedakova's syntax can turn even simple declarative sentences into incomprehensible sequences of apparently unrelated words. Not for nothing does she admire Khlebnikov. And Mandel'shtam. In Anna Akhmatova's work, she has been most drawn to the riddles of *Poema bez geroia* (*Poem Without a Hero*, 1940–1962), rather than to the early love lyrics, or even *Requiem* (1936–1940). Sedakova uses textual difficulty to slow down the reader's work of sense-making. Her poems take apart and play with the constituent elements of thought and of poetry; she also playfully rethinks the elements of self, the topic to which I turn in the second part of this paper.

New readers, among whom I would count myself, rehearse crucial aspects of Sedakova's poetic. The slow steps in coming to comprehend an idea – her richest subject – can be viewed as a miniature version of what happens to a reader in the presence of one of Sedakova's poems. These poems also reflect in remarkable ways on the idea of beginnings, not just the sources for a specific poem, but also the starting moment for poetry's ideas. One point of departure for this essay will be an investigation of how beginnings work in Sedakova's poetry, including consideration of how, in her view, thoughts begin. This is not precisely the same question as asking how her poems begin, though we shall look at the beginnings of some of her long poems. Sedakova fixes her concern on how thoughts begin, and in that way she makes herself into a specific kind of meditative poet. It is perhaps too early to pin down precisely what kind of poetry results, but one can already see that it exists in a tense relationship to the elegy.[3] Where elegy defines the present in terms of the past, her poems nearly always envision the present and imagine a future. Where elegy mourns what is lost, Sedakova celebrates what is, even in the face of loss. Where elegy often equates thinking with having memories, these poems reveal an interplay between fresh stimulus and reverberating associations. In her emphasis on processes of thinking, and in the mental work required to discern her patterns of imagery, Sedakova does not differ from many better known twentieth-century poets, some of whom have clearly influenced her (Rilke, Eliot, Mallarmé, Mandel'shtam). There are many others, including her near contemporaries, with whom future scholars will want to compare her (among American poets, John Ashbery and Jorie Graham come to mind, especially in terms of how they represent thought). But my own focus will be on Sedakova herself, with some comparisons to poets in the Russian tradition (Anna Akhmatova and Elena Shvarts): my goal is to describe how thinking works in Sedakova's poetry, particularly thinking about the self.

Sedakova's shorter lyrics present a good point of departure. They offer vivid details of atmosphere and mood; where they are less than transparent is in their images for ignorance and incompleteness, as in this brief poem, 'Zhenskaia figura' ('The Figure of a Woman', 1982):

> Отвернувшись,
> В широком большом покрывале
> стоит она. Кажется, тополь
> рядом с ней.
> Это кажется. Тополя нет.
> Да она бы сама охотно в него превратилась
> по примеру преданья —
> лишь бы не слушать:
> — Что ты там видишь?
> — Что я вижу, безумные люди?
> Я вижу открытое море. Легко догадаться.
> Море — и все. Или этого мало,
> чтобы мне вечно скорбеть, а вам — досаждать
> любопытством?[4]

As translated by Andrew Wachtel, the poem reads:

> Having turned away,
> She stands in a large
> and voluminous shawl. It seems there's a poplar
> next to her. It seems that way. There's no poplar.
> But she would be willing to turn into one
> Just like in the legend
> If only not to hear:
> – What do you see there?

    – What do I see, you lunatic people?
    I see the wide open sea – That's easy to guess . . .
    The sea and that's all.
                Or is that too little,
    for me to eternally grieve, while your curiosity's piqued?[5]

This poem is one of seven in a cycle called *Stely i nadpisi* (*Stellae and Inscriptions*, 1982); each lyric seeks the story behind nearly rubbed out figures and words on ancient stones. These poems never descend into lament of what has been lost (they are not, then, elegies). Instead, they contemplate the inscrutability of an emblem, of a simulacrum or near resemblance that, as in this example, looks like a poplar tree, but is not.

Compare the uncertainties of another poem from this cycle, 'Mal'chik, starik i sobaka' ('Little Boy, Old Man, and Dog'). I quote only a few lines:

> Мальчик, старик и собака. Может быть, это надгробье
> женщины или старухи.
>   Откуда нам знать,
> кем человек отразится, глядя в глубокую воду,
> гладкую, как алебастр?[6]

(Little boy, old man, and dog. Perhaps this is the gravestone | of a woman or an old woman. | How can we know | how a person will be reflected back, when looking into deep water | that is smooth as alabaster?)

Sedakova stresses that we cannot know what we see here, nor can we know what someone else sees. Her poems often include these quick observations about ignorance and limited knowledge; for example, in a longer verse to be discussed in a moment, there is the line 'But *what* he sees, only he can know' ('No *chto* on vidit – znaet tol'ko on').[7]

In 'Mal'chik, starik i sobaka', a person looks into deep water, and similarly the woman described in 'Zhenskaia figura' stares out into the open sea. Liquids often course through Sedakova's poetry; one of her philosophical lyrics is entitled 'Vino i plavanie' ('Wine and Swimming'). Water in her poems can lie stilly as reflective surface and enigmatic depth; water also often rolls past a motionless viewer, which is an important thing to note in a body of poetry where objects are often motionless, where there is little physical action. In 'Zhenskaia figura', the action consists of a visual perception and its attendant emotion. The reader's task is to figure out how they connect. We are given one clue, a passing reference to a legend. The legend can in fact be recovered, from Greek and Latin sources: the daughters of the Sun weep beside a river into which their brother, Phaeton, has fallen. Out of pity for their tears, the gods turn the daughters into black poplars, and their tears now flow as amber coming out of the tree bark.[8] 'Zhenskaia figura' does not actually tell this story. Sedakova typically elides the moment of relevant narrative and, in 'Zhenskaia figura', she turns her poem away from us, just as the woman described has turned away.[9] The most interesting rhythmic pattern in this poem (it plays with three-footed rhythms throughout) is the echo of the first and final lines – 'otvernuvshis'' | 'liubopytstvom' – anapaests that link the sight of someone who has turned away to curiosity. We are left conscious about our own aroused interest in someone who explains nothing of herself to us.

   Is the figure of the woman a figure for the poet? Certainly the posture of looking away connects them. But the emotions differ: a querulous claim to be eternally grieving contrasts sharply with Sedakova's typical celebrations. Yet we cannot but be curious about the similarity, it is as if we are offered the spectacle of something starting to resemble something else. The poem adds to our curiosity when the figured woman imagines transforming herself. Compare Sedakova's assertion that metamorphosis is the central activity of poetry (she calls it transformativeness, an activity that should affect feelings of both poet and reader).[10] Has she turned herself into this grieving woman, for the few lines of the poem? Has she produced a partial self, a simulacrum of self, a speaking subject whose words that directly address a reader include an element of ventriloquism? Alternatively, does the figured woman have such an intense presence in her own right as to make her an independent subject? The frequency of bits of conversation in Sedakova's poetry might alert us to the presence of polyphony; a reading that used Bakhtin's theories about voice and discourse would suggest that

such poems make space for multiple subject positions. Let me
leave these alternatives hanging for the moment, raising as they
do issues of subjectivity and impersonation to which I shall
return.

What we need to do in the mean time is to look at some of
the longer poems, for it is here that difficulties of meaning
become more intense and, I believe, more intriguing. I will be
discussing three long poems, too long for full citation here, but
let us at least look at the opening stanza of each one. First,
'Gornaia oda' ('Mountain Ode'), a poem published in Sedakova's 1986 Paris volume *Vrata, okna, arki* (*Gateways, Windows,
Arches*):

> Где высота сама себя играет
> на маленьком органе деревенском
> и на глазах лазурь изображает,
> но голосом не взрослым и не женским —
> а где-нибудь в долине удивленной
> водой, перебегающей повсюду,
> Моравии, Баварии зеленой
> перемывая чистую посуду,
> там в каменный кувшин с колоколами
> упрятано готическое пламя.[11]

(Where sublimity plays its own tune | on a small village organ | and
draws out azure before the eyes | in the voice of no adult or woman –
| somewhere in the surprised vale | in water, overflowing everywhere,
| from Moravia, green Bavaria, | washing once again the pure vessel,
| there into the stone jug with bells | has been hidden the Gothic
flame.)

Next, the first stanza of a poem entitled 'Pervye stansy' ('First
Stanzas'), part of a cycle entitled 'Stansy v manere Aleksandra
Popa' ('Stanzas in the Manner of Alexander Pope', 1980).
These lines are then the beginning of a poem that itself initiates
a cycle, and they interest us as well because the poem is
dedicated to Elena Shvarts.[12]

> Поэт есть тот, кто хочет то, что все
> хотят хотеть: допустим, на шоссе
> винтообразный вихрь и черный щит —
> и все распалось, как метеорит
> Есть времени цветок, он так цветет,

что мозг, как хризопраз, передает
в одну ладонь, в один глубокий крах.
И это правда. Остальное — прах.[13]

(A poet is one who wants what everyone else | wants to want: on a roadway, say, | a screw-shaped whirlwind and a black screen | all disintegrated, like a meteorite. | Time has a bloom, it flowers in a way | that the brain, like chrysoprase, can transmit | flat, in one handful, in one profound crash. | And this is the truth, all else is dust.)

One more opening stanza, this from a poem called 'Piatye stansy' ('Fifth Stanzas'). Originally, it was to have been part of the same cycle as 'Pervye stansy', but it now initiates a sequence of five poems with the title 'Iamby' ('Iambs', 1984–5).[14] Thus it, too, is the beginning of a beginning.

Большая вещь — сама себе приют.
Глубокий скит или широкий пруд,
таинственная рыба в глубине
и праведник, о невечернем дне
читающий урочные Часы.
Она сама — сосуд своей красы.[15]

(A great thing is a refuge for herself, | a deeply secluded monastery or a broad pond, | a mysterious fish in the depths | and a righteous man, reading about the never-ending day | in his Book of Hours. | She is herself a vessel for her own beauty.)

These three openings may share little beyond the inscrutability I have been discussing; certainly they illustrate it better than what must now seem the simpler poem, 'Zhenskaia figura'. I have made them seem even more obscure by juxtaposing three openings without giving an account of what follows, though readers who know each poem in its entirety will recognize how the poems continue in ways that perplex, rather than elucidate. Among other things, there is a confusing range of reference. In 'Gornaia oda', for example, mixed into the imagery of height and mountain views are repeated references to flowing water, and the first three stanzas cascade through evasive syntactic twists and turns. We do not know who the speaker is, we cannot be sure of the world of reference, rippling as it does through myth (the Holy Grail), geography (in references to Moravia and Bavaria), cultural history (the Gothic), decidedly biblical tones (especially later in the poem), images that refer to writing and to poetry (including voice, sound, game, language, and dream) and specific poetic allusions (starting with the title, a revision of Mandel'shtam's 'Grifel'naia oda' ('Slate Ode', 1923)). Catriona Kelly has rightly called Sedakova's poetry syncretic.[16] The dominant image in 'Gornaia oda', height, soon includes its opposite, for example when it refers to the Orpheus–Eurydice myth, and through words like ravine, falling, descent, lying down. By the poem's end, ascent has turned horizontal, vertical movement has grown round: the last stanza begins by predicting that all will vanish like a road, an unwilled path along which we depart lying down ('Vse, chto ischeznet – budet kak doroga. I lezha my ukhodim v put' nevol'nyi').[17]

Our first instinct, to follow the thematic and literary clues in an initial stanza, is thus only partly helpful, and it opens as many questions as it answers, surely. Let us return to the beginning, now with a closer focus on syntax, lexicon and image. The first line of 'Gornaia oda', 'Gde vysota sama sebia igraet', has a grammatical structure of subject doubling as object. My English version conceals the mirroring effect, which in Russian is doubly strong here – the Russian words literally mean 'Where sublimity itself plays itself'. This syntax appears in the other two long poems as well. Repeated words and images generally slow thought down and let it look at itself, and this mirroring effect of grammatical subject and object intensifies the repetition and the slow glance back. The first sentence of 'Piatye stansy' is another good example of these reflexive sentences, all the more so because it is a refrain. We hear those words, 'Bol'shaia veshch' – sama sebe priiut', three times in the course of the poem, and then hear a final version, 'Bol'shaia veshch' – utrata iz utrat' ('A great thing is a loss to end all loss'). The fourth hearing has a dramatic change in imagery, from the inviting enclosure of a refuge to the evocation of a loss beyond measure, but it preserves the reflexivity of the idea, transforming a haven that surrounds itself into a verbal repetition that makes loss seem to come out of itself.

Earlier comments in this essay about Sedakova's rejection of
the elegy may provoke readers to want to stop me now, to say
that here, indeed, is an eruption of elegy. I agree, though one
should specify that this joyous poem *contains* elegy. Containment
is the great theme of 'Piatye stansy': the first strophe ends with
an instance of grammatical and imagistic enfolding that is
telling.[18] In the line 'Ona sama – sosud svoei krasy', we hear
both the grammar of reflexivity discussed above, and a syntax
of containing or placing one thing inside another. This sentence
structure merits closer inspection, both as a grammatical
construction and as philosophical precept.

Sedakova herself shows us the importance of this phenomenon of containing in poetry. In an essay on Anna Akhmatova's
Poema bez geroia, Sedakova emphasizes what she calls *vnutripolozhnost'*, the placing of one thing inside another, as the deep motif
that appears at all levels of *Poema bez geroia*.[19] It is quite obvious
that the same thing is true of Sedakova's poems – that is,
several levels of meaning and structure are often governed by a
single, often metonymic association. This particular structure,
something inside something else, can be found in the syntax,
diction and imagery of several of Sedakova's poems. 'Piatye
stansy' offers us images like these: vessel, home, seashell,
parentheses, a cup, a scoop, a cellar, mouth, a door, a garden, a
cistern – all as containers, as things that surround and enclose.
Other poems, though less extensively, use the same pattern. In
'Gornaia oda', a Gothic flame is concealed in a stone jug, a bell
hides deep in a ravine and then sways back and forth in a
crevice, wine fills a gaping cavity, and one longs to sleep inside
the deep roots of trees as anxiety rolls around in a bell-shaped
sack and language itself descends into the grave. These structures do not dominate 'Gornaia oda' (where they are modified
by equally powerful transits of height and verticality, and where
things are as likely to be over and under one another as they
are to be inside them).

By comparison, in 'Piatye stansy', the stronger focus on forms
of containment permits a curiosity about how containment
begins. We see repeatedly the moment of insertion, the process
of something being placed into something else. In 'Piatye

stansy', the most important scenario of containing is a mind
containing a thought, vividly imaged when the 'thing' enters
into the creaking house of the poet's mind, its way lit by a
magic lantern ('tak v razum moi, v ego skripuchii dom | ona
idet s volshebnym fonarem ...'). Here the thought is a won-
drous thing, its light magical. The mind takes on the luminous
qualities of the thought it contains. Thought imaged as light is a
traditional philosophical topos, but for Sedakova thought is not
just the result of direct sense experience, as it would be for
Locke, nor is it entirely produced by the mind's own work, as in
Heidegger.[20] Thought happens both ways, it responds to the
sensory stimulations that penetrate the mind, and it has secret
vessels of its own in which thoughts take on different shapes.
Thus the poem ends:

> и будущее катится с трудом
> в огромный дом, секретный водоем ... [21]

> (and the future rolls laboriously
> into the gigantic house, the secret cistern ...)

These lines describe thought entering the poet's mind, but what
Sedakova particularly wants us to note is that the mind has its
own 'secret cistern', the mind is an enormous, but not an empty
house.

She gives us an image that helps describe both the mind and
the thought that enters it. In her essay about *Poema bez geroia*,
Sedakova uses the image of the Russian *matreshka* doll to
describe Akhmatova's repeatedly putting one thing inside
another. In her verse, too, Sedakova reveals each doll as
containing another similar and only slightly smaller doll within.
There is something inside thought itself, we are being taught.
Sedakova's capacious images serve her well here: thought is a
large thing, a seashell large enough to contain the ocean, a
vessel for scampering beasts, chirping birds, growing stars.[22] As
she writes in 'Pervye stansy',

> жизнь просторна, жизнь живет при нас,
> любезна слуху, сладостна для глаз,
> И славно жить как будто на холмах
> с любимым другом ехать на санях ... [23]

(life is spacious, life lives around us, | wonderful to the ear, sweet to the eye, | And it is splendid to live, like being in the hills | riding on a sled with a dear friend . . .).

Is this concept of thought large enough to contain the concept of self? That would be a more substantial requirement than in, say, the straightforward self-fascination of the Romantic poets, since (at least in my view) Sedakova takes the problem of subjectivity as a site of diversionary tactics, obstacle courses and play. She assumes many masks and poses, and her voice as a poet moves through multiple forms of ventriloquism. For Sedakova, the self is not a stable, knowable entity; it is, like the nearly effaced inscriptions of 'Stely i nadpisi', something that one must work to establish; it is a constantly changing shape, metamorphosing through a flux of identities that are themselves unstable. Because she is concerned with how thought works, Sedakova is also always asking what we do when we think about the self, where our ideas of self start, how our very processes of thinking keep a 'self' in constant play. In Sedakova's poems, thinking always includes the self-conscious moment when the thought, as it were, looks back at itself; but I want to suggest as well that in her view thinking becomes most urgent and most troubled when the *thinker* must reflect back on herself.

This claim might seem suspect. Sedakova's poems appear utterly uninterested in subjectivity, that is, in the presentation of a private world of emotion and introspection. Her poems do not begin with the word 'I', to use the standard Nadezhda Mandel'shtam made famous in her criticism of the early Akhmatova, though one might note that this is mostly because none of Sedakova's poems takes for granted that we know which self it is that 'I' refers to: there is no knowable coherent self that pre-exists the writing of a poem.

My passing reference to Akhmatova is quite deliberate, not only because the use I have made of Sedakova's essay on *Poema bez geroia* shows that Akhmatova has especial meaning for her poetry, but also because Akhmatova's treatment of the lyrical subject is so much a touchstone for twentieth-century Russian poets, especially women poets. One usually thinks of Akhmatova's early short lyrics of emotional intensity in this regard, but for Sedakova (as for other contemporary Russian women poets), Akhmatova's middle and later poems that use cultural masks are more important.[24] Akhmatova concealed references to her own tragic fate in familiar stories about Cleopatra, Lot's wife and Dido, among others. The idea of the self, the identity of self with story, is not called into question in such Akhmatova poems as 'Lotova zhena' ('Lot's Wife', 1922–4) or 'Shipovnik tsvetet' ('The Sweetbriar Blooms', 1946–64),[25] rather it becomes a challenge to Stalin's Russia, where integrity and individual identity were routinely denied to nearly all citizens.

Sedakova would define her own generation quite differently: rather than danger, lethargy seems to be the threat to her world.[26] The sleepy dream from which 'we' have awakened in 'Gornaia oda' can be read as such a generational reference. The lines refer to 'airy water', where

говорят, мы жили, как другие,
как снег в горах, как реки в летаргии[27]

(we lived, they say, like the others, | like snow in the mountains, like lethargic rivers).

There is only one poet of her generation for whom Sedakova has unqualified praise, and that is Elena Shvarts.[28] Given my claim about the relationship between historical location and the form of subjectivity in Akhmatova, we might expect to find a presentation of self in Shvarts that has more in common with Sedakova – that is, I am implicitly arguing that forms of subjectivity change as history changes. Shvarts and Sedakova are quite precisely of the same generation, only a year apart in age (Sedakova was born in 1949, Shvarts in 1948). And we find in their work quite a different sense of subject and self-identity from what Akhmatova so famously deployed. Shvarts, I would argue, has pushed Akhmatova's narratives of impersonation to their limit. In addition to a poetic sequence of several lyrics (in her Cynthia poems), Shvarts has written an entire novel in verse, all in the voice of a slightly crazed nun, Lavinia.[29] As Sedakova will do, Shvarts introduces the possibility of play with these personae, and, also like Sedakova, her masks can involve religious figures.[30] Shvarts gives us poems as if they were written by these invented personae. Rather than poems *about* Cynthia or Lavinia, we read the poems they are imagined to have written. A kind of layering of the self results; Shvarts revels in a structure of impersonation that repeatedly unmasks the self to reveal still further forms of masking.

Sedakova is equally capable of building up such a storeyed edifice, as we have seen: it is the way in which she imagines thought itself. A layered presentation of subjectivity emerges especially vividly in her poem to Shvarts. She commences with this conceit: 'Poet est′ tot, kto khochet to, chto vse | khotiat khotet″ ('The poet is someone who wants what everyone | wants to want').[31] We recognize the circularity, the repetition of word and sound to create the impression of reflexivity. But what is also quite striking is her definitional stance. We feel how impossible it would be for her to begin the poem with a claim about her own wants or wishes. Desire belongs to someone else. The syntax distances, and the gesture of self-definition here is profoundly relational.

The circle of syntax and verbal structure is thus not finally confining. In the very impositions of limits and definitions, a certain liberation into a radically different kind of subjectivity happens here. As Sedakova says a few lines later in the poem, speaking produces sounds that seem to describe arcs of enclosed meaning, but the poet can break out of that enclosure:

> Какой же друг? я говорю, мой друг —
> и вижу: звук описывает круг,
> потом другой, и крутит эту нить,
> отвыкнув плакать, перестав просить.
> Мой друг! я не поверю никому,
> что жизнь есть сон и снится одному —
> И я свободно размыкаю круг:[32]

(But which friend? I say: my friend, | and I see: the sound describes a circle, | then another, and it turns this thread | unused to crying, having ceased to ask. | My friend! I believe no one | who says that life is a dream dreamed by one alone – | And I freely break open the circle:)

Notice the heavily accentuated word 'drug' (and recall the pleasures of a sleigh ride with a friend in lines from this poem cited earlier). These words are spoken to someone repeatedly called 'moi drug', and Sedakova defines herself in terms of this friendship with Shvarts.[33]

The emotional content of this word 'drug' is crucial here. It spins a web where crying, begging have ceased. Why? Perhaps because these emotions of sadness, desperation, regret – the stuff of elegy and lament – are to be allowed into this poem under the aegis of Shvarts's own intensely, even violently emotional verse. As in the poem 'Zhenskaia figura', Sedakova makes suffering her theme momentarily. In 'Pervye stansy' we see the face of a beggar walking through a train, and glimpse the face of the returning prodigal son.[34] Thus the poem ends:

> Желанье — тайна. О, желанье — пасть
> и не поднять несчастного лица,
> не так, как сын перед лицом отца:
>
> как пред болящим — внутренняя боль.
> И это соль, и осолится соль.[35]

(Desire is a secret. O, the desire to fall down | and not to raise an unfortunate face, | not like the son before the father's face: || like an interior pain before one who hurts. | It is salt, and salt pours on to salt.)

Desire asserts itself, but again only in a syntax of definition. And then, the undiminished language of longing (signalled in poetry as 'O!'), a desire to fall, to suffer, but to look up to a comforter who is equally in pain. We have stumbled one more time on the syntactical reflexivities discussed above (in that final line, 'I eto sol', i osolitsia sol''), but now coupled with an emotional self-containment that can change our reading of Sedakova. Faced with pain, she acknowledges it, states simply that it *is*. But it confers no distinctiveness on its sufferer.

Before I looked at this poem, I would have said that her poems are not psychological in the way that Shvarts's are. I would have thought that Sedakova starts from a place where subjectivity seems not to exist,[36] where there is is no coherent psyche to explore as if it were the territory of desire and belief. Instead, I would now argue that Sedakova disperses bits of psychic information across richly seen landscapes, as in 'Gornaia oda'. Pieces of the self look out from the crevices of a cave or are perched on mountain tops (and in this respect she most resembles Jorie Graham).[37] It is the lesson of 'Pervye stansy' that Sedakova can find bits of self reflected in the world around her, but also in the psyche of the poet to whom her words are addressed. She is deeply empathetic, a self-transforming poet in more ways that I once thought.

This dispersed psyche conceals a deeper insight into Sedakova's poetry of the self, one that emerges when we juxtapose her fascination with acts of enclosure with the sentiments about desire expressed in her poem to Shvarts. The self of her poetry, I would argue, is always concealed within something or someone else. It is contained by an invented persona, an addressee, a figure of the landscape, a grammatical structure. And the layers that hide that self produce a kind of distancing that is felt most keenly in Sedakova's reluctant expressions of desire. It is as if the clay or leaves or skin or fabric that shield the self from exposure also protect its desires. And desire is then projected outward, on to all of us except the poet, who then look back at her with our own versions of distanced desire (we want to want the poet, she says). What I have also implicitly argued by beginning with statements about the difficulty of Sedakova's work is that our desire is for meaning, for a surer sense of any individual poem's range of reference, for some organizing trope or image to help us figure out what the poet so intensely wishes us to hear.

In keeping us from instant or even eventually full gratification of these desires, Sedakova maintains aspects of her inner world as inaccessible and protected from even the most searching gaze of the reader. Who, after all, are the readers of these poems? In her earlier poems, when Sedakova was virtually unpublished, we can perhaps sense the imagination of an intimate audience, a circle of like-minded intellectuals (she was part of the Tartu/Moscow intellectually (rather than politically) dissident movement, where lengthy apartment gatherings were the scene of heated discussion and enormous creative and scholarly ferment); but in the more recent work, as her audience widens toward those who do not share the familiar frame of reference, we may begin to sense a new self-consciousness about the readership. It is not that new layers of self-protection are added, but rather that Sedakova seems almost to sense that her habitual ways of writing have a newly useful potential for concealment, for a 'haven' in an all-too curious world. A poem like 'Zhenskaia figura' thus thematizes this will to keep some stories of the self buried: the *matreshka* dolls that mark Sedakova's reading of Akhmatova are an inexact figure for her own work, in this sense, because there is no final, innermost doll, no core of self-revelation that we can come upon if we keep prying the toys apart. Moreover, the sequence of revealed identities is much more surprising and more variegated than in conventionally identical *matreshka* dolls.

Nowhere is this more apparent than in the 1994 volume of Sedakova's poetry, a thick collection of hundreds of poems where she shows herself to have enormous diversity in both poetic styles and poetic selves. My own early difficulties in assembling material and trying to imagine a sequence for composition can now be put aside, as readers delve into a book of poems verified by the poet herself. It is sequenced in a rough chronology that shows her development as a poet, and divided according to the 'books' of poetry that ought to have appeared every few years. New approaches to her work can now be considered: for example, the dense repetition of images and locations (home, garden, mirror) and sources (the Bible, saints' lives, medieval romance, Dante, Pushkin, Baudelaire, Mandel'-shtam, Rilke) invites a structuralist analysis of Sedakova's 'poetic world'. The appearance of a cycle of elegies as the concluding group of poems in the 1994 collection demands a refinement and reconsideration of my conviction that Sedakova writes against the elegiac tradition, if only to make sense of why she would move now to write so differently of death and loss (themes that were present in earlier work, but variously contained and framed). Reassessment of the elegiac aspect of her work will also afford a clearer sense of Sedakova's place in Russia's tradition of poets who write about thinking. Evgenii Baratynskii (1800–44) defines this lineage for most twentieth-century poets (like Mandel'shtam and Brodskii, who so greatly admire him), but his elegies focus almost oppressively on psychic pain and the inevitability of death. Sedakova adroitly draws on Baratynskii's work, as in her references to pain and disease in passages discussed in this essay, but she rejects his apparent assumption that genuine thinking can only happen in the presence of grave dangers to mind, spirit, and body.[38] Countering Baratynskii's weighty example, Sedakova has happy recourse to the eighteenth-century metaphysical traditions that enliven the odes of Mikhail Lomonosov (1711–65) and especially Gavrila Derzhavin (1743–1816), as Andrew Wachtel has recently argued.[39] In so doing, she partakes in their joyous celebration of the capacities of language, exulting in her own intellectual agility and creativity all the while.

As in other national traditions (one thinks of the pre-eminence of Donne and Eliot in English metaphysical poetry, for example), Russian poetry of thought has principally featured male practitioners; among many of these, it can be argued that thought itself has been associated with masculinity. In Baratynskii's poetry, for example, the virility and toughness of incisive thinking almost requires a repudiation of the feminine (and thus his early love lyrics, which justify the abandonment of once-loved women by recounting the poet's disillusion and despair, have rightly been shown to set the stage for his mature philosophical meditations). Sedakova had a feminine predecessor in the Russian tradition, however, the intrepid Karolina Pavlova (1807–93). Like her, Pavlova was richly educated in foreign languages and cultures, but her poetry was not nearly so cloaked in protective allusion and inscrutable emblems. But Pavlova, in her more limpid and musical verse, just as surely as has Sedakova in her more conversationally inflected lines, made Russia's nascent metaphysical tradition her own. Like Sedakova, she records the emotions that surge as thoughts enter the poet's mind, and, like Sedakova, she explores the paths by which thoughts define a self, even a self who dares to claim the identity of 'the poet'. Silver Age poets, led by Valerii Briusov, rediscovered Pavlova at the start of this century, but they also domesticated and softened her image in the process (to be fair, one might note that they also respected her skill in versification and indeed were drawn to her technical innovations). Perhaps now, with the example of a late twentieth-century meditative poet equally undaunted by her masculine predecessors, we can also begin to reassess Pavlova's contribution to Russia's poetry of thought. That would be yet another benefit of knowing Sedakova's work – admittedly secondary to the pleasures that come of reading her for her own sake.

With the arrival of her carefully edited collection of poetry, Sedakova makes her claim on our attention even more irresistible. The textual inaccessibility that characterized the first decade of efforts to read her work recedes from view, and we come to recognize personal inaccessibility as one of several poetic personae that inform her verse. We begin to encounter in Sedakova a major poet, one whose work will repay our attention with the immense joy that great poetry contains.

NOTES

Travel to the Bath conference where this paper was first presented was supported by an Amherst College faculty research award. My colleagues in the Department of Women's and Gender Studies responded to a later version, and their comments were extremely helpful for this final revision. I am grateful as well to friends and colleagues who helped in the research for this essay and offered useful criticisms, including Joan Dayan, Ol'ga Demidova, Catriona Kelly, Elena Rabinovich, Dale Sinos and Rebecca Sinos.

1   It might appear that Sedakova has collaborated in this unavailability: she used to say she was not involved in the publication of her work, but even now, when Russian journals are more open to her, portions of larger cycles keep appearing, as if to tantalize with their gaps. Examples of fragmentary publication include 'Iz knigi "Dikii shipovnik": legendy i fantazii', *Znamia*, 8 (1992), pp. 103–10, where we get the second and sixth legends, but no others; 'Iz *Stansov v manere Aleksandra Popa*', *Druzhba narodov*, 9 (1992), pp. 114–20, where we get poems 1, 3 and 4. I have learned, however, that these publications were shaped by editors who made cuts against which Sedakova herself protested (from a conversation with Ol'ga Sedakova, London, May 1994).

2   Kent Johnson and Stephen M. Ashby, eds., *Third Wave: The New Russian Poetry* (Ann Arbor, MI: University of Michigan Press, 1992), p. 130.

3   Nowhere would this seem to emerge more vividly than when Sedakova names a poem an elegy. See the witty poem 'Elegiia smokovnitsy', included in Sedakova, 'Potomu chto vse my byli', *Novyi mir*, 5 (1990), pp. 161–4. In her recent work Sedakova has turned more often to poems titled elegies (she had completed a volume called *Elegii* by 1990), though with results that meditate on the possibility of the elegy, as in 'Stansy na smert' kotenka', especially its third stanza, where death is named a disease of the mind ('bolezn' uma'), a sharp challenge to the mind's dullness. See Ol'ga Sedakova, *Stikhi* (Moscow: Gnozis/Carte Blanche, 1994), pp. 229–32, 259–68, 274–6, 299–316. In general, I use this more reliable, recent text for citations in this essay, but I also mention journals or earlier collections in these notes, since the 1994 collection was (at least at the time of this writing) not easily available.

4   Sedakova, *Stikhi*, p. 47; see also Ol'ga Sedakova, *Kitaiskoe puteshestvie. Stely i nadpisi. Starye pesni* (Moscow: 'Carte Blanche', 1990), p. 28.

5   Johnson and Ashby, *Third Wave*, p. 133.

6   Sedakova, *Stikhi*, p. 245; *Kitaiskoe puteshestvie*, p. 27. For the English, I give in this case my own, literal translation (the whole poem is also translated by Andrew Wachtel in *Third Wave*, pp. 132–3). Other good translations of Sedakova appear in Gerald S. Smith, ed., *Contemporary Russian Poetry*, (Bloomington, IN: Indiana University Press, 1993), pp. 268–79; and in *Glas*, 4 (1993), pp. 221–7. A slim volume of her verse has appeared with Russian originals and English translations: Olga Sedakova, *The Silk of Time: Shelk vremeni*, ed. Valentina Polukhina (Keele: Ryburn Publishing, Keele University Press, 1994). Unless otherwise noted, all translations from Sedakova's originals will be my own.

7   Sedakova, *Stikhi*, p. 228; Sedakova, 'Iz *Stansov v manere Aleksandra Popa*', p. 115.

8   J. G. Frazer, ed. and tr., *Pausanias's Description of Greece*, 6 vols., II (London: Macmillan, 1913), p. 72. The particular image here, of the way that amber is produced from tears, is itself a striking example of the contrasts between fixity and movement that the poem elsewhere takes up.

9   The enigma here might be related to that of femininity itself, as described in Sigmund Freud, 'Femininity', in Freud, *New Introductory Lectures on Psychoanalysis*, trans. James Strachey (New York: Norton, 1965), pp. 99–119.

10 O. Sedakova, 'Zametki i vospominaniia o raznykh stikhotvoreniiakh, a takzhe POKHVALA POEZII', *Volga*, 6 (1991),

pp. 135–64; cited material is on p. 159. A condensed version of this essay appears in Sedakova, *Stikhi*, pp. 317–57. I refer below to this essay as 'Pokhvala poezii' in its journal version.

11 Sedakova, *Stikhi*, p. 182; see also Sedakova, *Vrata, okna, arki* (Paris: YMCA Press, 1986), p. 8.

12 In the first publication of the poem (in Sedakova, 'Iz *Stansov v manere Aleksandra Popa*', p. 114), it was entitled 'To Elena Shvarts'. Not so in the version that appeared in Sedakova's book, and thus which she herself supervised much more closely. See Sedakova, *Stikhi*, p. 225.

13 *Ibid.*

14 Because 'Piatye stansy' first appeared on its own (in *Nezavisimaia gazeta*, 15 February 1992, p. 7), my first efforts to make sense of it might be of interest. I also had at the time poems 1, 3, and 4 of 'Stansy v manere Aleksandra Popa' also published in 1992, and they seemed the apparent context. Each poem, or set of 'stanzas', is composed of 8–12 strophes 8 lines long, all rhymed couplets in 5-footed iambs, with one of the strophes a single couplet. 'Piatye stansy' seemed to me to be the fifth poem in the cycle – thus its title. It has the same stylistic features, except that the strophes are six lines in length rather than eight; it has the closing couplet. What seemed to refute this conclusion was that when 'Piatye stansy' appeared in *Nezavisimaia gazeta*, it had two titles: 'Muzykal'nyi korm' and a subtitle, 'Iz tsikla "Iamby"'. Presumably, the former was the newspaper's title, the latter Sedakova's, though I wondered if it might not refer to a larger book of which the Pope stanzas were a part. I resolved these questions in the usual two ways: I asked Sedakova, who confirmed that 'Piatye stansy' was first conceived as part of the Pope cycle, but took on a life of its own. It was to be part of a new cycle called 'Iamby', dedicated to Aleksandr Blok. (Conversation with Sedakova, London, May 1994.) And I awaited the appearance of her thick volume of poetry, *Stikhi*, which confirms Sedakova's explanation to me; the dedication to Blok is not present, though the very title, of course, echoes his own cycle *Iamby* (which appeared as a separate book in 1919).

The naming of the five 'stansy' by a number also has resonances with the poetic practice of both Mandel'shtam and Akhmatova; it recalls his 'Chetvertaia proza' ('Fourth prose'), so named because it was his fourth major piece of prose; and Akhmatova's *Sed'maia kniga* (*Seventh Book*), her ill-fated volume of verse that never appeared in the 1940s. Susan Amert has also observed that the 'seventh' referred to in Akhmatova's *Poema bez geroia* (*Poem Without a Hero*) is the seventh elegy in the *Severnye elegii* (*Northern Elegies*). See

Susan Amert, *In a Shattered Mirror: The Later Poetry of Anna Akhmatova* (Stanford, CA: Stanford University Press, 1992), p. 112.

15 Sedakova, *Stikhi*, p. 255. Though I give my own literal translation, there is a splendid rhymed version, from which I have borrowed some locutions, by Catriona Kelly: see *Glas*, 4 (1993), pp. 221–3. Kelly's translation is also available in Sedakova, *The Silk of Time*, pp. 57–61 and in Kelly, *An Anthology of Russian Women's Writing, 1777–1992* (Oxford: Oxford University Press, 1994), pp. 390–3.

16 Catriona Kelly, *A History of Russian Women's Writing, 1820–1992* (Oxford: Clarendon Press, 1994), p. 424. Kelly's chapter on Sedakova (pp. 423–32) is certainly the best introduction to her work available in English (or in Russian, for that matter). The first real discussion of Sedakova, while not an overview, appeared in the important essay by Mikhail Epstein, 'Metamorfoza (o novykh techeniiakh v poezii 80-kh godov)', in Epstein, *Paradoksy novizny: O literaturnom razvitii XIX–XX vekov* (Moscow: Sovetskii pisatel', 1988), pp. 139–76. Another important early, brief discussion of her work was the statement by Viacheslav V. Ivanov that prefaced the first Soviet publication of Sedakova: see Ol'ga Sedakova, 'Solovei, filomela, sud'ba', *Druzhba narodov*, 10 (1988), pp. 120–5. Sergei Averintsev's short, resonant essay, 'Gore, polnoe do dna', appears in Sedakova, *Stikhi*, pp. 358–63.

17 Sedakova, *Stikhi*, p. 186; *Vrata, okna, arki*, p. 12.

18 In the poem to Elena Shvarts, we find a more circular syntax: 'Poet est' tot, kto khochet to, chto vse khotiat khotet'' ('A poet is one who wants what everyone else wants to want').

19 Sedakova, 'Shkatulka s zerkalom, ob odnom glubinnom motive A. A. Akhmatovoi', *Trudy po znakovym sistemam*, 17, *Uchenye zapiski Tartuskogo gosudarstvennogo universiteta*, 641 (1984), pp. 93–108; see p. 94. Sedakova also notes that the idea of containment enfolds different spans of time. This observation is quite useful in describing *Poema bez geroia* with its shifting time frames and narrative planes. By comparison, Sedakova's poetry makes little use of temporal contrast. This is part of her larger pattern of rejecting narrative, rejecting a temporal sequence of beginning, middle and end. As I suggest here, she more typically uses the structure of repeatedly starting over again.

20 I mention Heidegger because his name occurs with suspicious frequency in Sedakova's interviews and prose writings as the example of 'the philosopher'. A more immediate source for 'Piatye stansy', however, is St Augustine, thus the poem's reference to 'mediolanskii sad' (Mediolanus is the ancient name for Milan), where one of St Augustine's epiphanies occurs.

21 These images are also notable for their contrasts. This recalls one of Sedakova's observations about Akhmatova's *vnutripolozhnost'*: the things that are put one inside the other in *Poem Without a Hero* are often sharply contrasting. Sedakova, in 'Piatye stansy,' likewise places a treasure in a sleeping powder, fiery constellations deep in the mountains, and the future rolls into an enormous house.

22 This is a poet who takes pleasure in the observed world, and it is not for nothing that Keats figures prominently among poets whose images she repeats (as in 'Fifth Stanzas', where the 'nighttime door of midnight beauty just slightly ajar' ['poludennoi krasy nochnaia dver' | raskryta nastezh"] recalls Keats's 'casement ope at night, | To let the warm Love in!' from 'Ode to Psyche'; the choice of this Keats poem is surely no accident, given its concluding paean to the pleasures of thought in a world where material realities cannot be so joyous). See *The Poems of John Keats*, ed. Jack Stillinger (Cambridge, MA: Harvard University Press, 1978), p. 366. Among other quotations from Keats, the line 'Neslyshimaia muzyka zvuchnei' translates from the 'Ode on a Grecian Urn': 'Heard melodies are sweet, but those unheard | Are sweeter' (*The Poems of John Keats*, p. 372). Sedakova's most explicit use of Keats is in 'Kuznechik i sverchok', with its epigraph 'The poetry of Earth is never dead' (see *Vrata, okna, arki*, p. 64), a line from Keats's sonnet 'On the Grasshopper and the Cricket' (no capital letter on Earth, according to *The Poems of John Keats*, p. 88). On this poem, with a reading that contrasts Sedakova's poetics with Keats's, see Kelly, *A History of Russian Women's Writing*, pp. 426–7.

23 Sedakova, *Stikhi*, p. 225; 'Iz *Stansov v manere Aleksandra Popa*', p. 114.

24 See Amert, *In a Shattered Mirror*, pp. 10–13 (for a discussion of Akhmatova's use of literary masks) and pp. 131–64 (for a richly detailed analysis of Akhmatova's Dido); and T. V. Tsiv'ian, 'Antichnye geroini – zerkala Akhmatovoi', *Russian Literature*, 7/8 (1974), pp. 103–19. I have discussed the importance of this aspect of Akhmatova's work for subsequent women poets in 'The canon and the backward glance: Akhmatova, Nikolaeva, Lisnianskaia, Petrovykh', in Helena Goscilo, ed., *Fruits of Her Plume: Russian Women's Writing* (Armonk, NY: M. E. Sharpe, 1993), pp. 113–34.

25 Clearly 'Shipovnik tsvetet' is a crucial poem for Sedakova. See the cycle 'Dikii shipovnik' (in *Stikhi*, pp. 13–98); a few of these poems appeared in 'Iz knigi "Dikii shipovnik"' and in other journal publications. In the journal variant, though not in *Stikhi*,

the cycle has an epigraph from Pushkin, 'I tainye stikhi obdu-
myvat' liubliu ...' and we might read the emphasis on *secret* verse
as another link to Akhmatova, who called her poetry writing
tainopis'; Akhmatova's life-long interest in Pushkin is also relevant.
For an excellent essay on the volume 'Dikii shipovnik', see D. S.
[V. A. Shaitanov], 'Ol'ga Sedakova: Novyi put'', in Sedakova,
Vrata, okna, arki, pp. 113–28.

26 See Sedakova, 'O "Bronzovom veke"', *Grani*, 130 (1983),
pp. 274–8; 'Pokhvala poezii'; also relevant are characterizations
of other Russian poets in her interview with Valentina Polukhina,
'A rare independence', in *Brodsky Through the Eyes of his Contemporaries* (New York: St Martin's, 1992), pp. 237–60.

27 Sedakova, *Stikhi*, p. 183; *Vrata, okna, arki*, p. 9.

28 See 'A rare independence', p. 251; 'Zametki i vospominaniia',
p. 141; and 'O "Bronzovom veke"', pp. 276–7. That last has the
most specific comments about Shvarts. It refers to her 'inspired,
solitary lyrics', continuing: 'Only in her work do we come close to
glimpsing the true spirit speaking a clear language.'

29 Both cycles are discussed briefly in Barbara Heldt, 'The poetry of
Elena Shvarts', *World Literature Today*, 63, 3 (Summer, 1989),
pp. 381–3. Appended to that essay are translations of two poems
from the Lavinia cycle, expertly rendered by Michael Molnar
(p. 384), but the entire cycle is available only in Russian: Elena
Shvarts, *Trudy i dni Lavinii, Monakhini iz ordena Obrezaniia serdtsa*
(Ann Arbor, MI: Ardis, 1987). Molnar has translated some of the
Cynthia poems as well: see Michael March, ed., *Child of Europe: a
New Anthology of East European Poetry* (London: Penguin, 1990),
pp. 197–202. For the full cycle, see Shvarts, *Tantsuiushchii David*
(New York: Russica, 1984), pp. 54–68. Additional very good
translations of poems by Shvarts, including two poems from the
Lavinia cycle, are available in *Contemporary Russian Poetry*,
pp. 246–57. A separate collection of Shvarts's verse has now
appeared in English, with some of the above translations reprinted and many more besides: Elena Shvarts, *'Paradise': Selected
Poems*, tr. Michael Molnar with Catriona Kelly (Newcastle-upon-
Tyne: Bloodaxe Books, 1993).

30 Both Sedakova and Shvarts use religious themes (without, in my
view, actually 'being' religious – by which I mean that the world-
view of the poetry taken as a whole subverts rather than
reinforces a stable religious order of being). See Sedakova's
comments criticizing the way she has been labelled a religious
poet in 'A rare independence', p. 240.

31 Sedakova, *Stikhi*, p. 225; 'Iz *Stansov v manere Aleksandra Popa*',

p. 114; the sentence is precisely repeated in the cycle's coda, p. 242 ('Iz *Stansov*', p. 120. The coda had been published separately in Sedakova, *Vrata, okna, arki*, p. 7, and translated in Smith, *Contemporary Russian Poetry*, p. 278.

32 Sedakova, *Stikhi*, p. 226.

33 Sedakova has commented on the importance of a familiar addressee in her poems, and 'moi drug' appears as an appellation in other lyrics (to Ivan Zhdanov, for example).

34 The latter also brings to mind Sedakova's fantasia on the theme of the prodigal son, thus it is a reference that points back to herself as a poet; see 'Vozvrashchenie bludnogo syna', in Sedakova, *Stikhi*, pp. 20–4, partly published as 'Kantsona-fantaziia na temu: vozvrashchenie bludnogo syna', in 'Iz knigi "Dikii shipovnik"', pp. 105–6. That poem also addresses the prodigal son as 'drug moi' (p. 21; 'Iz knigi', p. 105).

35 *Stikhi*, p. 228.

36 I am making this difference starker than it actually is, I should say: Sedakova *does* have poems that involve dramatic impersonations, both on small scale, e.g. 'David poet Saulu' ('David Sings to Saul'), and large, as in the Tristan and Isolde cycle; but we would be hard pressed to find a coherent speaking subject in those poems, or even to find sufficient references to familiar myth to retell the story. This is especially true in the Tristan and Isolde cycle, which Sedakova herself described as 'improvisations' and a 'suite'. See Sedakova, *Stikhi*, pp. 101–28; for the characterizations of the cycle, see the brief note that precedes the version in Sedakova, *Vrata, okna arki*, p. 23 (this note is absent in *Stikhi*).

37 Among Graham's poems, those in her most recent volumes especially exemplify this idea of a scattered self. See Graham, *Region of Unlikeness* (Hopewell, NJ: Ecco Press, 1991) and *Materialism* (Hopewell, NJ: Ecco Press, 1993).

38 For excellent accounts of Baratynskii's particular form of metaphysical poetry, see I. Semenko, *Poety pushkinskoi pory* (Moscow: Khudozhestvennaia literatura, 1970), pp. 221–91; L. Ia. Ginzburg, *O lirike*, second edition (Leningrad: Sovetskii pisatel', 1974) pp. 51–126; and Sarah Pratt, *Russian Metaphysical Romanticism: the Poetry of Tiutchev and Baratynskii* (Stanford, CA: Stanford University Press, 1984), esp. pp. 1–37.

39 Andrew Wachtel, 'The youngest archaists: Kutik, Sedakova, Kibirov, Parshchikov', forthcoming in Stephanie Sandler, ed., *Rereading Russian Poetry*.

CHAPTER 17

Women's space and women's place in contemporary Russian fiction

Helena Goscilo

> Space is always suddenly bethinking itself: I am here, and here, and over there! It is forever cropping up somewhere at the back of your head. Not in front, but behind: sneaking up on you from the rear.
>
> (Abram Tertz, *A Voice from the Chorus*[1])

TIME AND SPACE: OPPOSITION VERSUS UNION

In a recent issue of *New Left Review*, an article by a geographer named Doreen Massey deplores the tendency among current sociologists and cultural commentators to privilege time over space.[2] Surveying the most influential publications that engage the time/space issue, Massey chides Ernesto Laclau and Frederic Jameson for (1) opposing spatiality to temporality in a characteristic manoeuvre of reductionist binarism and (2) depoliticizing the realm of the spatial by equating it with stasis. Massey's critique of these related conceptualizations derives in large measure from her gender consciousness, specifically her awareness that a dichotomous dualism formulated as presence and absence (A/not-A) has come under most articulate and sustained attack from feminists, whose efforts to dismantle gendered binarism are too well known to warrant exposition here.[3]

Dichotomous conceptualization of the A/not-A variety (exemplified in the polarized gender distinctions cemented into most western thought) militates against change and, Massey correctly argues, inevitably not only prioritizes the first term of the dualism over the other, but also defines only the first positively.[4] Accordingly, time is conceived in terms of 'change, movement, history, dynamism' ('male' categories), while 'space, rather lamely by comparison, is simply the absence of these things'[5] (that is, the lack that western thought, with Freud's aid, has identified as 'female').[6] For Jameson as for Laclau, the temporal (i.e., dislocated, changing history) carries connotative associations with transcendence, while the spatial (i.e., the cyclical rhythm of simple reproduction) evokes immanence. In this 'system of interconnected dualisms',[7] dynamism, dislocation, History and transcendence are coded as male (Father Time), thereby predicating stasis, cyclical reproduction, and immanence as female (Mother Earth).

Rather than upgrading the status of space within the dualistic configuration, Massey concentrates on exposing the anachronistic assailability of the scientific assumptions fuelling the space/time opposition.[8] She legitimately contends that by conceptualizing space as a passive arena in which objects interact (as posited in Newtonian physics), one overlooks a major principle of modern physics, which maintains that 'the underlying reality consists of a four-dimensional space-time', with the identity of things *constituted through interactions* that in turn *create or define* space and time.[9] While I heartily endorse Massey's refutation, I propose the adoption of a richer, more concise and appealing alternative to an explicit dismissal of Newton in favour of Einstein: namely, Bakhtin's chronotope theory,[10] which Massey's otherwise informed and thoroughly reasoned article utterly ignores, perhaps out of ignorance.

The indissoluble link between time and space, as Bakhtin sensibly noted, is a prearranged marriage of true convenience, for each category unavoidably charges and is charged by the other. Today's psycho-babble would label the relationship one of co-dependency. A divorce signals the end of narrative, which, in a sense, means the end of existence (a nod to Kant[11]). My discussion imposes a temporary and incomplete separation of that genuinely 'dynamic duo', however, in so far as I downplay temporality (without bypassing it, however), so as to focus on space.[12] Instead of subscribing to the ludicrous notion of space as an *innately* gendered phenomenon, I examine how contemporary Russian women's fiction genders space.

Throughout history, the socio-political circumstances specific to a given culture have bred associations, which subsequently became sedimented in that culture's collective psyche, between certain locales and gender, while leaving other areas negotiable, neutered, or neglected. If one may generalize, somewhat sweepingly, that conventional gender disposition has allied women with domestic or private space (the home, the kitchen and the nursery) and men with public or open space (be it the bank, the courtroom, or the great outdoors), one needs as a preliminary step to refine that broad claim by acknowledging, at a minimum, that the male study or workshop belongs to domestic space, even if it produces items for public consumption. Furthermore, class plays a decisive role in such a comprehensive mapping, for female farm labourers inhabit a radically different space from aristocratic salon hostesses, such as Mariia Volkonskaia and Evdokiia Rostopchina. So Coventry Patmore's 'Angel in the House' (1855–6) – that icon of Victorian segregation – cannot blind us to the Floosie or Fiend in the Field, the temptress of Tolstoi, threshers and tractor drivers in rural areas, as prefigured by Thomas Hardy's Tess of the d'Urbervilles.

GENDERED SPACE: HOSPITAL/ITY AND HOSPITAL/IZATION

The distinctive chronotope of the prison in nineteenth-century poetry and fiction (by Byron, Hugo, Stendhal, Dickens and Dostoevskii) evolved into its modern variant in the camp literature authored by Primo Levi, Aleksandr Solzhenitsyn, Varlam Shalamov and Georgii Vladimov.[13] Drawing on a stable gendered tradition, the masculinized prison camp chronotope has its feminized counterpart in the chronotope of the hospital, which figures prominently in recent Russian women's prose, yet lacks comparable antecedents. History and cultural convention partly account for that absence: the privileged classes in Russia, who during the privacy-oriented era of tsardom dominated literature as both subject and source, summoned doctors to their homes whenever they required medical attention. Patients were treated and women delivered in the familiar, personal comfort of their own beds. Thus hospitalization, as a relatively late cultural phenomenon, occurs infrequently in literature of the nineteenth and early twentieth centuries. Moreover, whether out of squeamishness or ignorance, authors approach it obliquely, gingerly reporting it as an event occurring 'behind the scenes', instead of launching into protracted descriptions of a hospital routine or patients' sufferings.[14] Exceptions occur principally in fiction concerned with war, such as Tolstoi's *Sevastopol'skie rasskazy* (*Sevastopol Sketches*) and *Voina i mir* (*War and Peace*), and countless Soviet war novels, where the hospital mirrors the battlefield, inasmuch as it tests masculine fortitude in the face of mortal combat with a quieter version of the same dread enemy: death itself.[15]

By contrast, the civilian hospital functions as a major chronotope in numerous female texts of the last two decades, which conceptualize it primarily as carceral space. In Irina Velembovskaia's story 'V trudnuiu minutu' ('Through Hard Times'), a male patient in a district hospital tellingly confides to the female protagonist held there overnight: '"A hospital is just another prison. At least if you talk to someone it's cheerier"' («Больница — вторая тюрьма. Хоть поговоришь с человеком, и то веселее»).[16] Similarly, the heroine of Inna Varlamova's novel *Mnimaia zhizn'* (*A Counterfeit Life*) calls the women in her cancer ward 'branded prisoners, chained to the wheelbarrows of their disease' (прикованные к тачке своей болезни каторжницы).[17]

The prison analogy operates in a number of ways. Hospitalization means confinement (if not enforced incarceration), a spatial restriction that, in narrative terms, places a special burden on time. Given the relative stasis intrinsic to a hospital or prison setting, which imposes varying degrees of constraint on customary movement, time necessarily alters its contours and significance. It swells and decelerates, permitting the epistemological and narrative luxury of perceiving things close up and in slow motion. As regimen acquires inordinate ascendancy over the lives of patients and personnel, time undergoes domestication through regular repetition that in the context of near-immobility formalizes activities into ritual. On the surface, this imposition of pattern dictated by the clock creates the illusion of meaningful order and control over circumstances that humans fundamentally cannot govern: the creation and cessation of life. In short, the hospital chronotope structures an existentialist condition along domestic lines. It conventionalizes the shocking juxtaposition of birth and death by organizing them into kindred activities differentiated merely according to the micro-space they occupy within the larger macro-unit of the hospital.

Moreover, the systematized codes of behaviour constructed by hospital personnel, along with their medical skill, enable them to exercise power over the patient. The latter, conversely, upon entering this highly regulated environment, abrogates virtually all power – over her own body, her schedule, her social milieu, and, ultimately, her fate. Rendered helpless by virtue of signing or being signed into an institution adminis-tered according to what often seem arbitrary rules, the patient typically learns to subordinate her desires to the group impera-tive. In her passive role of dependency upon the presumed skill of strangers, she is less active than acted upon. Hence the unlimited potential for the transformation of the patient into a victim (as, for example, in Liudmila Petrushevskaia's 'Svoi krug' ('Our Crowd', 1988).[18]

Since physical incapacity or weakness limits external mobil-ity, the 'action' that transpires in narratives with a hospital setting tends, from the patient's perspective, to become inter-iorized. Hence the preponderance, in this brand of fiction, of philosophical exchanges and psychological analysis and dis-covery (as in Tat'iana Nabatnikova's 'Na pamiat'' ('In Memor-iam', 1984).[19] Inasmuch as ultimate questions of existence – literally, those of life and death – are decided in a hospital, it affords an ideal venue for psychological revelations, critical turning-points, and opportunities for access to self-knowledge (as in Varlamova's A Counterfeit Life). And from a purely practical standpoint, a hospital stay provides the contemporary Russian woman respite from the endless round of professional and domestic duties that keep her running, like Alice through the Looking Glass, in order to stay in the same place. In that sense, hospital may be synonymous with haven, as in Petrushevskaia's 'Skripka' ('The Violin', 1973).[20]

In addition to closed space and a highly regularized external time that liberates an internal, reflective narrative time, a hospital setting entails division along gender lines. That differentiation accurately reflects real-life conditions in Russia and elsewhere, for medical decorum prescribes the segregation of men from women. In a broader sense, too, medicine is a gender-marked field, for nursing and orderly work – the performance of 'the dirty and disgusting things that men usually disdain' (процедуры, от которых мужчины обычно уклоняются, оставляя женщинам все нечистое, отвратительное), as I. Grekova puts it[21] – remain female professions in Russia. Since the majority of Russian doctors are also women, the hospital ward in most women's fiction appears as an emphatically female sphere.

Within this context each patient interacts with two overlapping social groups: the chiefly female hospital personnel, stratified roughly according to principles informing any social hierarchy, and the fellow patients brought to a common human level through the democratizing forces of medical need. A third group, normally the only one containing male members, consists of family, friends, or associates from the outside world. These visitors either open up the perimeters of the ward on to a wider social environment of which they serve as a reminder, or themselves become assimilated into the narrower self-contained community, at least for the duration of their visit. They remain largely alien and 'other', 'outsiders' figuratively as well as literally, despite their intimacy or blood ties with the patients. Their primary narrative function – as catalysts to emotional crises or occasional passive observers on the sidelines – precludes their substantial input in sustaining the work's temporal-spatial centre. In Varlamova's novel, for instance, the protagonist's 'home and all her past ... had been left far behind, had receded into the distance' (дом и все прежнее ... безвозвратно отстало, оторвалось).[22]

Hospital conventions force representatives of all walks of life – of various political, intellectual, religious and moral convictions, of different class, background, race and age – to coexist, if only temporarily, side by side. Hence the equation of a woman's hospital ward with a microcosm of the female segment of society. Moreover, a more encompassing social picture characteristically emerges indirectly from patients' conversations, which supply the more comprehensive purview in which to contextualize women's individual and collective fates. Paradoxically, a hospital ward, precisely by virtue of its spatial circumscription, automatically implies the larger context that it ostensibly excludes.

Among the numerous contemporary Russian women's narratives relying on the hospital chronotope, the most memorable are Liudmila Velembovskaia's 'Through Hard Times' (1965), Petrushevskaia's 'The Violin' (1973) and 'Pania's Poor Heart' ('Bednoe serdtse Pani', 1988), Varlamova's *A Counterfeit Life* (1978), Viktoriia Tokareva's 'Nothing Special' ('Nichego osobennogo', 1981),[23] Grekova's *Ship of Widows* (*Vdovii parokhod*, 1981) and 'The Break/Crisis' ('Perelom', 1987), Iuliia Voznesenskaia's *The Women's Decameron* (*Zhenskii Dekameron*, 1986),[24] Natal'ia Sukhanova's 'Delos' (1988),[25] Elena Makarova's 'Preserving Life' ('Na sokhranenii', 1976),[26] Nabatnikova's 'In Memoriam' ('Na pamiat'', 1984), and Marina Palei's *Losers' Division* (*Otdelenie propashchikh*, 1991).[27] The commonality unduly emphasized by the juxtaposition within such a listing should not blur the appreciable differences among these texts or their authors. Some, such as Varlamova, Voznesenskaia, Petrushevskaia and Makarova, exploit the potential of the chronotope more fully than others (for instance, Velembovskaia). Furthermore, works dealing with sickness or injury (Tokareva, Nabatnikova) must be distinguished from those focusing on pregnancy (Sukhanova, Makarova, Palei), for by definition the assumptions, expectations and norms of the two diverge. United, nonetheless, through the shared element of the hospital chronotope, the narratives all offer a critique of the appalling conditions prevailing in Russian hospitals: outmoded equipment, ramshackle maintenance of buildings, understaffing, lack of essential medicines, insuffiently trained or outright incompetent personnel, insanitary conditions, widespread bribery, indifference to patients and indigestible food. In Grekova's 'Break/Crisis', the immobilized doctor, like the other patients, has to bribe the nurses for practically every service they perform; a husband in *A Counterfeit Life* quite openly pays a nurse to take care of his wife, and her response of 'That's too much money' confirms that receipt of funds for fulfilling standard nursely duties is accepted procedure; in *Ship of Widows* the victim of a stroke is tended not by the staff, but by her son, who takes up temporary residence in the hospital so as to provide her with the attention normally identified with a nurse's or orderly's responsibilities; in 'Nothing Special', 'The Violin' and 'Through Hard Times', food brought by patients' friends and family supplements the meagre or inappropriate diet supplied by the hospital facilities.

In 'Pania's Poor Heart', doctors misdiagnose pregnancy as a tumour, and the mistake goes undetected for months. Varlamova observes in *A Counterfeit Life*, where liver cancer causes the death of a patient treated for stomach cancer, that 'on Saturdays and Sundays you couldn't possibly find any doctors – it was more like a hostel than a hospital' (в субботу и воскресенье врачей днем с огнем не найдешь, не больница, а вольница).[28] In 'Nothing Special', Tokareva notes:

the nurse went off in a huff because she'd been humiliated in front of a patient. And patients ranked lower in the hospital than did nurses and even orderlies ... The hospital observed its own procedures, according to which what was needed could never be found, and what wasn't, could.

(медсестра ушла обиженная, потому что ее унизили при больной. А больные считались в больнице более нижним чином, чем медсестра и даже санитарки ... В больнице жили свои порядки, по которым не находилось того, что нужно, а было то, что не нужно.[29])

Of one surgeon, Tokareva says, 'Her patients survived purely by chance, not owing to, but in spite of, Raisa's intervention. It

was said that Raisa had got her job through some high
connection, and to remove her was impossible' (Ее больные
выживали совершенно случайно, не благодаря, а вопреки
Раисиному вмешательству[30]). Sukhanova's story, in which an
assistant's dilatoriness during an operation costs a newborn
baby's life, exposes universal administrative indifference to
problems of the most basic sort:

Every day something stopped working: water pipes, plumbing, elec-
trical wiring. I'd go to the public health department, the executive
council, the local Party branch – no one would listen.

(Каждый день что-нибудь отказывало: водопровод, нака-
лизация, электропроводка. Ходил в горздрав, в исполком, в
горком — уши затыкали.[31])

These flaws in the microcosm of the hospital may be
generalized into the pervasive deficiencies, the perennial
shortages and the staggering inefficiency that blight Soviet-
Russian society at large, and particularly its service sector.

Owing, no doubt, to the deplorable standards of hygiene
maintained in public facilities, as well as to prudishness,
entrenched practices that would strike most western cultures as
irrational or outmoded isolate expectant mothers from friends
and family – including the expectant father – before, during
and after delivery. As a highly revealing section of Sukhanova's
'Delos' argues, despite official Soviet glorification of motherhood, male-dominated society and literature find it expedient
to ignore the actual process of giving birth:

[I]n general it's considered improper to write about such things as
labour and pregnancy: that could put a damper on male passion ...
Our masculine reasoning tells us that labour is not an appropriate
subject for literature. But it's the women who pay for this reasoning in
the delivery rooms.

(роды, беременность — о них и вообще писать неприлично: у
мужчин, пожалуй, так и страсть притупиться может ... Наш
мужской разум подсказывает нам, что роды не тема для
литературы. Но именно женщины вот в этих родзалах платят
за разум.[32])

In effect, Russian women give birth in complete isolation, often
without sedatives and anaesthetics, prevented from sharing

their experience with anyone close to them. Neither doctors nor medical staff evince any sensitivity to the psychological effects of such separation, for by and large the hospital cultivates not a bedside, but a broadside, manner. For example, in *Ship of Widows*, the staff examining Anfisa Gromova, who anticipates going into imminent labour, comment, ' "[T]his one'll be quick – she's an elephant, not a woman!" ' («у этой скоро. Не женщина, слон»),[33] and her vocal anxiety about the baby withheld from her after delivery elicits the rebuke, ' "Hush! This isn't a market-place! There are a hundred of you in here, and you're the only one making a fuss ... We're all working here and you howl like a pig!" ' («Тише, тут не базар. Сто вас лежит, ни одна не позволяет, что ты ... Мы работаем, а ты орешь как порося?»).[34] Gossiping nurses in Tokareva's 'Nothing Special' carelessly allow a patient to overhear a conversation about how the doctor operating on her made a gross error in his incision. Fazmetal'skii, the head of obstetrics and gynaecology in Palei's *Losers' Division*, routinely ridicules and insults the peasant women on whom he cold-bloodedly performs abortions.

This official indifference to female psychology contrasts dramatically with the support and affirmation women generally find among their wardmates, even if the latter also prove a source of conflict and tension. Female bonding results in part from the extent to which life within a ward is laid bare for group consumption. Few, if any, secrets remain unguessed or unrevealed. Furthermore, the leisurely, externally uneventful pace of hospital existence permits the exchange of biographies and confidences, which unites women through the revelation of hardships that seem less individual than endemic to their gender. The same configuration of unimaginable, brutal sufferings repeats itself in the histories of women from the most diverse backgrounds, as witnessed in *The Women's Decameron*, where a shipyard worker, a doctor of biology, an engineer, a music teacher, an airline stewardess, a 'dissident wife', a Party functionary and a 'tramp' have no difficulty arriving at a common understanding as they share and evaluate each other's life stories. A parallel cross-section of female society appears in

A Counterfeit Life, 'The Break/Crisis', and 'Preserving Life', where empathy also forges relations among representatives of widely divergent allegiances and temperaments, particularly regarding the highly problematized, gendered issue of abortion.

Although contemporary Russian women's fiction identifies giving birth, abortion and sickness as essentially female problems, their solution, however spurious, seems to reside in the hands of men. Despite the feminization of the medical profession in empirical reality, masculine figures of authority rule the world depicted in the narratives under analysis. The so-called 'good doctor Volodia' in 'Pania's Poor Heart' takes it upon himself to deliver Pania's baby, contrary to her request for an abortion on the grounds of ill health, advanced years and an overburdened domestic situation; the ultimate decision as to when the homeless, pregnant, single young woman in 'The Violin' should leave the ward apparently belongs to the 'paternal' head physician; the strongly opinionated pro-natalist chief of the maternity hospital who performs the complex operations in 'Delos' is a bachelor, and the best surgeon entrusted with the most complicated operations in Tokareva's 'Nothing Special' is also male. In Grekova's *Ship of Widows*, nurses cannot curb the protagonist's agitation without appeal to a higher guardian of discipline: the male doctor who instantly silences her by accusing her of hooliganism. Although his female assistant arranges the abortions that Dr Fazmetal'skii in Palei's *Losers' Division* cannot or refuses to handle, his decisions and status in the hospital override hers. And Grekova's 'Break/Crisis' boasts two powerful male personae who determine the middle-aged heroine's life: the hospital chief and the omniscient 'eagle-like' Dr Chagin, who neatly resolves all of her personal and medical dilemmas.

Among the many insights emerging from the hospital chronotope, the most dispiriting from a feminist standpoint is that Russian men wield power, while women by force of habit subordinate self-fulfilment to the series of gendered moral imperatives pragmatically elided with countless aspects of Soviet institutions and officially promulgated for the presumed well-being of the entire society. By exploring the conditions of women as patients (and eternally patient), the feminized chronotope of the hospital in women's prose materializes the gender-specific dynamics of policy-sanctioned victimization. If within the masculine prison/camp chronotope a paradoxical access to spiritual enrichment and independence rescues malehood from the dehumanizing processes that accompany loss of liberty (as, for example, in Solzhenitsyn's *V kruge pervom* (*The First Circle*) and Abram Tertz's *Golos iz khora* (*A Voice from the Chorus*[35]), hospitalization seems to vouchsafe women primarily physical 'rewards' of an ambiguous kind – recovery of health, the vaunted delights of maternity, the termination of 'unwanted' pregnancies. Moreover, the psychological cost of these 'benefits', in the form of moral anguish, humiliation by medical staff, and complete loss of privacy in the midst of existential isolation, belongs to the commonplace realm of *byt* – the everyday world of humdrum existence – and therefore lacks the moral 'grandeur' of men's philosophical struggle against the more blatantly repressive constraints of a time/space structure officially acknowledged as totalitarian.

Whereas the prevalence of the hospital chronotope may be generalized across the full spectrum of recent Russian women's fiction, one would be hard put to adduce other categories of gendered space shared by the majority of contemporary female writers. Accordingly, hereafter my essay abjures universalizing statements that erase distinctions, to focus on space in the works of Liudmila Petrushevskaia, Tat'iana Tolstaia, and several representatives of 'novaia zhenskaia proza' ('new women's prose').

PETRUSHEVSKAIA'S 'HOME': ILLUSION, LIMINALITY AND INCARCERATION

While given to dissolving temporal markers, Petrushevskaia's drama and prose not only meticulously particularize, but densely psychologize, space. As her urtext, 'Through the Fields' ('Cherez polia', 1983),[36] makes clear, for Petrushevskaia the Home (*teplyi dom*) represents the irresistible illusion of existential security – a retreat from the perils of nature and history.[37] Her works teem with two-way traffic, as desperate loners seek sanctuary in a family domicile from the impersonal horrors of the outside world, while those suffocated by the emotional traumas of betrayal and indifference from their 'loved ones' flee in desperation from the imprisonment of a putative 'home'. Hence the prominence of the threshold as a locus of spiritual liminality in Petrushevskaia's works (emphasized in the pointedly titled 'Lestnichnaia kletka' ('The Stairwell') and in the universal search for a 'place to stay' in numerous stories and plays, where the spiritually dispossessed hope to be 'taken in': 'Rasskazchitsa' ('The Story Teller', 1972),[38] 'The Violin', 'Our Crowd'). These unfortunates do, indeed, get 'taken in' – metaphorically, inasmuch as they mistake the armies of Genghis Khan for the Salvation Army.

In a sense, the impulse to entrust one's soul to a healing environment (always illusory) merely plays a dephysiologizing variation on the hospital motif in Petrushevskaia, who obsessively checks all of her hearsay mothers (unwanted complications) into hospitals. Characteristically, mothers either remain in their wards or die, just as the spiritually wounded never recover from their malaise. In that regard the 'Izilirovannyi boks' ('Isolation Box') for terminally ill cancer patients in her one-act play is a matrix metaphor for Petrushevskaia's world-view. Each inhabitant is 'sentenced to death' ('prigovorennaia k smerti'),[39] utterly alone, with all hopes reduced to fantastic delusions.

Isolation or defensive immurement within the domestic domain is a related Petrushevskaian topos. As characters barricade themselves in locked rooms to escape from or defy their abusive cohabitants, home becomes carceral or punitive space – a prison that punishes those on both sides of the door, as in 'Gigiena' ('Hygiene')[40] and *Vremia noch'* (*Night Time*). In the latter, for example, the protagonist/narrator attempts to wreak subtle psychological revenge on her family by conspicuously isolating herself in her tiny room, while suspecting her mother, who, in turn, holes herself up in her bedroom, of attempting suicide behind her blocked door:

grandmother's door was blocked from inside, I had had difficulty opening it just a crack, the door was blocked by the desk ... why had she barricaded herself in? ... I tumbled into her room, she was sitting listlessly on her sofa (it's mine now). Had she been planning to hang herself?

(дверь бабушки приперта с той стороны, я с трудом приоткрыла щель, дверь была приперта письменным столом ... зачем она забаррикадировалась? ... Я ввалилась в ее комнату, она сидела бессильно на своем диванчике (теперь он мой.) Вешаться собиралась?[41])

Petrushevskaia transforms the fabled refuge of home into a claustrophobic environment of spiritual laceration, sadistic exposure and ceaseless emotional vampirism. She revises the genre of the family romance into a horror story.

Similarly, Petrushevskaia adroitly travesties the communal domestic feast (fundamental to the genres of the symposium and the idyll, with their harmonious gathering), degrading it into a grotesque anti-communion. So-called friends and family members assemble at table to enact Dostoevskian scandals, with hysteria, physical violence, seedy revelations and exposés of nasty or criminal deeds that erode and sunder relationships instead of reaffirming them. As 'Our Crowd' and 'A Raw Leg' ('Syraia noga') illustrate, Petrushevskaian groups convene on pseudo-festive occasions not to celebrate, but to annihilate. The final Easter feast in 'Our Crowd' culminates not in a resurrection, but in the heroine's beating her son until he bleeds, while the party in 'A Raw Leg' disintegrates when the host smashes his wife into bloody unconsciousness in the bathroom.[42]

Anyone seeking an antidote to the cloying sentimentality of the Victorians' idealization of domestic space as a tranquil haven from the push-and-slash of competitive public energies can do no better than to read Petrushevskaia's fiction or drama, for she envisions home as the quintessential site of psychic warfare and emotional evisceration, materialized in multiple forms of physical violence.

TOLSTAIA: SPACE AS BIOGRAPHY AND CREATIVE FREEDOM

Tolstaia's treatment of space is more varied, and differentiated according to age and character type. Within Tolstaia's associative construction of locale, older women tend to inhabit cramped apartments that document their lives via the objects amassed in them: outmoded furniture, kitschy bibelots, photographs and various mementoes that infuse space with subjective history and catalyse narrative (as, for example, in 'Milaia Shura' ('Sweet Shura', 1985).[43] In cinematic terms, these overloaded, enclosed spaces exemplify 'closed form', intimating the inward turn of the dweller's life as she retreats increasingly into the rich holdings of memory. Protagonists like Shura are the curators of their own biographies, displayed in confined quarters that recall antiquated museums. A variant on this subjectivized historical space is the attic (so central to ' "Na zolotom kryl'tse sideli ..." ' (' "On the Golden Porch ..." '), overrun by the fantastic bric-à-brac that holds magical allure for the young, but for the adult represents inertness and somnolent desuetude.

Of all Tolstaian narratives underscoring the identification of domestic space and old women, 'Samaia liubimaia' ('Most Beloved', 1986)[44] makes that connection most explicit: as the dacha in which Zhenechka thrived sags and grows dilapidated with time's passage, so does Zhenechka; each, in Tolstaia's words, 'quietly ages' (*tikho stareet*).[45] This Usher-like synonymousness emerges in such passages as the following, in which Zhenechka's spirit (voice) blends into, and becomes indistinguishable from, the dacha's atmosphere:

Zhenechka's voice lies cosily on the tablecloth, unhurriedly telling the telephone book, ashtray and apple core about its joys and worries ... her soul flows from the telephone receiver in an even stream, spills over the tablecloth, evaporates like smoke ...

(Уютно лежал на скатерти голос Женечки, неторопливо повествуя телефонному справочнику, пепельнице, яблочному огрызку о своих радостях и волнениях ... ровным потоком текла ее душа из телефонных дырочек, растекалась по скатерти, испарялась дымком ...[46])

In the same story, Tolstaia extends 'feminine space' to include the garden as a symbolic gauge of nurturing capacities, or the ability to raise the next generation along with healthy blooms. Space in such instances is emphatically temporalized, for Tolstaia suffuses it with temporal markers in the form of objects that stimulate elegiac memories of a past valorized largely through its transitoriness. Hence the prevalence of the Edenic garden in her earliest stories.[47]

Curiously, whereas the association between old women and apartments offers poignant occasion for poetic/lyrical reflections on the part of Tolstaia's narrators, young women's devotion to domestic space, its contents and embellishment, tends to connote philistinism, an acquisitiveness that Tolstaia satirizes with implacable hostility: for example, in 'Ogon' i pyl'' ('Fire and Dust', 1986),[48] 'Spi spokoino, synok' ('Sweet Dreams, Son', 1986),[49] and 'Poet i muza' ('The Poet and the Muse', 1986).[50] What accounts for her ironic treatment of that attachment is the absence of historical significance. With no profound personal experience animating rooms and their contents into valued participants in an individual life, the desire to possess and expand that ahistorical space inevitably acquires negative moral overtones.[51]

In contrast to this apparently conventional conflation of woman and home is Tolstaia's colourful counter-gendering of a space traditionally coded as male: that is, the adventure space of open seas, unchartered peregrinations unconstrained by teleology (what Bakhtin calls adventure-time[52]). That expansiveness of movement, unsurprisingly, accompanies sexual freedom, most notably in 'Fire and Dust', where the audaciously named Pipka happily embarks not only on involuntary voyages to exotic lands but also on casual intercourse of the unambiguous kind. A comparably magical and unfettered female character, Tamila in 'Svidanie s ptitsei' ('Rendezvous with a Bird'), occupies the fairytale space of mythic mountain, dragon kingdom and so on, that entertains all possibilities.[53] Both Pipka and Tamila, significantly, are associated with imagination, with the 'creative space' that is synonymous with a no-woman's land of original narration (a temporal artistic form). Through the chronotope of creativity (that is, storytelling), Tolstaia empowers both Pipka and Tamila with movement through boundless time and space. And that creativity, as in Lewis Carroll's *Alice in Wonderland*,

entails a self-metamorphosis articulated through richly elaborated spatial categories that more often than not take precedence
over the temporal.[54] In other words, Tolstaia's perspectivism
cannot accommodate a space devoid of temporality and a time
untethered to space.

NEW WOMEN'S PROSE: MOVING OUT/DOORS

If the 'new women's prose' may claim to have ushered in any
innovations regarding gendered space, it probably would be by
analogy with the movement of painters called *Peredvizhniki*
('Itinerants'). As did Repin and other representatives of the
'Itinerants' with their canvases, the younger generation of
writers has brought women's prose outdoors. Bella Ulanovskaia
in the minutely detailed topographies of her hunting sketches,
Larisa Vaneeva in her ecologically-conscious rhapsodies on the
wonders of nature, Valeriia Narbikova in her flights to the
liberating stretches of the seashore, and Svetlana Vasilenko in
her vivid renditions of traumatized landscape all transfer their
female protagonists from bounded interiors into outdoor
environments that interact with or mirror their psyches. This
extension of female space functions as a kind of prophylactic
against the automatic elision of womanhood with the domestic
sphere. Ulanovskaia, in fact, tends to situate her female
protagonists amidst untamed nature, in scenarios evoking
typically masculine confrontations with the 'great unknown' as
a rite of passage, while Vasilenko frames her heroines' intensely
sensual self-awareness in public settings contaminated by the
apocalyptic aura* of a post-nuclear world.[55] Above all,
unpredictable mobility, a restless movement that signals
psychological displacement – accentuated, moreover, by abrupt
narrative shifts – marks such otherwise diverse texts as Valeriia
Narbikova's *Ravnovesie sveta dnevnykh i nochnykh zvezd* (*The
Equilibrium of Light of Diurnal and Nocturnal Stars*, 1989),[56]
Vaneeva's 'Antigrekh' ('Antisin'),[57] and Vasilenko's 'Za
saigakami' ('Going After Goat-Antelopes'). By amplifying
female space the 'new prose' has reconstituted woman's
perspective as subject and object: her purview is not confined to

domestic and professional matters, nor her existence reduced to that of a stock character in the stale tragi-comedy of contemporary *byt*. Her week is *not* like any other.

One might say that when women 'knew their place', they occupied a circumscribed, convention-bound space; contemporary Russian women's fiction has remapped that territory along imperialistic lines, so as to encompass a broader range of possibilities for women's being. By so doing it has wrested womanhood from the stasis and immanence of gendered not-A status, thereby qualifying as one of the few glasnost phenomena to effect an authentic perestroika.

NOTES

Sections on the hospital chronotope draw on an earlier article of mine: see Helena Goscilo, 'Women's wards and wardens: the hospital in contemporary Russian women's fiction', *Canadian Woman Studies* 10, 4 (Winter 1989), 83–6. This chapter appears in a slightly different form in Helena Goscilo's forthcoming *Changing Figures: Russian Womanhood During and After Glasnost* (© by the University of Michigan, 1995), and is reproduced here by permission of the University of Michigan Press.

1 Abram Tertz (Andrei Sinyavsky), *A Voice from the Chorus*, trans. by Kyril Fitzlyon and Max Hayward (Glasgow: Fontana/Collins, 1977, p. 327.
2 Doreen Massey, 'Politics and space/time', *New Left Review*, 196 (November–December 1992), pp. 65–84.
3 The earliest, most original, and thought-provoking attempts belong to Mary Ellmann, *Thinking about Women* (San Diego, New York and London: Harcourt Brace Jovanovich, 1968), and Hélène Cixous and Catherine Clément, *The Newly Born Woman*, trans. by Betsy Wing (Minneapolis, MN: Minnesota University Press, 1988).
4 In deconstructionist parlance, the second term becomes the repressed or the 'unsaid'.
5 Massey, 'Politics and space/time', p. 72.
6 A woman, in Freud's theory of penis envy, may be minimally defined as a man lacking a penis. On Freud's views on women and femininity, see the Introduction in Elisabeth Young-Bruehl, *Freud on Women: a Reader* (New York: Abbeville Press, 1990), pp. 3–47.

7   Massey, 'Politics and space/time', p. 74.

8   *Ibid.*, p. 75.

9   *Ibid.*, pp. 76, 79.

10   Entitled 'Forms of time and the chronotope in the novel', the essay is contained in M. M. Bakhtin, *The Dialogic Imagination*, translated by Caryl Emerson and Michael Holquist (Austin, TX: University of Texas Press, 1981), pp. 84–258.

11   As Bakhtin notes, Kant in the 'Transcendental Aesthetics' of his *Critique of Pure Reason* defines space and time 'as indispensable forms of any cognition': see Bakhtin, *The Dialogic Imagination*, p. 85.

12   Throughout, I studiously avoid the hackneyed metaphorical use of 'space' favoured by deconstructionists and feminists, principally on account of its bathos and vagueness. On such a use, see Elaine Showalter, 'Women's time, women's space', in Shari Benstock, ed., *Feminist Issues in Literary Scholarship*, (Bloomington, IN: Indiana University Press, 1987), p. 37.

13   Although the prison memoirs of Evgeniia Ginzburg and Irina Ratushinskaia suggest that the genre is not totally alien to women writers, the literary tradition is nonetheless male. Perhaps one can draw a limited analogy between the risks undertaken by men in political and military crises with those that women face in the more everyday circumstances of giving birth. That parallel is implicitly drawn in Ernest Hemingway's *A Farewell to Arms*, in which Frederic Henry's life is under constant threat in battle (the arms of war), yet Catherine succumbs to death during childbirth ('love's arms'). See also the discussion of 'public' versus 'private' space in Dorothy O. Helly and Susan M. Reverby, eds., *Gendered Domains* (Ithaca, NY: Cornell University Press, 1992).

14   Mental hospitals, however, proliferate in earlier fiction, probably because they signal intellectual malaise and invite symbolic interpretation, just as certain physical sicknesses lend themselves to metaphoric usage. See Michel Foucault, *Madness and Civilization. A History of Insanity in the Age of Reason*, trans. by Richard Howard (New York: Random House, 1965); Susan Sontag, *Illness as Metaphor* (New York: Vintage, 1977/1979) and *AIDS and Its Metaphors* (New York: Farrar, Straus and Giroux, 1988/1989).

15   Amidst the plethora of military medical settings, Solzhenitsyn's *Rakovyi korpus* (*Cancer Ward*) and Boris P'etsukh's 'Anamnez i Epikriz' ('Anamnesis and Epicrisis', 1989) stand out as rare exceptions in male prose.

16   Helena Goscilo, ed., *Balancing Acts* (New York: Dell Publishing Company, 1991), p. 193; Irina Velembovskaia, *Zhenshchiny*

(Moscow: Sovetskii pisatel', 1967), p. 264. Whenever an English translation is available, I cite from the English source first, then from the Russian.

17 Inna Varlamova, *A Counterfeit Life*, trans. by David A. Lowe (Ann Arbor, MI: Ardis, 1988), p. 37; Inna Varlamova, *Mnimaia zhizn'* (Ann Arbor, MI: Ardis, 1978), p. 40.

18 L. Petrushevskaia, 'Svoi krug', *Novyi mir*, 1 (1988), pp. 116–30; translated by Helena Goscilo, in Helena Goscilo and Byron Lindsey, eds., *Glasnost: an Anthology of Russian Literature under Gorbachev* (Ann Arbor, MI: Ardis, 1990), pp. 3–24.

19 T. Nabatnikova, 'Na pamiat'', in *Domashnee vospitanie* (Moscow: Sovremennik, 1984); 'In Memoriam', trans. by Catharine Theimer Nepomnyashchy, in *Soviet Women Writing*, ed. by Jacqueline Decter (New York: Abbeville Press, 1990), pp. 117–30.

20 L. Petrushevskaia, 'Skripka', *Druzhba narodov*, 10 (1973), pp. 151–3; translated as 'The Violin', in Goscilo, *Balancing Acts*, pp. 122–5.

21 I. Grekova, *Ship of Widows*, trans. Cathy Porter (London: Virago, 1985), p. 160; I. Grekova, *Vdovii parakhod*, *Novyi mir*, 5 (1981), p. 139.

22 Varlamova, *A Counterfeit Life*, p. 39; Varlamova, *Mnimaia zhizn'*, p. 42.

23 V. Tokareva, 'Nichego osobennogo', *Novyi mir*, 4 (1981), pp. 113–33.

24 Julia Voznesenskaya, *The Women's Decameron*, trans. by W. B. Linton (London: Methuen, 1986); published in Russian as Iuliia Voznesenskaia, *Zhenskii dekameron* (Tel Aviv: izd. 'Zerkalo', 1987).

25 N. Sukhanova, 'Delos', *Novyi mir*, 3 (1988), pp. 69–84.

26 E. Makarova, 'Na sokhranenie', in her *Otkrytyi final* (Moscow, 1989).

27 M. Palei, *Otdelenie propashchikh* (Moscow: Moskovskii rabochii, 1991).

28 Varlamova, *A Counterfeit Life*, p. 37; Varlamova, *Mnimaia zhizn'*, p. 39.

29 *Balancing Acts*, p. 78; Viktoriia Tokareva, *Letaiushchie kacheli. Nichego osobennogo* (Moscow: Sovetskii pisatel', 1987), pp. 562–3.

30 *Balancing Acts*, pp. 84–5; Tokareva, *Letaiushchie kacheli*, p. 567.

31 Helena Goscilo and Byron Lindsey, eds., *Wild Beach and Other Stories* (Ann Arbor, MI: Ardis, 1992), p. 148; Natal'ia Sukhanova, 'Delos', *Novyi mir*, 3 (1988), pp. 69–70.

32 Goscilo and Lindsey, *Wild Beach*, p. 153; Sukhanova, 'Delos', p. 73.

33 Grekova, *Ship of Widows*, p. 50; Grekova, *Vdovii parakhod*, p. 86.

34 Grekova, *Ship of Widows*, p. 51; Grekova, *Vdovii parakhod*, p. 88.

35 Solzhenitsyn's *The First Circle*, trans. Michael Guybon (London: Collins and Harvill, 1968) consistently develops the paradox of prison as the ideal venue for attaining spiritual freedom. See

statements to that effect volunteered by Nerzhin, Prianchikov, Adamson and Sologdin. Comparable passages may be found in Tertz, such as the following:

> I like the slow tempo of our existence here compared with the usual rhythm of life which people outside willy-nilly adopt in order to be in time for the bus, the office or the cinema. The mind, therefore, works somehow more naturally in camp – it doesn't have to calculate all the time how to get ahead of somebody else ... And existence opens its blue eyes all the wider.

See Abram Terts, *Golos iz khora*, in Terts, *Sobranie sochinenii v 2 tt.*, II (Moscow: SP 'Start', 1992), p. 668.

36 L. Petrushevskaia, 'Cherez polia', *Avrora*, 5 (1983), pp. 113–14; 'Through the Fields', trans. Stefani Hoffman, in Sergei Zalygin, ed., *The New Soviet Fiction* (New York: Abbeville Press, 1989), pp. 235–8.

37 On this, see Natal'ia Ivanova, 'Bakhtin's concept of the grotesque and the art of Petrushevskaia and Tolstaia', in Helena Goscilo, ed., *Fruits of her Plume: Esays in Contemporary Russian Women's Culture* (Armonk, NY: M. E. Sharpe, 1993); see also Helena Goscilo, 'No ray of light in the kingdom of darkness: Petrushevskaia's vision', paper delivered at the American Association for the Advancement of Slavic Studies Conference in Arizona, 1992.

38 L. Petrushevskaia, 'Rasskazchitsa', *Avrora*, 7 (1972), pp. 11–13.

39 Liudmila Petrushevskaia, *Cinzano*, trans. by Stephen Mulrine (London: Nick Herne Books, 1991), p. 318; Liudmila Petrushevskaia, *Pesni XX veka* (Moscow, 1988), p. 234.

40 L. Petrushevskaia, 'Gigiena', *Ogonek*, 40 (October 1988), pp. 27–9.

41 L. Petrushevskaia, 'Vremia noch''', *Novyi mir*, 2 (1992), pp. 65–110 (p. 101).

42 L. Petrushevskaia, 'Syraia noga', in *Tri devushki v golubom* (Moscow: 'Iskusstvo', 1989), pp. 101–2.

43 T. Tolstaia, 'Milaia Shura', *Oktiabr'*, 12 (1985), pp. 113–17. This and other of Tolstaia's stories referred to below are published in her collection *Na zolotom kryltse sideli...* (Moscow: Molodaia gvardiia, 1987); Tatyana Tolstaya, *On the Golden Porch and Other Stories*, trans. by Antonina W. Bouis (London: Virago, 1989).

44 T. Tolstaia, 'Samaia liubimaia', *Avrora*, 10 (1986), pp. 92–110.

45 Tatyana Tolstaya, *Sleepwalker in a Fog*, trans. by Jamey Gambrell (New York: Alfred A. Knopf, 1992), pp. 106, 110; Tat'iana Tolstaia, *'Na zolotom kryltse sideli ...'*, pp. 102, 105.

46 Tolstaya, *Sleepwalker*, p. 111; Tolstaia, *Na zolotom kryltse sideli* ..., p. 106.

47 See Helena Goscilo, 'Paradise, purgatory and post-mortems in the world of Tat'jana Tolstaja', *Indiana Slavic Studies*, 5 (1990), pp. 97–114.

48 T. Tolstaia, 'Ogon' i pyl'', *Avrora*, 4 (1986), pp. 82–91.

49 T. Tolstaia, 'Spi spokoino, synok', *Avrora*, 10 (1986), pp. 94–101.

50 T. Tolstaia, 'Poet i muza', *Novyi mir*, 12 (1986), pp. 113–19.

51 On this, see Helena Goscilo, 'Monsters monomaniacal, marital, and medical: Tolstaia's use of regenerative gender stereotypes', in Jane Costlow, Stephanie Sandler and Judith Vowles, eds., *Sexuality and the Body in Russian Culture* (Stanford, CA: Stanford University Press, 1993).

52 Bakhtin, *The Dialogic Imagination*, p. 87.

53 Tolstaya, 'Rendez-vous with a Bird', in *On the Golden Porch*, pp. 119–33.

54 Pipka, for instance, appears in many shifting guises, all inseparable from precisely delineated locales: pathetic orphan at Rimma's house, irresistible seductress in her own Perlovka dwelling, victim, prize, and adventuress on the ship and remote islands where she has sexual relations with a series of different men, a smiling beauty in Australia, or a bright-burning flame turned to coal on the Iaroslavl Highway. Tamila's changing identity likewise depends on the nature of the space she occupies, whether it be magic mountain, semi-enchanted garden, or rumpled bed. On the role of movement through space and its relevance to gender and potential for change, see Nina Auerbach, *Woman and the Demon* (Cambridge, MA and London: Harvard University Press, 1982), *passim*.

55 For samples of these writers' prose, see Larisa Vaneeva, ed., *Ne pomniashchaia zla* (Moscow: Moskovskii rabochii, 1990); Svetlana Vasilenko, ed., *Novye amazonki: sbornik zhenskoi prozy* (Moscow: Moskovskii rabochii, 1991), as well as the three anthologies of translations entitled *Soviet Women Writing; Women's View, Glas: New Russian Writing*, 3 (1992) and Helena Goscilo, ed., *Lives in Transit* (Ann Arbor, MI: Ardis, 1995).

56 V. Narbikova, *Ravnovesie sveta dnevnyk i nochnykh zvezd* (Paris, 1989); also published in Moscow by Vsesoiuznyi modezhnyi knizhnyi tsentr, 1990.

57 Larisa Vaneeva, 'Antigrekh', in *Novye amazonki*, pp. 224–52.

Index

CAMBRIDGE STUDIES IN RUSSIAN LITERATURE

General editor MALCOLM JONES

Editorial board: ANTHONY CROSS, CARYL EMERSON,
HENRY GIFFORD, BARBARA HELDT, G. S. SMITH,
VICTOR TERRAS

Printed in Germany
by Amazon Distribution
GmbH, Leipzig